Aspiring to Home

ASIAN AMERICA
A series edited by Gordon H. Chang

The increasing size and diversity of the Asian American population, its growing significance in American society and culture, and the expanded appreciation, both popular and scholarly, of the importance of Asian Americans in the country's present and past—all these developments have converged to stimulate wide interest in scholarly work on topics related to the Asian American experience. The general recognition of the pivotal role that race and ethnicity have played in American life, and in relations between the United States and other countries, has also fostered the heightened attention.

Although Asian Americans were a subject of serious inquiry in the late nineteenth and early twentieth centuries, they were subsequently ignored by the mainstream scholarly community for several decades. In recent years, however, this neglect has ended, with an increasing number of writers examining a good many aspects of Asian American life and culture. Moreover, many students of American society are recognizing that the study of issues related to Asian America speak to, and may be essential for, many current discussions on the part of the informed public and various scholarly communities.

The Stanford series on Asian America seeks to address these interests. The series will include works from the humanities and social sciences, including history, anthropology, political science, American studies, law, literary criticism, sociology, and interdisciplinary and policy studies.

A full list of titles in the Asian America series can be found online at www.sup.org/asianamerica.

Aspiring to Home

SOUTH ASIANS IN AMERICA

Bakirathi Mani

STANFORD UNIVERSITY PRESS
STANFORD, CALIFORNIA

Stanford University Press
Stanford, California

© 2012 by the Board of Trustees of the Leland Stanford Junior University. All rights reserved.

No part of this book may be reproduced or transmitted in any form or by any means, electronic or mechanical, including photocopying and recording, or in any information storage or retrieval system without the prior written permission of Stanford University Press.

Library of Congress Cataloging-in-Publication Data

Mani, Bakirathi, author.
  Aspiring to home : South Asians in America / Bakirathi Mani.
    pages cm. — (Asian America)
  Includes bibliographical references and index.
  ISBN 978-0-8047-7799-5 (cloth : alk. paper) —
  ISBN 978-0-8047-7800-8 (pbk. : alk. paper)
  1. American literature—South Asian American authors—History and criticism. 2. South Asian Americans in literature. 3. Immigrants in literature. 4. South Asian Americans—Ethnic identity. 5. South Asian American arts. I. Title. II. Series: Asian America.
  PS153.S68M36 2012
  305.891'4073—dc23
                                      2011027977

Typeset by Westchester Book Group in 11/14 Adobe Garamond

For my family

Contents

Acknowledgments — ix

Introduction: Becoming South Asian — 1

1. Postcolonial Locations: Jhumpa Lahiri's *Interpreter of Maladies* and *The Namesake* — 30

2. So Far from Home: Documenting Immigrant Lives in *Knowing Her Place*, *Calcutta Calling*, and *Bangla East Side* — 75

3. Beauty Queens: Gender, Ethnicity, and Transnational Modernities at Miss India USA — 122

4. The Art of Multiculturalism: Diasporadics, Desh Pardesh, and Artwallah — 163

5. "Somewhere You've Never Been Before": The American Romance of *Bombay Dreams* — 208

Epilogue — 253

Notes — 265
Works Cited — 287
Index — 305

Acknowledgments

This book has accumulated so much in the decade it took toward publication. David Palumbo-Liu, Paulla Ebron, and Purnima Mankekar were my first readers, and it is to them I give my first thanks. David's belief in my work and its place in Asian American studies was a touchstone throughout the process of writing. I am indebted to the Program in Modern Thought and Literature at Stanford University, and the generous funding and intellectual flexibility that the program provided. Prior to Stanford, I learned a tremendous amount from my teachers at the Centre for Historical Studies at Jawaharlal Nehru University, particularly Neeladri Bhattacharya, who showed me how to think within and outside of disciplinary frameworks.

Many of the ideas in this book matured in the process of teaching at Swarthmore College, and for that my gratitude goes to the Department of English Literature. My colleagues welcomed this project with all its detours away from literature; for their camaraderie outside the office, I thank Peter Schmidt, Patty White, Kendall Johnson, and Nora Johnson. Swarthmore has been a congenial place to establish interdisciplinary ties, and so I also thank my friends in the Gender and Sexuality Studies Program, Film and Media Studies Program, Asian Studies Program, as well as the Department of Sociology and Anthropology. The Mellon Tri-College Faculty Group for Women of Color, and Mellon Tri-College Faculty Group in Colonialism, Culture, and Politics enabled me to converse with colleagues across the three colleges. Teaching postcolonial theory and Asian American studies, often in the same classroom, was central to the evolution of this project; the curiosity of my students made this a better book.

A South Asia Initiative Research Grant and a Richard Weiland Fellowship from Stanford University supported the initial phase of research for this project. At Swarthmore College, the Eugene M. Lang Faculty Fellowship as well as the Mary Albertson Faculty Fellowship gave me two full years of sabbatical funding, including one wonderful year in Brooklyn. Faculty research grants from the Provost's Office provided funds for follow-up fieldwork in California and New York. A Minority Faculty Research Grant from the Christian and Mary Lindback Foundation also aided my research, and a year as a visiting scholar at the Center for the Study of Ethnicity and Race at Columbia University sped its conclusion. A Tri-College Mellon Grant enabled me to establish a network of Asian American studies scholars in Philadelphia. I also benefited from sharing my work with colleagues in Asian American studies, American studies, South Asian studies, and Women's studies at the University of California at Berkeley, the National University of Singapore, Dartmouth College, Yale University, Ohio State University, Bowdoin College, the University of Minnesota, the University of Pennsylvania, and the University of Michigan.

Friends and colleagues from across the country gave generously of their time in reading full drafts of the manuscript. David Eng, Suvir Kaul, Allan Isaac, and Lok Siu participated in a Mellon-funded seminar at Swarthmore in 2009; their belief in the project encouraged me to complete revisions. Lisa Arellano, Ritty Lukose, and Kyla Tompkins also read selections, and gave heartfelt support. At various stages in the writing process, Daniel Kim, Inderpal Grewal, Ania Loomba, Werner Sollors, and Robyn Wiegman lent an ear and sound advice. Kathy Chetkovich worked with me through a year of developmental editing. As many academic writers know, the process of anonymous review can often be unsettling. For their insightful comments on the manuscript, my deep appreciation goes to those readers who made themselves known, including Kandice Chuh, Lok Siu, Gayatri Gopinath, Martin Manalansan, and Celine P. Shimizu.

I treasure the companionship of my childhood friends from Tokyo; their openness to new experiences is what I have learned most from. Gitanjali Mathias, Yogita Goyal, Katrina Moore, Reiko Akakura, Anne-Yoshié Narahara, and Marlisa Butler have been companions for nearly thirty years.

Though we live in different ways and in different places, I am grateful for the life we share. The ideas for this book began in 1992, in a series of late-night dormitory conversations with Sushant P. Rao. Though we have followed divergent careers, his enthusiasm for my work has been no less sustained. My two years in Delhi would have been lonely without the warm company of Jisha Menon, Bhavani Raman, Aparna Balachandran, Latha Varadarajan, Naina Dayal, and Rochelle Pinto. Some of them came along to the United States later, and I take so much pleasure in our continued friendship.

San Francisco was the first city in the United States that felt like home to me, and for that I want to acknowledge the friends who made my life there and subsequently on the East Coast so vivid: Lalaie Ameeriar, Falu Bakrania, Tara Carr, Manishita Dass, Maya Dodd, Gauri Gill, Nicole Fleetwood, Arati Karnik, Rajan Lukose, Ritty Lukose, Celine Shimizu, Sameer Pandya, and Miriam Ticktin. I cannot begin to thank each of them for their vibrant intelligence and compassion. From Delhi to Philadelphia, the ways that Ania Loomba and Suvir Kaul live their lives as scholars and as teachers has been an inspiration. More important, they have become friends. Lisa Arellano's friendship exceeds every description of that word. She has been a sister to me during our time at Stanford and in the years thereafter.

I have written this book with all my families in mind. In the course of writing I gained a family in Southern California. The Ruiz and Avalos clans provide me with so much joy, especially through my beautiful nieces and nephews. Dilly and Manek Daver, along with their children and grandchildren around the world, raised me with enormous affection and boundless generosity. I hope that my research reflects the good deeds, good acts, and good words that the Davers live by. My uncles and aunts in India, in particular Mani Mama and Mami, Raman Chittappa and Meera Chithi, have been tremendously supportive of my career and personal life, despite its idiosyncracies. I am optimistic that this book reflects the diasporic lives that our family increasingly inhabits.

My parents, Pushkala and A. P. S. Mani, taught me about leaving home through their own experiences. Their journey from Kerala to Bombay, from Bombay to Tokyo, and after thirty-four years from Tokyo back to Kerala, is nothing short of epic. To write of their capacity to embrace change would take another book. Their love for their children has been of the deepest kind, for it enabled us to make our way into new worlds. My brother, Parameshwar

Mani, has lived his life with strength and resilience in Tokyo, London, Boston, and Dubai. With his partner, Takako Ohyabu, he takes our family into the future.

Mario Ruiz entered this project after much of my initial fieldwork was complete. But the manuscript became a book only when he became a part of my world. Throughout the long days and nights of writing he took me into his arms and showed me what it means to belong. He is my love, my heart, and my home.

Aspiring to Home

Introduction

Becoming South Asian

> We are here to pervert—excuse me, to *preserve*—our culture.
>
> —Teju Patel, addressing the Miss India USA pageant

As I walked into the Miss India USA pageant, I momentarily felt out of place. Inside the hotel banquet room, speaker systems buzzed with static as emcees commandeered the microphone and audience members chattered loudly with their friends. Glancing through the program booklet, I noticed that the preparation for the evening exceeded the actual events onstage. The pageant was not simply about who won the contest, but about the community itself. Threaded through the talent and fashion shows were stories about local immigrant entrepreneurs whose small businesses funded the contest; about parents who invested their time and money into the display of their daughters; and about the young women who aimed to win the crown. Throughout the evening, the pageant organizers, beauty queens, and emcees appeared to represent an upwardly mobile immigrant group. Yet while the pageant promoted a singular narrative of ethnic and national community, those who gathered at the event came from diverse backgrounds. The contestants represented more than twenty states across the United States, and as many regions of origin within India. They were Hindu and Sikh, Muslim and Christian; they spoke Telugu, Hindi, Punjabi, and Malayalam. The audience included first- and second-generation immigrants from India, as well as Fijians and East Africans of subcontinental origin. Despite my initial hesitation, I was compelled by the spectacle of belonging generated at the pageant. As an Indian national from Japan, an academic, and as a feminist who rejected the objectification of female bodies, I considered myself to be unlike the immigrants who attended and participated in this event. Yet like other audience members, I too became part of the powerful performance of community that was staged by the contestants. Their efforts to win the crown represented an aspirational narrative of belonging, enunciated through popular music, fashion, and dance.

Historically, beauty pageants have been occasions for Asian immigrants to proclaim their allegiance as Americans.[1] At Miss India USA, what struck me were the disparate claims to class and citizenship that were made by a heterogeneous group of immigrants. The pageant was nominally a charity fund-raiser, but it required large investments of capital and labor on the part of contestants and organizers. The lavish setting of the hotel ballroom signaled the wealth of this immigrant group, but pageant sponsors included struggling small-business owners as well as white-collar professionals. Though the judges spoke eloquently about what it meant to be Indian, such singular notions of national identity were challenged by the diverse religious and linguistic backgrounds of the contestants. Moreover, the majority of the young women onstage identified as American citizens, claiming regional identities as Texans or Californians who proudly represented their states of residence.

The visible contradictions embodied by the pageant contestants, organizers, and audience members came to a head at the end of the show. Just before the winners were announced, Teju Patel, an emcee for the evening, came onstage and proclaimed, "We are here to pervert—excuse me, to *preserve*—our culture." The audience reacted with shock and titters of disapproval as Patel struggled to regain his composure. Caught in the spotlight, Patel's comment exemplifies the ways in which immigrants both preserve and pervert notions of belonging. For those immigrants who organized this public event, identity is staged as a coherent national and cultural construct. Cultural identities came to life through Bollywood songs and dances, a Hindu-centric iconography, and the colloquial use of Hindi. These acts of cultural preservation reproduced a homogeneous ideal of nationhood—that is, one constituted through dominant religious, ethnic, and linguistic ideas of what it means to be "Indian." Yet for the contestants as well as their supporters in the audience, the pageant perversely generated another notion of identity, one that enabled them to think of themselves as "Americans." They viewed the pageant as a universal rite of passage that accounted for their racial difference and showcased a middle-class immigrant group. Perversely still, such claims to racialized citizenship were articulated through the gendered idiom of Indian popular culture.

Who won the pageant quickly became secondary to the question of what it meant to be Miss India USA. For the judges—a motley collection of Indian embassy officials and Hollywood casting agents—the title crown was reserved for those women who preserved an idea of India, cast as Hindu and Hindi-speaking. For audience members from Fiji and Africa, and for those who belonged to religious and linguistic minorities in India, the notion of a single "Indian culture" was itself perverse. As for the contestants, who juggled multiple demands from the organizers and audience members, performing onstage illustrated their agency as diasporic subjects of the Indian state and as ethnic minorities in the United States. What drew together this disparate assemblage of immigrants was not a shared belief in "culture" or "tradition," but a collective investment in producing community, one that sustained an upwardly mobile narrative of South Asians in the United States.

The contentious relationship between preserving and perverting culture at this public event brought to the foreground how the production of diasporic community is not simply a question of ethnic identity: instead, it is a problem of locality. Locality is the means through which first- and second-generation immigrants, of varying regional, religious, and linguistic backgrounds, come to experience what it means to belong. In critical race and ethnic studies, belonging is commonly articulated through claims to place that are characterized by generational divides. Within this framework, first-generation immigrants from India may readily identify as "Indian," whereas their second-generation offspring claim to be "American." The transition from one place to another is represented through narratives of ethnic adaptation and assimilation, or captured by the formation of new ethnic identities (such as desi, a Hindi/Urdu term meaning "of the homeland"). However, each of these constructs of ethnic identity reverts to a clearly demarcated geographical site, whether a "homeland" on the subcontinent or the United States. Such claims to place fail to capture the affective experience of creating transnational communities *across* differences of generation, national origin, religion, and language. Locality exceeds nationalist frameworks of belonging by exploring how the affective experience of migration produces new forms of race- and class-based community. For those diasporic subjects who come to understand themselves as immigrants and as middle class through the experience of living in the United States, locality engenders the production of South Asian communities.

Locality is a phenomenology of belonging that operates as a category of subjectivity as well as a means of establishing community. In *Modernity at Large*, the anthropologist Arjun Appadurai defines locality as a "structure of feeling, a property of social life, and an ideology of situated community" (189). As a structure of feeling, locality is the practice of establishing relations of affinity with those seen as similar to oneself, often through a series of shared experiences and rituals. Locality is also embodied as a property of social life, one that is central to making identity and community visible and distinct. Because locality operates as an ideology of community, it does not specify the geographical boundaries of group identity. Instead, locality acquires a phenomenological quality that is "relational and contextual rather than scalar or spatial" (178). Moving away from quantitative assessments of immigrant groups in discrete geographic locales, locality signals a shift toward the affective nature of establishing identity in a diverse range of sites, including domestic, public, and virtual spaces. For many immigrants, the production of locality is a means of transforming lived space into the place of home(land). However, the forms of belonging that emerge from the production of locality are distinct from claims to countries of origin. Immigrants identify as South Asian because of their experiences as racial minorities in the United States, rather than in relation to citizens of nation-states in South Asia. The experience of being South Asian is fundamentally about localizing transnational ideologies of class and race, for immigrants who take on the project of producing locality find themselves struggling against the authority of the state and its requirement of national allegiance. Locality is therefore integral to processes of globalization, for it elucidates how communities are generated through the interplay between local racial formations and global movements of capital. Yet the fact that locality must be repetitively embodied, across multiple sites, makes it an "inherently fragile achievement" (179) that is liable to repetition, degeneration, or erasure.

For many subcontinental immigrants, locality is embodied through the production and consumption of popular culture: through reading literature and watching films made by other South Asians; performing at and attending cultural events; and participating in online forums. These everyday practices of identifying with other immigrants—a process that requires negotiating differences of language, caste, and region—lay the groundwork for formations of diasporic community. In this sense locality is distinct from theories of cultural citizenship that subject immigrants to the regime of the state.[2] Viewed through the parameters of citizenship, subcontinental immigrants are identified by (and identify primarily through) nation- and faith-based constructs of identity as Indian, Pakistani, Bangladeshi, or Sri Lankan; as Muslim, Hindu, or Sikh. By contrast, locality outlines the affective conditions through which immigrants create subjectivity and community based on a shared experience, in this case an experience of migration. These new forms of community require negotiating certain forms of difference (such as national origin, religious faith, or language) and reproducing others (such as class). As such, the production of locality is also complicit in reinforcing class-based notions of nationhood. Immigrants come to identify as South Asian within domestic frameworks of race and ethnicity in the United States, as well as in relation to neoliberal formations of citizenship in South Asia. The troubling elisions incurred in the production of locality highlight how it can be a profoundly generative experience of belonging for some immigrants but not for others. These elisions also alert us to the ways in which locality can itself be perverted, often productively, by those who are otherwise excluded from dominant representations of what it means to be South Asian.

Throughout this book I examine literary, visual, and performative texts created by and about middle-class South Asians, whose educational achievements and material wealth are frequently glossed as the "solution" to America's racial problems.[3] Representations of middle-class immigrants circulate widely in mainstream U.S. public culture in the works of writers such as Jhumpa Lahiri and filmmakers like Mira Nair, at art festivals and Broadway shows, on television and in online communities. These upwardly mobile stories of scientists, entrepreneurs, and engineers come to stand in for what it means to be South Asian despite the increasing numbers of working-class and undocumented immigrants from the subcontinent. Such popular cultural texts are frequently critiqued for their assimilationist representations of a heterogeneous immigrant group. These texts also contribute toward the erosion of working-class narratives of migration as well as the reification of patrilineal and masculinist notions of middle-class mobility. However, shifting our attention away from how these texts represent immigrant identity and toward questions of how such texts are consumed for the production of locality highlights the affective and material practices through which immigrants become South Asian. The circulation and consumption of South Asian popular culture generate narratives of race and class that bind together a fragile coalition of immigrants who are otherwise divided by generation, national origin, religion, and language.

Because these popular cultural texts are produced and consumed within a domestic racial framework, the experience of being middle class means that South Asians are simultaneously aware of their position as minorities in the United States while also complicit in embodying multicultural ideologies of nationhood. These public discourses of multiculturalism range from the well-worn paradigm of the "melting pot" or "salad bowl" that portrays immigration as a voluntary act, to more recent neoliberal formulations that produce highly differentiated ethnic, religious, and sexual communities, coded as "color-blind" or "post-racial."[4] Both pluralist and neoliberal forms of multiculturalism are a means of managing racial and class difference within the state, even though the rhetoric of a "color-blind" society purports to move beyond race. Across these diverse rhetorics of multiculturalism, the emphasis on individual "choice" is particularly appealing to immigrants who, as bourgeois subjects in their countries of origin, are familiar with the prospect of full citizenship. Such enabling fictions contrast with the heightened racial surveillance of immigrant groups, particularly Sikhs and Muslims, after September 11, 2001. Yet for middle-class South Asians, multiculturalism continues to be the principal framework through which to advance their claims to being American. Multiculturalism is experienced not as an abstract legal formation but as a rhetoric of subjecthood, one that remains compelling even as many subcontinental immigrants are deliberately and consistently excluded from visions of universal citizenship. The flexible operation of multicuturalism and its alliance with narratives of upward mobility reveal unexpected linkages between domestic ideologies of nationhood and transnational practices of citizenship. As Viet Thanh Nguyen writes, "Compliancy and accommodation are flexible strategies that were and *remain* important political choices for Asian Americans that are overlooked by assumptions about Asian American identity as being inherently, or desirably, oppositional" (26, emphasis in original).

However, whereas Nguyen explores the ramifications of Asian American capital accumulation within the domestic paradigm of U.S. race relations, I explore how the embodiment of class mobility by South Asians is intimately linked to postcolonial formations of citizenship in South Asia. In the early twenty-first century, middle-class immigrants experience postcoloniality as an exceptional state of citizenship. More than a decade after the institution of market reforms on the subcontinent, the emergence of neoliberal ideologies of statehood in India, Pakistan, and Bangladesh has transformed what it means to be a citizen.[5] For elite diasporic subjects, access to state power in South Asia is established through modes of transnational capital accumulation and consumption. In turn, these same middle-class immigrants are routinely recruited into the expansive public sphere of the postcolonial state. Such "exceptional" immigrants can claim privileges (in terms of rights to property) that are not afforded to citizens on the subcontinent.[6] Many immigrants also deploy their capital investments to advocate for political change in their countries of origin. Such diasporic political movements fundamentally refashion the spatial and temporal distance between the postcolonial citizen and the immigrant.[7] Equally important, however, are the ways in which the circulation of neoliberal ideologies of citizenship transforms the formation of communities in diaspora. While subcontinental immigrants in the United States may retain regional- or faith-based categories of identity (as Tamil or Punjabi, Hindu or Muslim), the proliferation of market-based notions of individual autonomy also means that immigrants can identify with each other through a shared experience of class as South Asians. Class mobility thus becomes crucial to the production of locality, for it is through a gendered (primarily male and bourgeois) experience of class that immigrants negotiate the difference between postcolonial and multicultural citizenship.

Locality challenges the ways in which we think through racial identities in the United States. By moving away from the representational politics of ethnicity and toward the affective experience of class mobility, locality takes seriously the intimate and often vexed relationship between domestic racial formations and global structures of capital. It also highlights the compelling power of state-sponsored nationalisms, experienced as ideologies of multicultural belonging and as neoliberal constructs of postcolonial citizenship. Middle-class immigrants do not reject multiculturalism as a dominant ideology of subject formation (identifying as South Asian *instead of* as American). Rather, they identify as South Asian *because* they desire to be American. Such intense feelings of belonging are often misrecognized as narratives that codify South Asians into a "model minority." What these experiences reveal, instead, are the ways in which diasporic identities and communities are produced in relation to nationalist ideologies of the state inasmuch as they are embodied as a response or retaliation to state power. Understanding the production of locality demands that we consider not only the ways that immigrants embody racial difference within the state: more important, it requires that we also understand how diasporic subjects locate themselves within multicultural and postcolonial constructs of nationhood.

Examining South Asian localities thus necessitates an alternative method of analyzing diasporic subject formation, one that is equally attentive to the rhetoric of community formation and its embodied practice. Because South Asian identities and communities are forged through a diverse set of experiences, across differences of religion, gender, and sexuality, I draw upon an equally diverse set of methodological tools. Drawing upon ethnographic practices of participant observation, I explore how becoming South Asian is an everyday practice of belonging among specific communities of immigrants: across first-generation professionals and second-generation political activists, on the East and West coasts, among queer and straight immigrants, as well as between Muslims, Sikhs, and Hindus. Locality is expressed in the series of affinities that I generate between immigrant subjects, the popular culture that they create and consume, and my own intervention as participant and audience member at public events. But such affective relations of identity are also expressed through writing and performance, and so I also analyze literary texts as rhetorical acts of producing community. Drawing upon popular fiction and film made by South Asians, I examine how these texts are rendered as quintessentially American stories of ethnic assimilation. By historicizing these same narratives in relation to the politics of modern South Asia, I demonstrate how these fictional and cinematic works also tell stories about a diasporic community that is shaped by memories of the 1947 partition of the subcontinent, recollections of nationalist movements for Bangladeshi independence, and participation in Hindu-Muslim communal riots.

In the chapters that follow, I integrate the literary and the ethnographic in order to unravel the constraints of form and genre that shape the ways in which we look at diasporic popular culture. I read documentary films by and about South Asians not for the "truth" of their representation of immigrant lives, but as ethnographic narratives that articulate the disjointed production of locality between filmmaker, viewer, and documentary subject, all of whom identify variously as South Asian. Some of these documentary films circulate online and generate vibrant debates on blogs and websites about who and what is South Asian. Similarly, I consider a Broadway show about Indians in India in terms of its political implications for racial and class identities in America, by interviewing first- and second-generation actors, dancers, and audience members who participated in the making of the musical. I bend the formal constraints of popular culture by examining the work of South Asian visual artists not only as aesthetic depictions of identity but as archival texts about immigration that generate a collective viewing experience. By consistently situating literary, visual, and performative objects within a larger ethnographic field, I examine the ways in which South Asian localities have been produced and consumed across the turn of the twenty-first century.

Between 1999 and 2009 I attended public events organized in cities across the United States by immigrants of Indian, Pakistani, Bangladeshi, and Sri Lankan origin. Held in venues ranging from abandoned warehouses to marquee theaters, these community productions varied in genre and scale. Some of these public events, such as art festivals and musicals, traveled between the United States and Canada, as well as between the United States, the U.K., and South Asia. These disparate venues of cultural production were linked through a network of immigrant artists, activists, and audience members who themselves circulated across disparate national sites. Many of the participants that I interviewed self-identified as South Asian and as middle class; many more did not. How immigrants identified as South Asian, when they did not, and what it meant to embody South Asian subjectivities became the focus of my study. My engagement with South Asian public culture demonstrates how locality is experienced relationally and contextually, as an ideology of situated community that includes my own diasporic experience.

South Asians in Asian American Studies

Theorizing locality requires expanding the historical and geographical scope of Asian American studies, since the political history of South Asia and the class-based migrations of South Asians are uneasily situated within the epistemology of the field. Asian American studies is commonly narrated as a community-based movement for racial equality that emerged out of decolonization in the third world (in particular, the war in Vietnam). Yet the impact of South Asian anticolonial nationalism on Asian American politics is rarely discussed, even though these same movements against British imperialism shaped the broader context of the civil rights movement.[8] The absence of subcontinental immigrants from this early history of the field is also central to the racial dissonance embodied by South Asians. Although more-recent scholarship in the field represents first- and second-generation South Asians as examples of Asian American activism, these works remain oriented toward correcting an original absence. While studies of South Asian American literature and culture expand the representational claims of Asian American studies, they also retain an additive model of critical discourse.[9] Within this context, South Asians are represented as one more ethnic group that is "like" other Asian Americans, despite the divergent histories of race, class, and empire that characterize immigrants from Asia.

Because such representational politics inadequately capture the specific processes of what it means to be South Asian, locality provides a more capacious means of attending to the phenomenology of racialized experience. As postcolonial subjects, South Asians embody a history of empire that remains outside the purview of Asian American studies, even as scholars increasingly attend to the expansive scale of the U.S. empire in East Asia as well as in the Pacific Rim.[10] As ethnic minorities, the ways in which South Asians are gendered and racialized in the United States diverge from established perspectives on East and Southeast Asian immigrants.[11] Although scholars across the humanities and the social sciences have vigorously debated the relationship between the domestic and the diasporic as sites for the production of Asian American subjectivity, with few exceptions these debates have not taken into account the specificity of South Asian diasporic history, culture, and politics.[12]

Reorienting the purview of Asian American studies westward toward the subcontinent requires thinking through the unexpected relation between frameworks of racial politics in the United States and formations of postcolonial nationhood in South Asia: a relationship that comes to the forefront in the localizing practices of South Asians. As racial minorities who also participate in neoliberal politics on the subcontinent, middle-class South Asians demonstrate the conflation and overlap between distinct narratives of nationhood. The ties that bind these two narratives of belonging are not immediately visible, for unlike immigrants from Southeast and East Asia whose lives are directly impacted by U.S. imperialism in the region, there is no visible history that tethers the United States to the subcontinent. Instead it is a complex narrative, one that is triangulated through the legacy of British colonialism on the subcontinent. As the historian Antoinette Burton suggests, the cultural practices of South Asian immigrants facilitate "American identification with and disavowal of the British imperial legacy" (147). These real and imagined relationships between the United States and South Asia emerge in the domain of South Asian popular culture, which powerfully reshapes the topography of Asian America.

In *Immigrant Acts*, Lisa Lowe examines a series of Asian American aesthetic texts—literature, visual art, cultural festivals, and theater—that critically engage with U.S. race and ethnic politics. Although Lowe focuses on cultural texts, her readings resist assimilation into the aesthetic of multiculturalism. Instead, she argues that Asian American popular culture functions as a site of "minority cultural production" that produces "effects of dissonance, fragmentation, and irresolution" within canonized forms of national culture (31). By highlighting the legislative and material processes through which Asian immigrants are racialized by the U.S. state, Lowe reveals the contradictions inherent in universal notions of U.S. citizenship. Her readings of Asian American literature and performance leads her to contend that "the contradictory history of Asian Americans produces cultural forms that are materially and aesthetically at odds with the resolution of the citizen to the nation" (30). The Asian immigrant, at once intrinsic to and excluded from the U.S. state, emerges in Lowe's readings as an oppositional figure who contests multicultural discourses of citizenship.

My reading of literary and ethnographic texts draws upon Lowe's foundational work but differs in two important aspects. First, I argue that South Asians are racialized as minority subjects through their engagement with U.S. as well as subcontinental nationalisms. Second, instead of operating as a site of critique, South Asian diasporic popular culture is aligned with dominant discourses of multicultural citizenship. Popular fiction and film created by South Asian immigrants almost invariably reproduce middle-class narratives of migration, despite the heterogeneous experiences that characterize subcontinental immigrants. Likewise, at the public events I attended, middle-class immigrants of diverse national and regional origins on the subcontinent collaborated to embody unitary notions of "tradition" and "culture." South Asian communities emerge through this erosion of national, religious, and class difference, a process that is intensified by the assimilative tendencies of multiculturalism.

To propose that South Asian localities are shaped through the discourse of multiculturalism is also to acknowledge that resistance—so central to theorizing Asian American subjectivity—is an insufficient mode of understanding racial formation. For scholars in the field, "resistance" also operates as a powerful phenomenology of belonging, one that is central to the epistemic conditions of critical race and ethnic studies. Resistance frames the discursive claims made by Asian American studies within an antiracist and anticapitalist politics; it is also symptomatic of our collective commitment to theories of social justice. What this has meant in practice, however, is that Asian American popular culture is consistently framed as a site of oppositional politics.[13] Producing such narratives of opposition to the state constrains the ways in which we understand the dynamic production, consumption, and circulation of popular culture, particularly when the state and its ideologies of race, gender, and sexuality shape the form (if not the content) of these cultural texts.

These genealogies of racial resistance and models of ethnic community formation shape a number of works on South Asian immigrants in the United States. In their introduction to a special issue of *Amerasia Journal* titled "Satyagraha in America," the editors Biju Mathew and Vijay Prashad advocate the critical perspectives afforded by South Asian immigrants, in particular by the "children of 1965" (xii). Framing domestic movements for racial equality in the spirit of Gandhi's anti-imperialist call for satyagraha or "truth-force," Prashad and Mathew view South Asian youth as racialized subjects and diasporic popular culture as a domain of progressive politics. More important, the volume established a model of activism for scholars of South Asian American studies.

In the decade since the publication of Mathew and Prashad's volume, scholarship on South Asian Americans has evolved from an emergent field of research into an established domain of cultural criticism. However, in the humanities, research on South Asian diasporas continues to be defined by arguments for racial, gender, and sexual subjectivities that reject, rather than reproduce, dominant formations of U.S. citizenship. For example, in her book *Impossible Desires*, Gayatri Gopinath employs a queer diasporic reading of South Asian popular culture. By reading literature and film produced by South Asian immigrants as queer texts, Gopinath rejects the primacy of nationalism as an ideology of diasporic selfhood and community. While I share Gopinath's concern with deconstructing the hierarchical relationship between nation-state and diaspora, our archives of popular culture are diametrically opposed. Instead of emphasizing queer diasporic cultural texts, I focus precisely on those bearers of heteronormative patriarchy who make it "impossible" to occupy minority subject-positions. This is the cultural archive of the U.S. immigrant bourgeoisie, whose literary, cinematic, and ethnographic texts consolidate representations of South Asians as an upwardly mobile, assimilated group. Working from the center of popular culture rather than from its margins, I examine the ways in which middle-class immigrants re-embody dominant constructs of ethnicity and nationhood. One of my objectives is to understand how South Asian immigrants continue to circulate and consume heteronormative narratives of belonging, despite the visibility and centrality of queer diasporic cultural production.

In the social sciences, an oppositional politics of ethnicity likewise remains integral to research on South Asian immigration. Writing against quantitative studies of ethnic assimilation published in the 1970s and 1980s, recent scholarship has emphasized how South Asians are integral to movements for social change.[14] Focusing on youth cultures, working-class immigrants, and minority religious groups, scholars such Sunaina Maira, Shalini Shankar, and Nitasha Sharma have positioned South Asian immigrants as resistant subjects. Their ethnographic work highlights the unequal relations of power between working-class and undocumented immigrants, and middle- and upper-class professionals.[15] Together, these works also emphasize how new ethnic identities (such as desi) exceed pluralist narratives of multiculturalism. From this perspective, to be South Asian is to reject liberal ideologies of U.S. nationhood, even though the stakes of refusing to participate in the nation have distinct consequences for different groups of South Asians.

Positioning South Asians in opposition to dominant modalities of citizenship limits the ways in which we can understand how ideologies of multiculturalism and neoliberal state formation shape practices of belonging. In literary criticism as well as in the social sciences, the turn away from popular narratives of multiculturalism has resulted in a narrowed scope for South Asian American studies. Despite the strength of its interdisciplinary interventions, over the past decade the field has been increasingly characterized by its reliance on "good" and "bad" subjects of immigration.[16] The "good" subjects (those who embody resistant racial, gender, sexual, or class subjectivities) are positioned against and in relation to "bad" subjects who conform to the status quo (male immigrant bourgeoisie, Hindu right-wing nationalists). South Asian American studies is defined by this binary logic, within which the "good" subjects of immigration operate as models of collective struggle against a neoliberal state. The forms of solidarity that are enunciated through this process generate a teleological narrative of progressive politics within which minority subjects resist assimilation to the United States.

By contrast, the immigrants that I interview and the literary and cinematic texts I study do not necessarily express a resistant ideology of race and citizenship. Nor do the chapters coalesce into a coherent narrative of struggle, one that culminates in the expression of a solidarity-based politics. Instead, the ways in which middle-class immigrants embody locality reveals how South Asian communities accede to hegemonic ideologies of belonging. Rather than distinguish between a "dissenting" citizenship and a "complicit" citizenship, I argue that the formation of South Asian communities is immersed in multicultural as well as neoliberal notions of nationhood.[17] The production of locality requires that we engage with multivalent narratives of identity and community, some of which converge with dominant notions of what it means to be American. In this regard, "South Asian" is itself an interpellative term, one that brings into being the very communities that I study. For first- and second-generation immigrants who disidentify with pluralist narratives of multicuturalism, identifying as South Asian may engender an oppositional politics, creating forms of transnational community outside the domain of the state. Yet for those who identify strongly with the promise of full citizenship in America, such affective relations to place may engender partial identifications or misidentifications with regimes of ethnic pluralism. In both instances, disidentification does not operate as a form of disavowal, but rather as a reengagement with dominant structures of race and citizenship.[18]

In their essay "The Remaking of a Model Minority," Jasbir Puar and Amit Rai note that "underlying the debate about SAAS [South Asian American studies] is an assumption that it is a coherent subfield centered on the study of South Asian American subjects and, implicitly, that the community-studies model needs to continue to be the basis for the new work that will 'correct' the neglect of certain ethnic groups" (99, note 4). They point out that insisting on a "community-studies model" obscures the fact that the field itself relies on an unstable subject of study. Puar and Rai's response is to queer the field of South Asian American studies—that is, to pervert the very assumption of a single community or identity shared by South Asians. I share in their effort to deconstruct representational notions of South Asian community, but my own approach is somewhat different. By focusing on the production of locality, I examine how middle-class South Asians are at once complicit with normative frameworks of citizenship in the United States and generate notions of selfhood and community that question these same frameworks. This back-and-forth movement between assimilation and resistance, as well as between nationalist discourses in the United States and on the subcontinent, is central to what I see as the formation of South Asian community.

Locality reflects the practice of an oppositional ethnic politics but makes a different intervention in Asian American studies, one that expands upon the capacity of multiculturalism, as a rights-based discourse of identity, to generate a collective experience of belonging. In the chapters that follow, I turn to those sites of cultural production and to those immigrant subjects whose self-fashioning have not always aligned with progressive politics. Among my objectives is to clarify what we understand as "progressive," particularly as this political rhetoric inflects emerging forms of racial and class identity. As I demonstrate in my readings of South Asian art festivals, self-consciously activist venues for diasporic cultural production can unexpectedly reproduce pluralist discourses of multiculturalism. In contrast, those forms of South Asian popular culture that may be viewed as retrograde, such as the Miss India USA pageant, dynamically reconfigure the transnational terrain of racial subjectivity. The ideological contradictions that are inherent within each of these venues demand our attention, for they call into question a linear and necessarily progressive correlation between immigrant art and cultural politics. Reading these various texts also requires us, as scholars and teachers of ethnic studies, to reflect upon our own investments in progressive representations of race and ethnicity. Our discomfort with these varied forms of South Asian popular culture emerges not only from its distorted representations of ethnic community, but also from the fact that ethnicity itself is constituted alongside normative ideologies of class and nationhood.

Theorizing South Asian localities thus requires turning away from emancipatory narratives of resistance, and toward more complicit notions of multicultural belonging.

Genealogies of Locality

The term "South Asian" has been widely used by students and academics since the 1990s to refer to immigrants from across the subcontinent: Bangladesh, India, Pakistan, and Sri Lanka, and to a lesser extent, Nepal and Afghanistan. On university campuses across the United States, South Asian student associations aim to be pan-regional and pan-religious, and remain predominantly middle class. Importantly, these associations do not necessarily claim to be secular, for South Asian student associations tend to organize around Hindu religious festivities and cultural events. In a different political register, the term "South Asian" is frequently claimed by progressive activists who work to advance the legal status of subcontinental immigrants in the United States: these include antiracist coalitions, labor unions, domestic-violence prevention groups, and gay and lesbian social networks.[19] Many of these groups point to the broad geographical distribution of their membership in terms of national origin, as well as the services they provide for members from various linguistic backgrounds and religious faiths.

The activist Naheed Islam warns us, however, that identifying as South Asian in the United States elides differences between and within countries on the subcontinent. By focusing predominantly on the history, culture, and politics of India, many South Asian groups marginalize Muslim communities within India, as well as the Islamic states of Pakistan and Bangladesh (and often ignore altogether minority Buddhist, Christian, and Jain communities). Islam writes against universalizing experiences of immigration, for while migration can enable new political solidarities, it can also reinscribe hegemonic relations of power between individuals from the subcontinent.[20] The new solidarities that are forged through immigrant experience reveal how identifying *as* South Asian is not necessarily the same as identifying *with* South Asia, the region or its people. Becoming South Asian is a form of locality that is produced through ideologies of racial and class mobility in the United States. In contrast, South Asia is a geographical construct produced through the long history of colonial and postcolonial nationalist movements on the subcontinent, and an academic field of study that emerged in tandem with U.S. foreign policy during the cold war.[21] Translating the uses of "South Asian" as a class-based experience of migration in relation to the geopolitical construct of the subcontinent highlights the limitations of transnational claims to citizenship.

Given the diverse regional, religious, and national origins of immigrants, "South Asian" is one of many terms of ethnic identity that has circulated among subcontinental immigrants in the United States. The sociologist Monisha Das Gupta has persuasively argued that since the late nineteenth century, working-class and middle-class immigrants from India, Pakistan, and Bangladesh have struggled to occupy legible racial constructs and in turn produce ethnic identities for themselves. Whether as "Caucasian," "Asian Indian," "Asian American," or "Muslim," racial categorization for South Asian immigrants has operated as a disciplinary apparatus of legality and as flexible constructs of identity. Moreover, these shifting constructs of race elucidate how different generations of South Asian immigrants understand their locality in the United States, as well as in relation to political movements in South Asia. From early twentieth-century Punjabi Sikh immigrants who were mistakenly labeled "Hindoo," to middle-class professionals who petitioned to be categorized as "Asian Indian" in the 1980 census, to immigrants who are (mis)recognized as "Muslim" after 2001, the crooked lines of South Asian racialization generate a nonlinear narrative of locality. Delineating the ways in which subcontinental immigrants are incorporated into and ejected from legal formations of race-based citizenship demonstrates how notions of belonging are split across class, gender, sexuality, religion, and national origin.

The popular history of South Asian immigration originates with Punjabi Sikhs, Hindus, and Muslims who migrated as farmworkers to the West Coast in the early twentieth century. Many Punjabis married Mexican women (who were also racialized as "brown"), and their families became central to the growth of agricultural industries in northern and central California.[22] During this period, the landmark case of *United States v. Bhagat Singh Thind* (1923) legislated South Asian immigrants as nonwhite, thereby limiting property ownership and rights to citizenship for subcontinental migrants. Scholars of Asian American studies frequently cite *Thind* as an early example of Asian immigrant racialization by the U.S. state.[23] However, the specific case of *Thind* is also compounded by the fact that Indian immigrants were colonial subjects of Britain for the first half of the twentieth century. Thus the claims to U.S. citizenship made in *Thind* cannot be considered in isolation from simultaneous claims to British citizenship made by other South Asian immigrants to North America, in particular those Sikhs who migrated to Canada on the *Komagata Maru* in 1914. The *Komagata Maru* was a chartered ship that steamed from Punjab to Vancouver via Hong Kong and Japan, a voyage that directly challenged Canadian immigration policy, which required that immigrants make a "continuous journey" from their country of origin. The policy effectively barred migrants from the Indian subcontinent, even though Indians, like Canadians, were also British subjects. When the *Komagata Maru* was banned from anchoring in Vancouver and its passengers were refused entry to Canada, the ship's journey became testament to the unequal claims to citizenship embodied by imperial subjects. Upon its return to Calcutta, British police detained the *Komagata Maru* for fear of political violence. As a consequence of these events, many of the ship's passengers later became leaders of the transnational Ghadar movement against colonial rule.[24] The *Komagata Maru* episode emphasizes how imperial discourses of racial difference intersect with race-based claims to citizenship. Viewed within a broader North American context, linking the history of the *Komagata Maru* to *Thind* reframes South Asians as simultaneously colonial subjects and racialized immigrants.

These early histories of migration feature prominently in contemporary South Asian popular culture, most notably at the art festivals that I discuss in Chapter 4. Films about the *Komagata Maru* as well as artwork depicting early Punjabi immigration to California cross over from art festivals in Canada to the United States, and then from the U.S. East to West coasts. Such cultural texts are central to forging a common sense of South Asian locality between artists and audience members at the festival sites. However, the commodification of early South Asian immigrant histories through the exhibition of films and artwork also generates a homogeneous history of migration, one that is claimed at the festivals by second-generation South Asians of various religious, national, and class backgrounds. Even as young immigrants collaborate with each other to produce a common history of South Asian ethnicity, their consumption of these aesthetic texts eclipses the structural differences between British imperial migration to North America, early twentieth-century Punjabi immigration to California, and the migration of professionals to the United States in the mid-to-late twentieth century.

In 1965 the reform of the Immigration and Nationality Act marked a break from earlier histories of South Asian migration and initiated the first wave of professionally trained immigrants from the subcontinent. Also known as the Hart-Celler Act, the Immigration and Nationality Act abolished quotas based on national origin. The Hart-Celler Act was central to the advancement of science and technology industries during the cold war, as the U.S. state incorporated the knowledge and labor of South Asian doctors, engineers, and scientists. Many middle-class immigrants struggled with identifying their place within U.S. racial formations, for "in India they had been the beneficiaries of full citizenship on account of their class, caste, and in some cases, male privilege."[25] Unlike immigrant activists in the early twentieth century who advanced race-based claims to U.S. citizenship, however, this new group of immigrants advocated for citizenship on the basis of ethnicity. Some groups of middle-class immigrants worked to redefine their racial categorization on the U.S. census as nonwhite, or "Asian Indians" in order to gain civil rights provisions and full citizenship. At the same time, this wave of immigration established a popular narrative of South Asians as an upwardly mobile and assimilated ethnic group, whose educational and economic achievements made them a so-called model minority.[26]

Such representations of upwardly mobile male immigrants predominate in the works of Jhumpa Lahiri, which I discuss in Chapter 1. However, reading Lahiri's fiction as merely a story of becoming American limits the ways in which we can understand how post-1965 immigrants continue to participate in nationalist movements on the subcontinent at the same time that they inhabit racialized notions of U.S. citizenship. Even as Lahiri's middle-class protagonists acclimate to living in America, that very notion of belonging is often shaped through their actual and remote participation in the 1971 Bangladeshi War of Independence, which in turn invokes memories of the 1947 partition of the subcontinent and the 1905 colonial partition of Bengal. Prioritizing political events in South Asia that mark the everyday lives of immigrants in America enables us to reconceptualize narratives of ethnic assimilation as a practice of localizing postcolonial history.

More-recent waves of immigration from the subcontinent demand a different analytic perspective, one that is necessitated by the changing demographic of South Asian communities. Between 1990 and 2000 the population of South Asians (both foreign and U.S.-born) more than doubled, and certain communities, such as Bangladeshis, tripled in number.

Indian Americans continue to be the largest group of immigrants from the subcontinent and constitute the third-largest Asian immigrant group in the United States, after Chinese Americans and Filipino Americans.[27] The class composition of South Asian communities also shifted significantly. Family reunification provisions and green card sponsorship, as well as the influx of undocumented immigrants, have created large working-class populations of South Asians in the service industry and manufacturing sectors. Immigration has been amplified by neoliberal economic policies in Bangladesh and India, which have created new job opportunities on the subcontinent and destroyed others.[28] These demographic shifts demonstrate the difficulty of identifying as South Asian in the early twenty-first century, particularly across differences of religion, national origin, class, and language. In Chapter 2 I consider several documentary films that demonstrate the irregular production of South Asian locality, especially when alternative constructs of community—such as being working class, Muslim, or mixed race—take precedence.

Any contemporary examination of South Asian identity and community necessarily contends with the altered racial and political landscape of the United States after September 11, 2001, particularly in terms of its implications for Muslim South Asians, as well as those immigrants who are misrecognized as Arab or Muslim, including Hindus, Christians, and Sikhs.[29] The legal scholar Muneer Ahmad argues, "The events of September 11 have proven the attempt of Arab and South Asian elites to escape the debasement of race by way of class to be the impossibility that those in the working class have always known it to be" (111). As racial profiling impacts all classes of South Asian immigrants (though it does not affect all classes equally), Ahmad discusses how South Asians come to be identified as terrorists, informants, and non-Americans. In Chapter 5 I examine the difficult locality of Muslim, Sikh, and queer immigrants through an ethnographic reading of the Broadway musical *Bombay Dreams*. I discuss how the portrayal of a "secular" and "modern" India in the musical relies on the hypervisibility and subsequent invisibility of Muslim, Sikh, and queer characters onstage, a narrative that is amplified by the concurrent erasure of Muslim Americans offstage. Because the musical was incorporated as entertainment programming for the Republican National Convention (RNC), I also discuss *Bombay Dreams* as a spectacular performance of U.S. nationalism. *Bombay*

Dreams was staged in New York City just one year after the institution of Special Registration procedures that mandated the surveillance of immigrant men from Pakistan and Afghanistan, among other countries. For those RNC attendees who supported Special Registration and other legislative acts to keep Americans "safe and secure," the nationalist narrative that shaped *Bombay Dreams* was uncannily similar to their own representation of America.

The locality of Muslim immigrants demands our continued analysis as U.S. imperialisms are renewed, even in a so-called post-racial age. Throughout the book I situate September 11, 2001, as one nodal point in the broader historical framework of immigration from the subcontinent. The aftermath of the attacks has had intensive legal ramifications for South Asians who are racially profiled, detained, and deported, and for prospective immigrants who apply for travel, work, and student visas, as well as permanent residency. To focus singularly on the ways in which this historical event reshapes racial and religious identities, however, limits our understanding of how multiculturalism works to incorporate and eclipse other forms of difference. This is particularly important in the current political moment, in which religious difference invites both intellectual consideration and social panic. In my ethnographic and literary readings I emphasize how locality is not contingent on a single historical event, but is produced in relation to a shifting set of political and social structures in the United States as well as on the subcontinent. Such a transnational perspective enables us to understand how immigrants creatively deploy neoliberal structures of class mobility in South Asia in order to inhabit their identities in the United States. That middle-class immigrants claim to be American even as working-class and Muslim immigrants are denied rights in the United States highlights how differential relations of power are reproduced and eclipsed within diasporic communities in the name of becoming South Asian.

Sites of Production

The cultural texts at the core of this book were created by first- and second-generation South Asian immigrants between 1999 and 2009, a period marked by the rapid expansion of race-based claims to citizenship in the United States and class-based ideologies of citizenship in South Asia. Over the course of the decade, the imperialist claims made by U.S. foreign policy in South Asia and the Middle East were manifest domestically through the violent rhetoric around immigrants from these regions, particularly working-class, non-English-speaking, and undocumented immigrants. Yet even within this charged racial context, cultural commodities from South Asia such as music and fashion have garnered a wide following, and South Asian actors, including many Muslim South Asians, have gained prominence in the mass media.[30] Such commoditized representations of South Asians as an upwardly mobile immigrant group are codified further in U.S. political culture. The recent elections of Bobby Jindal and Nikki Haley, both second-generation Indian immigrants, as Republican governors of Louisiana and South Carolina, respectively, demonstrate how the difference of race continues to be absolved into universal ideologies of American citizenship. Whereas for Haley and Jindal their victories exemplify a "post-racial" moment in American politics, the very exceptionalism of their election demands our renewed attention to multiculturalism as a flexible discourse of nationhood that manages race, religious, and class difference.

The primacy of class mobility as a vehicle for "universal" citizenship also resonates in South Asia during the same period. Economic and social "reforms" instituted in India and Bangladesh in the 1990s under the directive of the World Bank and International Monetary Fund generated neoliberal notions of citizenship, which in turn became central to the expansion of a middle-class consumer citizenry. The citizen-consumer has become the paradigmatic face of popular culture in South Asia, particularly in commercial Hindi (or Bollywood) films, as well as in music and television.[31] At the same time, in response to economic liberalization, a series of riots, protests, and terrorist attacks in South Asia actively contested the relation between state sovereignty and minority ethnic, religious, and linguistic groups. A major site of rupture between the Indian nation-state and its citizen-public was the Hindu-Muslim riots in Bombay in 1992 and Gujarat in 2002, both of which codified the dominance of Hindu nationalism in India despite its post-independence secular constitution. Similarly in Pakistan, the 2008 terrorist attacks in Islamabad and sporadic assassinations of political figures reflect the rise of Islamist movements, but also highlight class divides between those who are the beneficiaries of global capital accumulation and those who are not. These contentious events are often interpreted as a threat to modernization in South Asia and operate as a pretext for more intimate relations of global capital (via foreign aid and weapons transfers agreements) that bind together South Asia with the United States. South Asian immigrant groups are central to this process, both for their remittance of funds toward state security and reconstruction and for their personal investments in reproducing ideologies of what it means to be secular and modern.

Situating contemporary South Asian popular culture within this broader geographical context illuminates how the ties that bind South Asia to the United States are triangulated through the legacy of British imperialism, the rising power of the U.S. military, and the increasingly neoliberal orientations of the United States and nation-states in South Asia. Such political convergences highlight the ways in which the postcolonial history of the subcontinent is never far from the formation of South Asian identities and communities in America. As immigrants, South Asians become ethnic subjects through pluralist discourses of multiculturalism that codify their religious and racial difference. As diasporic subjects, South Asians participate in postcolonial constructs of nationhood on the subcontinent in ways that inflect their racialized and classed locations in the United States. Both these frameworks of national belonging are embedded in global movements of class and capital, and yet their claims to locality take distinct forms. The ways in which immigrants work to coherently embody these two distinct narrative frameworks—and when they fail to do so—constitutes the process of becoming South Asian.

I map the production of locality through these diverse routes of belonging. Bringing together art and literature, documentaries and blogs, activism and community events, I examine works produced by South Asian immigrants in the United States throughout this decade of cultural and political foment. This archive of cultural texts highlights the demographic shifts that impact the shape of South Asian communities: from the migration of middle-class professionals to the growing numbers of working-class immigrants from India, Pakistan, and Bangladesh; from multiracial South Asians to transnational adoptees; from progressive youth groups that identify as secular, to young Muslim immigrants who define themselves through their practice of faith. As I move from popular fiction and film toward sites of performance, I also make a methodological shift from representations of immigrant communities toward an analysis of the phenomenological conditions under which such communities come into being. I organize these distinct cultural texts chronologically in order to emphasize the historical (or material) and affective ties that bind immigrants to one another. The intensity of experience that brings together different groups of subcontinental immigrants also emphasizes the fragility of locality, as differences of class and national origin, region and religion, gender and sexuality are obscured by the affective conditions of creating community. Fusing literary criticism with ethnographic participant observation, I underscore the ruptures between the rhetorical production of locality and its embodied practice. Throughout, I situate myself in relation to this cultural archive as reader, viewer, and consumer, one whose own experience of locality is produced in tandem with the subjects I study.

Chapter 1, "Postcolonial Locations," situates the work of Jhumpa Lahiri, author of the short-story collection *Interpreter of Maladies* and the novel *The Namesake*, in relation to contemporary nationalist movements in South Asia. Lahiri's fiction is frequently represented as a narrative of immigrant assimilation and adaptation. I argue instead that Lahiri's works underscore the exigency for a different temporal and spatial landscape of Asian American literature, one that rehistoricizes the conditions of postcoloniality for first- and second-generation immigrants. In my reading of *Interpreter of Maladies*, I delineate an uneven historical framework that binds together post-partition South Asia with postwar America. As Lahiri's first- and second-generation protagonists negotiate disparate national events in their everyday lives (the 1971 Indo-Pakistan War and the Vietnam War; Nehruvian plans for socialist development and the 1969 lunar landing), they embody postcolonial localities. The synchronous temporalities that link South Asia to the United States are also evident in Lahiri's novel, as I read *The Namesake* in relation to the Russian writer Nikolai Gogol's short story "The Overcoat." The intertextual relationship between these two literary works engenders a postcolonial critique of America, even as Lahiri's male protagonists reproduce an experience of class mobility. As Ashoke Ganguli, an engineering student in newly independent India, avidly reads "The Overcoat," he identifies with the anti-imperialist politics that undergird Nikolai Gogol's work. Ashoke's critique of imperialism is fostered within the context of India's leadership of the Non-Aligned Movement during the same period, in particular the internationalist principles and alternative to cold war politics that the movement offers. For Ashoke, his repeated reading of "The Overcoat" is a means of embodying a critical postcoloniality even after his migration to the United

States. While his son Gogol initially rejects "The Overcoat" in order to claim his American citizenship, in the aftermath of Ashoke's death Gogol turns toward his namesake as a means of aligning himself with his father's immigrant past, thereby expanding the historical contours of his own American story.

Chapter 2, "So Far from Home," examines documentary films by emerging and established South Asian filmmakers as ethnographic, autobiographical, and historical texts. Whereas in Lahiri's fiction locality is experienced as a temporal feeling through various historical narratives that bind South Asia with the United States, in these films locality emerges as a spatial construct that is diversely embodied by middle- and working-class immigrants. Ranging from Mira Nair's early documentary on subway newsstand vendors in New York, to a feminist intervention in a multigenerational middle-class family, to a PBS documentary about Indian adoptees in Minnesota, to a collaborative video on young Bangladeshi Muslims in Manhattan, the films map the changing demographics of South Asian immigration from the 1990s to the present. Despite the heterogeneous experience of migration across these communities, however, each filmmaker portrays immigration as a "choice" between living in South Asia or in the United States, a narrative that is eventually resolved through the protagonists' identification as American citizens. I reframe these documentaries as ethnographic texts by considering the ways in which the filmmakers and viewers—themselves first- and second-generation immigrants—become an integral part of their cinematic projects. As filmmakers conflate their own class and racial identities with those of their subjects, and as viewers insist on seeing the documentaries as normative representations of middle-class migration (as indicated by their online commentaries), I highlight how differences in class, national origin, gender, and religion are steadily eroded in the collaborative attempt to identify as "South Asian." These collaborative identifications are only made possible through a distorted spatial logic of locality, as filmmakers and viewers remain invested in a geographic and political divide between the subcontinent and the United States. Yet attending to the dissonances between the aural, visual, and oral narratives within each film alerts us to another logic of locality, one that ties together South Asia and America through the transnational constructs of religion, class, and gender embodied by the documentary subjects.

26   *Introduction*

The production of locality is also the subject of Chapter 3, "Beauty Queens." At the Miss India USA pageant in San Jose, California, I explore the disjuncture between the rhetoric of community that is articulated and embodied by the young contestants for the crown, as well as by their supporters and funders. Within Asian American studies, beauty pageants are often cited as paradigmatic representations of gendered citizenship. Through an ethnographic and archival analysis of the pageant, I shift our perspective from questions of representation toward the experiential qualities of belonging that are differentially embodied across generation, religion, and region of origin. Whereas the contestants embody a gendered notion of India onstage and position themselves as multicultural American citizens offstage, the organizers and audience members are also complicit in the performance of community. Given the expansive notions of class and capital that shape South Asian identities in Silicon Valley at the turn of the twenty-first century, I highlight how the high-tech entrepreneurs who fund and attend the pageant become the new face of the "model minority." These narratives of capital accumulation obscure the increasing numbers of undocumented and underpaid immigrant workers who labor in the same technology industries, as well as an earlier history of working-class Punjabi immigration to California. The close organizational ties between the Miss India USA pageant and Miss India contests in India codify these structures of upward mobility, as both pageants reproduce notions of a feminine, modern, and "global" India. For the young female contestants who must straddle two disjunct narratives of national belonging, their experience of locality is forged through the circulation of ideologies of sexuality, modernity, and class mobility.

In Chapter 4, "The Art of Multiculturalism," I move from the transnational production of locality toward its domestic practice. In this chapter I focus on annual art festivals organized by young immigrants between 1999 and 2005 in Toronto, New York, and Los Angeles. These festivals are designed to be progressive political events, bringing together artists and activists of Sri Lankan, Pakistani, Bangladeshi, and Indian origin. By highlighting the exhibition and consumption of visual artwork across these festival sites, I also delineate a broad ethnographic field of self-identified South Asians. Each festival is differently funded by state and/or private grants, oriented toward distinctly Canadian or U.S. public discourses of multiculturalism, and draws upon diverse local immigrant histories. Yet across these festivals, organizers, artists, and audience members collude to create homogeneous notions of community. Because these festivals emerge out of local racial formations, they also highlight the disjuncture between identifying as South Asian—articulated as a domestic experience of racialization—and identifying with the history and cultural politics of contemporary South Asia. I argue that the affective conditions of creating South Asian community are produced through a collective experience of "feeling good" rather than "feeling guilt." Such positive feelings, which emerge from progressive activism, in turn obscure the disparities between histories of subcontinental emigration, between experiences of racialization, and between the divergent groups of immigrants who assemble at these festival sites. Looking at the ways in which artworks are consumed by organizers and audience members enables us to understand how the festivals generate commodified notions of South Asian ethnicity and codify neoliberal constructs of race- and class-based community.

I conclude the book by situating South Asian localities within the domain of U.S. multiculturalism. In Chapter 5 I examine the Broadway musical *Bombay Dreams*. A love story between a poor boy and rich girl in the Bombay slums, this blockbuster production featured subcontinental immigrants in all its lead roles. For these actors and dancers, the musical offered a breakthrough into mainstream popular culture. For the middle-class immigrants who went to see the show, the musical symbolized the emergence of a global India, staged through Bollywood songs and dance. I read *Bombay Dreams* as a performative text about contemporary representations of India in America; as a social text about how an "ethnic" musical was translated into an "American" story; and as an ethnographic text about the ways in which actors and dancers came to collectively identify as South Asians even as they performed as "Indians" onstage. Situated within its immediate historical context, however, the musical also delineates the political and economic ties that bind together South Asia and the United States after September 11, 2001. Bombay and New York are both global cities, celebrated for their ethnic, racial, and religious diversity and as sites for class and capital mobility. Onstage, such representations of Bombay as a "secular" and "modern" city rely upon the erasure of Muslim, Sikh, and queer characters. Offstage, *Bombay Dreams* provoked a fierce debate around the meaning of multiculturalism in America. Because the musical was incorporated into the 2004 RNC as part of its entertainment programming, *Bombay Dreams* was also the site of public protests against the deportation and surveillance of Muslim Americans after 9/11. While the musical was advertised as "Somewhere You've Never Been Before," for the South Asians who viewed, protested against, and worked in the show, *Bombay Dreams* produced an intimately familiar sense of place—a place that was located in the United States.

For those subcontinental immigrants who create and participate in these popular cultural texts, South Asia comes ever closer to America. The convergence between postcolonial notions of nationhood and multicultural ideologies of race defines each of these sites of cultural production. Collectively, these texts advance a popular narrative of South Asians as an upwardly mobile immigrant group. Unraveling these dominant representations of race and class thus requires attending to the phenomenological qualities of locality as an emplaced architecture of feeling, differentially embodied by a heterogeneous group of immigrants. The work of producing locality illustrates the continued allure of multiculturalism, which operates across these texts as a means of inhabiting race- and class-based claims to America. While South Asians continue to invest in nationalist discourses of belonging, the promise of full citizenship remains elusive. Particularly for those immigrants who are minoritized by national origin, class, gender, sexuality, and religious faith, the difficulty of identifying as South Asian elucidates how locality remains liable to repetition and failure. By opening out this range of cultural texts to an unconventional strategy of reading, one that prioritizes the relationship between filmmaker and viewer, between author and reader, and between performer and audience, I show how the uneven embodiment of locality by South Asians preserves and perverts normative frameworks of ethnicity in the United States.

Throughout this book, I position myself as a critic and consumer of South Asian popular culture, as one who takes pleasure in the act of consumption. However, that pleasure is mediated through the process of participating in these venues of cultural production. Over the past decade I have come to understand how my desire to identify with other South Asians hinges on the possibility that such collaborative endeavors can provide a place for me to belong. Yet the fact that I frequently feel out of place within the forms of community engendered by these popular texts demonstrates how being "South Asian" can never be a universal experience. Instead, South Asian diasporic communities remain intimately linked to dominant ideologies of national origin and class, gender, and sexuality. Untangling the relationship between narratives of racialization and experiences of identification requires not only that I disidentify with the communities that I study, but equally important, that I continue to position myself (contingently, and sometimes unsuccessfully) within sites of South Asian cultural production. By delineating nonlinear paths of belonging, I locate not only my own entry point into the world of South Asian diasporic popular cultures, but also the ways that readers, viewers, and audience members enter these texts unexpectedly.

ONE

Postcolonial Locations

Jhumpa Lahiri's Interpreter of Maladies *and* The Namesake

> "Mr. Sen says that once I receive my license everything will improve. What do you think, Eliot? Will things improve?"
> "You could go places," Eliot suggested. "You could go anywhere."
> "Could I drive all the way to Calcutta? How long would that take, Eliot? Ten thousand miles, at fifty miles per hour?"
>
> —Jhumpa Lahiri, "Mrs. Sen's"

In Jhumpa Lahiri's story "Mrs. Sen's," the newly married wife of an Indian immigrant complains to Eliot, a young boy in her charge, about how far removed she is from Calcutta. Mrs. Sen understands her own locality in terms of distance, which she comprehends in spatial as well as phenomenological terms. For Mrs. Sen, distance is an affective condition, one that is felt through the sheer number of miles that demarcate her family home from her current residence in Rhode Island, and which is also felt through her absence from the rituals of daily life in Calcutta. Even as Eliot encourages Mrs. Sen to secure her driver's license—a quintessentially American emblem of freedom and mobility—she remains unconvinced of the utility of such a legal document. In her first and only drive without a license, to procure a freshwater fish similar to what she ate in Bengal, Mrs. Sen crashes her car. Not only is it not possible to drive from Rhode Island to Calcutta; it is also impossible to return to a time before her marriage, to a time before her migration. It is impossible, in other words, for Mrs. Sen to go back to a time when she was unbound by America. Even as Mrs. Sen describes her experience in the United States through metaphors of spatial distance, her locality is also a temporal condition, one that ties together her immigrant experience in the United States to her continued participation in everyday life in South Asia.

In Asian American literary studies, the historical relationship between South Asia and America is often represented through narratives of migration, narratives depicted in terms of individual journeys out of the subcontinent. Mrs. Sen, for example, comes to the United States for a job—not her own but her husband's. The rather dour Mr. Sen works in a tenure-track position at a local university, and so the couple's trips to Calcutta as well as their time together in Rhode Island are bound by the calendar of academic life. Their migration is part of the larger wave of professional immigration spurred by the 1965 Hart-Celler Act and its abolition of "national origins" quotas for skilled Asians. This legal provision forms the temporal conditions of *Interpreter of Maladies* and *The Namesake*, both texts that feature stories of middle- and upper-middle-class Bengali immigrants. However, mapping the distance between the United States and the subcontinent is not only a matter of highlighting the legislative practices that recruited South Asian immigrants. Writing the relationship between South Asia and America also requires attending to the temporalities that differentiate colonial and postcolonial histories of the subcontinent from imperial histories of the United States. What it means to be South Asian is not singularly defined by U.S. immigration law, but also by ongoing movements for decolonization, independence, and modernization on the subcontinent. For South Asians who embody these differential histories, the time of immigration engenders a postcolonial subjectivity that binds the history of nation-states on the subcontinent to the racial formation of the United States. Mrs. Sen's postcoloniality is evident in her extensive preparations for the nightly meals she shares with her husband; in the closets full of saris that were given to her as dowry; in the ways that she expends time to find ingredients that remind her of home. Postcoloniality becomes one name for the phenomenology of locality that South Asian immigrants produce and inhabit in their everyday lives.

Accounting for a postcolonial reading of South Asian subjectivity requires broadening the geographical as well as historical framework of Asian American studies. As an immigrant group, South Asians are marginalized from normative histories of Asian American studies that originate in the civil rights and ethnic studies movements of the 1970s, even as such movements for Asian American representation were informed by histories of decolonization in South Asia.[1] While contemporary fiction by South Asian immigrants is now regularly featured in Asian American literature courses, the specific histories of independence and partition on the subcontinent do not figure into the domain of Asian American literary studies. The disjuncture between the exclusion of South Asia from the geographical framework of Asian American studies and the incorporation of South Asians as ethnic and literary subjects in the field is a problem of locality, one that is constituted by the intellectual parameters of the discipline. Unlike former and current U.S. territories in the Caribbean and the Pacific, South Asia is not part of what Allan Isaac calls the "American Tropics," the chain of empire that binds the United States to Asia throughout the nineteenth and twentieth centuries. The spatial boundaries of Asian American studies, which once focused exclusively on East Asia and has more recently shifted to include Southeast Asia and the Pacific Rim, is defined by the contours of U.S. imperial policy: wars in Japan, Korea, and Vietnam; the annexation of Hawai'i; the colonization and ongoing military occupation of the Philippines. From this perspective South Asia remains outside the proper geographic domain of Asian America, for there is no documented history of U.S. colonialism in the region. Locating South Asians within Asian American studies thus requires a longer temporal and spatial perspective, one that is triangulated between the legacy of British imperialism, decolonization movements on the subcontinent, and the emergence of the United States as a global power.

Over the past decade postcolonial theory has been deployed by Asian Americanists as a critique of U.S.-as-empire (by literary theorists such as Isaac and Kandice Chuh), and as a category of naming ethnic subjects (by critics such as Jenny Sharpe, Lata Mani, and Ruth Frankenberg). Postcolonial critiques of U.S. imperialist expansion in East and Southeast Asia have importantly drawn attention to the Pacific Rim as a site of contested histories and subjectivities. As Kandice Chuh notes in *Imagine Otherwise*, postcolonial theory highlights "the ways that national identities come into being through negotiations with global nexuses of relations of power" (117). However, in most cases this scholarly consideration of Asian American postcoloniality operates from the United States outwards—that is, by prioritizing local (continental U.S.) conditions as the starting point from which the ethnic subject becomes a postcolonial subject. For those immigrants whose histories of migration are conditioned by U.S. colonial intervention in Asia—such as Korean, Vietnamese, or Filipino Americans—postcolonial theory reveals how local conditions of ethnicity and race are bound to global events. However, such a scholarly maneuver of reaching outward from within—of incorporating histories of war and neocolonialism into a reflexive critique of U.S. nation-formation—has the unintended effect of reinscribing the imperialist geography of the United States. While a postcolonial critique of empire broadens the intellectual scope of Asian American studies and American studies more generally, it has a limited effect on decentering the United States as the primary terrain on which diasporic ethnic and racial subjectivities are formed.

In my reading of popular South Asian literature, I move away from using the term "postcolonial" as a name or claim to ethnicity. Instead, I ask a different set of questions about the relationship between postcolonial theory and Asian American studies. Taking seriously the difference posed by South Asians, I deploy Lahiri's work as a means of rehistoricizing the conditions of postcoloniality. For first- and second-generation South Asians, how does postcoloniality operate as a phenomenology of belonging? In what ways does the history of British colonialism in South Asia come alive in the United States, as an act of memory and as a condition of everyday life? What would it mean, in other words, to theorize immigrant subjects as postcolonial outside the imperial domain of the United States? Asking these questions shifts our focus away from the dominant American studies narrative of the U.S.-in-Asia, toward understanding how colonial and postcolonial histories on the Indian subcontinent produce new life forms in the United States. Broadening the parameters of what constitutes a postcolonial Asian America reorients our location as scholars of Asian American literary and cultural studies. Because I direct our attention to histories of other colonialisms rather than limiting scholarly inquiry to those imperialist narratives produced by the United States, I enlarge the scope of "Asia" within "Asian America." I emphasize that my intellectual engagement with South Asian history is not in the service of identifying Asian Americans as essentially Asian. Instead, it is a means of provoking a more dynamic conception of where and what "Asia" is, and how that enlarged spatial formation impacts the shape of immigrant communities in America. It requires being cognizant of the ways in which histories of colonialism *outside* the directive of the United States continue to structure racialized identities produced *within* the U.S. state. Postcoloniality is not a fixed or an essential historical condition but a means of performing locality, one that South Asian immigrants repeatedly, if not consistently, embody.

In my readings of Lahiri's short stories, I demonstrate how first- and second-generation immigrants embody postcoloniality as a structure of feeling integral to their identification as Americans. In her ethnography of Indian immigrants in New Jersey, Keya Ganguly argues that postcoloniality is embodied through a series of material practices, for example, through memory (via oral narratives of immigration) and consumption (of foods and cultural texts that remind immigrants of "home"). Such acts of consumption consolidate and reproduce postcoloniality, even as second-generation immigrants contest many of these practices (by rejecting food or literary or visual texts). Likewise, in *Interpreter of Maladies* the postcolonial subjectivities of South Asian immigrants emerge through acts of everyday life: by watching the nightly news on television, reading books, preparing familiar foods. These rituals also function as "invented traditions," generating normative constructs of nationhood in diaspora.[2] The process of sharing such intimate acts with other immigrants from the subcontinent creates ties of fictive kinship among South Asians who, for reasons of religion, national origin, or language, may not otherwise have forged a community. Postcoloniality operates as a material practice that constitutes and defines a "South Asian" immigrant community, one that may be different from normative constructs of nationhood on the subcontinent. Participating in such rituals of production and consumption is the means through which diasporic subjects reconcile the difference between their national, religious, and regional identities on the subcontinent and their ethnic and class identities in the United States.

The postcolonial time of immigration is also structured in relation to nationalist and decolonization movements on the subcontinent. In *The Namesake* as well as in *Interpreter of Maladies*, I situate the post-1965 migration of South Asians in relation to contemporaneous historical developments in South Asia. The formation of South Asian immigrant communities during the 1971 Bangladesh Liberation War, for example, recalls both the 1947 partition of the subcontinent and the 1905 partition of colonial Bengal by the British. Further, the fact that the Bangladesh Liberation War was central to U.S. foreign policy in South Asia during the cold war links the project of post-independence nationhood on the subcontinent to the expanding parameters of U.S. imperialism in Asia. In this context Lahiri's protagonists identify variously as Bengali, Hindu, Bangladeshi, Muslim, Pakistani, and Indian, as the conditions of subcontinental nationhood are constantly being renegotiated through wars and riots. That these regionalist, national, and religious constructs are consistently inadequate to capture forms of ethnic and class identification in America demonstrates the difference between histories of postcolonial modernity and the temporality of U.S. citizenship.

Reading contemporary fiction by South Asian immigrants as postcolonial literature is not only a means of recuperating diasporic texts into the story of "other" nationalisms (including narratives of Indian, Bangladeshi, and Pakistani independence); more important in my view is the fact that such a historicized reading of immigration rewrites the story of what it means to be American. Realigning the relationship between immigration, postcoloniality, and citizenship enables us to see the ways in which South Asians produce and inhabit locality. In turn, such narratives of locality draw attention to how the contradiction between the immigrant and the citizen—what Lisa Lowe has centrally defined as the difference of race—can be obscured by class, particularly in terms of the middle-class backgrounds of Lahiri's fictional subjects.[3] Her protagonists are university professors and librarians, executives and architects, students and teachers. As bourgeois subjects, these men (for with few exceptions Lahiri's protagonists are largely male) are accustomed to embodying the full privileges of citizenship. The problem of locality arises when, as immigrants, they recognize that access to U.S. citizenship is determined by race, and when, as diasporic subjects, their participation in historical events in South Asia is curtailed by distance. For such immigrants, embodying postcoloniality is a means of stitching together racialized and classed locations in the United States with the practice of politics on the subcontinent. Insofar as Lahiri's protagonists identify as South Asian, their embodiment of locality cannot be reconciled within hegemonic formations of U.S. citizenship. Together, these temporal and spatial narratives of diaspora shape the postcolonial topographies of Asian America.

The Time of Citizenship

In the pastoral setting of New England, the protagonists of *Interpreter of Maladies* are out of place in the new world they inhabit. News from home, whether Bangladesh, Pakistan, or India, comes via the television set, letters, and the occasional phone call. Neighbors and teachers are oblivious of familial and national struggles that shape immigrant lives: civil wars and insurgencies fought on the subcontinent, wives left behind, the death of extended family members. Against this backdrop, recent immigrants come to terms with the mundane challenges of life in America, learning to drive on freeways and dutifully carving jack-o'-lanterns on Halloween. In my reading of the stories "The Third and Final Continent" and "When Mr. Pirzada Came to Dine," I examine the ways in which immigrants bind together their experiences as racial minorities in the United States with their religious and national identities in South Asia. Each of these short stories establishes the difference between, first, the racialized immigrant subject and the U.S. public sphere and, second, the diasporic subject and colonial/postcolonial histories on the subcontinent. For first-generation immigrants who leave the subcontinent, political movements in South Asia divide existing national homelands and create new ones. For their second-generation descendants, the logic of American citizenship provides no space for multiple homelands. The fact that South Asians are bound by competing logics of nationhood without fully resolving their citizenship to either geographic site reveals the ambivalent embodiment of locality.

"The Third and Final Continent" begins in 1969, four years after the passage of the Hart-Celler Act. In this short story the unnamed narrator travels from Calcutta to London in 1964 to study and work, and five years later moves from London to Boston, where he has secured a job as a librarian at the Massachusetts Institute of Technology (MIT). In the time between his student life in England and employment in the United States, the narrator has agreed to an arranged marriage in India, and he travels from Calcutta to Boston by air rather than by ship. The narrator's arrival in Boston coincides with the day that the first American men land on the moon: a journey declared by the local newspaper as "traveling farther than anyone in the history of civilization.... The voyage was hailed as man's most awesome achievement" (179). The ways in which the narrator's own life experience is consistently subordinated to the arrival of men on the moon demonstrates how the public history of America—the pedagogical project of U.S. citizen-subjects—is disjunct from the private histories of first-generation immigrations.

As Vijay Prashad asserts in *The Karma of Brown Folk*, the passage of the Hart-Celler Act was integral to building the military infrastructure necessary for the United States to compete against the Soviets. The "special skills" provision of the 1965 act initiated the passage of trained scientists and engineers from Asia. These immigrants, who were largely male, consolidated the health care, defense, and technology industries in the United States.[4] The 1965 act also drew upon a labor pool of skilled professionals in South Asia, for its passage coincided with the Indian government's investment in building educational infrastructure for engineering and the sciences. Part of Jawaharlal Nehru's broader nationalist vision of creating a progressive citizenry, these scientific institutions recruited students from across India in order to develop a cadre of technocrats who would advance India's claims to modernity.[5] However, Nehru's socialist projects also incorporated five-year plans (based on the Soviet model) to develop the national economy, plans that did not accommodate the growing numbers of skilled graduates from these national science and engineering institutions. The migration of professionally trained immigrants from the subcontinent, therefore, was shaped by the globalization of capital that linked together the economic demands of the U.S. state with the educational infrastructure of post-independence India. From this standpoint, the rise of the United States as a global superpower—evident in the successful lunar landing—was intrinsically linked to the irregular modernization process of the postcolonial Indian state.

This history of modernity and migration is almost entirely absent from "The Third and Final Continent," for the narrator relates his journey as a singular and unique event. Although he is neither a scientist nor an engineer, the narrator's work at MIT in library science substantiates the fact that he is also part of an emerging technocratic class. Lahiri's intimate description of the narrator's personal encounters in the United States emphasizes the individuality of his experience. Situating the narrator within the changing racial formation of the United States in the late 1960s, however, also illustrates how his gendered and classed experience of migration acquires a normative value. Given the widespread popularity of Lahiri's fiction in mainstream U.S. literary cultures, I explore how this story of middle-class mobility stands in for a universal narrative of South Asian immigration.

The short story centers on the encounter between the narrator and his landlady, Mrs. Croft. Their relationship is determined not only by the contractual legal conditions that bind together landlord and tenant, but also by their different locations in the United States. Mrs. Croft is 103 years old, a tiny, wrinkled woman who rarely ventures outside her home. In contrast to the narrator, she is a native of Cambridge, Massachusetts, has owned her home for decades, and is rooted in a city that is still foreign to the newly arrived narrator. At the same time, Mrs. Croft is also the antithesis of the modern and young America that the narrator has come to expect in a country whose progress is symbolized by the lunar landing. Although it is 1969, Mrs. Croft retains nineteenth-century notions of etiquette, forbidding "lady visitors" in the narrator's room and admonishing her sixty-eight-year-old daughter for dressing inappropriately (186). The arrival of an Indian tenant in Mrs. Croft's home does not faze her in the least. Yet she is consistently awed by news of men on the moon. Every evening when the narrator returns from work, Mrs. Croft exclaims, "There is an American flag on the moon!" Soliciting a response to her declaration, she commands the narrator to "say 'splendid!'" Although the narrator is initially "baffled and somewhat insulted by the request," he nonetheless yells, "Splendid!" (179). Each night Mrs. Croft reiterates the same command, declaring with "equal measures of disbelief and delight" that there is an American flag on the moon; each night the narrator must cry out "Splendid!" in response (182).

For the narrator, the voyage of his own journey as an immigrant far surpasses the lunar landing. Indeed, by the time Mrs. Croft expresses her pleasure at the American flag staked on the moon, the narrator knows that the flag is long gone, having fallen shortly after the astronauts returned to earth. It is the narrator, by contrast, who continues to stake his claim to America, a country that is as unfamiliar to him as the moon. The contrast between the narrator's youth and Mrs. Croft's old age, between his immigrant subjectivity and Mrs. Croft's claim to citizenship, and between the narrator's racialization as "Indian" and Mrs. Croft's (unstated) whiteness structures the narrative tension of the short story. Lahiri consolidates this series of binaries in order to deconstruct U.S. claims to global power. The lunar landing is so brief that it can only be a symbolic triumph in the cold war arms race; the fact that the flag on the moon falls shortly after the astronauts depart foreshadows the impending American defeat in Vietnam and the failure of the U.S. empire in Southeast Asia.

Although the story is set in 1969, Lahiri's narrative is curiously devoid of other national and world-historical events that shape the encounter between the narrator and Mrs. Croft. It is the year of the Stonewall rebellion, which is frequently cited as an origin point for mainstream gay and lesbian movements in the United States.[6] One year after the death of Martin Luther King Jr., Stonewall can also be viewed as part of the comprehensive civil rights struggle that King and others initiated. That same year the United States, still embroiled in the ongoing war in Vietnam, began bombing Cambodia, prompting a series of public protests and student movements that swept across Asia and Europe. Later that year the Woodstock music festival came to symbolize the countercultural youth movement, even as the racial and class homogeneity among festivalgoers remained unaddressed. None of these events become part of the conversation between the narrator and Mrs. Croft. Instead, their nightly exchange returns to the lunar landing, as if this achievement triumphs over all others in American history.

In a rare critical essay discussing her own work, Lahiri notes that for the ancient Mrs. Croft, "modern life has itself become a baffling foreign language, one she neither participates in nor understands."[7] While Mrs. Croft remains sequestered inside her house, unable and unwilling to confront the world outside, the narrator's own life is saturated with new experiences. As an immigrant, he bears the burden of being a foreigner in an unfamiliar city. In contrast, Mrs. Croft is parochial in her knowledge. Though she exclaims over the American flag on the moon, professing a constant interest in this national event, she remains uninterested in the particular details of the narrator's life. For the narrator to assent to Mrs. Croft's exclamations on a nightly basis, he must reconcile the distance between his private history of migration and the public narrative of U.S. nationalism that culminates in placing men on the moon. A temporary accord is achieved through the narrator's nightly reiteration of "Splendid!" At the same time, their contractual relationship as landlord and tenant demands nothing more than the eight dollars a week the narrator pays Mrs. Croft in rent.

In *The World Next Door*, the literary critic Rajini Srikanth suggests that Lahiri's story "allows for no easy alliances or rejections" of identity (231). Instead, the encounter between Mrs. Croft and the narrator is shaped by the distinct temporal localities that are embodied by both protagonists. Born in 1866, Mrs. Croft was an adult when in 1906 the U.S. Naturalization Act was extended to "aliens being free white persons and to aliens of African nativity and to persons of African descent."[8] During her lifetime she witnessed the expansion of the United States into Puerto Rico, the Philippines, and

Hawai'i, all the while giving piano lessons in Cambridge, one of many metropoles of U.S. imperial power. Mrs. Croft's life is testament to both the expansionist and exceptionalist claims of U.S. citizenship, which is reflected through her absolute disregard for her tenants' racial or national identity. The 1906 Naturalization Act was the contentious focus of judicial cases on Asian American citizenship, including most famously *Takao Ozawa v. United States* (1922) and *United States v. Bhagat Singh Thind* (1923). In *Ozawa* a Japanese immigrant who had lived in Hawai'i for twenty years was denied the right to citizenship on account of being nonwhite; likewise, in *Thind* a Punjabi Sikh immigrant was denied citizenship on the basis of race. Both Ozawa and Thind argued that they should be considered "white" due to their skin color as well as on the basis of prevalent racial origin theories. Scholars have extensively detailed the ramifications of the *Ozawa* and *Thind* cases for Asian immigration during the interwar period.[9] However, in "The Third and Final Continent," these race-based claims for Asian American citizenship are displaced by Lahiri's emphasis on the aftermath of the 1965 Hart-Celler Act. Because the narrator is recruited under the provisions of this revised immigration law, he is temporally dislocated from an earlier history of Asian American naturalization. Instead, his professional success and subsequent decision to apply for American citizenship is narrated in tandem with the emergence of the United States as a global power in the late twentieth century.

Whereas Mrs. Croft embodies a history of U.S. imperialism, the narrator is a postcolonial subject of empire. The relation of power between empire and colony is rescripted through the divergent subject-positions occupied by landlord and tenant, even though there is no direct colonial history that links the United States to India. For the narrator of "The Third and Final Continent," postcoloniality is negotiated not simply in terms of his migration to the United States, but also in relation to his experiences in post-independence India and in post-imperial Britain. As Kandice Chuh writes, "The United States may not be postcolonial in the ways that Britain or India may be, but it does nonetheless negotiate postcoloniality as a global condition."[10] As a postcolonial subject of India, the narrator feels no particular kinship to his birthplace, Calcutta. He remembers the city only in terms of his mother's madness and her increasingly abject living conditions. The demise of the narrator's family unit in the aftermath of his mother's death operates as a metaphor for the partition of India itself, a place that becomes unrecognizable to him. When the narrator arrives in London in 1964, he attempts to re-create a family by living with "penniless Bengali bachelors like myself" (173), but this shared living arrangement engenders a collective experience of isolation rather than belonging. His five years in London coincide with a period of intensified racial violence against South Asian, African, and Caribbean immigrants, symbolized by the rise of the conservative member of Parliament Enoch Powell. Powell's virulent attack on immigrants and his calls for their repatriation stoked widespread fears of miscegenation, culminating in the infamous "rivers of blood" speech that Powell delivered in 1968.[11] Though the narrator notes that he moved from London to Boston because he procured a job and a green card, his departure one year after Powell's speech may also be read as a response to heightened anti-Asian violence in Britain. Thus even as the narrator arrives in the United States in response to state-directed demands for skilled labor, he embodies another temporality, one that is shaped by the colonial and postcolonial encounter between the U.K. and South Asia. As such, the narrator's travels across three continents redirect linear narratives of Asian American migration that focus on points of departure in Asia and arrival in America.

However, despite the disparate temporalities embodied by the narrator and Mrs. Croft, "The Third and Final Continent" is frequently read as an assimilationist tale of coming to America. In part this is due to Lahiri's emphasis on the narrator's adjustment to life in Boston after the death of Mrs. Croft. By the end of the short story the narrator mentions that he and his wife, Mala, "are American citizens now, so that we can collect social security when it is time. Though we visit Calcutta every few years [. . .] we have decided to grow old here." The couple has a son who attends Harvard, and the narrator expresses concern as to whether the son will "eat rice with us with his hands, and speak in Bengali, things we sometimes worry he will no longer do after we die" (197). The narrator and his wife have become prototypical upwardly mobile immigrant subjects: they are citizens, property owners, and parents of an Ivy League student. As such, these last paragraphs of the short story consolidate a public myth of South Asians as a "model minority," a myth that is affirmed by Lahiri herself, whose debut publication won the Pulitzer Prize. Reflecting on "The Third and Final Continent," Srikanth writes, "Reinforcing the title's sense of an ultimate destination—beyond which there is no need to go, for one has arrived in the best of all possible locations—the story uncovers, in Lahiri's unobtrusive way, the protagonist's gradual understanding of himself as an emotional being" (233). Srikanth's characterization of America as an "ultimate destination," and the narrator's immigration as a metaphor for individual self-realization, substantiates a reading of the text as a universal story of becoming American. By domesticating the narrator's diasporic subjectivity within the framework of U.S. citizenship, Srikanth elides the narrator's location within a larger global history of South Asian postwar migration, which was initiated through British and American demands for skilled labor.

Given that "The Third and Final Continent" substantiates dominant representations of middle-class South Asian immigration, how can we locate the short story within the postcolonial turn in Asian American studies? I return to the narrator's encounter with Mrs. Croft, for their relationship is curiously devoid of an explicit acknowledgment of racial difference. In my view, the problematic absence of race determines both the narrator's postcolonial subjectivity and his contingent occupation of U.S. citizenship. However, race is not easily captured through categories of nationality or ethnicity. At no point in the story does the narrator identify as "Indian" or "Bengali" (nor, for that matter, is Mrs. Croft described as "white" or "American"). Notably, it is only his wife, Mala—with her saris, bindi, and henna designs on her feet—who is marked as racially "other" in this text. Throughout the short story, race does not operate as a measure of difference or distance from an ideology of American nationhood, even though race has consistently determined Asian American claims to citizenship. Instead, the primary difference between the native-born American symbolized by Mrs. Croft and the immigrant narrator is their embodiment of distinct temporal localities. Whereas Mrs. Croft's repeated celebration of the lunar landing reveals her static temporality as well as the ever-expanding domain (and subsequent failures) of the U.S. empire, the narrator embodies multiple temporalities simultaneously. He is old enough to have witnessed the independence and partition of the subcontinent; he moves to London during the demise of the British empire; and he is recruited to advance the United States' claims to be a global superpower. The narrator's postcolonial locality is forged through these three disparate histories. His story enlarges the geographical and historical scope of "Asia" in Asian America, and also underscores the expanding presence of America in Asia.

The narrator's journey reveals the disjuncture between a "foreign" past and a "citizen" present, disrupting a narrative trajectory that enshrines America as a "destined, natural result."[12] However, unlike the lunar landing that is lauded as a national event, the narrator can claim no public record of his achievements. As he reflects in conversation with his son,

> While the astronauts [. . .] spent mere hours on the moon, I have remained in this new world for nearly thirty years. I know that my achievement is quite ordinary. I am not the only man to seek his fortune far from home, and certainly I am not the first. Still, there are times I am bewildered by each mile I have traveled, each meal I have eaten, each person I have known, each room in which I have slept. As ordinary as it all appears, there are times when it is beyond my imagination. (198)

The expansive capacities of the narrator's imagination elucidate an intimate perspective on globalization. As an American citizen, the narrator's location within the domain of U.S. empire is skewed in relation to the demise of the British empire and the emergence of an independent Indian state. Reading this short story as a narrative of diaspora instead of as a story of assimilation illustrates how immigrants are located at the interstices of dissimilar rhetorics of nationalism and modernity. The ways in which middle-class immigrants unevenly reconcile these divergent notions of belonging delineates the postcolonial localities of South Asians in America.

Remapping South Asia in America

Whereas the first-generation immigrant narrator of "The Third and Final Continent" produces locality in relation to public narratives of U.S. history, the second-generation protagonist of "When Mr. Pirzada Came to Dine" embodies locality in relation to contemporaneous political events in South Asia. In "When Mr. Pirzada Came to Dine," the young narrator, Lilia, is treated to candy every night when her parents' acquaintance from the nearby university comes to join them for dinner. The story is set in the autumn of 1971, following months of violent repression in East Pakistan by the Pakistani armed forces during the Bangladesh Liberation War. Despite political upheaval on the subcontinent, Mr. Pirzada is a welcome sign of the familiar to Lilia's Indian parents, who in "search of compatriots [. . .] used to trail their fingers, at the start of each new semester, through the columns of the university directory, circling surnames familiar to their part of the world" (24). A Pakistani citizen, Mr. Pirzada has arrived at the local university on a grant from the Pakistani government to study the botany of New England. Because the fellowship does not provide for his wife and seven children, who remain in Dhaka, Mr. Pirzada is alone for the year and joins Lilia's family for meals on a regular basis. Every night Mr. Pirzada brings sugary treats for young Lilia, who is quietly charmed by the formality of his appearance and greeting.

In this suburban town north of Boston, memories of the subcontinent come alive through domestic rituals and objects: the chilis bought whole and frozen from Chinese markets; the music and games that Lilia's parents play with their friends; the familiarity and variety of meals prepared by Lilia's mother each night; and Lilia's grandmother's areca nut box, in which she stores Mr. Pirzada's confectionary treats.[13] Lilia's parents share these rituals of domesticity with Mr. Pirzada as a means of consolidating their own notion of diasporic community, despite differences of religion and national origin. As the evening news blasts images from East Pakistan into the carpeted comfort of the living room, however, this nostalgic recreation of homeland in Lilia's house begins to unravel. War between India and Pakistan becomes all the more likely as the number of East Pakistani refugees in India increases exponentially. As this violent drama over territory and national identity is played out on the subcontinent, Lilia, her family, and Mr. Pirzada are insistently reminded of the differences between them. It is because Mr. Pirzada is Muslim and his family is in East Pakistan that his wife and daughters are missing in the chaos of the civil war; and it is because Lilia's parents are Hindu Indians, from Calcutta, that they are enveloped in confusion when India declares war on Pakistan and commences to move its troops onto East Pakistani soil.

Mr. Pirzada, as Lilia's father notes, is not an "Indian man" (25). He is from Dhaka, and thus from East Pakistan, part of a country created when colonial India was partitioned at the time of independence. But because he is from Dhaka he is also, like Lilia's parents, a Bengali. East Pakistan was created out of the Muslim-majority population of the eastern regions of Bengal, and so Mr. Pirzada and Lilia's family are bound by language and custom, though not by religion. Pointing out Mr. Pirzada's difference from his own family, Lilia's father shows her that on the world map, the eastern and western wings of Pakistan are colored yellow, not orange like India.[14] For Lilia, who has been schooled in the geography of North America rather than the subcontinent, the bifurcated country of Pakistan looks as if "California and Connecticut constituted a nation apart from the U.S." (26).

Informed that Mr. Pirzada is East Pakistani and not Indian, Lilia tries to look for signs of visible difference between him and her parents, noting only similarities in appearance, language, and food habits. However, what is central to the text is the fact that the difference of being East Pakistani is also the difference of being Muslim. Mr. Pirzada's Muslim identity remains unrecognized by Lilia, who has not been raised in a religious household. Instead, Mr. Pirzada's idiosyncracies are read by Lilia as part of the difference of being "Indian"—characteristics that demarcate him from Lilia herself, who identifies as an "American." Mr. Pirzada's otherness in the short story thus does not register on the level of religious difference but rather in terms of a generational divide: he is an immigrant, and Lilia, born and raised in the United States, is not. However, for the reader the difference of Mr. Pirzada's Muslim identity is manifest throughout the short story in a number of material objects: the fez that he never removes, even inside Lilia's home; his coat, which has the Muslim name "Z. Sayeed, Suitors" stitched on the inside; and the pocket watch that Mr. Pirzada rests on the dining table each night.

The pocket watch comes to signify Mr. Pirzada's temporal difference from Lilia as they share their evening meals. Every night Mr. Pirzada winds his watch to check that it is set eleven hours ahead to the time in Dhaka as he watches the evening news. Lilia realizes with a start that the lives of his wife and daughters in Dhaka take precedence over his own immigrant experience: "Life, I realized, was being lived in Dacca first [. . .] Our meals, our actions, were only a shadow of what had already happened there, a lagging ghost of where Mr. Pirzada really belonged" (31). Though Mr. Pirzada never actively consults his watch, the fact that it simultaneously ticks with the watch on his wrist (set to Boston time) synchronizes life in Dhaka with Mr. Pirzada's experiences in the United States.[15]

However, Mr. Pirzada's attempt to establish a temporal synchrony between South Asia and America remains incomplete. With the spare watch set to Dhaka time, Mr. Pirzada watches the evening news, where reporters list the numbers of dead, abducted, and injured citizens in East Pakistan.

His wife and children have been lost to the conflict that he sees on-screen: telephone and postal services in Pakistan have collapsed, and Mr. Pirzada is unable to communicate with his family. Lahiri outlines the casualties of war in the first paragraph of her story: three hundred thousand people dead, teachers shot, women raped. A more detailed examination of the war, however, presents a different picture. In her reading of public cultures surrounding the Bangladesh Liberation War, Nayanika Mookherjee notes, "During the nine months of the war, the Pakistan Army [. . .] killed some three million Bengali men and women from all walks of life and social classes—intellectuals, journalists, students, workers and villagers. Amidst this carnage 200,000 to 300,000 women were raped" (73). Much of the Pakistani army's persecution of East Pakistanis, including Muslims and Hindus, took place during the infamous "Operation Searchlight" of March 1971.[16] As antiwar groups in Bangladesh have noted, the intensity of violence during the relatively short (ten-month) period of conflict in 1971 means that this series of events amounted to West Pakistani genocide against Bengalis in East Pakistan.[17] None of this information appears in the brief updates on the evening news, which is already filled with images from another war far away, in Vietnam. Mr. Pirzada watches the television reports intently, "as if someone were giving him directions to an unknown destination" (31). The destination of the war between India and Pakistan is, of course, Bangladeshi independence. However, because Mr. Pirzada remains bound to the terms of his fellowship in the United States, he is unable to influence the political outcome of the war. Instead he spends his time researching the deciduous trees of New England and watching the nightly news. Lilia cannot imagine Mr. Pirzada's ties to the "unruly, sweltering world we had viewed a few hours ago in our bright, carpeted living room" (32), for in her view South Asia has never seemed farther from America.

In historical accounts of the Bangladesh Liberation War, the protracted conflict between East and West Pakistan, and between Pakistan and India, is situated within a larger narrative of the cold war between the United States and the Soviet Union. White House documents pertaining to the Nixon administration's correspondence with the Pakistani general Yahya Khan demonstrate that Nixon aimed for the U.S. role in the conflict to "tilt" toward Pakistan. To that end the United States supplied military and other relief materials to the Pakistani government and sent a warship to the Bay of Bengal to warn the Indian government against pursuing war with Pakistan over Bangladesh. While the Nixon administration advocated aligning with Pakistan, the American public—confronted with television images of Bengali refugees and news updates of civilian deaths—supported the Bangladeshi cause.[18] In the meantime, the Indian government, led by Indira Gandhi, strategized to cope with the influx of nearly two million refugees from East Pakistan to the state of West Bengal, and employed guerrilla forces to initiate anti-Pakistani resistance from within Bangladesh.[19] India's covert presence in Bangladesh also ensured that the Indian state was able to suppress the cross-border leftist Naxalite movement that was organized by peasants and students against feudal regimes and the central government. Both the Indian army and the Pakistani army were culpable in the looting, harassment, and sexual assault of civilians in East Pakistan.[20]

The Bangladesh Liberation War was at the heart of the changing economic and political relationship between the United States and South Asia during the early 1970s. The mass popularity of a nationalist movement for an independent state of Bangladesh challenged U.S. foreign policy in the region, but it also initiated public support in America for the establishment of a new nation-state in South Asia. Given that the Bangladesh war occurred in tandem with the U.S. war in Vietnam, I highlight the simultaneity of these two sites of global conflict in order to illustrate the expansive reach of the United States in Asia. First, U.S. support for military regimes on the Indian subcontinent (particularly in Pakistan) was strategically linked to its ongoing imperialist maneuvers in Southeast Asia, as both the war between East and West Pakistan and the Vietnam War emblematized the U.S. fear of communism. Second, examining the Bangladesh Liberation War as a site for U.S. colonial intervention in Asia demonstrates how the scope of U.S. power extended to the decolonizing nations of South Asia.

In the first-person narrative of a ten-year-old girl, Lilia views the war in relation to the activities that compose her everyday life: her school, her friends, her participation in local traditions that mark the passing of the seasons. India declares war on Pakistan, for example, on Halloween. Lilia comes home expecting to find her parents sympathetic to her blisters from carrying sacks of candy and her sadness for the destroyed jack-o'-lantern at their doorstep; instead it is her parents who are sitting dejectedly in front of the television screen, and Mr. Pirzada who holds his head in his hands, reacting to the on-screen announcement of war.[21] Until Mr. Pirzada's arrival, Lilia is unaware of religious, ethnic, and nationalist movements on the subcontinent, which have already produced two successive partitions of Bengal—the 1905 partition of the province by the British colonial administration (a decision that was reversed in 1911) and the 1947 partition of the subcontinent into India and Pakistan, which divided Bengal into West Bengal and East Pakistan.[22] The war for the independent nation-state of Bangladesh is a third form of partition, which pivoted on the linguistic and political differences between a predominantly Urdu-speaking West Pakistan and the Bengali-speaking peoples of East Pakistan. None of these historical movements have been taught to Lilia, whose knowledge of British imperialism is limited to the American history she learns in school. There, each year students rehearse the history of American independence beginning with the Revolutionary War. "How can you possibly expect her to know about Partition?" asks Lilia's mother; to which Lilia's father responds, "But what does she learn about the world? [. . .] What is she learning?" (27). What Lilia is learning, of course, is the repetitive pedagogy of American citizenship. She and her classmates go on excursions to Plymouth Rock, visit Revolutionary War monuments, and make dioramas of George Washington. She can fill in blank maps of thirteen U.S. colonies, but unless prompted by her father cannot identify the independent nations of India and Pakistan on a world map. Incorporated into this narrative of U.S. citizenship, Lilia participates in an American national body that also defines itself against British imperialism. Yet her education makes no room for the ideological linkages between anticolonial movements in the United States and South Asia, or for that matter between British imperialism on the subcontinent and U.S. foreign policy in South and Southeast Asia.

In defense of her daughter's schooling, Lilia's mother notes, "We live here now, she was born here" (26). In Lilia's mother's estimation, the family's immigration to the United States marks a clear spatial and temporal demarcation between a past history of communal violence on the Indian subcontinent and their present lives, where the only kind of politics that Lilia watches filters through the television screen. Lilia's mother points out that her daughter does not need to experience the riots or curfews, or shortages of food and electricity that marked her own experience of partition. In her view, the fact that Lilia was born in the United States absolves her from participating in the making and unmaking of postcolonial South Asia. However, as Judith Caesar points out, this representation of America as a safe and secure homeland is a fallacy. "In the real America of 1971," Caesar writes, "there were indeed riots and violence, as Black ghettoes burned, police beat anti-war protesters, and students took over buildings on American college campuses. The family is oblivious of all this."[23] Whereas Lilia's mother attempts to establish temporal and spatial difference between South Asia and the United States, Caesar reminds us that in contemporary America, differences of race and class enable middle-class immigrants like Lilia's family to be absolved from the turmoil of domestic political movements.

For these South Asians, locality is a vexed process. Mr. Pirzada attempts to embody a synchronous temporality between East Pakistan and the United States, but his keen attention to the time of Bangladesh's birth is steadily diminished as news reports from East Pakistan become less frequent. For Lilia's mother, her own decision to immigrate to the United States absolves her daughter from political movements on the subcontinent and keeps Lilia at a safe remove from states of violence. As Caesar points out, in order to secure a middle-class existence, Lilia's mother must also deny the contemporaneous development of antiracist and anticolonial political movements in the United States. For Lilia's father, his disappointment in his daughter's education reveals the inconsistencies of anti-imperialist narratives of American independence. The exceptionalism of U.S. history is evident when Lilia is unable to see the transnational linkages between British colonies in North America and the legacy of British colonialism on successive partitions of the subcontinent. For Lilia, her sudden exposure to news reports on the war in East Pakistan initiates a complex process of embodying diasporic locality. Inasmuch as she has come to regard Mr. Pirzada as part of her own family, she also recognizes that he is a foreigner in her homeland. Lilia's recognition of Mr. Pirzada's differences (temporal, national, and religious) prompts her to learn more about the war in order to imaginatively locate herself in other homes.

Although Lilia dedicates herself to learning about South Asia, her peers and teachers in school marginalize the place of Asia in the American imagination. Throughout the duration of the Bangladesh Liberation War, her history teacher assigns students to research the Revolutionary War, seemingly oblivious of the birth of a new nation on the other side of the world. When

Lilia is found surreptitiously reading a book on Pakistan in the school library, curious to know more about Mr. Pirzada's birthplace, she becomes the object of pedagogical discipline:

> I slammed the book shut, too loudly. Mrs. Kenyon emerged, the aroma of her perfume filling up the tiny aisle, and lifted the book by the tip of its spine as if it were a hair clinging to my sweater. She glanced at the cover, then at me.
> "Is this book a part of your report, Lilia?"
> "No, Mrs. Kenyon."
> "Then I see no reason to consult it," she said, replacing it in the slim gap on the shelf. "Do you?" (33)

Admonishing Lilia for her academic interest in South Asia, Mrs. Kenyon deems the book irrelevant to Lilia's proper focus on American history. The book itself becomes an object of disgust (Mrs. Kenyon lifts it "as if it were a hair"), though for Lilia it is an object of desire. Mrs. Kenyon firmly deposits the history of postcolonial South Asia outside the temporal and spatial parameters of American citizenship, insisting that her class should only learn about the nation to which they express their allegiance each morning. It is only many years later that Lilia learns about the histories of colonialism, nationalism, and partition that shaped her family's experience of the war, from books available in the local library.

Juxtaposing Lilia's aborted venture into the academic study of South Asia against Mr. Pirzada's ongoing research in the United States produces two dissonant forms of diasporic locality. As the recipient of a Pakistani government research grant, Mr. Pirzada is an emissary of the Pakistani state, and it is in this capacity that he studies the botany of New England. However, the government that funds Mr. Pirzada's research is in disarray, and his presence in the United States during the war means that he is also separated from his family in Dhaka. Mr. Pirzada is thus a subject of the Pakistani state, but as a Bengali is also subject (virtually, via the television screen) to the liberation movement for Bangladesh. As a result, Mr. Pirzada's desire to embody a simultaneous lived time between Dhaka and the United States fails precisely because the nationalist project of the Pakistani state has failed. Within the subcontinent, what it means to be Pakistani is split along the eastern and western wings of the state; what it means to be Bengali is split along lines of Hindu or Muslim religious affiliation. The idea of a postcolonial citizenry on the subcontinent is consistently being reshaped, evident in the fact that Mr. Pirzada's two watches never tell the same time.

By contrast, Lilia is disciplined into becoming the proper subject of the U.S. nation-state. Unlike Mr. Pirzada's government grant, the public school that Lilia attends makes no room for geographies and histories outside the United States, including those countries within the domain of the U.S. empire. Lilia's desire to learn outside the parameters of her classroom is evidence of her racialized location in the United States, as a citizen unable to reconcile her family history to the national narrative of America. At the same time, however, Lilia's intimate engagement with Mr. Pirzada and her pedagogical interest in modern South Asia incorporates her into an alternate national body, a citizenry on the subcontinent that occupies a postcolonial time. Shaped by a racialized experience of U.S. citizenship as well as by subcontinental national politics, Lilia produces and embodies a postcolonial locality.

The difficulty of reading second-generation immigrants like Lilia as postcolonial subjects was anticipated nearly two decades ago by the feminist scholars Lata Mani and Ruth Frankenberg. Mani and Frankenberg argue that South Asians in the United States are more accurately characterized as "post–civil rights" rather than as "postcolonial." They contend that the use of "postcolonial" to describe South Asians in the United States flattens the history of empire that binds together the U.K. and South Asia. Further, they insist that scholars attend to the particularities of the historical, political, and social relationship between the imperial metropolis and its former colonies. Mani and Frankenberg's argument for a different periodization—or, a different measure of temporality—for South Asians in the United States has been taken up by other literary scholars, including Jenny Sharpe. In her essay "Is the United States Postcolonial?" Sharpe argues that the term "postcoloniality" should be limited to British Asian immigrants, as it does not adequately capture the neocolonial relationship between the United States and India. "Postcolonial," in her view, should be limited to the aftereffects of British colonialism in India and used to characterize the historical location of subcontinental immigrants in Britain. Sharpe is concerned with "the refashioning of postcolonial studies as a minority discourse," as she argues that eliding the distinction between postcolonial studies and ethnic studies "risks playing into a liberal multiculturalism that obfuscates the category of race"

(186). More recently, however, historians such as Antoinette Burton have persuasively argued that the United States has supplanted Britain as an imperial power in the Indian imagination since the mid-twentieth century. In her book *The Postcolonial Careers of Santha Rama Rau*, Burton examines the biography of the title character, the daughter of an Indian diplomat who lived in the United States from the 1940s onward. Reading Rau's books and essays, Burton demonstrates that Indian immigrants to the United States experience postcoloniality as a transnational subjectivity produced through the intersecting histories of postwar America, post-imperial Britain, and post-independence India.

In alliance with Burton, I explore postcoloniality as a structure of feeling rather than a temporally or spatially bound condition of citizenship. Lilia's curiosity about the differences between Mr. Pirzada and her parents, her visceral response to the loss of his family members, her concern for Mr. Pirzada and shame at her own inability to console him demonstrate the affective charge of postcolonial histories. Such histories are delineated in the short story through the transnational linkages that bind together India, Pakistan, Bangladesh, and the United States in 1971. Postcoloniality is also an ongoing pedagogical project, one that Lilia must surreptitiously educate herself in at the school library. Her inability to reconcile the history she learns in school with her own knowledge of the Bangladesh Liberation War ruptures an assimilationist narrative of U.S. immigration. Despite her mother's desire to leave behind memories of partition on the subcontinent, in Lilia's case migration does not engender emancipation from past lives. Instead Lilia's intimate encounter with Mr. Pirzada generates a form of locality based on their joint occupation of postcolonial time. Their affective relationship binds together what the literary critic Suvir Kaul describes as the differences between "memory and nationality, between belonging and citizenship."[24]

The difference between belonging and citizenship structures not only the postcolonial localities of Lilia and Mr. Pirzada, but also the nascent forms of South Asian diasporic community that are generated by Lilia's family. During the twelve days of war between India and Pakistan, Lahiri describes how Lilia's parents and Mr. Pirzada operate "as if they were a single person, sharing a single meal, a single body, a single silence, and a single fear" (41). In New England, Lilia and Mr. Pirzada's shared Bengali heritage is what brings them together, as similarities of language and cultural practice provide the impulse to act as if they were the same body. Yet on the subcontinent, the difference between Lilia's Hindu family and Mr. Pirzada's Muslim background is precisely what has split their countries apart. The horror of the Bangladesh Liberation War is evident not only in the scale of military conflict, but in the fact that the imagined community that Lilia's parents and Mr. Pirzada so actively cultivate in the United States, of people from their part of the world, is being severed and reformed at "home."[25] As the war consolidates the boundaries of the new nation-state of Bangladesh, it clarifies the distance between Hindu Bengalis in India and their Muslim counterparts in what was formerly East Pakistan. It also establishes the difference of citizenship between Lilia's family, who are legal residents of the United States, and Mr. Pirzada, who as a Bengali is no longer a legitimate citizen of Pakistan.

The contentious relation between religious faith and secular citizenship not only demarcates boundaries between nation-states but also shapes the composition of linguistic and cultural communities in South Asia. Lilia's confusion about what it means to be "Bengali" and "Muslim," or "Indian" and "Pakistani," is in fact echoed in a novel by another South Asian writer, Amitav Ghosh. In *The Shadow Lines*, Ghosh describes the anxiety of the unnamed young male narrator who witnesses a Hindu-Muslim riot during the late 1960s. Though the riot takes place in Calcutta, on the Indian side of the border, the conflict is stoked by popular movements in East Pakistan for the liberation of Bangladesh. The narrator realizes with horror that the boundaries that demarcate Pakistan and India—boundaries that he is thoroughly familiar with and takes for granted, having grown up in the era after partition—threaten to reproduce themselves between the minority Muslim and majority Hindu communities within Calcutta. As Ghosh writes, the narrator is consumed by a fear that is "without analogy":

> That particular fear has a texture you can neither forget not describe [. . .] it is not comparable to the fear of nature, which is the most universal of human fears, nor to the fear of the violence of the state, which is the commonest of modern fears. It is a fear that comes of the knowledge that normalcy is utterly contingent [. . .] It is this that sets apart the thousand million people who inhabit the subcontinent from the rest of the world—not language, not food, not music—it is the special quality of loneliness that grows out of the fear of the war between oneself and one's image in the mirror. (204)

Lilia is also consumed by the fear that normalcy is "utterly contingent," her anxiety aroused by concerns over Mr. Pirzada's family and their safety during the war. However, unlike the narrator of *The Shadow Lines*, Lilia is literally unable to see the differences between herself and Mr. Pirzada. What distinguishes her from Mr. Pirzada is not simply a matter of Lilia's American citizenship and Mr. Pirzada's Pakistani passport. Nor is it a question of racial difference, which Lilia encounters during her experience of trick-or-treating in her suburban neighborhood.[26] More fundamentally, Lilia is unable to recognize the difference between what constitutes a Bengali subject in India and in Pakistan. As Suvir Kaul argues in his reading of *The Shadow Lines*, the "fear of oneself" conditions South Asians to come together at the very moment that it tears the notion of South Asia apart. Likewise, Lilia's parents and Mr. Pirzada identify with each other as if they were images in a mirror, momentarily sharing a "quality of loneliness" that emerges from a shared experience of violence from a previous partition that split apart the subcontinent. Even though Lilia's parents identify with Mr. Pirzada as another Bengali, their formation of a secular community in diaspora is consistently impeded by religious and linguistic nationalisms on the subcontinent. The communal differences between Hindus and Muslims on the subcontinent led to the formation of India and Pakistan in 1947; less than thirty years later, the cleavage between Urdu- and Bengali-speaking Muslims, as well as the lopsided economic relationship between East and West Pakistan, engendered the movement for the liberation of Bangladesh. These differences of religion and language, class, and geography on the subcontinent do not translate into Lilia's everyday life in America, and as such her identification as a U.S. citizen remains intact even as Mr. Pirzada's identity as a Pakistani national dissolves.

Toward the end of the short story Mr. Pirzada returns to Dhaka and writes to Lilia's parents to inform them that his wife and children are safe. As it turns out, the family had taken refuge in the Indian city of Shillong for the duration of the war. Like Dhaka, Shillong is a city that has been subject to partition under the British administration and during the post-independence era.[27] Mr. Pirzada's family is among the tens of thousands of Bangladeshi refugees who sought shelter in India, and whom in turn the Indian state mobilized as part of its own militarized defense of the border with East Pakistan. Mr. Pirzada's nascent citizenship as a Bangladeshi therefore continues to be forged through his contingent embodiment of diasporic locality. Because he is a Bengali Muslim, his home became East Pakistan during the 1947 partition; because he is from Dhaka, he has inadvertently become Bangladeshi. But because his wife's family is originally from Assam, in northeastern India, Mr. Pirzada continues to be subject to the hegemony of the Indian state. The contested claims to Shillong established during the Bangladesh war by indigenous groups, refugees, and migrant Bengalis demonstrate how borders and boundaries on the subcontinent are consistently redrawn. The 1971 war not only brings into relief the linguistic and cultural differences that demarcated Muslims in East Pakistan from West Pakistan; it also emphasizes the heterogeneity of religious, linguistic, and ethnic groups that continue to redraw domestic and international boundaries in South Asia. For Mr. Pirzada as well as for Lilia and her parents, the specter of partition continues long after the formal conclusion of war. As a new map of South Asia emerges in the aftermath of Bangladeshi independence, regional and national identities are consistently re-embodied by those on the subcontinent as well as abroad.

In her reading of "When Mr. Pirzada Came to Dine," Kavita Daiya argues that for Lilia, "'America' becomes an ambivalently charged nation-space, which needs to be provincialized and which also *enables* her to dream of a transnational, non-nationalist South Asian American politics" (197). Daiya's point is that Lahiri's emphasis on subcontinental politics provincializes the United States because the emergence of the new nation-state of Bangladesh takes precedence over the daily lives of immigrants. But as the historian Dipesh Chakrabarty contends in his book *Provincializing Europe*, "conceptualizing practices of social and political modernity in South Asia often requires us to make the [. . .] assumption: that historical time is not integral, that it is out of joint with itself" (16). In my reading of "When Mr. Pirzada Came to Dine" I have outlined how Lahiri renders simultaneous national-historical events in South Asia and the United States "out of joint," particularly in terms of the temporal dissonance that is embodied by Lilia and Mr. Pirzada. Equally important, however, is the fact that the time of immigration, the story of an American national time, remains the dominant narrative throughout this short story. Because the emergence of Bangladesh is always rendered in sync with the daily events of Lilia's life (her schooling, Halloween, Christmas), the historical time of South Asia is rendered secondary to immigrant time. Though Mr. Pirzada keeps an eye on his spare watch set to Dhaka time, the time that takes precedence in Lilia's life is the national time of America. Even as Lilia recognizes her racialized difference from universalized notions of U.S. citizenship, her teacher continues to reproduce exceptionalist narratives of American history that are not dislodged by contemporaneous events in South Asia. The United States is not only *not* provincialized; its own history remains the dominant narrative into which reports from other countries (and other times) are incorporated. Ultimately the only memory of the Bangladesh Liberation War that Lilia retains are the leftover objects from Mr. Pirzada: a greeting card that he sends her family, and the decaying sweets that she has accumulated from his visits.

In contrast to Daiya's claim that Lilia dreams of a "non-nationalist Asian American politics," my contention is that Lilia is thoroughly incorporated into the nationalist ideologies of both South Asia and the United States. She is subject to nationalist, ethnic, and religious politics on the subcontinent, and she is also disciplined into histories of American exceptionalism. The narrative of postcoloniality that emerges in "When Mr. Pirzada Came to Dine" is triangulated between Lilia's pedagogical inculcation into the history of post-independence South Asia, her exposure to television and popular media representations of the subcontinent in the United States, and her recognition of exclusionary narratives of American history. Lilia is a postcolonial subject not because she rejects nationalist ideologies, but rather because she re-embodies and alters hegemonic structures of citizenship. Her creative embodiment of postcolonial subjectivity emerges in her intimate encounter with Mr. Pirzada, through the momentary convergence between the political histories of South Asia and the teleology of U.S. citizenship.

Naming and Belonging in The Namesake

The topography of postcolonial localities expands significantly in Jhumpa Lahiri's novel *The Namesake*. Published four years after *Interpreter of Maladies*, *The Namesake* captures the intergenerational relationship between the protagonist Gogol Ganguli and his parents. In comparison to Lahiri's short stories, which focus on a single historical event, *The Namesake* encompasses a wider temporal scale that spans more than three decades. For Gogol's parents, Ashima and Ashoke, their son's name is an unexpected consequence of living in the United States. Though they expected Ashima's grandmother to choose a name for their child, her letter from Calcutta never arrives. Ashoke is left to record the name of his favorite writer, the Russian author Nikolai Gogol, on the official record of his son's birth. Originally a "pet" name to be used in the privacy of family and other intimates, "Gogol" also comes to function as a "good" name in the public domain of school and work.[28] For the young Gogol, his name is a constant reminder of his parents' difference in America: it represents their tastes, preferences, and customs, a way of being that marks how foreign they are in his world. As an adult, Gogol legally changes his name to Nikhil, but even this name fails to resolve his identity. As a pet-name-turned-good-name, "Gogol" comes to stand for both the history of Ashima and Ashoke's migration from India and Gogol Ganguli's claims to the United States.

The Namesake follows a linear temporality of migration that tracks Gogol's life from birth to adulthood, spanning the years between 1968 and 2000. During this period the demographic composition of South Asian immigrants to the United States broadens significantly, encompassing not only middle-class professionals and their descendants, but also an increasing number of workers in the manufacturing and service sectors, as well as dependent family members. In 1970 the U.S. census recorded fifty-one thousand Indian immigrants; by 2006 that number had increased thirty-fold, to nearly one and a half million.[29] As immigrants from the subcontinent increased in number, so too did regional, linguistic, and religious organizations that catered to distinct subcontinental communities, such as Bengali and Telugu cultural associations, Punjabi Sikh religious groups, and Gujarati business organizations. Thus in the novel, the expanding numbers of South Asians in the United States is represented through a contracted social sphere: that of upwardly mobile Bengali-speaking immigrants on the East Coast. Ashoke is a university professor and Ashima a librarian; their son attends Yale and later Columbia. Like so many of their friends, the Gangulis own a comfortable home in the suburbs of Boston. As a portrait of South Asian immigrant life, the fictional Ganguli family stands in for the hegemony of middle-class narratives of migration.

Despite Lahiri's portrayal of this narrow demographic of South Asians in the United States, Gogol's story is often recuperated into a broader coming-of-age narrative about the assimilation of ethnic subjects into a multicultural America. Reviews of the novel emphasize Gogol's so-called identity crisis, analyzing the difference between his parents' identities as "Indians" and his own claims to being American.[30] As Sunaina Maira has argued, popular representations of Asian American immigration reproduce a "pathologized focus on 'intergenerational conflict' in immigrant families."[31] In the case of *The Namesake*, the generational conflict between parent and child is reflected in a bifurcated division between old and new worlds, private and public life, India and America. Notwithstanding the fact that Ashima and Ashoke are also U.S. citizens, Gogol's resolution of his "identity crisis" via his love affairs, marriage, and subsequent divorce is represented as a quintessential story of becoming American.

However, the linear temporality of Gogol Ganguli's life contrasts with Lahiri's use of an alternate temporal narrative, one that is suggested by her incorporation of Nikolai Gogol's short story "The Overcoat." Instead of framing the novel as a coming-of-age narrative centered on the life of Gogol Ganguli, I examine the relationship between *The Namesake* and "The Overcoat," two literary texts separated by more than a century and a half. "The Overcoat" circulates throughout *The Namesake* as an anachronistic referent that expands the geographical and historical scale of the novel. Set in imperial Russia, "The Overcoat" is one of Ashoke's favorite stories as a young man in India. A page from the story literally saves his life during a train accident, and in the aftermath of this event he names his son after its author. Yet for Gogol Ganguli, "The Overcoat" is simply a relic of a past time. He cannot identify with the story or its author, nor can he identify with its role in his father's life in India. Ashoke gives his son a copy of Nikolai Gogol's short stories, but the book remains buried in Gogol's bedroom for nearly two decades. Lahiri's consistent references to "The Overcoat" in *The Namesake* thus produces a temporal dissonance within the novel, for the time and place of the short story appears to be out of sync (or as Chakrabarty would note, "out of joint") with the novel's emphasis on the immigrant time of the Ganguli family. Bringing together these two distinct temporal narratives reveals the ways in which the teleology of migration in *The Namesake* is altered by its relationship to a literary text that circulates across time and across space, from imperial Russia to post-independence India, from postcolonial India to contemporary America.

As a story about South Asian locality, *The Namesake* can be read in multiple registers. The primary narrative in the novel delineates Gogol's emergent identity as an American citizen-subject. As a child he draws pictures of tombstones at a local cemetery, collecting these remains as if they were part of his own family. As a teenager he changes his name so as to escape the association with his father and with Nikolai Gogol. And as an adult, Gogol gains class mobility through a series of heterosexual romantic relationships. Though Gogol is born a U.S. citizen, Lahiri emphasizes how he consistently works to secure his identity as an American. The secondary narrative of the novel underscores the experience of his first-generation immigrant parents. As ethnic subjects, Ashima and Ashoke adapt to their new homeland: they endure the loss of their parents, raise two children, and purchase a suburban home. Though Ashima and Ashoke are never fully at ease in America, Lahiri emphasizes how they come to rely on other immigrant Bengalis for sustenance and comfort, thereby creating new forms of ethnic community. Situating the primary and secondary narratives of *The Namesake* in relation to each other highlights how the production of locality is differently embodied across generations.

My concern is with another narrative of locality, one that is uncovered through the novel's strategic alliance with Nikolai Gogol's "The Overcoat." I focus on Ashoke Ganguli's avid reading of Nikolai Gogol's works as a student in Calcutta in the 1960s. Ashoke, as Lahiri describes, "openly reveres Marx and quietly refuses religion" (21). Ashoke's reading of "The Overcoat," which is itself an allegory for Czarist Russia, generates a critique of imperialism from the third world. It also illuminates a form of locality that cannot be domesticated into universal notions of U.S. citizenship. In Calcutta, a city defined by its leftist politics, and in a decolonized country characterized by socialist five-year plans, Ashoke's reading of "The Overcoat" evokes the transnational politics of the Non-Aligned Movement.

Forged as a response to the cold war, the Non-Aligned Movement emerged in the aftermath of the Bandung Conference of 1955, which produced a unified third world alliance in opposition to U.S. and Soviet spheres of influence. As the Indonesian leader Sukarno noted: "We are united by a common detestation of colonialism in whatever form it appears. We are united by a common detestation of racialism. And we are united by a common determination to preserve and stabilize peace in the world."[32] In the aftermath of Bandung, the Non-Aligned Movement offered decolonized nations an ideological alternative to alignment with the United States or the Soviet Union. For Ashoke, the historical context of the Non-Aligned Movement informs his reading of a Russian short story, one that is centered on the rejection of imperialist and feudal claims to power. The fact that Ashoke continues to read Nikolai Gogol in the United States and names his American-born son after the author demonstrates the ways in which Ashoke embodies a postcolonial critique of U.S. citizenship.

Less than a decade before his migration to the United States, a young Ashoke travels from Calcutta to Jamshedpur to visit his blind grandfather, a retired professor of European literatures. The grandfather has requested the company of his grandson to read English-language newspapers every morning. The daily act of reading the newspaper aloud incorporates Ashoke and his grandfather into an imagined community, as joint participants in the project of postcolonial nationhood. Complementing this act of national imagination is his grandfather's second request: to read Dostoyevsky and Tolstoy in the afternoon—not contemporary Indian authors but the great Russian writers whose literary fiction is emblematic of what it means to be modern. On this occasion Ashoke will also receive an inheritance of sorts, the vast store of European and American novels that are housed in his grandfather's bookcase. Ashoke boards the overnight train to his grandfather's home engrossed in a book of Nikolai Gogol's short stories. His journey is soon interrupted by an accident: the train is derailed, and Ashoke is left for dead under a pile of corpses. In his hand he clutches a single page from "The Overcoat." Fluttering in the wind, the sheet of paper signals rescuers and leads to his long recuperation in Calcutta, and his eventual decision to study in the United States.

"The Overcoat" is the story of Akaky Akakyevich, whom Nikolai Gogol describes as "a Civil Servant who cannot by any stretch of the imagination be described as in any way remarkable" (5). Akaky's name itself is unremarkable, for it is a repetition of his father's name and thus carries with it the burden of genealogy without any distinctive identity.[33] The theme of reproduction is extended throughout the short story: Akaky is employed as a civil servant in St. Petersburg, and his only responsibility is to copy government documents. The act of duplication is his single greatest source of pleasure; even when requested, Akaky cannot bear to change a single word in the text. Indeed, it seems as if "his very lack of identity is the source of his happiness."[34] However, this lack of identity or request for anonymity changes when Akaky decides to buy a new overcoat. As he scrimps and saves toward this goal, the thought of owning a new overcoat fills Akaky with a sudden and overwhelming desire: "His whole existence [. . .] somehow [seemed] to have become fuller, as though he had got married, as though there was someone at his side, as though he was never alone" (28). However, Akaky's personal transformation is short-lived. On the first night that he wears his new overcoat, he is accosted by thieves and robbed of his coat. Akaky complains to the police and various members of the imperial bureaucracy, but he is cowed into submission by their brutality. Exposed to the cold Russian winter and consumed by anxiety, Akaky dies shortly thereafter. For many weeks following his death, the ghost of Akaky is rumored to haunt St. Petersburg, stripping citizens of overcoats in all shapes and sizes.

Ashoke identifies intensely with Akaky Akakyevich, whose existential predicament mirrors his own life. Akaky's government job reflects the thankless clerical occupation of Ashoke's father; Ashoke's mouth waters at the prospect of the celebratory meal that Akaky eats the night he wears his new overcoat, despite the fact that Ashoke has never tasted such food in his life. Although the young Ashoke has never been outside of India, much less anywhere outside of Bengal, he travels beyond these regional and national boundaries through his consumption of this literary text. In her reading of *The Namesake*, Judith Caesar writes that "one can read the story [of 'The Overcoat'] as a kind of parable about identity theft and shifting identities, in which Akaky goes from being no-one, to being an overcoat, to being a ghost, and finally to being, perhaps, a version of the very person who robbed him [. . .] The true protection seems to lie in not being known, not being knowable."[35] The fact that Akaky briefly inhabits and then loses his overcoat moves Ashoke, who also wishes to inhabit an identity outside the space of family, home, and nation. But while Akaky can lose himself inside his overcoat, Ashoke has no such protective cover. His problem is that he embodies too many public identities. He nurtures an academic interest in engineering and a passionate love of literature; he is a dutiful son to his parents but also yearns to move away from home; later in life he is both Bengali and American, and known by both his good name as well as his pet name, Mithu.

Reading "The Overcoat" provides no immediate resolution for Ashoke's sense of self. However, the fact that he is immersed in the text when his train derails demonstrates how the short story's critique of imperial Russia is duplicated in the circumstances of the train accident. Like Akaky, who works in the service of the modernizing regime of Czarist Russia in the mid-nineteenth century, Ashoke is an engineering college student, part of an emerging technocratic class that is integral to the modernizing project of the Indian state. The project of postcolonial modernity relies, in turn, upon the apparatus of colonial administration established by the British during the nineteenth century. One such apparatus is the Indian railway system, which was built to extend British administrative control of the subcontinent. After independence and partition, the railways continued to be a dominant mode of mass communication and transportation in India, literally mapping the national body of the state.[36] Whereas Nikolai Gogol suggests that brutal government bureaucrats caused Akaky's death, Ashoke's near-death incident is caused by the inefficiency of the Indian government. The train guard's portable phone at the site of the accident fails to work, and the first rescuers are local villagers rather than government-designated rescue workers. Indeed, in *The Namesake* the train wreck signals the derailment of Indian modernity, symbolized in the newspaper headline that declares, "Holiday-Makers' Tryst with Death" (19)—ironically referencing Nehru's famous declaration in 1947 that independent India faced a "tryst with destiny."[37] In the aftermath of the accident it is Ashoke who makes a tryst with destiny as he decides to migrate overseas: he imagines "walking away, as far as he could from the place in which he was born and in which he had nearly died" (20). Ultimately, it is his engineering degree that gains him, along with so many other South Asian immigrants in the mid-1960s, admission to the United States.

However, Ashoke's immigration cannot be easily reconciled with an assimilationist narrative of U.S. citizenship. His identification with "The Overcoat," as well as with other contemporary Russian and English writers, delineates an alternative narrative of locality, one that is based on a critique of the state. Ashoke's consumption of these literary works is amplified by the historical context of the Non-Aligned Movement, which also dissents from the imperialist formation of the United States, and which in turn informs Ashoke's later identification as a Marxist. Focusing on Ashoke's reading choices as a young man clarifies how he embodies at least two distinct ideologies of citizenship. On the one hand, he is a postcolonial subject who identifies with Nikolai Gogol's tacit critique of imperial rule. This ideology of postcoloniality emerges directly from the relations of empire that bound Europe to South Asia during the nineteenth and early twentieth centuries, but it is also informed by India's socialist engagement with the Soviet Union after independence. On the other hand, Ashoke also inhabits liberal-universal ideologies of citizenship, which are propagated by the same set of literary texts. These notions of citizenship rely on fictional depictions of the modern subject, such as the figure of Akaky Akakyevich. The fact that Ashoke identifies strongly with Akaky despite their visible differences of space, time, and race demonstrates how Ashoke inhabits universal narratives of citizenship even prior to his immigration to the United States. As an immigrant, Ashoke continues to embody both a postcolonial and a liberal-universal notion of subjectivity, which is codified through his sustained interest in modernist literature.

Like Ashoke, who inherits his love of modernist literature from his grandfather, the author Amitav Ghosh has also written extensively about his veneration of his grandfather's bookcase in his essay "The March of the Novel Through History." As a young boy, Ghosh regularly pilfers from the bookcase and is amazed at the "thoroughly international" collection of authors to be found there (294). Though a quarter of the novels in the bookcase were in Bengali, the others were English translations from a wide variety of countries: "Russian had pride of place [. . .] The great masterpieces of the nineteenth century were dutifully represented, the novels of Dostoevsky, Tolstoy, and Turgenev [. . .] But these were the dustiest books of all, placed on shelves that were lofty but remote" (290). The books more prominently displayed were winners of the Nobel Prize for literature. As Ghosh writes, the Nobel Prize heralds the advent of a cosmopolitan or world literature that "embodies differences in place and culture, emotion and aspiration, but in such a way as to render them communicable" (292). Many years later these books influence Ghosh's decision to become a writer. As Inderpal Grewal notes, Ghosh's essay suggests that the European novel "created cosmopolitan readers as well as writers."[38]

The fictional bookcase that Ashoke is due to inherit in *The Namesake* is almost identical to Ghosh's grandfather's bookcase, for it also features Russian writers along with major British and American authors. As a teenager Ashoke "had gone through all of Dickens. He read newer authors as well, Graham Greene and Somerset Maugham [. . .] But most of all he loved the Russians" (12). Reading these authors while walking through the crowded streets of Calcutta, Ashoke is oblivious of the overwhelming historical and geographical differences between his own urban landscape and that of the novels. Despite what Ghosh describes as differences in "place and culture," Ashoke identifies with the protagonist of "The Overcoat," a relationship that links a modernist text set in imperial Russia with the fictional experiences of a man in postcolonial India. Through the sustained act of reading, Ashoke embodies a transnational narrative of locality that rhetorically links India with imperial Europe, and nineteenth-century Europe with twentieth-century America.

Ashoke's reverence for his grandfather's books opens out the geographical and historical framework of *The Namesake*. Exploring these broadened parameters of the novel requires that we, as readers, also be equally cosmopolitan in our reading of the text. Unlike "When Mr. Pirzada Came to Dine" or "The Third and Final Continent," *The Namesake* does not revolve around a single historical event that binds together South Asia and the United States. Instead, the extended temporal and spatial scale of the novel is generated through its intertextual relationship with Nikolai Gogol's work. Because Ashoke reads "The Overcoat" during the early 1960s, Nikolai Gogol's critique of imperial power resonates with the decolonizing ethos of the Non-Aligned Movement. But Ashoke's affinity with Akaky Akakyevich also highlights the faltering project of postcolonial modernity, particularly as the Indian state provides Ashoke with engineering skills but also provokes him to leave the country. Like that of the unnamed narrator of "The Third and Final Continent," Ashoke's arrival in the United States in the late 1960s is located not only in the aftermath of the Hart-Celler Act, which is the dominant historical narrative for middle-class South Asian immigrants. His migration must also be read in terms of the limitations of socialist regimes of modernization in India, which is metaphorically connoted in *The Namesake* through the train accident. Viewed from this perspective, Ashoke's migration from India to the United States does not signal his abandonment of one project of national citizenship for another, but instead illustrates his difficult occupation of both. For Ashoke, naming his only son "Gogol" is one way of reproducing an alternate narrative of locality, a means of renegotiating his embodiment of postcolonial Indian nationhood within the universalizing demands of U.S. citizenship. As Ashoke informs his son many years later, quoting from Dostoevsky, "We all came out of Gogol's overcoat" (78).

In contrast to his father's veneration of Nikolai Gogol, Gogol Ganguli hates his namesake. Throughout his awkward teenage years Gogol feels that his given name is symptomatic of his discomfort between worlds. It is not simply the fact that his full name is neither Russian, nor Indian, nor American; instead, what is most disturbing is the fact that his name collapses the distinction between public and private lives. With a "good" name supplementing his pet name, Lahiri writes that Gogol "could have had an alternative identity, a B-side to the self" (76). But as Gogol, there is no other identity that he can take refuge in, no distinction between an intimate interior life and the public persona he exhibits at school and work. As a teenager Gogol is unaware of the circumstances of his father's accident, and the first time that Gogol is forced to confront his namesake is in high school. In his English class Gogol learns of the circumstances of Nikolai Gogol's life and death: the writer, struggling with depression, reputedly died of self-imposed starvation as a means of purging himself of homosexual desire.[39] Hearing his teacher read these details aloud in the classroom, Gogol feels betrayed. Without an alternate name to shelter him, he feels that his life (his small circle of friends, his inexperience with women) is exposed to public view. Like Akaky Akakyevich, Gogol feels as if he wants to disappear into the protective cover of an overcoat, and yet he refuses to read the story that gave him his name.

Used as a noun and a verb, the word "namesake" is variously defined as "A person or thing that has the same name as another"; "that shares the same name as someone or something else previously mentioned"; "named after or for."[40] As Nikolai Gogol's namesake, Gogol mistakenly assumes a synchronous temporality between himself and the writer. In Gogol's view, the fact that he shares his first name with the writer means that his name is never uniquely his own: it contains histories preceding his birth, histories that link him to his parents' lives in India. On the occasion of Gogol's fourteenth birthday, when Ashoke presents him with a copy of "The Overcoat," Ashoke casually remarks that he feels a "special kinship with [Nikolai] Gogol" because "He spent most of his adult life outside his homeland. Like me" (77). While Ashoke feels an affinity with Nikolai Gogol's exile, Gogol Ganguli rejects any association to his father's migration or to the writer's. Unlike Ashoke, Gogol identifies as an American, one whose claims to citizenship are disrupted by the temporal conditions of his name.

In *A Critique of Postcolonial Reason*, Gayatri Spivak argues for the reintroduction of the word "catachresis," which she defines as a "false but useful analogy" (179). Discussing the term in relation to J. M. Coetzee's novel *Foe*, Spivak describes the pedagogical process through which Friday, the African "native informant" in the novel (who is tongueless, and therefore speechless), is taught the word "Africa." She writes, "*Africa* is only a timebound naming; like all proper names it is a mark with an arbitrary connection to its referent, a catachresis" (189). Confronted with the word "Africa," Friday denies its pedagogical repetition, choosing instead to write the four letters "h-o-u-s." Whether finally "hous" comes to stand in for "house" and is made synonymous to "Africa" remains unclear in the narrative of *Foe*.

In *The Namesake*, the word "Gogol" also functions as a time-bound naming. It is a name that is bounded by time and space, a diminutive pet name that was meant to be used only by family members and other intimates. However, "Gogol" also threatens to transcend the domestic sphere, for it is a name that occupies multiple public histories, including the biography of the writer Nikolai Gogol, as well as the circumstances of Ashoke's train accident. The problem with "Gogol," therefore, is that it is a name in excess of its proper temporal and spatial boundaries. "Gogol" is a name that is repetitively invoked at home, at school, and most importantly by Gogol Ganguli himself. When as an adult Gogol confronts the history of his namesake, he refuses to identify with his name and chooses instead another word, the proper name of "Nikhil." The question of whether "Nikhil" can be made synonymous to "Gogol" structures the dominant narrative of *The Namesake*. Gogol Ganguli's incomplete transition to Nikhil reflects the sustained temporal disjuncture between immigration and citizenship, one that cannot be resolved through a simple change of name.

When Gogol officially changes his first name to Nikhil at age eighteen, he aims to embody an entirely new temporality that is distinct from the history of his namesake. He learns by reading an issue of *Reader's Digest* that changing one's name is "a right belonging to every American citizen" (99). As such, Gogol's legal application to change his name is not only a personal rite of passage; it is also emblematic of consenting to the rights and constraints of U.S. citizenship. By changing his name to Nikhil, Gogol joins the ranks of thousands of men and women who changed their names upon arrival in America. As Lahiri writes, "European immigrants had their names changed at Ellis Island, [and] slaves renamed themselves once they were emancipated" (97). Paradoxically, though Gogol feels that "Nikhil" is a unique and appropriate name for his adult self, it is in fact the original "good name" that Ashoke and Ashima selected for him, a name that he had rejected as a child. Moreover, though Gogol aims to distinguish himself from his namesake by changing his name, he once again echoes the biography of Nikolai Gogol, for the author shortened his surname from Gogol-Yanovsky at the start of his writing career.

As Nikhil, Gogol attempts to embody a new sense of locality that is aligned with his own experience of American citizenship. However, "Nikhil" also functions as a catachresis, a useful (but ultimately false) analogy. Unlike the name Gogol, which was bound to his father's life, Nikhil is altogether bereft of a sense of history. Describing Gogol's freshman year at Yale in the immediate aftermath of his name change, Lahiri writes, "There is only one complication: he doesn't feel like Nikhil. Not yet. Part of the problem is that the people who now know him as Nikhil have no idea that he used to be Gogol. They know him only in the present, not at all in the past" (105). As a college student Gogol is initially thrilled by the absence of his namesake, for being Nikhil enables him to engage in a series of sexual relationships. Yet it is worth noting that even at Yale, Gogol cannot escape from an imperial past. The university is named after Elihu Yale, a British merchant who served in the East India Company and was formerly governor of Fort St. George in Madras (now Chennai). While Gogol's upward class mobility in the United States is secured by his attendance at this elite institution, Elihu Yale's considerable wealth was amassed through exploiting contacts with traders in Madras during the late seventeenth century. Yale's illegal profiteering, against the directives of the East India Company, enabled him to patronize the founding of the American university.[41] The fact that Gogol continues to be haunted by the ties that bind South Asia to America is evidence that a name change alone cannot alter the past. Even as Nikhil, Gogol remains subject to narratives of colonial and postcolonial India. As Spivak comments, "All longings to the contrary, it [the proper name] cannot provide the absolute guarantee of identity."[42]

Gogol ultimately fails to be known as Nikhil. Within his immediate family, this new name remains unfamiliar, and Ashima's (and later, his wife Moushomi's) continuous references to "Gogol" threaten to expose his past. More important, Gogol himself becomes dissatisfied by the absence of a family genealogy in the name Nikhil. Though Gogol-as-Nikhil stakes his claim as a U.S. citizen, the multiple temporalities connoted by his given and chosen names are impossible to accommodate within assimilationist models of American citizenship. Just as Ashoke inhabited multiple localities—as a postcolonial subject of India and as an immigrant to America, as a critic of imperial rule and a modern subject of the state—so too does Gogol. He is a racialized immigrant and an assimilated citizen; his names reflect the possibilities of a life gained in the aftermath of the train accident and also remain bound to past lives. What differentiates Gogol's embodiment of locality from his father's is not time but space. In contrast to his parents, who crossed continents, the spatial topography of Gogol's life is remarkably constricted, limited to the northeast corridor between Boston and New York. After the death of his father, Gogol reflects: "He had spent years maintaining distance from his origins; his parents, in bridging that distance as best as they could. And yet [. . .] he has always hovered close to this quiet, ordinary town [. . .] for most of his adult life he has never been more than a four-hour train ride away" (281).

As Gogol compares his own negotiation of time and space with that of his parents, he realizes that it is not spatial distance but intimacy that he desires. Despite the fact that his entire adult life has been oriented toward distinguishing himself from his parents, Gogol has never lived more than a brief train journey away from home. It is Ashoke and Ashima who have left behind their homes and families in India, and it is they who have willfully given up their pet names to be known in the United States only by their good name. After the death of his father and impending retirement of his mother, Gogol recognizes that no one else will call him by his pet name. He will now always be known as Nikhil, the name that offers only a partial narrative of self. Without a namesake that explains his birth or the circumstances that persuaded his father to leave India, Gogol is unmoored from a sense of ethnic community. Toward the end of the novel, Gogol rediscovers the copy of "The Overcoat" that his father had given him as a gift. By reading this short story, Gogol attempts to reconcile the distance between himself and his namesake, between his claims to a single national domain and the transnational subjectivities embodied by his father.

The circulation of "The Overcoat" within *The Namesake* illustrates the difficulty of establishing a name and a claim to identity. For Ashoke, reading "The Overcoat" establishes a contradictory relationship to the postcolonial Indian state, one that ultimately persuades him to leave India. By identifying with Akaky Akakyevich's predicament over his stolen overcoat, a situation that is exacerbated by the cruelty of the Russian imperial bureaucracy, Ashoke begins to disidentify with the bureaucratic organization of the modern Indian state. At the same time, his avid consumption of the modernist literary canon engenders a transnational subjectivity, one that is amplified by the contemporary politics of the Non-Aligned Movement. Gogol's parameters of identification are somewhat narrower, and informed almost exclusively by personal rather than public histories. His disidentification with his father's narrative of migration persuades him to adopt a new name, Nikhil. Yet Nikhil is a catachresis, a name that cannot reflect the unresolved transition between immigrant and citizen. Tracing the patrilineal circulation of "The Overcoat" across four generations (from Ashoke's grandfather to Ashoke, and from Ashoke to his son) demonstrates the conditions of postcoloniality and modernity that continue to structure Gogol's locality in the United States. In this sense, the relationship between *The Namesake* and "The Overcoat" refashions dominant narratives of what it means to be American.

Importantly, what it means to be South Asian in America had already undergone a transformation during the three decades of Gogol's fictional life, as immigration reforms in the 1980s and 1990s radically shifted the demographic composition of subcontinental communities. By the time of the novel's conclusion, South Asians were no longer only scientists and doctors but also newsstand vendors, taxi drivers, and workers in the high-tech as well as manufacturing industries. These changes in social and class composition among South Asians are not reflected in *The Namesake*, either through minor characters or events. It is also telling that Lahiri concludes the novel in 2000, a year prior to the September 11, 2001, terrorist attacks that transformed the political landscape for South Asians in America. Reading these absences into *The Namesake* is a necessary critique of its hegemonic and middle-class narrative of immigration. However, analyzing the novel through a singular national framework that emphasizes historical change in the United States limits the rhetorical implications of the text. Instead, I generate a narrative of locality in relation to postcolonial histories of the subcontinent; fictional depictions of imperial Russia; and racial and class politics in America. The ties that bind these disparate geographies are partial and fragmentary, not least because Gogol's reading of "The Overcoat" remains incomplete at the conclusion of the novel. At the same time, the widened temporal scope provided by Nikolai Gogol's short story engenders a postcolonial critique of *The Namesake*, one that conditions how we read and write narratives of South Asian immigration. By linking disparate projects of modernity and citizenship, an intertextual reading of the novel and the short story highlights how the localities of South Asian immigrants cannot be incorporated within hegemonic representations of U.S. citizenship.

Topographies of Diaspora

In an essay reviewing early twentieth-century histories of South Asian migration to the United States, the anthropologist Purnima Mankekar contends that scholars in the field require a "bifocal" perspective on diaspora: "This notion of political bifocality foregrounds the capacity of diasporic subjects to build alliances with struggles for social justice in both our 'homes' [. . . It provides] a first step out of the binary between 'homeland' (associated with origin and authenticity) and 'diaspora' (tied to tropes of loss, exile, and inauthenticity) and, more centrally, between the subject positions of citizen and immigrant."[43] In Mankekar's view, such an analytical perspective emphasizes the convergence rather than dissimilarities between the citizen and the immigrant by examining how political histories of labor migration in South Asia are linked to immigration laws in the United States. In my reading of Jhumpa Lahiri's works, I extend the framework of bifocality to consider how diasporic subjects negotiate distinct ideologies of citizenship in both their "homes," particularly as notions of citizenship are linked to colonial and postcolonial projects of modernity. In the case of "When Mr. Pirzada Came to Dine," the subject-positions of Lilia and Mr. Pirzada briefly converge during the Bangladesh Liberation War, when both citizen and immigrant are confronted by nightly images of violence. Mr. Pirzada uses his pocket watch to keep an eye on the time in Bangladesh, to participate in the birth of a new nation on the other side of the world. But his attempt to keep time fails to bridge the geographical distance between South Asia and the United States, where a Pakistani government fellowship keeps him away from his family in Dhaka. For Lilia, seeing the impact of the war on her family provokes her to read about the political history of the subcontinent. However, none of the books in her school library detail how the war in Bangladesh is framed by the larger geopolitical conditions of the cold war, nor is Lilia aware of the ideological relationship that links the Revolutionary War in the United States with anticolonial movements in South Asia. The short story also produces other unexpected convergences, for during the 1970s, movements for ethnic self-determination in the United States are coterminous with nationalist movements in Bangladesh. At universities such as the institution that employs Mr. Pirzada and Lilia's father, students and faculty are engulfed in debates over Asian American studies, Native American studies, African American studies, and other emerging interdisciplinary fields as the civil rights movement continues to put forward the legislative claims of racial and sexual minorities. Thus even as nations on the subcontinent continue to be riven by ethnic, linguistic, and religious movements, the national idea of America is also ruptured by racial and class differences. Bringing this domestic history of anti-imperialism in line with the anticolonial and nationalist politics of South Asia in "When Mr. Pirzada Came to Dine" requires us, as readers, to also maintain a bifocal perspective.

Such an analytical framework demands a more nuanced understanding of empire, one that links the consolidation of British imperialism in the late nineteenth and twentieth centuries with the expanding territorial reach of the United States during the same period. The story of Mrs. Croft and the unnamed narrator of "The Third and Final Continent" is one example of what Lisa Lowe, in a different context, has called "the intimacies of four continents." Lowe tracks the migration and circulation of Chinese indentured laborers between Europe, the Americas, Africa, and Asia in the early nineteenth century in order to examine the conditions of modernity engendered through the figure of the Chinese "coolie." She defines intimacy in three contexts: First, as "spatial proximity or adjacent connection," the logic of political economy through which slave labor became the foundation of wealth for nation-states in Europe and North America. Second, as "sexual and affective intimacy in the private sphere," which includes relationships such as domestic servitude that disrupt the binary between public and private relations of power. Third, Lowe defines intimacy as "the variety of contacts among slaves, indentured persons, and mixed-blood free peoples," which produces political, sexual, and intellectual connections that in turn incite revolt and rebellion (193–202). The coolie becomes a representational figure for reimagining the relationship of empire between the Americas, Europe, Asia, and Africa through the migration of indentured and slave labor.

In "The Third and Final Continent," the narrator is a professionally skilled worker, one of many thousands of men who migrate in the aftermath of the 1965 Hart-Celler Act. The conditions of his work as a librarian are utterly distinct from the exploitation of the coolie, and yet historians such as Vijay Prashad have argued that middle-class South Asians are also girmitiyas, or indentured workers, who are contracted to work for the U.S. state.[44] During his lifetime, the narrator has been a colonial subject of Britain; a postcolonial subject of the Indian state; a worker and student in London; and a new migrant to the United States. He arrives in America with permanent residency and with the professional skills that later generate upward class mobility. However, his intimate relationship with Mrs. Croft is engendered through the contractual economic relationship between landlord and tenant, and enacted through the nightly conversations they have within the private sphere of her home. Whereas for Mrs. Croft the lunar landing signifies the advent of a distinctly American future—what she might describe as a "splendid" future—for the narrator that same event signals the impending failure of empire. The labor of Asian American scientists and engineers made the lunar landing possible, for their collective work helped create the technological infrastructure for the cold war. Thus while Mrs. Croft marvels at the arrival of American men on the moon, the narrator recognizes that it is his arrival, along with so many other immigrants, that has altered the landscape of America. His achievement merits no public record; in this regard, the figure of the unnamed narrator is akin to the Chinese coolie who, as Lowe remarks, is absent from early historical records of the Americas.[45] The fact that the narrator's life story is absent from the domain of national history highlights how the subject-position of the immigrant continues to contradict universal notions of citizenship. Focusing on unnamed figures like the narrator of "The Third and Final Continent" is not simply a move toward the "recovery and recuperation" of a lost history, but rather a means of supplementing absence with "new narratives of affirmation and presence."[46]

These narratives of presence generate a different topography of Asian America, one that is shaped through the intersection of the complex histories of partition, independence, and secession that characterize contemporary South Asia. Locating Lahiri's popular fiction at the intersection of these national histories reorients the geographical framework of Asian American studies. The postcolonial theorization of Asian America is enabled not only by attending to the expansion of U.S. empires in East and Southeast Asia but also through the different temporal frameworks embodied by South Asian immigrants. These histories, as Chakrabarty claims, are "out of joint," impossible to reconcile with dominant narratives of assimilation to America. Lahiri's *The Namesake* is characterized by such temporal dissonance, which is embodied first through Ashoke and then through his son Gogol. Their joint consumption of Nikolai Gogol's "The Overcoat" reconfigures what is otherwise an intergenerational portrait of immigration. For Ashoke, Nikolai

Gogol's short story articulates a critique of imperialism that resonates with the Non-Aligned Movement, and which characterizes leftist Indian nationalism in the 1960s. Ashoke aims to pass this political legacy on to his son, but for Gogol his namesake impedes claims to American citizenship. Gogol's attempt to change his name alerts us to the power of nationalism as a normative modality of belonging. However, his subsequent failure to fully inhabit his new name demonstrates how nationalist frameworks rarely capture the contradictions of diasporic subjectivity.

As a phenomenology of belonging, locality is distinct from citizenship. None of the fictional protagonists in these three texts identify as anything other than "Bengali," "Pakistani," "Indian," or "American," and yet in my readings each of these national constructs remains fundamentally incomplete. Equally important, there is no room in any of these categories for notions of religious or class difference. Such ethnic and national constructs remind us of the power of dominant regimes of identification, but also illustrate how the everyday life of South Asian immigrants consistently exceed singular categories of identity. Sustaining locality among South Asian immigrants is, like the brief friendship between Lilia and Mr. Pirzada, a fragile endeavor. It is nearly impossible to bind together diasporic experiences that are characterized by different histories of migration and shaped by distinct national politics on the subcontinent. However, by prioritizing the convergence between histories of migration and empire, I demonstrate how South Asians inhabit postcolonial localities that inform their relationship of identity with the U.S. state.

In the decades between 1965 and 2005, U.S. immigration laws produced a different demographic profile for South Asian immigrant communities, differentiated not only by national origin but also by changing notions of racial, class, gender, and religious identity. In Chapter 2 I move from the fictional characters of Lahiri's work to the cinematic subjects of public television and film documentaries. Shifting from literature to film, and particularly from fiction to documentary films, requires a different method of inquiry. I continue to emphasize the temporal dissonance embodied by South Asians, but I also examine how locality is produced through the spatial disjunctures that characterize the visual relationship between the subcontinent and the United States. If Lahiri's protagonists move from the "old world" to the "new," the protagonists of the documentary films move from third world to first world.[47] Because these documentaries circulate as public pedagogical texts, the filmmakers deliberately disrupt representations of upwardly mobile, middle-class South Asian immigrants. However, the widespread circulation and consumption of these films reveals the dominance of assimilationist notions of U.S. citizenship. The ways in which first- and second-generation immigrants negotiate the geographical, political, and historical boundaries between South Asia and America—or how they create lived spaces as South Asians *in* America—is the subject of the following chapter.

TWO

So Far from Home

Documenting Immigrant Lives in Knowing Her Place, Calcutta Calling, *and* Bangla East Side

In Mira Nair's documentary film *So Far from India*, Ashok, a subway newsstand vendor in New York City, returns to his hometown of Ahmedabad in western India to visit his family. It is Ashok's first trip to India in two years. He left twenty days after marrying his wife, Hansa, and so the trip is also Ashok's first occasion to meet his toddler son, Manan. Throughout his visit Ashok is inundated with advice from both sides of his family. His sisters tell him to return "home," back to his privileged place as the youngest and only son of their large family. But his sister-in-law implores him to take Hansa and Manan to the United States in order to subsequently sponsor green cards for the rest of the family. Hansa's sister asserts, "You are the engine that has to pull a whole train of cars to America." Despite her insistence, Ashok leaves Ahmedabad without his wife and child, promising to send for them in six months or a year or more. After his return to New York, his family constantly writes to him asking what he requires from Ahmedabad. To their queries Ashok responds, "I want nothing from India." For Nair, who is physically and audibly present throughout the film, Ashok's story is a ubiquitous tale of migration. "When you leave to find your own way in another country," she says in a voice-over, "it is hard to return and find comfort in what you left."

Moving from fictional narratives about upwardly mobile South Asians to documentaries about emerging immigrant groups challenges popular representations of who and what is South Asian. The shift in genre from literature to film also requires a different modality of reading, one that attends to the site of documentary film production, its circulation as an aesthetic and pedagogical text, and its consumption by South Asian and non–South Asian viewers. The films I examine in this chapter focus on underrepresented communities of South Asians—workers, women, adoptees, and Muslims. From the filmmakers' perspective, these documentaries challenge normative histories of South Asian migration; because they are screened at film festivals and in the classroom, the documentaries also aim to establish relations of identity between the filmmaker, documentary subject, and viewer. Yet such aspirations of solidarity are frequently undermined by the cinematic form of the documentary, which reveals rather than sutures differences of class, gender, and generation.

So Far from India, released in 1982, is among the earliest films made by a South Asian filmmaker about new immigrants from the subcontinent. While Ashok's occupation as a subway newsstand vendor reflects the changing demographic profile of South Asians, Nair's voice-over commentary (as translator and interpreter for the viewer) underscores the class difference between filmmaker and documentary subject. In *So Far from India* the difference of class is folded into a visual rhetoric of spatial difference between India and the United States. Throughout the film these two countries are represented by a series of binaries. "India" is represented through Hansa's domestic labor and becomes the site of home, family, and tradition. "America" comes to life through Ashok's conspicuous consumption of brand-name goods and stands for individuality and autonomy. Though both Nair and Ashok travel between countries, only Ashok's anxiety is reflected in the film. He is hesitant to reconcile his family life in India with his autonomy in the United States, but Nair has no such qualms. She migrates freely between both countries, returning to Ahmedabad to interview Ashok's family after his departure. Nair's mobility is enabled by her middle-class subjectivity, but this class difference is not the subject of the film. Instead Nair turns her camera onto Ashok, who frames his dilemma as a "choice" between identifying as an Indian or as an American. Yet even as Ashok proclaims that "I want nothing from India," the visual narrative and aural voice-over of the film significantly contradict his oral testimonial. Nair depicts interconnected networks of labor and capital that link India and the United States, and which in turn link the U.S.-based viewer to the film. These same networks of capital accumulation engender the hierarchical relation between Nair and her documentary subject. In this documentary, as in many others by South Asian filmmakers, locality emerges through a contradictory set of visual, aural, and oral narratives.

Within the pedagogy and practice of Asian American studies, documentary films are central to modes of self-representation. Such films circulate widely in Asian American film festivals, as well as on public television programs as "authentic" testimonials of ethnic community.[1] Throughout the 1980s and 1990s, Asian American independent filmmakers created an extraordinary number of documentary features that showcased autobiographical stories of migration. These narratives were critical to correcting mainstream perceptions of Asian immigrants as a "model minority" and directly commented on ethnic, racial, and sexual stereotypes, particularly of Asian American women and queer immigrants.[2] Within this milieu, South Asian independent filmmakers have also used documentaries to showcase the heterogeneity of immigrant groups. The number of documentaries by first- and second-generation South Asian filmmakers has proliferated over the past twenty years, reflecting the diverse religious, economic, and linguistic composition of immigrant communities, as well as the enlarged public sphere of South Asian diasporic cultural production.[3] These two decades also span a period of rapid historical and social change in South Asian immigrant communities. Following the migration of middle-class professionals in the 1960s, structural changes in the U.S. service economy and immigration laws led to an influx of working-class immigrants in the 1980s. In the 1990s the population of working-class and undocumented immigrants from Bangladesh, Pakistan, and India continued to increase in metropolitan areas across the East and West coasts, as well as in the U.S. South. However, this demographic trend obscures the arrival of another group of South Asian immigrants: transnational adoptees, many of whom have been adopted by white American families in suburban and rural areas, particularly in the Midwest. More recently, younger South Asian filmmakers have collaborated with a number of emerging immigrant groups, such as student and workers' organizations. Such documentaries operate as educational programming that emphasizes how South Asians forge ethnic and religious identities, particularly in the aftermath of September 11, 2001. Despite the collective nature of these cinematic projects, social and political differences among South Asians deeply impact the process of filmmaking. For many South Asian filmmakers as well as for their documentary subjects, creating visual representations of immigrant life requires negotiating a complex set of differences around class, religion, language, and national origin.

South Asian documentaries operate simultaneously as autobiographical, historical, and ethnographic texts. All of the films I discuss in this chapter are directed by filmmakers who self-identify as South Asian and as feminist. As autobiographical texts, these films open up the relationship between the director and the documentary subject, both of whom identify as immigrants. At the level of racialization, therefore, the subjectivity of the filmmaker converges with that of the documentary subject. However, in terms of political and class identities, the documentaries are frequently characterized by a relationship of dissonance between the protagonists on-screen and the filmmaker off-screen. These dissonant identities are manifest through relations of trust and betrayal, intimacy and estrangement that impact the oral testimonials and voice-over narratives recorded in each film. The notion of producing an "authentic" documentation of South Asian experience is thus distorted from the outset through the heterogeneous social field that defines the encounter between filmmaker and documentary subject.

As historical texts, the documentaries map the changing demographic composition of South Asian communities, defined as much by shifts in class-based migration as by the emergence of new immigrant groups. Despite the highly specific narratives of immigration that are made visible in each film, the ways in which questions of identity are resolved remain remarkably similar. Across the documentary films, migration is represented as a "choice" between identifying as South Asian or as American. The only possible resolution of this so-called crisis of identity is through the protagonists' identification as American citizens. However, citizenship offers only a partial resolution to the question of locality, for the protagonists continue to embody memories of the subcontinent and negotiate relationships with family members who remain in South Asia. For these protagonists, locality operates as a phenomenological quality that cannot be recuperated into singular constructs of nationhood. Even as the filmmakers reproduce linear narratives of assimilation, the locality of the documentary subjects exceeds the teleology of U.S. citizenship.

Finally, the films operate as ethnographic texts. Immigrants from the subcontinent obviously feature as ethnographic subjects in each film, but I am equally interested in how the documentaries circulate online (via publicly accessible websites) and off-line (in film festivals and in the classroom) among immigrant groups. By examining records of viewer experiences posted on blogs and websites, I explore the debates that these films generate over what constitutes an "authentic" narrative of South Asian migration.[4] The fact that these films are eagerly consumed by other South Asians in the United States, despite differences of national origin or class, demonstrates the collective investment of viewers in reproducing certain dominant narratives of immigration. From this perspective, the proliferation of assimilationist narratives emerges not only from the oral testimonials of the documentary subjects, or from the filmmakers' attempts to resolve the "identity crisis" posed by their subjects. Assimilation is also the rhetoric through which viewers describe their own resolution of locality, particularly when viewers are themselves second-generation South Asians. Throughout the chapter, I emphasize the convergences and dissimilarities between viewer and film, between documentary subject and filmmaker, and between the filmmaker and viewer. The irregular relationships forged in each instance showcase the difficulty of creating, embodying, and sustaining a collective notion of what it means to be South Asian.

In comparison with the literary texts that I discussed in Chapter 1, the production of locality in South Asian documentary films is figured through notions of space rather than time. As Appadurai notes, spatial boundaries are critical to the ways in which members of a community define themselves *as* a community and establish boundaries in relation to other groups. The documentaries that I examine engage with the spatial characteristics of locality in three distinct ways. First, I explore how the filmmakers deploy a visual rhetoric of spatial distance that amplifies the political and historical differences between South Asia and the United States. Such notions of distance and difference are evident in *So Far from India* primarily through Nair's gendered representations of India and the United States, but they are also visible in Indu Krishnan's documentary *Knowing Her Place*. *Knowing Her Place* is the story of Vasu, a middle-class woman who has migrated on multiple occasions between Madras (now called Chennai) and New York City. Though Madras and New York are both densely populated metropolises, many of the scenes in Madras are shot within airy, bright interior spaces: large living rooms, open kitchens, light-filled courtyards. Krishnan sidelines the urban commotion of Madras in favor of an expansive perspective on middle-class, upper-caste Hindu South Indian domesticity that is embodied by Vasu. By contrast, Krishnan portrays New York through a series of exterior shots (subways, buildings, supermarkets). When Krishnan interviews Vasu in her New York apartment, the interior spaces are filmed in artificial light, thereby appearing both cramped and invasive. Such visual tropes of difference codify the spatial distance between South Asia and the United States, even though Vasu's oral testimonial consistently binds these two sites together.

Second, I examine the ways in which documentary filmmaking has itself become a collaborative venture, one that establishes spatial and racial boundaries between who is South Asian and who is not. For example, the recent film *B.E.S. (Bangla East Side)* was conceived as a project with Bangladeshi immigrant teenagers at a public high school on the Lower East Side of Manhattan. The directors of the film, Fariba Alam and Sarita Khurana, collaborated with youth in an after-school program to develop testimonials of Muslim American experiences after September 11, 2001. The film showcases the strong relations of identity that bind together the filmmakers with the documentary subjects, despite the fact that the Bangladeshi youth are first-generation immigrants and Khurana and Alam are second-generation Americans. Moreover, while Alam identifies as Bangladeshi American and Khurana is of Indian descent, the documentary subjects tend to identify themselves as Bengalis. Yet through the collaborative process of making the film, Alam and Khurana demarcate the contours of a South Asian identity, one that is embodied by the directors as well as documentary subjects despite differences of class, religion, and national origin.

Third, I underscore the ways in which the documentary subjects unexpectedly produce and inhabit South Asian localities in the United States. In *Calcutta Calling*, the filmmaker Sasha Khokha interviews teenage girls born in Calcutta who have been adopted by white American families in Minnesota. All these young women identify strongly as Christians, and thus their stories of coming to America (as well as the testimonials of their parents) reflect what I call a "salvation narrative," one that confirms the United States as the ultimate destination of immigrants. When the adoptees visit Calcutta with their adoptive families, their shock, unease, and confusion only strengthens their identification as American citizens. However, upon their return to Minnesota the adoptees maintain intense bonds of affection and affinity with each other, proclaiming that they want to create and inhabit a country full of "adopted Indian girls." The oral testimonials collected in *Calcutta Calling* thus generate an alternate narrative of locality, one that exceeds the narrative of American citizenship embodied by the adoptees' family members as well as by Khokha herself.

Examining the production of locality in each of these films requires critically engaging on multiple and interconnected levels with the filmmakers and documentary subjects. In *So Far from India* and *Knowing Her Place*, the filmmakers depict the protagonists as sovereign subjects, as individuals with their own stories. Yet Nair and Krishnan's characterization of their protagonists as autonomous agents is critical to the directors' own sense of autonomy as feminist filmmakers. Narrating the relationship between Nair, Krishnan, and their documentary subjects highlights the limits of liberal-feminist modes of representation. In *Calcutta Calling* and *B.E.S.*, the filmmakers focus on youthful protagonists who reflect new forms of multiculturalism in the United States. As such, the transnational adoptees documented by Sasha Khokha in *Calcutta Calling* as well as the Bangladeshi youth interviewed by Fariba Alam and Sarita Khurana in *B.E.S.* are depicted as challenging dominant representations of South Asians as a model minority. However, the resistant subjectivities embodied by these youth are in turn central to Khokha, Alam, and Khurana's own self-representations as second-generation and mixed-race South Asians. Viewing each film highlights how locality is generated through the dynamic encounters between filmmaker and documentary subject. The heterogeneous quality of what it means to be "South Asian" emerges through the uneven circulation and consumption of visual narratives on- and off-screen.

Locating the Feminist Subject

So Far from India was released in 1982, just two years after a racial category was established for South Asian immigrants in the U.S. census. The formation of the category "Asian Indian" in the 1980 census was the result of community-based mobilization by the Association of Indian Americans (AIA), a group of professional, middle-class immigrants in the United States. The AIA argued for a distinct racial and ethnic category in the census, one that was differentiated from "Caucasian" and "Hindu" under which South Asians had been previously counted. The category of "Asian Indian" was meant to secure rights to full citizenship for all immigrants from the subcontinent, but in fact it reified the hegemony of Indian immigrants in the United States and led to the undercounting of other immigrant groups (such as Pakistanis, Bangladeshis, and Sri Lankans) who did not identify with the construct of "Asian Indian." Equally important, while the AIA contended that South Asians were a racial minority in the United States, their concern was with middle-class immigrants—doctors, professors, engineers—who had experienced racial discrimination in the workplace.[5] Ashok, the protagonist of *So Far from India*, occupies a contradictory position within the racial and political landscape generated by middle-class Indian immigrant groups. On the one hand, as an "Asian Indian" he is entitled to full representation and rights to citizenship by the U.S. state. On the other hand, he is a working-class immigrant, and thus his labor is fully ignored by the mainstream Indian immigrant community.

The class disparity between working-class and middle-class immigrants, which I suggest is reflected in the vexed encounter between Nair as filmmaker and Ashok as documentary subject, is central to contemporary formations of South Asian identity. By the 1980s the number of immigrants such as Ashok who worked as newsstand vendors, cab drivers, or domestic workers was increasing rapidly in urban areas across the United States. Their presence is frequently traced to family reunification preferences in the 1965 Hart-Celler Act. However, in contrast to those professional immigrants who are extolled by the mainstream U.S. press and within South Asian community organizations for their individual merit (whether academic or entrepreneurial), working-class immigrants are frequently derided by middle-class immigrants for their lack of skill. More broadly, the class schism between professional and working-class South Asians is represented through personal narratives of "success" or "failure," which is indeed how Ashok himself narrates his experience in the United States. However, such individualistic narratives eclipse the relational dynamic between primary and secondary labor markets in the United States. Whereas the secondary labor market is "characterized by poor pay, poor job security, minimum benefits or none at all, hazardous working conditions, and minimal opportunities for promotion," the primary labor market is characterized by secure positions often occupied by native-born Americans.[6] In Nair's film, instead of a broader discussion of family reunification policies, or a structural account of the primary and secondary labor markets for immigrants, the emphasis is on Ashok's individual story.

While *So Far from India* tracks Ashok's journey from New York, the story of his migration begins in Ahmedabad, the largest city in the state of Gujarat, in western India. Ashok is the only member of his immediate family living overseas, but in Ahmedabad, Nair informs us, one in three households has a relative working in America. Ashok's family has a storied presence in Ahmedabad, where for generations the men in his family worked as spice merchants employed by the local royal family. After independence and partition in 1947 the family was divested of its property, settling into a life of more modest means. Ashok's father, Thakorbhai, entertains Nair with a nostalgic account of his youth, reading from journal entries that are dotted with descriptions of the Hollywood films he saw as a young man. Singing lyrics from the "The Continental," the song popularized in the 1934 movie *The Gay Divorcee*, Thakorbhai recounts his admiration for Ginger Rogers and Fred Astaire and for the magic of the Hollywood musical. America comes alive through the enchantment of its entertainment industry, but for Thakorbhai's son there is no time for leisure. Ashok is born into a different world, growing up in a newly independent country that disabled a colonial system of princely states and instituted in its place a socialist central government. His departure for New York in the 1980s comes at a time when the Indian economy is beset by structural inefficiencies: extensive regulation and protectionism by the state has led to rampant corruption.[7] Confronted with the dismantling of the national economic system, Ashok cannot afford to remain nostalgic like his father. Instead, his participation in a global system of privatized capital is contingent on forgoing the feudal patronage system that benefited his family. As Ashok confesses to Nair, "You forget everybody in America. Who's your uncle, who's your brother? Your life is your own."

Throughout her depiction of Ashok's journey, Nair maintains a temporal and spatial divide between two countries. "India" is represented through long shots of Ashok's large ancestral home and wide shots of street scenes in Ahmedabad. In contrast, "America" is connoted through the cramped, dark interior spaces of the New York subway and Ashok's apartment. Nair's deployment of an oppositional aesthetic between India and the United States is projected onto a developmental discourse between third and first worlds. India is characterized by domestic production, as Hansa constantly cooks and cleans for Ashok's family; America is the site of conspicuous consumption, where Ashok spends lavishly on new items of clothing. India is also gendered feminine through Nair's depiction of Hansa's household work, as well as by a predominance of female relatives. By contrast, the United States is masculinized through Ashok's aggressive embodiment of autonomy. Despite the fact that Ashok and his wife hardly spend any time together during his trip to India, Ashok professes to feeling "a little love" for her. He informs Hansa's family that her and the couple's son's pending migration is a matter of finances: as soon as Ashok has earned enough, they can join him. Yet upon returning to the United States, Ashok tells Nair that bringing his family to New York is not simply a question of money. He is wary of becoming emotionally and financially responsible for Hansa's extended family and thereby compromising his newfound autonomy.

Ashok's narration of his "identity crisis" is amplified by Nair's voice-over as well as by her visual imagery, which depicts Ashok's identity as a "choice" between India and America. Although Ashok is the apparent subject of this documentary, it soon becomes clear that he is incapable of straddling the breach between the two countries. In fact the only subject on-screen who moves easily between these two sites is Nair, the filmmaker. Nair, not Hansa, follows Ashok on his journey from the United States to India and back again; moreover, during her interviews with Hansa, we hear Nair speak, as she dubs over Hansa's voice in English. Positioned against the entrenched geographical divide that separates Ashok and Hansa, Nair is characterized by her ability to converse across difference. Nair's mobility is, of course, a function of class as well as gender. The dissonance between her own middle-class status and Ashok's working-class background translates into Nair's ability to move freely between male and female spheres in Ahmedabad. She is equally conversant with Ashok and his male relatives in the sitting room of the family home as she is with Hansa in the narrow confines of the kitchen. Whereas for Ashok his tenuous job security in the United States and lack of facility in English depict his incomplete identification with America, Nair's middle-class position enables her to occupy a relation of belonging to both India and the United States. Working within a binary representational framework of "choice," Nair unexpectedly curtails Ashok's agentive capacity. Instead, *So Far from India* frames Nair's own upward mobility as the legitimate subject of the film.

Nearly a decade later, Indu Krishnan's documentary film *Knowing Her Place* (1990) also tracks the journeys of its immigrant protagonist, Vasu.[8] Vasu's story is unusual: as a child she was raised in Queens, New York, and moved when she was twelve with her parents to Madras. In the aftermath of her father's death Vasu entered an arranged marriage at age sixteen and then returned with her husband to Queens. Alternating between scenes shot in New York and in Madras, the film documents over a two-year period Vasu's relationship with her husband and teenage sons in the United States, and with her mother and grandmother in India. Throughout, the visual narrative of the film and Vasu's oral testimony are mediated by Krishnan's voice-over. Krishnan's documentary initially appears to reaffirm hegemonic representations of middle-class South Asians: Vasu's father was a scientist, and her husband is a mathematics professor. However, *Knowing Her Place* aims to challenge the dominant role of immigrant men by focusing on the gendered dimensions of Vasu's story. In the initial scenes of the film, Vasu appears to seamlessly transition between her homes in New York and Madras: in both cities she adeptly fulfills her roles as wife, daughter, and mother. Yet Krishnan's extensive interviews with Vasu unexpectedly precipitate a crisis about where Vasu belongs. Given the abrupt transitions between India and the United States that marked Vasu's childhood and adolescence, she speaks of having to choose between two cultures. Despite the fact that Vasu's sons, Ashok and Gopal, as well as her husband, Raghu, claim to have no conflict over their own identities, Vasu herself is gripped by the feeling of belonging nowhere.

The cinematic narrative of *Knowing Her Place* operates on familiar grounds of resolving Vasu's "identity crisis," but in fact Vasu's life story exceeds this framework. Although Krishnan attempts to chart the transition from being Indian to becoming American across three generations of Vasu's family, Vasu's story cannot be captured within this narrative of assimilation. Instead, her subjectivity is produced through a series of disparate visual and rhetorical relationships that remain unresolved in the film. By examining the relationship between Vasu's oral testimonials and Krishnan's conversations with Vasu's husband and children, between Vasu's experience and that of her mother and grandmother, and between the visual narrative of the film and Krishnan's voice-over, I argue that *Knowing Her Place* captures formations of locality outside nationalist frameworks. Even as Krishnan's voice-over and Vasu's oral testimonials appear to express the dilemma of choosing between two cultures, I explore how the rhetorical framework of "choice" limits our perspective on Vasu's gendered and racialized experience.

In the opening scenes of the film, Vasu turns to the camera to inform Krishnan that "it takes a long time to figure out where you belong [. . .]

that is the pain of being, sort of, a second-generation Indian child." Shortly thereafter, Krishnan tells the viewer that Vasu attempted to commit suicide during their initial period of acquaintance. Situating this crisis as the locus of the cinematic narrative, Krishnan interviews Vasu's mother as well as her husband and sons as a means to track Vasu's life before and after her suicide attempt. Throughout, Krishnan establishes a binary relationship between India and the United States. In India Vasu is portrayed as obedient and deferential; in America she is outspoken and progressive in her social outlook. Likewise, within the context of her family in New York, Vasu is described as "Indian" at home (reproducing values of domestic virtue and filial piety) and "American" in her workplace (she teaches in an adult education program). The camera mirrors this contrast between India and the United States by depicting two places that could hardly be further apart: the open-air markets filled with fruit, flowers, and vegetables that stand in for Vasu's India contrast with the bustling supermarkets and subway trains that characterize New York. As Vasu negotiates these two distinct national-cultural entities, she also operates as the pivotal generational link in her family's transition from being Indian to becoming American. However, although Krishnan notes at the outset that Vasu appeared to have found "a balance between two cultures," the hybrid identity that Vasu ostensibly embodies is immediately disrupted by her suicide attempt.[9]

Why does Vasu try to kill herself? In interviews with several members of Vasu's family and with Vasu herself, Krishnan attempts to uncover the reasons behind Vasu's depression. Vasu describes her anger at leaving Queens when she was twelve, and her resentment toward her mother for marrying her off at sixteen. More than twenty years later, Vasu says that her feelings about marriage are "very bitter" and that her relationships with her husband and teenage children are deteriorating. These fraught-but-familiar psychological responses constitute Krishnan's narrative of Vasu's life, but they provide only a partial means of understanding the complexity of her experience. What is equally important is that Vasu's migrations have been determined by her participation in a series of overlapping patriarchal relationships that revolve around the containment of her sexual desire. When asked what was wrong with the parties that Vasu wished to attend as a young girl in Queens, her mother mentions the possibility that boys and girls would "slowly start kissing" at such parties, and that Vasu would be in the company of those who were too young to know about the consequences of their sexuality.

Not coincidentally, Vasu moves with her parents to India just before the onset of puberty. It is only in the aftermath of her marriage, in the context of a sanctioned heterosexual relationship, that Vasu moves back to Queens with her husband. As an adult, Vasu continues to be pathologized by her husband and sons, often subject to their verbal and emotional abuse. Treating Vasu's feelings as a case of individual neurosis, Raghu maintains that Vasu exaggerates her conflict, while her sons Gopal and Ashok rebut their mother's questions about cultural identity by pointing out their own assimilated ease.

In one particularly painful scene, Vasu prepares an elaborate Thanksgiving meal for her family but is verbally humiliated by her husband and sons when they fail to recognize her considerable domestic labor. Rather than appreciating their mother for preparing a multicourse meal, Gopal and Ashok belittle her cooking, shaming her for spending so many hours in the kitchen. The visual composition of the scene is sympathetic to Vasu, as the camera lingers on the lines of disappointment that crease her face and the shifting weight of her body as feelings of anger and resentment settle inside her. Meanwhile, the oral narrative of the film focuses on Vasu's children, who mock her with their mouths full of her carefully prepared food. Her husband chortles with laughter at the head of the table. Krishnan's voice-over is absent from this scene, and it remains unclear to the viewer whether, as a guest at the Thanksgiving dinner, she intervened in this ritual humiliation of Vasu or remained silent.

In her reading of *Knowing Her Place*, Lata Mani notes that this scene makes visible how middle-class men and women experience immigration differently. This gender difference accounts for the husband's and sons' incomprehension of Vasu's dilemma, and Raghu's perception, in particular, that Vasu imagines her crisis. Mani writes, "Raghu feels no conflict, but then why should he? His passage to the United States has been relatively smooth, thanks to class and male privilege. Vasu's benefits from her class position, on the other hand, are tempered by her femaleness" (34). In Mani's view, the film highlights how South Asian women in diaspora are expected to reproduce nationalist ideals of patriarchal tradition.[10] As feminist scholars including Inderpal Grewal and Caren Kaplan have argued, the persistent identification of women with nation, and concurrently with static notions of "tradition" and "culture," evades the impact of globalization. The filmmaker's impulse to resolve Vasu's "identity crisis"—a narrative that is reified by the film's protagonists as well as its critics—obscures the fact that such a resolution only replicates the fixed divide between private and public spheres, between the home and the world, and between India and the United States. By the end of the documentary, the crisis that precipitated Vasu's suicide attempt is assuaged by Vasu's decision to devote more time to her career, as well as through her resolve to reorganize labor relations in her household. Vasu becomes more "modern" as she is transformed into a career woman, and she is "liberated" by her husband's increased participation in domestic labor. In both instances *Knowing Her Place* charts Vasu's transformation from an "Indian" to an "American."

Rather than focusing on a static divide across gendered experiences of migration, however, I pay close attention to the discordance between the visual, oral, and aural narratives within the film. Such disparities reveal the ways in which the filmmaker and her documentary subjects, as well as viewers, may be complicit in this story of ethnic assimilation. By emphasizing the disparity between Vasu's oral testimonial of her experience and the depiction of her domestic labor, we can see how Vasu's story engenders a question of locality. In *Knowing Her Place*, locality is not simply a matter of representing Vasu as either Indian or American, but a means of theorizing the everyday experience of gender, class, and generation that shape immigrant subjects. Rather than asking why Vasu attempts to commit suicide—a question that assumes that Vasu can freely make other choices—we can better understand the film by asking: what are the conditions under which Vasu is prompted to choose between India and the United States?

The paradox of the film lies in the fact that Vasu's story of migration is structured by her experience of gender inequality, and yet her labor as a wife, daughter, and mother reproduces patriarchal notions of domesticity. A liberal-feminist critique of the film, such as Lata Mani's, recognizes how Vasu is made into an object of patriarchal discipline, a cinematic narrative that is echoed by Vasu's oral description of her experience at home and her subsequent emancipation in the workplace. However, it is important to recognize that Raghu does not actively discipline Vasu into adhering to a "traditional" idea of Indian femininity, nor do her sons expect her to dress or comport herself in a particular way. Their nonverbal embodiment of male privilege may be read as an assumption of patriarchal power, but what is equally important for my purpose is the filmmaker's investment—and our own complicity as viewers and as critics—in maintaining the binary structure of the cinematic narrative.

The teleological narrative of *Knowing Her Place* is produced through Krishnan's consistent spatial and rhetorical demarcation between India and the United States, or what Vasu experiences as her inability to transcend the difference between the private domain (of home, family, domesticity) and the public sphere (of work and professional development). Krishnan's investment in maintaining a spatial divide between India and the United States is mapped in the film through Vasu's identification as an "Indian" in India (by going to Hindu temples, wearing saris, speaking Tamil) and as an "American" in the United States (by working as a teacher, speaking fluent English, and occasionally wearing Western clothes). At one level, the film's depiction of India as the private or "spiritual" world and America as the public and "material" world enhances the cinematic narrative of identity crisis, one that the viewer and filmmaker satisfactorily resolve through Vasu's apparent choice to become an "American."[11] At another level, however, Vasu's sustained attempt to negotiate these two distinct national cultures reflects her enmeshment in projects of domestic patriarchy in both sites, for her embodiment of femininity is contingent on her sustained identification as wife, daughter, and mother. When Vasu embodies notions of sexuality that are not aligned with so-called traditional depictions of femininity—for example, when she unties her hair, drinks, and smokes—she does not do so in the presence of her family but at a bar, far removed from the sanctity of home. Whereas for middle-class immigrant men like Raghu there is no distinction between assuming patriarchal privilege in the private as well as public sphere, for Vasu maintaining the spatial demarcation between material and spiritual worlds structures the most intimate aspects of her everyday life, conditioning the sites and forms of expressing pleasure and desire.

Producing a different narrative of Vasu's experience, one that does not duplicate hegemonic tropes of assimilation, requires examining the similarities and differences that emerge through the spaces between her oral testimonial, Krishnan's voice-over, and the viewers' own investment in the film. As I have noted, Krishnan's portrayal of Vasu's "choice" to become American obscures the fact that Vasu's continued location in India and the United States relies upon her participation in reproducing patriarchal structures of domesticity. Moreover, while Krishnan structures *Knowing Her Place* as a narrative of emancipation (from Vasu's initial suicide attempt to her recuperation two years later), throughout the film Vasu continues to inhabit domestic arrangements that are defined in large part through the gendered division of labor and property. In the aftermath of her suicide attempt she does not, for example, divorce her husband or leave her children; instead she attempts to become a *better* mother and wife. While Mani contends that the difference of Vasu's gender challenges dominant representations of South Asian migration, I argue that Vasu's continued participation in the patriarchal structure of the family challenges the viewers' investment in the emancipatory discourse of the film.

An easily overlooked scene between Vasu and her ninety-year-old grandmother in Madras illustrates the complexity of Vasu's transnational locality in India and the United States. Directly in front of the camera, Vasu prompts her grandmother to speak about her relationship with her husband. Vasu's grandmother, old, frail, and shivering under the cool air generated by a ceiling fan, begins to provide an outline of her married life. The grandmother, who was married at age eleven, is initially distracted by explaining her household finances: how much her husband would earn, and how much they saved, more so because she could bring rice and other staples from her village. Vasu interrupts to ask about her grandfather's reputed temper, specifically whether there was any truth to the stories that he used to beat her. Her grandmother waves away Vasu's question, but assents that her husband did hit her. When Vasu asks her grandmother why she never protested, her grandmother suddenly becomes animated and retorts, "What good would it do? [. . .] If I went back to my father my three sisters would never get married, and the rumor would spread that there was something wrong with us [. . .] girls." Emphatically underscoring her decision to remain in her marriage, Vasu's grandmother points out the limited conditions of the "choice" available to her. To exit an abusive relationship would return her to the safety of her parents' home; but actually returning home would destroy her sisters' prospects for marriage.

Vasu's conversation with her grandmother vividly brings to life the ways in which her experience at home exceeds the public narrative of "choice" that is produced by Krishnan's documentary. Like her grandmother, Vasu inhabits a patriarchal division of labor that creates an emotionally abusive context for her marriage. She is subject to violence precisely because she is female, and yet Krishnan insists on framing this as a conflict between two cultures. As Krishnan narrates, Vasu describes herself as a "cultural schizophrenic": "she didn't know which way to be, Indian or American. She felt trapped." Having noted the claustrophobic conditions of Vasu's domestic life, Krishnan refuses to present an alternate way of understanding her subjectivity. Although Vasu is consistently depicted as having to choose whether to belong to India or the United States, the parameters of such a choice are false because Vasu operates within distinct structures of patriarchy in both national sites.

In *Real and Imagined Women*, Rajeswari Sunder Rajan examines the conditions under which particularly painful narratives of gendered subjectivity—for example, the subject of sati, or widow burning—are produced. While some scholars have argued for understanding the sati as the object of competing discourses of Indian nationalism and British imperialism, and others have noted the rhetorical conditions under which the sati is effectively caught between the rhetoric of subjectivity (as one who intends to die) and objectification (as one who must be saved from dying), Rajan argues that we must understand the sati as a subject-in-pain: that is, the sati is formed at the moment of her burning.[12] As one whose subjectivity is constituted through her pain, the sati embodies "a dynamic rather than a passive condition, on the premise that the subject in pain will be definitionally in transit towards a state of no-pain" that is her death. By arguing that pain constitutes the subjectivity of the sati, Rajan reads the sati "as one who acts/reacts, rather than as one who invites assistance" (22). In Rajan's view, because the sati does not give her consent to burn on her husband's funeral pyre, nor is she coerced to join him in his death, the subjecthood of the sati emerges precisely at the moment when her agency appears to be extinguished.

By invoking Rajan's provocative reading of the subject of sati, I do not wish to imply that Vasu's attempt to commit suicide is comparable to the act of sati, nor universalize the heteronormative conditions of marriage within which Vasu constructs a sense of self. Rather, Rajan's essay helps us to think through an alternative idiom of feminist agency in the film. Subject to mental and emotional abuse from her husband and sons, Vasu is visually depicted as a body-in-pain. Vasu's psychic abuse is not revealed through marks on her body but rather through her oral testimonial. Further, Vasu participates in self-abuse, primarily through her alcohol dependence. Though these signs of domestic and self-inflicted abuse are clearly legible in the visual narrative of the film, Krishnan's voice-over (her verbal commentary along with her silences) denies the existence of Vasu's abused body.[13] In my own experience of screening this film in the classroom, Vasu's embodiment of mental and emotional anguish has on several occasions prompted a visceral reaction from my students. However, the voice-over narrative eclipses the materiality of this painful subjectivity to focus solely on the ways in which Vasu's identity is constituted through her choice between two cultures. Within this framework, we can only understand Vasu as either a victim or agent. On the one hand, in the context of her relationship with her husband and sons, Vasu is represented as a victim of patriarchal tradition. On the other hand, Krishnan films Vasu's oral testimony in order to represent her as a feminist subject who is ultimately able to recuperate her free will.

In contrast to both these readings, what I suggest is that we must reexamine the narrative conventions through which Vasu's gendered subjectivity is produced. As Vasu begins to negotiate her "traditional" role at home along with the increasing demands of her "modern" participation in the workplace, it is equally important to emphasize Vasu's desire to remain with her family, within its existing structure of power. Although Krishnan encourages Vasu to pursue psychotherapy in order to articulate her own demands and desires (or to inhabit a position of free will), Vasu's continued participation in a transnational configuration of patriarchy complicates Krishnan's aural and visual narrative of immigration-as-emancipation.

In "Feminist Theory, Embodiment, and the Docile Agent," Saba Mahmood examines the challenges posed to liberal-feminist notions of self and agency by women who embody nonliberal religious traditions, specifically Islamic discourses of piety. Mahmood discusses the challenges posed to feminists by women who wear the veil or who practice ideals of modesty that, in conventional Western feminist discourse (as well as in secular-liberal third world feminism) are viewed as antithetical to feminist practice. Suggesting that "we think of agency not as a synonym for resistance to relations of domination, but as a capacity for action that historically specific relations of subordination enable and create" (203), Mahmood argues that the gendered embodiment and practice of nonliberal notions of piety expands our understanding of agency. In her view, liberal feminists depict agency as either a capacity for resistance or subversion of dominant patriarchal traditions. In contrast Mahmood suggests that women's participation in Islamic revivalist mosque movements (which involves to varying degrees their pursuit of ideals of shyness, modesty, and humility) encourages us to think beyond the "prescriptive" conditions of liberal-feminist theory.[14] Indeed, while such practices apparently ensure the subordination of women to a dominant and patriarchal religious discourse, Mahmood notes that they also draw our attention to the ways in which "individuals work on themselves to become the willing subjects of a particular discourse" (210).

In *Knowing Her Place*, Vasu's decision to invest more time in her career and share domestic responsibility with her husband and children is narrated by Krishnan as well as by Vasu as part of the process of becoming American. However, we can also look at this set of practices as the means through which Vasu works on herself to become the "willing subject" of a particular discourse, in this case the hegemony of national patriarchy. Although Vasu feels trapped by her marriage, one of the ways she attempts to resolve this dilemma is not by breaking out of a set of domestic responsibilities, but instead by reinhabiting them. She demonstrates a capacity for agency not by resisting but rather by refining her responsibilities as mother and wife. Vasu's transnational locality (neither Indian nor American) is thus constituted through her intensive participation in domestic arrangements that, at least in part, seem to initiate her suicide attempt. There are, of course, ways in which Vasu appears to subvert her family's expectation of gendered norms: for example, by smoking or drinking alcohol. Yet Vasu's inhabitation of her roles as wife and mother is not about straightforwardly resisting domesticity but rather realigning notions of home and family with her own understanding of what it means to be a better mother and wife. In this light, Vasu's testimonial in *Knowing Her Place* reworks the conditions of the film's narrative movement from repression to liberation, and from tradition to modernity. Instead, Vasu produces and inhabits a more complex notion of gendered agency that challenges our understanding of the "choice" that is made central to this film.

Shifting the narrative framework of the film away from a story about being Indian or becoming American enables us to understand alternate forms of locality. Although Vasu's depression is symptomatic of the psychic pain of patriarchy, she engenders a new sense of self by re-embodying her role as wife and mother. Toward the end of the film Krishnan interviews Vasu, Raghu, and Ashok two years after Vasu begins psychotherapy. As Vasu narrates the shifting configuration of her family—her decision to refrain from controlling her children, her newfound ability to view her husband as a partner—Krishnan films scenes of Raghu massaging Vasu's hair, and Ashok deferring to his mother in conversation. The new Vasu that emerges in these scenes complements her own narrative of developing an autonomous sense of self. At the same time, these scenes suggest that Vasu continues to inhabit patriarchal configurations of the (national) family. Although Raghu now assumes a greater share of domestic labor, he continues to be the primary breadwinner of the family, while Vasu's work outside the home is relegated to a matter of personal interest. Instead of following Vasu's transition from "traditional" to "modern" woman, from immigrant to citizen, viewing Vasu's complex embodiment of agency unexpectedly produces a different narrative of locality, one that contests both liberal-feminist and nationalist conceptions of gendered selfhood. Developing a means of "seeing" the subject of *Knowing Her Place* requires us to read against the grain of the oral and aural narratives of the documentary. Such a practice of reading demands—on the part of the viewer, critic, and filmmaker—a means of recognizing forms of locality that exist outside the binary spatial framework of the film.

Krishnan's voice-over narrative provides one way of opening out the relations of identification that structure the documentary. In *Knowing Her Place*, Krishnan is visible both as the empathetic feminist filmmaker who brings Vasu's story to life and as a documentarian whose own story of migration (as an Indian, upper-caste, and Tamil-speaking woman living in the United States) is closely aligned with Vasu's. Yet given that Krishnan's commentary frequently diverges from the materiality of Vasu's experience, the film also reveals the ways in which Krishnan's relationship to Vasu is characterized by a profound ambivalence. Although Krishnan deliberately encourages an intimate encounter between director and subject, she tells us from the outset, "It was kind of unsettling to bear her [Vasu's] intensity." Not only does Krishnan resist bearing the weight of Vasu's oral testimonial; she is also unable to contend with the fact that her interviews with Vasu's family members disrupt the overarching assimilationist narrative of the film. For example, when Krishnan interviews Vasu's older son, Gopal, what she portrays is a generational difference between an Indian mother and her American son. However, during that conversation with Gopal, Gopal not only claims to be American; more specifically he derides his mother's household labor, noting that her work for their family does not serve his "utility function." Here, the operative difference is not the divide between first- and second-generation immigrant; it is the gendered relationship between Gopal's public masculinity and Vasu's private labor. Remarkably, Krishnan resists highlighting the sexist implications of Gopal's remarks or linking them to Vasu's own testimonial of being marginalized in her family. Instead, Krishnan recuperates this interview into a linear narrative that culminates in Vasu's eventual recovery as an "American."

Noting the ways in which Krishnan's voice-over commentary is called into question by Vasu's experience, Lata Mani describes the discrepancy between the visual and aural narrative of the film as a "problem at the heart of feminist representational practice: the relation between the critic and the subject/object of her analysis."[15] Although Mani commends Krishnan for her empathy, she also notes that Krishnan's close relationship to her documentary subject interferes with the film's capacity to produce alternative narrative frameworks. Building on Mani's critique, I delineate another reading of Krishnan's collaboration with Vasu, one that turns on their shared background as Indian immigrants in the United States. While Mani praises Krishnan for her feminist intervention in revealing Vasu's vulnerabilities and those of her family, I read Krishnan's documentary collaboration with Vasu as a form of betrayal.

I take the term "betrayal" from Kamala Visweswaran's illuminating account of conducting ethnographic fieldwork in *Fictions of Feminist Ethnography*. Visweswaran theorizes her tentative alliance with informants, as well as the social ties between her informants via relations of difference, rather than similarity. The "central, unspoken betrayal" in her work, she writes, is "my own assumption of a universal sisterhood between women" (41). Betrayal thus operates as an allegory for the ways in which ethnographic narratives are constructed, performed, and narrated, and characterizes the complicity or collusion between ethnographer and informant in producing specific versions of knowledge. Like Krishnan, Visweswaran actively cultivates close relationships with the subjects of her study. Yet the intimacy of these relationships, critical to producing the confessional "truth" of ethnography, is also the means through which we come to understand the emergence of a particular form of knowing. In the process, Visweswaran describes her own discomfort as the keeper of the official ethnographic record but also as one who aids and abets her informants to produce so-called truthful narratives.

In my reading of *Knowing Her Place*, I suggest that Krishnan's work with Vasu also constitutes a form of betrayal. But who betrays whom? My use of the term does not imply that Krishnan trespassed Vasu's confidence or otherwise explicitly revealed information about Vasu that was not meant for public consumption. Rather, I use the category of betrayal to examine the limits of transnational feminist collaboration between filmmaker and subject, specifically when both are invested in producing a certain narrative of immigration about South Asians in the United States. As Krishnan tells us toward the close of her film, "In trying to understand Vasu's experience, I'd revealed her pain. I wondered then if it was my right as a filmmaker to make that pain public. But we both came to the conclusion that [. . . Vasu's story] might be of use to [people] who had similar questions of who they are and where they belonged." Uneasily occupying a relation of similarity and difference to Vasu, Krishnan in her voice-over diverges from the visual and oral narrative of the film. Although Krishnan's consistent framing of Vasu's experience as a cultural "choice" resonates with Vasu's own testimonial, the material practice of Vasu's labor inside the home suggests new ways of reading her gendered subjectivity. Retaining a documentary framework that emphasizes a choice between two cultures also betrays the ways in which Vasu's story demonstrates the limits of nationalist frameworks of identity. Given that neither Krishnan nor Vasu admits to the difference that gender makes to narratives of immigration, is there a way of understanding this film as an instance of collusion between filmmaker and documentary subject? If we read Krishnan as codifying a binary cultural framework through which Vasu narrates her own experience—a narrative of migration that Krishnan herself shares in—then the collaboration between filmmaker and subject becomes a betrayal of anticipated forms of knowledge for the viewer. Reading the various betrayals that take place in *Knowing Her Place* provokes us to question whether the realist conventions of the documentary film reveal the "truth" of Vasu's experience.

In her final voice-over, Krishnan remarks that "growing up in two cultures, or coming from one to live in another, is like moving in two directions at once, or like being in two places at once. For those who haven't experienced it, it seems a simple matter of picking and choosing the best of both worlds, but for some of us, it's more painful than that." The conditions of pain that produce Vasu's subjectivity contest a narrative of choice in this film. Her repeated trips back and forth between two countries revise narratives of assimilation by illustrating the ways in which domestic arrangements of patriarchy are reconstituted in India and the United States. Although Krishnan frames Vasu's oral testimonial as a story of being in between two cultures, the visual language of the film highlights how Vasu's participation in transnational structures of domesticity produces a sense of temporal and spatial continuity between two distinct sites. By arguing that Vasu reinhabits structures of patriarchal domesticity, I highlight the ways in which constructs of "free will" or "choice" eclipse gendered experiences of migration. Although Vasu's husband and sons appear exempt from the identity crisis that structures her life, for Vasu the imperative to distinguish between India and America ultimately leads to her suicide attempt. However, describing Vasu as suffering from clinical depression is only one way to understanding her identity. *Knowing Her Place* is also shaped by distinct ideologies of feminist agency, which are articulated by the filmmaker as well as the documentary subject. Both women struggle to produce a linear narrative of immigration that results in the emancipation of the gendered subject, a narrative that is more easily embraced by the liberal-feminist critic. Part of that struggle is embedded in the forms of betrayal that define Vasu and Krishnan's collaboration, and which illustrate how our knowledge of Vasu's identity is "multiple, contradictory, partial, and strategic."[16] Reading against the grain of Vasu's oral testimony and Krishnan's voice-over commentary reveals the transnational conditions of patriarchy that engender Vasu's locality. In turn, this dialectical process of reading exposes the ambivalent subjectivity of the filmmaker, whose own diasporic locality cannot be represented on-screen.

The National Family: Embodying Race and Citizenship

In Sasha Khokha's documentary video *Calcutta Calling*, three teenage girls adopted by white American families in Minnesota participate in a cultural program for adoptees that brings them to India. Adopted as infants from Christian orphanages in Calcutta, Kaylan Johnson, Anisha Pitzenberger, and Lizzie Merrill are overwhelmed by their first impressions of a country that they have no recollection of. Over a two-week period, the three girls go on elephant rides, see the Taj Mahal, and visit the orphanages and charity institutions from which they were adopted. Sponsored by the Ties Program based in Wisconsin, this tour of India is meant to provide the adoptees with exposure to the country of their birth.[17] As the Ties website notes, "More and more, [adoptive] parents are realizing that a heritage journey is one of the most significant factors in the identity building process of internationally adoptive children."[18] For Lizzie, Kaylan, and Anisha, the trip is also the first time that they encounter other Indian adoptees in the United States (or for that matter, Indians in India). Becoming fast friends during their trip, the girls continue to keep in touch after their return to Minnesota, eventually affirming their joint experience by getting their noses pierced at a local mall.

Calcutta Calling is one in a growing number of films that document the racial and national identities of transnational adoptees in the United States.[19] In Asian American studies, research on transnational adoption has proliferated in recent years as a means of examining the historical, social, and psychic encounters between the United States and East and Southeast Asia, regions deeply impacted by the imperialist expansion of U.S. power. Historically, the first large-scale adoptions were conducted between South Korea and the United States in the aftermath of the Korean War; more recently, adoptees from China and Russia have accounted for the largest number of transnational adoptions in the United States, along with a growing number of adoptees from Vietnam, Cambodia, and Central America. In many ways, adoption is emblematic of flows of capital and labor between industrialized states such as the United States and developing countries in Asia.[20] The anthropologist Ann Anagnost has delineated the global dimensions of adoption by focusing on the ways in which transnational adoptees reconfigure notions of kinship and race within the private domain of the family, examining the implications of these new definitions of kinship for the politics of U.S. multiculturalism. In his essay "Transnational Adoption and Queer Diasporas," David Eng notes that transnational adoption is increasingly seen as an alternative to domestic open adoptions. In this context he argues that the Asian adoptee serves to "triangulate the domestic landscape of black-white race relations" (11). As immigrants, the adoptees are legally and economically privileged over other immigrants from Asia; as racialized subjects, Asian adoptees are uneasily recuperated into the politics of Asian American nationalism.

India is among the most popular countries for adoptions in Asia, and yet transnational adoptees from India are almost entirely absent from these polarizing debates over racial identity and citizenship.[21] Unlike adoptees from South Korea, Vietnam, and Cambodia, Indian adoptees have no visible historical relationship to the United States that relies on the evidence of war and colonial occupation. However, many Indian-born children—including the teenage girls featured in *Calcutta Calling*—were adopted as infants from charitable organizations in India such as the International Mission of Hope

(IMH), which emerged in the aftermath of the Vietnam War. Based in Calcutta, IMH was founded by Cherie Clark, an American social worker who had been involved in the international adoption of Vietnamese children during the fall of Saigon in 1974 (Nixon's infamous "Operation Babylift," referenced in another Asian American adoption film, *Daughter from Danang*). Unable to continue her work in Vietnam, Clark founded IMH in 1977 under the auspices of Mother Teresa's Missionaries of Charity.[22] In the United States, IMH was linked to several adoption agencies, among them the Children's Home Society and Family Services, based in Minnesota, as well as Lutheran Social Services. At least two of the three teenagers interviewed in *Calcutta Calling* were directly adopted from the IMH through U.S.-based Christian social service organizations. Although *Calcutta Calling* was filmed many decades after the Vietnam War, the structural relationships between U.S. social service organizations and Indian charitable organizations that emerge out of the war in Southeast Asia demonstrate how U.S. foreign policy is central to the transaction of human capital between South Asia and the United States.

Current government policies in India, however, restrict transnational adoption to individuals of Indian descent. As part of the liberalization of the Indian economy in the 1990s, the Indian state asserted nationalist policies that prioritized domestic adoption for Indian adoptees, followed by adoptions by individuals of Indian descent living abroad, and lastly to non-Indian individuals applying to adopt from India.[23] The category of the "Indian" adoptee is also in question, as many infants taken into orphanages in Calcutta are the children of Bangladeshi refugees as well as of indigenous groups displaced by state regimes of modernization. Further, like many children adopted from orphanages in Asia and elsewhere, Indian adoptees are often not orphans at all. As with Chinese adoptees, the majority of Indian adoptees are girls. They frequently have one or more living parents and/or siblings, who are unable to provide for the child due to economic and social conditions. Moreover, the erasure of caste and gender differences by the Indian state in its effort to promote domestic rather than international adoptions eclipses the fact that a number of children in orphanages remain without adoptive parents due to color, religious, or caste prejudice among Indians.

What is striking about *Calcutta Calling* is not only that it documents a little-known demographic group of South Asians in the United States, but that it highlights the ways in which these adoptive children are shaped by distinct rhetorics of nationalism: on the one hand, multicultural ideologies of the American national family, and on the other hand, the postcolonial and neoliberal politics of the Indian state. Situating Kaylan, Anisha, and Lizzie's experiences in Calcutta in relation to their everyday life in Minnesota complicates the rhetoric of transnational subjectivity and racialized citizenship. Like *So Far from India* and *Knowing Her Place*, *Calcutta Calling* relies on visual tropes of difference that highlight the spatial distance between India and the United States. However, unlike the earlier two films, the protagonists have no memory of their past lives in India, nor do they travel frequently between the two countries. In their oral testimonies, the young women consistently identify as "Americans," as opposed to "immigrants." In this context the cinematic narrative does not reproduce hegemonic tropes of immigration-as-assimilation. Moreover, because Khokha does not occupy an audible or visible role in the film, the camera is exclusively focused on the three women and their family members, as well as accompanying tour guides and social workers in India. As Indian adoptees in America, these young women embody a unique historical relationship that ties two countries together. Upon their return to Minnesota, however, the three teenagers develop primary relationships to each other instead of to their country of "origin." *Calcutta Calling* reworks the narrative framework of immigration in order to emphasize how "home," for these documentary subjects, lies in new formations of locality in the United States.

As the only persons of color in their schools and communities, the three young women are ambivalent about their racial difference. With the exception of Lizzie, whose lesbian parents have adopted a second child from India, the teenagers' parents incorporate the adoptees into white, Christian, and heterosexual formations of the American family. Kaylan's mother, for instance, tells Khokha in the opening scene, "I don't think of Kaylan as being Indian at all. She's just my daughter. I don't see the, the color difference, or the things at all. I don't know how she sees herself." Hesitating to name the visibility of racial difference ("the things"), Kaylan's mother assimilates Kaylan into universal narratives of kinship ("she's just my daughter"). Kaylan herself identifies India primarily in terms of food or religious icons such as Mother Teresa. Similarly, Lizzie says, "I identify more as white, but I'm not as materialistic, I think, as a lot of Americans are." Constructing their affiliation to India through tropes of orientalism—spirituality, religiosity, and ethnic foods—the girls and their parents evade the visibility of racial difference. Even Anisha, who confesses that among her friends in high school, "I think I stick out really, really bad," later describes herself as "completely American, I'm just brown." For Anisha, who grew up in a small town with little sustained contact with other people of color, "being brown" carries no meaning as a form of politicized subjectivity. Instead, "America" is the sign of the multicultural national body, into which Anisha's differences are subsumed. If *Knowing Her Place* made visible the difference that gender makes in narratives of migration, *Calcutta Calling* examines the place of racial difference in the life experiences of these three girls and their families. Like Vasu's husband and sons, who cannot see the physical and mental violence that they enact onto her body, in *Calcutta Calling* the racialized body becomes a visible subject that is consistently obscured by the protagonists and their families. By contrast, for the viewer, racial difference becomes a primary means of "seeing" the film, as the camera pans across a high school auditorium full of white midwesterners in the opening scene, finally settling on Anisha's brown body.

Moving between scenes shot in India and in the United States, *Calcutta Calling* relies upon images that establish a visual contrast between the two countries, as well as between brown Indian bodies and white Americans in the United States. However, this trope of spatial and racial difference is thrown into question when the families visit India through the Ties Program. Whereas in the United States the adoptive families refuse to recognize the racialization of their children, in India it is precisely the adoptees' racial difference that signals their incorporation into an alternate national family. Anisha's mother panics when she realizes that she cannot recognize her own daughter, who drifts away into a crowd during their sightseeing tour. As she explains, "I got real nervous when I realized I couldn't see Anisha. She was blending in pretty good."[24] For the adoptees themselves, however, their visit to India does not generate feelings of racial or national identification. Instead, the young women disidentify with India, particularly in terms of their class locations. Recoiling from the sensory excess of urban density, noise, pollution, and poverty that permeates their trip, Anisha asks, "Doesn't it feel good knowing that we get to go home to Minnesota?" Kaylan responds, "Seriously, if I ever had to live here I would die." Although prior to the trip Anisha had vividly described her feelings of racial alienation, in India she appears not to recognize (or "see") her mother's fears of racial assimilation.

In a pivotal scene, the adoptees visit a local orphanage and play with the children they meet there. Anisha helps a young boy color in a paper sketch of a child, encouraging him to color in the child's hair blond and leave his skin a pale white. Upon completion of the coloring project, Anisha is prompted to note the visual contrast between the young Indian boy and the paper figure he holds up to the camera. Though Anisha is embarrassed to recognize this contrast, she explains that she didn't think about what colors she was using, as she grew up accustomed to coloring in blond and white paper figures. Together, Anisha and the young boy shade over the initial drawing with brown and black crayons. Finally the young boy grins as he holds up his completed picture and Anisha proclaims, "It looks more Indian, you know." Anisha's awkward identification with Indians in India highlights the ways in which the adoptees occupy complex configurations of race and class. In Minnesota, Anisha, Lizzie, and Kaylan embody forms of racial visibility that are incorporated into a panoramic portrait of the multicultural American family. In India, however, Anisha's embarrassment—her recognition of the unconscious disparity between the white figure in the painting and the skin tones of the young boy and herself—does not create a feeling of racial solidarity with the children at the orphanage. Instead, Anisha's proclamation that the redrawn figure "looks more Indian" (that is, more like the young boy who colored it) is evidence of her difference from the orphans, for in contrast to them she identifies as a middle-class American citizen.

The difficult negotiation of race, family, and nation—or the substitution of the family for the nation—is consistently reiterated in the film through the trope of the salvation narrative. By refiguring the public history of transnational adoption in order to emphasize private stories of "rescuing" adoptees from their countries of origin, salvation narratives amplify the distance between third and first worlds, and the difference between starvation and liberation. Visually evoked through images of destitution and poverty, salvation narratives eclipse the agency of the adoptees themselves, who are often figured as charitable causes. In this context, adoption operates as a privileged route of immigration, and the salvaged adoptee must make good on the opportunities afforded to her to succeed. "God chose me out of all those babies to come here [to the United States] and live this life," Anisha recounts. "I always tell myself—I'm not supposed to be here, but I am, so I'm gonna live it up." Salvation narratives are thus also a form of immigration narratives, with the difference being that the adoptees' families frequently do not recognize their children as immigrants.

As Eng writes, it is "crucial to link transnational adoption not just to humanitarian or religious narratives of love, altruism, salvation, and redemption but also to specific pre– and post–World War II histories of imperialism, immigration, racialized exploitation, and gendered commodification."[25] In *Calcutta Calling*, the salvation narrative that links India and the United States mitigates structures of capital movement as well as race. The three teenagers visit India with their adoptive parents through the U.S.-based Ties Program. Advertisements on the Ties website describe the organization as an "Adoptive Family Homeland Journey." As portrayed in the film, the Ties Program encourages adoptees and their adoptive families to find their cultural "roots" in India, while at the same time consistently underscoring their citizenship as Americans. During their visit to tourist sites such as the Taj Mahal, as well as to orphanages in Delhi and Calcutta, an unnamed Indian social worker who accompanies the families speaks at length about the adoptees' birth mothers, who in her words "sacrifice" a relationship with their children in order to give them a better life. Framing the birth mother's contribution to the adoptive family as a voluntary act, the social worker reiterates the geopolitical distance between India and the United States by figuring the adoptees as privileged immigrants. The adoptees are able to go to "a more developed country than India," she says, and "it is all because of your karma [fate] in your past life." Most children who are left behind in India, she continues, cannot imagine the lives these young girls lead. The adoptees are thus marked from birth for immigration to the United States. The social worker's fatalism elides the conditions of economic and sexual production that compel women to give up their girl children, as well as the ways in which charitable and religious organizations mediate the transfer of human capital from developing to developed countries.

The birth mother is also erased from the historical narrative that brings the adoptees to the United States. In a conversation with Anisha's adoptive mother, who asks about the circumstances that would lead a woman to leave her baby at an orphanage, the social worker describes the birth mother as less than human. Noting that many women who give up their children are pregnant out of wedlock, the social worker declares that, "the woman didn't want her [the baby . . .] I believe it's like being an animal [. . .] The woman who left a child like that is just like another dog on the street or a cat on the street [. . .] You breed and you just forget about your child." While the same social worker initially characterizes the birth mother as a martyr who selflessly gives up her child for the chance of a better life, here she is condemned for her sexual and reproductive choices, which are represented as bestial acts. The social worker reproduces hegemonic structures of class and caste in her derogatory description of birth mothers and makes no room for women who are subject to sexual exploitation within their families or in their professions, including domestic and sex work. In so doing, the social worker codifies the rhetoric of the salvation narrative, representing Americans as saviors who salvage the adoptee from the bestial impulses of the birth mother (whose full names are often unrecorded in the adoption files). Equally important, in this story of maternal abandonment, the role of forgetting is reversed. Instead of the adoptee who has no memory of her birth in India, it is the birth mother who has forgotten about her child. Although Anisha and her peers participate in the Ties Program in order to recuperate a past history in India, in the absence of a birth mother the adoptee has no memory to recall, and no affective bond of belonging to this place left long ago.

As portrayed in *Calcutta Calling*, the India Ties Program facilitates a form of cultural encounter between India and the United States distinct from that depicted in other Asian American films that document the reunification of adoptees with their birth countries and birth mothers. Prominent films on Asian American adoption include the Oscar-nominated documentary *Daughter from Danang* and *First Person Plural*. In *Daughter from Danang*, Heidi Bub, a Vietnamese-American woman adopted by a single white mother in Tennessee, returns to Vietnam after more than twenty years. Heidi has been disowned by her adoptive mother, and her encounter with her birth mother and siblings begins as a tearful reunion. Yet that initial overflow of affect begins to unravel when Heidi realizes that she must provide financial support to her birth family, a demand that is couched within the rhetoric of filial piety. Unable to reconcile her birth family's request for material support with her own desire for emotional affection, Heidi finally rejects her birth mother. In *First Person Plural*, by contrast, it is the birth mother who eventually rejects her daughter, instructing the Korean-born protagonist of the film to respect and honor her white adoptive mother.[26]

In *Calcutta Calling* the central encounter is not between the adoptive children and their birth mothers, or between the adoptees and Indians in India. Instead, the cultural tour of India that is carefully scripted for the adoptees reinforces not only their salvation from India but also the fact that their rightful place is with their adoptive parents in America. This becomes particularly clear when Anisha, Kaylan, and Lizzie visit the IMH, the orphanage from which they were adopted, now an abandoned, empty building. The girls sift through the memorabilia of children left behind. The grounds are littered with photographs and correspondence with missionary organizations in the United States and dusty packages of medicine. Outside the building, however, the teenagers meet a woman who had formerly cared for orphans at the IMH and who, in her excitement, brings the girls back to her home. Pulling out sheaves of correspondence and photographs, she claims that she remembers these girls as infants and animatedly narrates her memories of them. Confronted by this affective storytelling, Kaylan and Lizzie fail to be persuaded. Back in the hotel room after their visit to the orphanage, Kaylan rejects the caretaker's nostalgic narrative, proclaiming, "That's all bullshit." Kaylan proceeds to say, "I played her game." By going along with the caretaker's belief that Kaylan was once an infant under her supervision, Kaylan enables the caretaker to believe that the orphans at IMH have been rescued. Kaylan herself, however, has no need for the caretaker's memory. Instead, she points out the historical inaccuracies that characterize the caretaker's account: the dates on the photographs do not match the year of her birth, nor do the babies in the photos look like her.

By refusing to identify with the nostalgia that characterizes their return to the orphanage, Kaylan, Lizzie, and Anisha must produce an alternate narrative of locality. As they come to realize, that narrative is increasingly difficult to create, given the adoptees' differences in terms of class and citizenship from the Indians that they meet on the street and in the orphanages. At a shopping mall, Lizzie offers a group of street children her half-empty container of soda. In response, the children insist on singing for Lizzie (and for the camera crew, who remain outside the frame). Their exuberant performance at once incorporates her into their public spectacle and reinforces the fact that she is their patron. Uncomfortably drawn into their performance, Lizzie tells Khokha that "you got this feeling that you were seeing someone you could have been. [It] makes me feel really isolated too: it's like I can't fit in anywhere. I can't fit in at home, and I can't fit in here. [Even after arriving in India] you're still isolated, you're still treated different." Identifying with the street children as "someone you could have been," Lizzie simultaneously retracts that racial identification by acknowledging differences of class and citizenship. Lizzie's negotiation of identity and difference from the objects of her charity mirrors the adoptive parents' relationship of familiarity with, and difference from, their children. At the same time, Lizzie's disappointment with being unable to "fit in anywhere" indicates her own desire for a historical narrative that brings her birth in India and present experience in America together. Notably, Lizzie does not claim an Indian identity at the risk of her American national subjectivity; instead what she and the other adoptees on the tour attempt to produce is an imagined historical narrative that makes India meaningful in their lives as Americans.

In an online interview for *Frontline*, the Public Broadcasting Service (PBS) documentary series, the director Sasha Khokha discusses her reasons for making the film. She herself is the child of an Indian father and Irish American mother, who considered adopting from India before unexpectedly conceiving their daughter. After Khokha's birth they relinquished their plans for adoption but continued to support orphanages in India. For Khokha, therefore, Anisha, Kaylan, and Lizzie are *her* version of "someone you could have been." Throughout the interview, Khokha compares her life story as a mixed-race South Asian with the young women's experiences of living in Minnesota and traveling through India. Despite their apparently shared background as Indian immigrants in the United States, it is the dissimilarity of their racial subjectivities that Khokha emphasizes: "When I first contacted the girls about the project, they were enthusiastic about meeting me—a young Indian American woman. But our differences were quick to surface. I am light-skinned on the outside, but have grown up feeling Indian on the inside. These girls have felt isolated by their skin color, but feel like Swedish Lutherans on the inside." As Khokha proceeds to note, the teenagers identified more with the lead camera operator, a young white man who, having grown up in rural Illinois, was able to understand their experience as Minnesotans. Although Khokha intended to make a film about what she described as "the Indian American experience," producing that common narrative of belonging between herself and her documentary subjects required negotiating a series of differences around issues of historical locality and racial authenticity. For instance, while Khokha identifies as a second-generation Indian immigrant, the adoptees have no recourse to established histories of immigration from the subcontinent. Further, despite being "light-skinned," Khokha notes that she embodies a more "authentic" experience of India (having traveled there on several prior occasions) than the girls themselves.[27]

Like Khokha, who attempted to produce an "Indian American" story that brought together her family's experience of adoption with the personal narratives of transnational adoptees, several other viewers of the film critically engaged with Anisha, Lizzie, and Kaylan's experiences. On the *Frontline* website, where Khokha's film was initially available online as a documentary video, viewers posted a number of comments that related the adoptees' stories to their own experiences of adoption, immigration, and traveling through India. Several commentators self-identified as adoptees who were also from the IMH in Calcutta; many wrote movingly about identifying with the young women on-screen. One such anonymous commentator writes, "I was surprised and comforted after watching it [*Calcutta Calling*], because the film encompasses my feelings about being adopted from India. I view myself as American first but the fact that I have links to another country can raise feelings of confusion." Several other commentators were parents of a transnational adoptee. Reena Kapoor, a U.S.-based mother of an adopted daughter from India, posted a comment on the website that read, "This journey [the Ties Program] was so important because it allowed them [the adoptees] to see where they came from and where they do NOT belong [. . .] even though they were born there."[28]

Although the majority of viewer responses perceived the adoptees as Americans, one anonymous commentator racialized the teenagers as Indians. Noting the film's focus on "Indians out of context in the frozen fields of Minnesota," the commentator writes of her own niece who, as a white American, is surrounded by Indian immigrants in the San Francisco Bay area. The documentary, she notes, "is simply a reverse image of what has happened in some American enclaves."[29] By establishing equivalence between her niece's experience in Silicon Valley (a region with a large number of professional and working-class South Asian immigrants) and the lives of transnational adoptees in rural Minnesota, the commentator collapses the differently racialized spaces that her niece and the adoptees occupy. More specifically, this comment historicizes the adoptees as immigrants from India: much like the immigrant workers who live in Silicon Valley, the adoptees are transactions of human capital between South Asia and the United States. By contrast, the families of the adoptees featured in the film do not recognize Anisha, Kaylan, or Lizzie as immigrants; instead, they characterize the young women as "gifts," transactions without financial value.[30] Comments on the PBS *Frontline* website from persons who identify themselves as Kaylan and Anisha's relatives describe the young women as spiritual and religious gifts. As spiritual subjects rather than racialized immigrants, Anisha and Kaylan can be seamlessly incorporated by family members into pluralist (and Christian) visions of the American national family. The disparity between Khokha's representation of the adoptees as immigrants, and the online postings that testify to the adoptees' spiritual integration into their American families emphasizes the ways in which the adoptees are uncomfortably located at the intersection of multiple narratives of belonging.

In an online blog edited by the U.S.-based South Asian collective *Sepia Mutiny*, a number of commentators responded to Khokha's film. In particular, bloggers and readers focused on the dilemma of locality occupied by transnational adoptees. *Sepia Mutiny*, which has been described as a "political community blog," details popular culture and current news and events of interest to those who identify in various ways as South Asian.[31] Abhi, a blogger on *Sepia Mutiny*, flagged *Calcutta Calling* under the title "All American Girls in Calcutta." In his initial posting, Abhi writes:

> While watching the film I KNOW you will have the same conflicted reactions as me. These girls were all raised in white families and in white neighborhoods. This is an entire step removed from Indian Americans that, despite being born here, still retain cultural ties to India through family and community. Except for their brown skin, these girls have no connection to Indian culture whatsoever. And yet [. . .] their brown skin instinctively causes you to unfairly judge their often shallow reactions as the film unfolds.

While Abhi acknowledges that as adoptees, Anisha, Kaylan, and Lizzie have experiences "an entire step removed" from those of second-generation Indian Americans, he pointedly notes that their "brown skin" invites readers of *Sepia Mutiny* to "instinctively" react to the film. Despite this assumption of a common racial identity, however, the adoptees' experience in India elicits an uncomfortable reaction from readers of the blog. Even though the young women have a biological relationship to India, their adoption by white families leads Alohi to proclaim that the adoptees have "no connection to Indian culture whatsoever."

The vexed reaction of this blogger to *Calcutta Calling* prompted several commentators to view the film online and leave postings that attempted to theorize the relationship between their own experiences as self-described South Asians, desis or mixed-race subjects, and the experience of the young adoptees.[32] As several commentators wrote, the teenagers' reactions to poverty in India resonated with their own experiences during visits to the subcontinent (including India and Pakistan). Indeed, the discomfort described in the initial posting appears to derive at least in part from the fact that Kaylan, Lizzie, and Anisha are *not* "an entire step removed" from the experiences of second-generation South Asians, but in fact occupy similarly racialized and historicized locations as immigrants. As one commentator put it, the fact that Anisha recognized her difference from her family and friends despite growing up in a white household suggested that her experience was consistent with how many South Asians grapple with being racial minorities in the United States. By confronting the complexities of their own relationship to the subcontinent, the readers of *Sepia Mutiny* turned to *Calcutta Calling* as a way of understanding how the adoptees—immigrants like themselves—produced transnational affiliations to both South Asia and America.

These varied responses to *Calcutta Calling* underscore the locality of the documentary subjects in public discourses of immigration, multiculturalism, and race. In relation to their families and communities in Minnesota, Kaylan, Lizzie, and Anisha's racial difference is subsumed within dominant representations of the (white) American national family. When the three of them are in India, assumptions of racial identification are transformed through the trope of salvation into differences of class and citizenship. At the same time, given that the adoptees reject a nostalgic relationship to Calcutta and (having been "forgotten" by their birth mothers) cannot recuperate a genealogy of origin in India, Anisha, Kaylan, and Lizzie do not identify as immigrants. Yet the postings on the *Frontline* website and on *Sepia Mutiny* insist on reading the experiences of these young women as a story about immigration to America.

"For the transnational adoptee," Eng writes, "where does history begin?"[33] In *Calcutta Calling*, the unique historical relationship between South Asia and the United States embodied by the protagonists is consistently reworked as narratives of immigration and assimilation by the filmmaker and by viewers. For the protagonists, their trip "back" to India does not produce a genealogical narrative of origin. During their time in Calcutta, they are prevented from forging relationships to their birth mothers, who—the social worker claims—have forgotten about their children. Nor do the protagonists identify with the nostalgic narrative of "home" offered by the caretaker at the orphanage. Instead, locality is produced through the new forms of racialized solidarity that these young women develop with one another. In a hotel room toward the conclusion of their trip, the excited trio exclaim over their shared physical characteristics. Anisha exults over the fact that "our hands on this side are white, [and on the other] side are brown, filled with brown lines!" Given their lack of interest in historical or cultural narratives that bind them to India, the teenagers find solace through their common experience of racialization in the United States. "I've always kind of associated myself with white people," says Lizzie, "which is kind of embarrassing—but when you get here, and you, like, meet *you* guys, and stuff, then you're like . . ." to which Anisha concludes, "It's, like, finally!" As transnational subjects, these adoptees identify with each other precisely through disidentifying with India (still marked by poverty and underdevelopment) and America (now read by Lizzie as "white"). For the young women, creatively producing and inhabiting a relationship of belonging with each other provides an alternative to the salvation narrative that previously explained their location in the United States.

Instead of the fraught choice between being Indian or becoming American that is at the heart of *So Far from India* and *Knowing Her Place*, the young women in *Calcutta Calling* reject dominant narratives of immigration in order to inhabit and produce an incipient form of transnational locality. Exuberantly claiming her friendship with Anisha and Lizzie, Kaylan proclaims, "We decided that we need to make our own country [. . .] of adopted Indian girls!" This newly imagined country, as Kaylan suggests, exceeds the rhetoric of national citizenship disseminated in postcolonial India and in a multicultural America. It also circumvents the spiritual rhetoric of "karma" offered by the social worker in India, and the commodity form of the "gift" proffered by the girls' relatives in the United States. Months after their return, Kaylan, Lizzie, and Anisha meet in a mall in Minneapolis, where they decide to get their noses pierced.[34] Happily ensconced back "home," Kaylan says, "We looked in the mirror and we were like, that's just how it's supposed to be." The protagonists' resolution of their own immigrant histories enables them to reinhabit a racialized relationship to their adoptive families as well as within the larger national body of America. *Calcutta Calling* brings to life the complex interrelationship between the visuality and embodiment of race, experienced across the subject-positions of the protagonists, the filmmaker, and the anonymous viewers.

Being Muslim in Multicultural America

A world apart from the snowy plains of Minnesota, *B.E.S.* (*Bangla East Side*) documents the lives of four teenage first-generation Bangladeshi immigrants on Manhattan's Lower East Side. Released in 2004, this short film profiles Mahfuja, Maroofa, Saleh, and Jemi, all of whom have arrived in New York within a span of five years. In that brief time, each of these young men and women has come to call New York home, though they still with great pride describe themselves as Bengalis. What is equally important to the teenagers, however, is their religious identity as Muslims. These young immigrants are acutely conscious of their racial and religious difference in a city impacted by the terrorist attacks of September 11, 2001. Mahfuja, for example, has taken to wearing a head scarf (hijab) for the past year, while Jemi speaks of the ways in which her classmates taunted another Muslim girl at school who wore a full veil (niqab). While Maroofa tells the filmmakers that the subject of 9/11 is off-limits in conversations at school, Saleh, the only man interviewed in the group, notes matter-of-factly that "you cannot raise your voice high" as Bangladeshis in a domestic climate that is characterized by terror and surveillance. As juniors and seniors in high school, however, the students do not limit themselves to discussing terrorism. Instead, they talk about the ways in which they have begun to acclimatize themselves to New York, despite occasionally missing Bangladesh, and of their plans to pursue the higher education and careers for which their families traveled to the United States.

B.E.S. was originally conceived as an educational video project for Bangladeshi immigrant youth that the filmmakers Fariba Alam and Sarita Khurana produced in the context of an after-school program. However, the film was subsequently circulated on university campuses as an "authentic" depiction of the lives of young Muslims after 9/11. *B.E.S.* was also among the first documentary films that captured the changing class and national composition of South Asians at the turn of this century. Immigrants from Bangladesh constitute the fastest-growing South Asian population across the United States, but recent Bangladeshi immigrants are also less likely to have secured full employment and advanced educational degrees. As Maroofa notes, 56 percent of all Bangladeshi immigrants live in New York City. In New York City between 1990 and 2000, the Bangladeshi immigrant population expanded by more than 400 percent, currently numbering 28,269 immigrants.[35] Despite the rapid growth of this community, Bangladeshis are discriminated against by South Asian immigrants and are also marginalized within the larger Asian American population. First-generation Bangladeshis have been disproportionately affected by hate crimes, job discrimination, and federal immigration policies post–September 11, in addition to being characterized more generally by lower income levels as well as higher rates of poverty.[36]

These statistical quantifications of Bangladeshi immigrants do not reflect the continued subjection of Bangladeshis, along with other Muslim and Arab American immigrant groups, to the disciplinary regimes of the U.S. state. In the aftermath of 9/11, such measures include the 2003 Patriot Act, which required immigrants from countries across South Asia and the Middle East to register with the U.S. government. These registration procedures were required of immigrant men who were undocumented as well as those who were permanent residents. The Patriot Act led to the detainment and deportation of hundreds of South Asian and Arab American immigrants and has been the subject of a number of recent art and filmmaking ventures. However, this disappearance of South Asian and Muslim immigrants from the urban landscape, particularly from New York City, is not addressed in *B.E.S.* Instead, the young protagonists of the documentary claim New York as home.

As an autobiographical and ethnographic text, *B.E.S.* brings to light the convergences between the filmmakers—also South Asian immigrants—and their documentary subjects. Alam and Khurana enjoy a playful relationship with the teenagers that is reflected in the visual and aural narrative of the film, as many of the scenes are shot within the teenagers' homes, and as the youth confide in the filmmakers on-screen. However, this narrative of identity and community is undercut by the dissonant biographies of the directors and their protagonists. Alam and Khurana are second-generation immigrants, whereas the four teenagers they interview are first-generation immigrants, whose parents run convenience stores and gas stations. While Alam is of Bangladeshi descent and uses Islamic iconography in her other artistic projects, Khurana is of Indian origin. Neither director primarily identifies as Muslim, although Muslim identities (variously defined) are of central importance to the Bangladeshi youth they interview. As such the documentary captures the shared investment of the filmmakers and protagonists in belonging to New York, but it also highlights how this diasporic locality is embodied unevenly across differences of generation, national origin, religion, and class.

Like *So Far from India*, *B.E.S.* focuses on working-class South Asian immigrants. And like that earlier film, the oral testimonials collected in *B.E.S.* also shift between depictions of everyday life in New York and on the subcontinent, in this case in Bangladesh. However, unlike previous documentaries on South Asian immigration, the visual landscape of *B.E.S.* is largely limited to the Lower East Side of Manhattan. This narrow slice of the city is brought to life with long shots of the dense urban neighborhoods where the teenagers live; the high school they attend; the mosques and public housing projects that define their notion of community. By focusing their lens on a single geographic site, Alam and Khurana work to locate the subjectivities of these young immigrants within the changing demography of New York City. In doing so they rework the spatial difference between South Asia and the United States by depicting how the urban space of New York is racialized by an emerging group of immigrants. Jemi, Maroofa, Mahfuja, and Saleh speak volubly to the ways in which their everyday lives are saturated with the visible presence of Bangladesh, for their imaginary homeland comes to life through a profusion of family and friends, music and video stores, and groceries.[37] Saleh, whose family lives just a block away from the school, points out the number of Bangladeshi families who live in the neighborhood. On the Lower East Side, Bangladeshis operate grocery stores and medical dispensaries, and gather at the local mosque. His two closest friends live in the same building, having moved from Bangladesh to New York at the same time. Walking through the neighborhood, once a tenement district for Jewish immigrants, Saleh exuberantly claims its streets, buildings, and alleys. It is this racialized urban space that comes to stand in for "Bangladesh" in the film. For Saleh, the topography of Bangladeshi immigrant life in Manhattan is a place of intimate familiarity. Although he nostalgically recounts his life on the subcontinent, it is New York City that has become home.

In her book, *Missing: Youth, Citizenship, and Empire After 9/11*, the anthropologist Sunaina Maira discusses the complex processes through which immigrant Muslim youth identify with America. Like Alam and Khurana, Maira works with working-class first-generation South Asian teenagers, who in her case attend public school in the greater Boston area. Through interviewing, tutoring, and sharing leisure time with these youth, Maira explores the ways in which Muslim youth identify with or dissent against hegemonic modes of cultural citizenship in the United States. Central to her work are the expanding parameters of the U.S.-as-empire, particularly after the terrorist attacks of September 11. In the heart of empire, she notes, immigrant subjects (including herself) produce and inhabit what she describes as "imperial feelings." As Maira argues, "empire is constructed through myriad interconnections between cultural representations, public discourses, state institutions, and social relations that shape identification with, support for, or dissent from imperial policies" (62). *Missing* is an important ethnographic counterpoint to the cinematic narrative of *B.E.S.*, which in the eyes of the filmmakers was also conceived as a critique of the "representations," "discourses," and "institutions" of the U.S. state. Indeed, *B.E.S.* explicitly reflects the marginalization of Muslim immigrants in America. In the opening scenes of the film, Jemi reacts to an image of George W. Bush on the television news. She enthusiastically challenges his claim to the presidency, commenting that she probably scored higher than him in her U.S. history classes. Her friends rally around her, yelling, "Yeah! *You* should be president!" Of course, the fact that Jemi was born outside the United States, in Bangladesh, means that she can never be president. In addition, the fact that Jemi is Muslim means that no matter how high she scored on her U.S. history test, in the public sphere she is racialized as non-American.

Within this current moment of U.S. domestic and global politics, Maira notes how Muslim teenagers produce extensive oral narratives that center on their romantic and social lives, as well as their dreams and aspirations for family and work. The narratives that Maira showcases demonstrate the myth of upward mobility, as well as how such myths rapidly dissolve when the teenagers confront obstacles at home and at work. In their part-time jobs, Muslim youth face racial and class-based discrimination, often from other upwardly mobile South Asians. At school they are the targets of racial and religious epithets, much like the young woman in a niqab described in *B.E.S.*

At home, some of the teenagers Maira befriends confront their family members, who oppose their romantic relationships with other South Asian Muslim or Hindu youth. Throughout her ethnography, Maira emphasizes how such narratives of striving upward (for better employment, better education, better romantic relationships) in fact operate as evidence of downward mobility for Muslim immigrants.[38]

The teenagers interviewed by Alam and Khurana in *B.E.S.* also extensively talk about their plans for life and work after high school. Many of these young men and women aspire to be the first college graduates in their families. Their desire for class mobility is palpable, and yet these youth and their family members continue to be targets of racial hostility. As a result, they spend time in the company of other Bangladeshi immigrants instead of socializing with different ethnic groups at school. However, in contrast to the youth interviewed by Maira, the teenagers documented in *B.E.S.* maintain their belief in the possibility of upward mobility. Throughout the film the oral testimonials of the young women (particularly Jemi) communicate a desire for public recognition. Why is upward mobility so central to the lives of these young immigrants? What might be our own investments as viewers in such narratives?

The dominant rhetoric of mobility for the protagonists of *B.E.S.* is the language of liberal multiculturalism, which is reinforced in their schools through educational and social programming. Because *B.E.S.* was made during an after-school program, the film is one such example of multicultural programming. The framework of liberal multiculturalism enables the students to maintain coherent notions of racial and religious identity in school as "Bengalis." In turn, the school encourages students to identify with their countries of origin as an integral component of identifying as "Americans." Within the curriculum of multiculturalism, the experience of immigration becomes central to universal formations of U.S. citizenship.[39] Consequently, the racial discrimination that unofficially characterizes the students' patterns of socialization within the school grounds are in fact officially incorporated into an educational rhetoric of pluralist multiculturalism. Instead of relegating differences of race, language, and national origin to the private realm of the home and family, at school such differences become central to the public production of newly American identities.

All four teenagers attend the same public school on Manhattan's Lower East Side. In the film the school is depicted as predominantly nonwhite: the teenagers' classmates are Asian American, Latino, and African American, as are faculty and other mentors. However, as a practicing Muslim, Jemi notes that it is difficult to socialize with non-Bangladeshis—she does not date or drink, and she does not care to affiliate with those who do. From her perspective, multicultural programming such as the annual International Day festivities at the high school assume primary importance, for it enables students like her to perform their "ethnic" difference and receive public recognition from other students. At the annual International Day, Jemi, beaming in her finery, performs an elaborate dance to recorded music of a popular Bengali song. Her performance is not simply a nostalgic reiteration of homeland but also a re-embodiment of a pluralist rhetoric of diversity. While Jemi identifies through her dance as a "Bengali" in school, for those non-Bengalis who watch her dance (including her teachers and peers), her performance is one more example of the expansive reach of a multicultural America.

The performance of Bengali-ness is thus central to the teenagers' claims to locality inside and outside of school. Whereas Jemi's dance is an explicit performance of being "Bengali," similar performances recur in the film within the domestic space of home. Maroofa, who is a fan of Indian popular film, dances along to Bollywood songs at home with her sisters and says, "We love to spend time together [. . .] that make[s] me connected to Bangladesh." Maroofa and her sisters avidly watch satellite television that broadcasts the latest films from India; they also shop for videos that feature their favorite film stars. Importantly (and ironically), Bengali-ness for these young women is constituted through cultural commodities from India, which reinscribes the hegemony of Indian popular culture within South Asian diasporas. Maroofa and Jemi's claims to being Bengali are not simply a reflection of their nostalgic or childhood desire for Bangladesh. Nor do they identify as "Bengali" as a substitute for identifying as "Muslim." To be Bengali is to inhabit a highly specific transnational subjectivity, one that is shaped by transborder movements of South Asian popular culture. As Jemi remarks, "It's kind of cool to be a Bengali because [. . .] you have that culture." In this instance "culture" is not an essential attribute of national belonging but a series of popular practices, which, like Jemi and Maroofa's dances, are repetitively enacted as a means of producing locality as South Asians in the United States.

The production of locality is, of course, not always a euphoric process. Throughout the film the students forcefully articulate how their embodied identities as Bengalis and as Muslims are also subject to verbal and physical violence. Jemi's father, for example, was murdered at a gas station, the victim of violent and anonymous crime. Jemi speaks of her father's death dispassionately, as he never lived with her family in Bangladesh; growing up, she hardly knew him. Yet it is his labor and his sponsorship of her permanent residency application that enabled her, together with her sister and brother-in-law, to immigrate to New York. Similarly, Mahfuja also lives with her siblings, as her parents have decided to move back to Bangladesh. Mahfuja is the only one of the young women who routinely wears a head scarf. For her it is a relatively recent practice, one that she does not share with other female family members or for that matter with the two directors of the documentary. Mahfuja is regularly harassed on the streets and at school. However, in her oral testimony she reflects that she has gotten used to wearing her head scarf and feels ashamed without it. As she walks along a narrow sidewalk on the way to school she comments, "I really, you know, love my religion [. . .] I don't think they're going to force me to take it [the scarf] off. This is my own thing, you know, First Amendment?"

As a visibly racialized and gendered subject walking through the public space of New York City, Mahfuja draws upon the vocabulary of U.S. civil rights in order to produce and inhabit her right to citizenship as a Muslim woman. Importantly, the question for Mahfuja is not whether she exercises a "choice" to identify as a Bengali or as an American. Instead she draws upon the multicultural rhetoric of U.S. citizenship in order to locate her gendered subjectivity as a Muslim within the national body of America. Mahfuja's assertion demonstrates how religion and race are "contingent and fluid" social structures, which together operate as "articulated discourses" that shape South Asian diasporic subjectivities.[40] For Mahfuja, there is no apparent contradiction between her right to citizenship as a racial minority and her public surveillance in a city that stigmatizes her embodiment of Islamic religiosity. Mahfuja's claim to doing "my own thing" calls into question what Maira terms "dissenting citizenship." Elaborating on dissent as a "feeling," Maira contends that dissenting feelings are "not simply caught in the binary of resistance and complicity but [are] expressed in ambiguous and hard to identify ways [. . .] we can try to understand dissent without falling prey to a romanticization of heroic protest or passive victimhood based on easy rhetoric or familiar tropes" (*Missing*, 214). Mahfuja's assertion of the First Amendment may be read as both a form of embodied dissent and a form of complicit engagement with the U.S. state. Her claims to locality along with that of her peers constitutes the ambivalent narrative of belonging in *B.E.S.*

Inside and outside their school environment, the teenagers' identification as Bengalis and as Muslims is consistently reproduced in ways that collude with, rather than explicitly contest, the rhetoric of U.S. multiculturalism. For these young immigrants, locality is as much about claiming a sense of belonging to the United States as it is about affirming a nostalgic relationship to a country of origin. To perform one's locality as a "Muslim" or as "Bengali" becomes, for Mahfuja and her friends, another way of identifying as American.

At the conclusion of *B.E.S.*, the video camera turns over into the hands of Maroofa's sister, who points it at Saleh, Mahfuja, Jemi, and Maroofa. Riding the subway together on the way home, the students suddenly shy away from being documented on film. Instead, they tilt the camera toward the viewer. Becoming subjects rather than objects of ethnographic filmmaking, the protagonists of *B.E.S.* focus their lens on us. Following this turn toward the viewer, I ask: In what ways do these documentaries of South Asian immigrants, by South Asian immigrants, facilitate relations of identification and disidentification between filmmaker, viewer, and documentary subject? What are the intersecting claims to locality that are produced on- and off-screen? It is important to note that none of the documentary subjects in this chapter explicitly identifies as South Asian. Vasu calls herself "Indian American," the transnational adoptees of *Calcutta Calling* identify as "American," and the teenagers in *B.E.S.* use the term "Bengali." However, each of these films makes visible the conditions under which first- and second-generation immigrants create narratives of locality. In the at-times-contentious dynamic established between filmmaker and documentary subject, and between subject and viewer, these films map the vexed relationship between visual narratives of migration and oral narratives of assimilation.

The stories of "choice" that so vividly come to life in Nair and Krishnan's films deeply resonate with popular representations of South Asian immigration. As Parminder Dhillon-Kashyap remarks, "Think of an Asian woman—what comes to mind? Arranged marriages? Domestic violence? Stuck between two cultures?"[41] In *Knowing Her Place*, Vasu's psychic condition is linked to all three of these tropes. Her oral testimony and Krishnan's aural voice-over converge in order to reproduce what appears to be a generic narrative of cross-cultural encounter: tradition versus modernity, home versus abroad, South Asia versus America. Such narratives are defined by the free will of the immigrant, who is portrayed by Krishnan (as well as by Vasu's husband and children) as an autonomous agent of her migration. Within this discursive framework, Vasu must choose between being Indian and being American. Krishnan centrally relies on the emancipatory promise of immigration in order to resolve the gendered, classed, and racialized conflict at the heart of her film. However, reading against the grain of Vasu's testimonial in *Knowing Her Place* demonstrates the extent to which the trope of "identity crisis" fails to explain the historical and psychic conditions of Vasu's depression. By engaging with the visual and aural narrative that provides evidence of Vasu's everyday life in New York as well as Madras, the viewer comes to see and hear how Vasu painfully inhabits conditions of patriarchal domesticity in both sites. Recognizing the transnational formation of her subjectivity requires the filmmaker and viewers, including myself, to underscore our complicity in and betrayal of notions of "universal sisterhood."

In the more recent short films by Khokha as well as Alam and Khurana, the question of "choice" dissolves from view when documentary subjects self-consciously situate themselves as American citizens. In *Calcutta Calling*, Anisha, Kaylan, and Lizzie insist on their rightful place in the United States. Despite their racial alienation from their adoptive families, the girls are also cognizant of their class difference in relation to Indians in India. These differences of race and class make the three adoptees subjects of betrayal. They are betrayed first by orphanage caregivers who narrate fictive memories of their infancy, and secondly by their birth mothers, who ostensibly have forgotten about them. In turn, the adoptees betray the myth of racial origin theories, for each of them rejects India as a biological homeland. For their adoptive families, the young women are "gifts," spiritual transactions that have no commercial value. Such narratives of salvation locate the adoptees within multicultural formations of American nationhood, figured as predominantly white and heterosexual. At the same time, reading online commentary on the films demonstrates how the adoptees are also claimed and disowned by South Asian immigrants. On progressive South Asian blogs, viewers identify with the adoptees' feelings of estrangement from India, but disidentify with the girls' claims to being American. Because the adoptees embody a complex history of capital and labor exchange between South Asia and the United States, they become a site for contentious debate around who and what is South Asian.

In *B.E.S.*, four first-generation immigrants from Bangladesh claim their identities as Muslims and as Bengalis in New York. By examining the ways in which these immigrant subjects creatively engage with public discourses of multiculturalism, *B.E.S.* maps the discursive relationship between a faith-based category of "Muslim" and the race-based construct of "American." For Mahfuja, Jemi, and Maroofa, their intimate embodiment of American citizenship is produced via their identification as Muslims and secured through their consumption of South Asian popular culture. Reading *B.E.S.* alongside contemporary ethnographic accounts of Muslim youth also highlights how the events of September 11, 2001, resonate differently for different groups of immigrants. In *Missing*, Maira posits 9/11 as the single most significant event that alters the landscape of South Asian immigrant experience. In *B.E.S.*, by contrast, it is one among many personal and political events that shape the subjectivities of the young protagonists. Their lives are also impacted by the death of family members, their turn toward religious faith, and their ambitions to go to college. In this regard my reading of the film expands upon the argument made by the sociologist Syed Ali. In his research on second-generation South Asian Muslims in New York City, Ali questions the singular historical impact of 9/11 on Muslim American cultural identity. He writes,

> While September 11th clearly affected many Muslim communities, especially Arab and Pakistani working-class communities, the idea that September 11 somehow *qualitatively* affects all Muslims in a way different from other events that had negative repercussions for Muslims in the US is not justified. Previous events, including the first Gulf War, the bombing of the Federal Center in Oklahoma City in 1995 and the 1993 bombing of the World Trade Center, all served as catalysts for a re-evaluation among Muslims about what it means to be Muslim. (392, note 7)

Similarly, I locate the teenagers interviewed in *B.E.S.* within a larger historical purview that is embodied by the documentary subjects as well as the filmmakers. Whereas Maira situates her informants entirely within the racial formation of the U.S. state, I delineate the fragile interconnections between the United States and Bangladesh that are visualized in the film through a series of personal narratives. The distinction of my approach is reflected in the fact that for the four teenagers, their identification as Bengalis is not only about what it means to be Muslim in the United States today. These young men and women are consciously subject to practices of racial profiling by the state, but the communities that they create are also shaped by the circulation and consumption of Bollywood music, movies, and dance.

The tension between dissenting and complying with frameworks of U.S. multiculturalism remains a central feature of South Asian localities. In Chapter 3 I extend my analysis by exploring the national, racial, and gendered identities embodied in the annual Miss India USA pageant. As upwardly mobile immigrants strategically deploy pluralist discourses of multiculturalism, their performance of ethnicity reveals how locality is produced in tandem with the U.S. state. Equally important, however, is their engagement with another set of nationalist ideologies: that of the neoliberal Indian state at the turn of the twenty-first century. How immigrants inhabit these multiple ideologies of nationhood, and when they embody dissent, demonstrates that locality is far more capacious than domesticated narratives of citizenship. Shifting my attention from viewer to audience member, I underscore how the triangulated relations between the contestants onstage, the audience members offstage, and the organizers of the show generate transnational formations of belonging.

THREE

Beauty Queens

Gender, Ethnicity, and Transnational Modernities at Miss India USA

At the 1999 Miss India USA pageant, more than six hundred people streamed into the ballroom of the five-star Fairmont Hotel in San Jose, California. The event was billed in the pageant booklet as of "great social and cultural value" and "the most glamorous Indian function in the country," and tickets had quickly sold out. Families and friends of the contestants, local businesspeople, community leaders, and pageant enthusiasts milled around their assigned tables and the cash bar, and the pageant finally commenced after an hour's delay. Stretching well past midnight, the pageant included fashion shows, music and dance performances, and speeches by local civic officials. Sponsored by the New York–based India Festival Committee, Miss India USA is the nationwide culmination of a series of state-level competitions, such as the Miss India New York, Miss India Texas, and Miss India Georgia pageants. The winner of Miss India USA goes on to represent the United States at the annual Miss India Worldwide competition; successful contestants have become actresses, television personalities, doctors, entrepreneurs, and homemakers. With its parade of young women, a talent show that displays the musical and athletic skills of its contestants, and its ceremonial pomp and splendor, the Miss India USA pageant is in many ways like any other beauty contest. Yet as the only national-level beauty pageant specifically for immigrants of subcontinental origin, the pageant also uniquely articulates the convergences between ideologies of nationhood on the subcontinent and in the United States.

Moving from fictional and cinematic narratives of South Asian immigrants on the East Coast to an ethnographic study of South Asian communities on the West Coast highlights how subcontinental immigrants at the turn of the millennium occupy shifting constructs of class, race, and gender. During the 1990s thousands of Indians and a smaller number of Pakistanis and Bangladeshis migrated to work in Silicon Valley's high-tech industry. As H-1B visa holders, these workers are officially categorized as "nonimmigrants," employed in specialized occupations for a temporary period by U.S. corporations.[1] Yet the exceptional conditions of class and capital mobility in Silicon Valley enable H-1B workers to stake their claim as immigrants in the United States. The Miss India USA pageant draws upon narratives of entrepreneurship and capital accumulation symbolized by this recent group of immigrants, even though South Asian immigrants to California throughout the twentieth century have been predominantly working class. The pageant also draws upon narratives of neoliberal economic reform in India, symbolized by the successful figure of the Indian beauty queen, now internationally recognized on the global pageant circuit. The Miss India USA pageant is thus located at the intersection of emerging formations of ethnicity and class in California, and neoliberal ideologies of gender and citizenship in contemporary India.

In this chapter I make use of ethnographic and archival methods to demonstrate how the beauty pageant operates as a multifaceted site for the formation of South Asian identities and communities. In addition to the Miss India USA pageant in San Jose, I attended various community beauty pageants between 1999 and 2004, interviewing participants as well as audience members. I also constructed an archive of Miss India USA and Miss India pageants in India between 1996 and 2006, during which time beauty pageants in India received unprecedented levels of international attention. Drawing upon coverage of the pageant world in Indian newsmagazines, immigrant community newspapers, and websites, I highlight the interrelationship between pageants in the United States and on the subcontinent. By tracking the flow of charity donations from the Miss India USA pageant to various nonprofit organizations in India, I outline the transnational circuits of gender, culture, and capital that bind together ethnic beauty pageants in the United States with the political and economic development of the Indian state. As an ethnographic and historical text, the beauty pageant brings to life the ways in which contestants, organizers, and audience members collude in the production of locality. The intense relations of identification and disidentification that are forged onstage and off, demonstrate how multiple and asymmetrical notions of belonging to America emerge at the pageant.

Historically, Asian Americans have hosted beauty pageants as part of ethnic festivals that promote the "culture" and "identity" of a particular immigrant group. Such events also demonstrate the assimilation of that group into mainstream American popular culture. The historian Judy Wu, for instance, discusses Miss Chinatown beauty pageants that were organized by local Chinese chambers of commerce in San Francisco during the 1950s and 1960s, countering dominant images of communism during the cold war. Likewise the sociologist Rebecca King-O'Riain examines contemporary Japanese American beauty pageants held on the West Coast, which are central to revising racialized notions of what it means to be nisei or sansei—that is, a second- or third-generation immigrant. Because ethnic beauty pageants are community-specific events, they are targeted toward first- and second-generation audience members. Though Asian American beauty pageants are modeled on national events such as the Miss America pageant, they often incorporate performances of "tradition" that are specific to the community, for example, dance performances or demonstrations of language competency.

The Miss India USA pageant is also oriented toward local communities of Indian immigrants, though, as I discovered, what it meant to be "Indian" was consistently challenged by the contestants onstage as well as by audience members offstage. Miss India USA is the only beauty pageant annually organized by South Asian immigrants in North America. In Canada the Ontario-based Miss Canada Pakistan Corporation occasionally sponsors the Miss Pakistan World contest, and while this pageant is open to Pakistani immigrants across North America, it is not officially endorsed by Pakistani community groups in the United States. Likewise, the Bangladeshi immigrant community does not sponsor beauty pageants. Among Sri Lankan Americans, beauty pageants are organized sporadically, primarily as part of trade conventions endorsed by government agencies (for example, the Tea Queen contest in Los Angeles in 2007 was sponsored by the Consulate General of Sri Lanka). Miss India USA is thus the only national contest that caters exclusively to first- and second-generation immigrants of "Indian origin."

As such, this beauty pageant underscores how Indians are the largest group of subcontinental immigrants in the United States and reinforces the hegemony of Indian popular culture within South Asian diasporas.

In my reading of the Miss India USA pageant, I discuss three issues critical to the production of South Asian localities. First, given that the 1999 pageant was held in San Jose, a city at the heart of northern California's thriving technology industry, Miss India USA consolidates new middle-class narratives of immigration. By evoking stories of Indian American entrepreneurial success in Silicon Valley, the pageant sponsors elided a longer history of working-class Punjabi migration to the West Coast in the early twentieth century. Because the pageant was sponsored by local small businesses, it endorsed notions of private enterprise and capital accumulation, reflected in the career aspirations of the contestants. The sociologist Pawan Dhingra has argued that the San Francisco Bay area is a primary field site for examining the rise of second-generation South Asian professionals. Such professional immigrants are central to the pageant, for they financially sponsor and judge various aspects of the event. I demonstrate how these upwardly mobile South Asian immigrants redefine what it means to be "ethnic" and "middle class" in California.

Second, the Miss India USA pageant functions not only as the crowning event of an acculturated immigrant community but also as a formative site for imagining gendered notions of nationhood and citizenship. In her study of the Miss America pageant, Sarah Banet-Weiser writes, "In order to manage and construct different styles and practices of citizenship, beauty pageants thus create imagined communities where nationalist discourse is produced as cultural tradition" (6). I argue that the organizers of Miss India USA attempt to create a coherent ethnic group within the larger racial formation of the U.S. state *and* a cohesive diasporic community in relation to an idea of India. These multiple ideologies of ethnicity and nationhood are articulated through the prominence of commercial Hindi, or Bollywood, film, song, and dance at the pageant.[2] During the talent show segment, the prolific use of Bollywood song and dance by the contestants represents the pluralist composition of the Indian state (across ethnic, linguistic, and religious groups) and its claims to a "secular" modernity. The contestants' sexualized performance of Bollywood songs, however, also demonstrates how Bollywood comes to stand in for popular idioms of Indian femininity in diaspora. The rhetorical link between the embodiment of Indian nationalism and the practice of multicultural American citizenship is thus forged through the performance of young women's sexualities.

Third, I explore the similarities in form and content between the Miss India USA pageant and the Miss India contests in India. The tremendous popularity of (and protests against) the Miss India pageants reflects the effect of neoliberal economic reforms in the Indian public sphere. Specifically, the emergence of the beauty queen as a figure of Indian modernity demonstrates how middle-class Indians participate in various popular ideologies of nationalism, among them right-wing Hindu nationalism (or Hindutva), Bollywood representations of the nation, and a "secular" democratic ideal of Indian nationhood. The circulation of notions of sexuality and modernity between the Miss India and Miss India USA pageants brings to light the highly contested relationship between, on the one hand, postcolonial India and South Asian diasporas and, on the other, South Asian diasporas and the racial formation of the U.S. state.

I attended the Miss India USA pageant in San Jose after receiving flyers advertising the event. The pageant was the first cultural program that I had attended in the San Francisco Bay area that was organized by first-generation immigrants for second-generation youth. As an intergenerational cultural production, the pageant "showcase[s] value, concepts, and behavior that exist at the center of a group's sense of itself and exhibit[s] values of morality, gender, and place."[3] Despite the ubiquity of beauty pageants at the international, national, and community levels, I was interested in the ways in which South Asian immigrants participate in pageantry as "places where cultural meanings are produced, consumed, *and* rejected."[4] Because the contest showcases the professional achievements of first- and second-generation immigrants, the winner of Miss India USA represents a model of multicultural U.S. citizenship. However, as a charity fund-raiser for economic and social initiatives in India, the pageant is also invested in the project of postcolonial Indian modernity. Set against the global popularization of beauty pageants, how is Miss India USA shaped by the demands, desires, and dreams of this local immigrant group? As young women participate in the display of Indian nationalism and American multiculturalism, their gendered performances illuminate the ways in which second-generation immigrants become South Asian. Although I watched from the sidelines, I found myself fully engaged by the spectacle of multiple nationalisms onstage. My ambivalent participation in this pageant—

along with that of the contestants and other audience members—revealed the dissonances within the production of locality offstage.

The Business of Identity: Race, Class, and Cultural Capital

The eighteenth annual Miss India USA pageant opened with great fanfare on a cool February night as the emcee announced four segments that would compose the contest: evening gown, Indian dress, talent show, and question and answer. In addition to the beauty contest, the evening also included a fashion show, performances of dance and music, a call for charity donations, and speeches by pageant organizers and former beauty queens, all entirely unrelated to the judging of the contest itself. Following a formal introduction of invited guests, the judges were introduced as "eminent, respected members of the Indian, American, and international community." That year, the judges included South Asians who worked in Hollywood as directors, actors, and producers; a casting agent for a major national television network; and a Hindi film actress.[5]

Approximately an hour into the show, the fifteen contestants for the crown made their first appearance onstage. As each young woman emerged onto the catwalk dressed in a floor-length Western evening gown, she was given a microphone to introduce herself. All the contestants uniformly greeted the audience with broad smiles, stating their names and the state they represented. Most of the women introduced themselves in terms of their regional identities (as Texans, Floridians, or Californians). However, one contestant named both a city in India as well as a state in America as her hometown: Miss India Virginia announced that she was from Fairfax County, Virginia, and New Delhi.[6] While each contestant walked down the runway, the emcee recited the contestant's astrological sign, her height (though not her age, weight, or body measurements), and her present occupation or intended profession. This brief introduction of the contestants was followed by another lengthy sequence of dances and speeches, prominently featuring young women—themselves dressed like pageant contestants—dancing to a fusion of hip-hop music and popular Hindi film songs. Throughout the evening, the podium at the far right of the stage was occupied by an emcee, Vidya Chandra Shekhar (Miss India USA 1986), who adeptly segued between segments by talking about her own past involvement with the pageant. Eventually the contestants came onstage again in "traditional wear," adorned in shararas, lehengas, and saris, walking down the catwalk individually and then assembling for a brief choreographed dance onstage. The women were reintroduced for the talent show, during which each contestant was allotted three minutes to perform a "talent," ranging from dance to dramatic monologue to martial arts. Five finalists were selected out of the fifteen contestants for the question-and-answer session. While the judges tallied the final results, the pageant wound down with performances by local dance troupes. The contest came to an end as pageant organizers clambered onstage to announce the runners-up and winner of Miss India USA. As the winning contestant was crowned, the ballroom floor opened out for dancing to live bhangra music.

Throughout the evening the pageant spilled across the grounds of the Fairmont Hotel as middle-aged South Asian men and women, wearing their finest clothing and jewelry, mingled in the hotel lobby. In the narrow hallway adjacent to the ballroom, local fashion retailers displayed designer Indian clothes at steep prices. The women's bathroom also became a scene of intense competition, as women of various ages, who had ostensibly come to support contestants for the title, exchanged compliments and comments on each other's dress and makeup as they beautified themselves. Inside the ballroom, proceedings were occasionally disrupted by the hoots, hollers, and whistles of groups of young South Asian men, who entered the ballroom intoxicated, flanked by their friends and girlfriends. During the fashion show that inaugurated the pageant, these young men (much to the consternation of the emcee) ogled the female models onstage, yelling from their seats, "Take it off! Take it off!" Importantly, not all of the audience members identified as Indian American—at my table the other guests included two women of South Asian descent from Fiji, their boyfriends and brother, as well as a middle-aged white American woman dressed in salwaar kameez who said, simply, that she came because she enjoyed seeing all kinds of pageants.

An annual event that continues to attract a large number of contestants at the state and national levels, the Miss India USA pageant had its origin in the India Festivals organized by the India Festival Committee (IFC), held in New York since 1974. These India Festivals were composed of classical and popular dance performances as well as music and fashion shows. The fashion show in particular proved to be a resounding success, leading

Dharmatma Saran, chairman of the IFC, to produce the Miss India New York pageant in 1980. With the financial support of Air India and a number of small Indian-owned businesses, Miss India New York became the first beauty pageant conducted specifically for and within the Indian American community. Two years later Saran solicited the participation of other regional Indian community associations to elect state-level beauty queens in order to hold the first Miss India USA pageant. As the prosperity of the sponsoring Indian American business communities grew, the pageantry of Miss India USA also increased in scale, moving out of basements and public park grounds into the ballrooms of five-star hotels in major cities across the United States.[7]

Organizations like the IFC are often described as "gatekeepers" that modulate the representation and dissemination of South Asian public culture. Members of these organizations, largely first-generation immigrants, uphold what they construe to be "authentic" and "traditional" notions of national culture. As Monisha Das Gupta notes, "through this act of naming who or what is South Asian, the communities' mainstream sections reproduce the idea that ethnic traditions are fundamentally antagonistic to U.S. values and practices. Yet, at the same time, their culture work reaffirms the American dream and its tropes of meritocracy, individual achievement, fairness and cohesion" (59). For the IFC, the Miss India USA pageant is an opportunity to reproduce so-called authentic notions of Indian culture among second-generation immigrants. The pageant is also a means to represent these same cultural traditions to a white American public. At the same time, the Miss India USA pageant reaffirms "tropes of meritocracy [and] individual achievement" by highlighting the educational and financial successes of its contestants. The pageant thus simultaneously disseminates idealized notions of "Indian culture" to a diverse South Asian community and locates upwardly mobile South Asians within pluralist ideologies of multiculturalism.

These divergent tropes of national belonging are unevenly reconciled in the rules that determine the racial identity of contestants. On the official Miss India USA website, the pageant stipulates that contestants must be "of Indian origin," between the ages of seventeen and twenty-five, unmarried, and childless. The racial category of "Indian origin" is defined further through regulations denoting that at least one parent must be of "Indian descent." Whether that parent can be multiracial, or identify as Pakistani or Bangladeshi, or from another South Asian diasporic community (such as from the Caribbean or East Africa) is unspecified. As a result, state- and national-level competitions routinely feature multiracial contestants as well as individuals from the larger South Asian diaspora. In addition, the contestant must be a resident of the state that she represents, although she need not have U.S. citizenship. Similar rules are duplicated at the state level, with the caveat that while regional representatives of the IFC are authorized to conduct Miss India beauty pageants outside of the Northeast tri-state region, the IFC appoints its own candidates from New York, New Jersey, and Pennsylvania and may also select candidates-at-large to participate in the national pageant. While the state- and national-level pageants do not stipulate physical requirements (there are no minimum height or maximum weight measurements), the pageant website maintains, "Since Miss India USA is a conservative pageant proper attire for all segments is mandatory. No vulgar attire will be permitted." Through this set of limitations on sexuality and racial identity, the pageant solicits contestants who reaffirm the IFC's sense of itself as a gatekeeping organization that not only promotes "Indian culture" but also attempts to determine who is "Indian."

In *Pure Beauty*, King-O'Riain discusses similar regulations around race and national identity for the Japanese American contestants who participate in regional Cherry Blossom Queen pageants. Contestant eligibility is determined by ancestral relation to Japan, though this notion of genealogy is supplemented by a "percentage rule" that is strikingly similar to blood quantum theories that determined notions of blackness for African Americans. Contestants for Japanese American community beauty pageants in California must be at least 50 percent Japanese (that is, they must have one parent of Japanese origin), but more important, the contestants must "look" visibly Japanese. The racial "look" of the contestants is determined by hair and skin color, as well as by the ways in which contestants conform to dominant popular notions of Japanese femininity through their speech, movement, and dress. King-O'Riain notes that the many multiracial contestants who participate in Japanese American beauty pageants over the past decade have challenged "not only the criteria for membership (*content*) of racial categories, but also the very definition of membership (*form*) of these same racial categories" (3).

At Miss India USA, official rules stop short of specifying blood quantum for measuring "Indian descent." However, the legibility and visibility of race is determined through the sexualized conduct of the contestants. While several contestants at both the state and national levels have been of mixed-race background (Miss India USA 1998, Nileem Shah, was of Indian and Italian American parentage), the bodily comportment of the candidates, amplified by their dress and accessories, generates visions of femininity that are popularized in Bollywood films. For the formal Indian wear segment of the pageant, the candidates wear elaborate lehengas and sheraras that approximate ornate bridal wear. Their hair is straightened or professionally curled, and the contestants' heavy makeup (along with a profusion of earrings, necklaces, and bangles) generates a glamorous but uniform effect of contained sexuality. Likewise, in order to maintain its reputation as a family-oriented and (as Saran describes it) "conservative" event, the pageant prevents women who have been married and/or have children from applying for the competition. In order to preserve these so-called family values, the pageant does not include a swimsuit round. Instead, the pleasure of watching the female contestants onstage derives from their bodily performance of sexual modesty, particularly during the Indian dress and talent show segments of the pageant.

These norms of racial, sexual, and gender identity are codified through the promotion of the pageant as a middle-class event, sponsored by local immigrant-owned small businesses. At the national- and state-level competitions, the pageant sponsors include travel agencies, jewelry stores, and insurance companies. As Robert Lavenda writes in his essay "It's Not a Beauty Pageant! Hybrid Ideology in Minnesota Community Queen Pageants," the result of the selection process is "that young women who appeal to members of the small-business community become candidates" (33). The contestants at Miss India USA embody values of hard work and upward class mobility, which are signaled through their plans for higher education and their commitment to the pageant industry (in terms of attending auditions, rehearsals, and so on). For audience members, the contestants represent idealized notions of youthful achievement. Lavenda proceeds to argue:

> Throughout this part of the pageant, the audience is invited to recognize the achievements of these young women [. . .] The audience is also invited to make the leap of taking these young women to stand for all young people in the community, a much trickier but important transformation, given what the pageant is about. After all, by extension, the achievements of the candidates are the achievements of the community itself, for it is the community that has formed them and has given them the opportunities to excel. (36)

Similarly, the entrepreneurs who sponsor, organize, and serve as judges for regional Miss India USA contests select a winner who stands in for the aspirations of this middle-class immigrant group. Successful contestants are rewarded with a variety of gifts (cash, scholarship money, jewelry, a round-trip ticket to India), underscoring their value to the local community.

At the 1999 Miss India USA pageant, a brochure distributed to audience members described the contest as a "platform for our children to express themselves and build their self-confidence." The infantilization of the contestants as "children" and the use of the possessive pronoun "our" enabled audience members along with the judges to invest in the stakes of the competition. The contestants were not simply regional representatives of discrete immigrant communities across the nation; together, they stood in for the singularity of the Indian immigrant experience. In return, the contestants incorporated pageant sponsors and organizers into the rhetoric of extended family. Several contestants referred to the pageant organizers through the idiom of fictive kinship, as "uncle" or "auntie." As an opportunity for "our children to express themselves," the pageant was also a primary site for local Indian American communities to produce and reward narratives of upward mobility. When the emcee Vidya Chandra Shekhar introduced the contestants onstage, all the candidates uniformly listed their intention to pursue careers in medicine, law, or engineering, professions that require extensive tertiary education and long-term financial investment. The hegemonic notions of nationhood and culture that are generated through such public rituals are central to Indian immigrants becoming better "Indians," but equally important, to becoming better Americans. The collective investment of immigrants in public displays of nationhood, whether through clothing or dress, education or occupation, is integral to the transformation of ethnic subjects into multicultural American citizens.[8]

Such notions of ethnic transformation were of particular import at the 1999 Miss India USA pageant because of its location in San Jose, in the heart of California's Silicon Valley. It was the first and only year that the pageant was held in northern California; all other pageants to date have been held in suburban New Jersey or New York or elsewhere on the East Coast. These regions have dense and established networks of middle-class South Asian immigrants, composed of corporate professionals and small-business owners. By contrast, organizing the pageant in San Jose marked a dynamic shift in the class composition of immigrant communities, for it highlighted the distinctive history of subcontinental migrations to the U.S. West Coast and, more specifically, the influx of skilled workers from South Asia to Silicon Valley at the turn of the twenty-first century.

In *Desi Land*, the anthropologist Shalini Shankar explores South Asian youth culture in Silicon Valley during the "boom" years of the technology industry in the late 1990s. As Shankar argues, South Asian immigrants in Silicon Valley produce and inhabit a mobile construct of class shaped by the influx of venture capital into the region. Inflated property values in California during this period, alongside the rapid growth of computer hardware and software industries, led many South Asians in the region to identify as middle class. These include those immigrants who worked in "gray collar" professions such as computer chip manufacturing or network security administration, in positions ranging from assembly-line workers to corporate executives, all of whom participated in similar acts of conspicuous consumption. The conjuncture of property appreciation and capital infusion into Silicon Valley underscores "how economies of late capitalism can destabilize traditional trajectories to class mobility and create new opportunities that complicate existing class categories" (11). In contrast to the fixed differences of class and geography that characterized earlier waves of migration, in the late twentieth century in Silicon Valley, South Asians participated in more-mobile networks of class and community. This dynamic social field directly contrasts with notions of upward mobility embodied by suburban middle-class professionals who arrived in the wake of the Hart-Celler Act (which I examined in Chapter 1) and circumvents the polarized narratives of "choice" that structure the localities of urban working-class immigrants who arrived in the 1980s and 1990s (which I discussed in Chapter 2).

Such an elastic notion of class identity, which is specific to the recent history of Silicon Valley, was central to the self-representation of those South Asians who participated in, sponsored, and attended Miss India USA. Throughout the pageant, the aspirational figure of the immigrant Internet entrepreneur circulated through the discourse of pageant organizers. Amar Walia, the chief pageant sponsor, noted in his opening speech:

We have the best-educated labor force of any country in the history of the world. And every day it gets better because we have more and more college graduates entering the labor force every day, and more and more people who are high school graduates dropping out of the labor force. Ladies and gentlemen, the Indo-American community has a big contribution in that! So how about a thundering applause for our parents, who stressed education, and for all of us who are vigorously continuing with the tradition.

Referring to the "Indo-American community" as a coherent class group, Walia portrayed Indian immigrants as carriers of "tradition" and as substitutes for the undereducated U.S. labor force, depicted as dropping out of the national workforce in droves. Evading structures of race and class discrimination that delimit access to higher education in the United States, Walia projected Indian Americans to the forefront of Silicon Valley as the ideal assimilated immigrant workforce.

Local government representatives also reaffirmed the importance of skilled immigrant labor as an engine for U.S. economic growth. Elaine Alquist, an Assembly member of the twenty-second district of California, appeared briefly onstage, declaring, "I really understand what it is to be very proud of your culture. I am the daughter of a Greek immigrant [. . .] like many of you I majored in mathematics." Alquist's remark, received with loud applause by the audience, portrayed Indian immigrants as repositories of an education-intensive culture whose technological and scientific skills contribute to a pluralist vision of America. Alquist's representation of South Asians as a model minority, based on the success of Internet pioneers, drew upon the longer legacy of professionals who migrated to build the scientific infrastructure for the cold war in the 1960s and 1970s. That the audience roared with approval at Alquist's comments demonstrates how middle-class experiences of migration—particularly, an aspirational narrative of accumulating capital—continue to circulate as the dominant narrative of South Asian immigration.

Alquist and Walia's triumphant rhetoric stood in sharp contrast to the heterogeneity of South Asian populations in northern California throughout the twentieth century. In her revisionist history of early South Asian immigration to the United States, Karen Leonard details the migration of Punjabi workers to the north American West Coast in the late nineteenth and early twentieth centuries. As Punjabis (largely Sikhs, but also Muslims and Hindus) migrated to work as farmers and railroad workers in California, Washington, and Oregon, existing immigration and antimiscegenation laws prevented workers from bringing their families to the United States and from marrying white American women. The subsequent marriage of several hundred immigrant Punjabis to local Mexican women created a community that Leonard calls "Mexican Punjabis" (also erroneously known as "Mexican Hindus"). Children of these marriages were raised primarily Catholic, identified to varying degrees as both Indian and Mexican, and continued to work in the agricultural professions that their fathers had established. Over succeeding generations, descendants of Mexican Punjabis increasingly married outside their community. Leonard analyzes this process as a series of "ethnic choices" made by new immigrants as they strategically adapted to an increasingly pluralist society in the United States. For many immigrants and their descendants, however, their "choice" to be Indian or American or Mexican, as well as their "choice" to identify as citizen or immigrant, was sharply curtailed by existing immigration legislation that discriminated against "Hindus" and that stripped first-generation immigrants of U.S. citizenship.

Just three hours south of Yuba City, where many Mexican Punjabis settled—and where a large working-class community of recent Punjabi Sikh immigrants continues to establish social and religious ties today—this early history of South Asian immigration was fully eclipsed by the pageant. Nor did the triumphant stories of capitalist success acknowledge the ongoing phenomenon of "body shopping" underpaid skilled immigrant labor from the subcontinent.[9] Instead, the pageant endorsed a historical narrative that focused on the recent success of largely male technology-industry workers, building upon and exceeding the rhetoric of the post-1965 "model minority." As Amar Walia proclaimed onstage, the pageant was "a crusade to make the Indian community a part of America." As the Internet economy becomes a central site for the globalization of capital, the portfolio of the high-tech entrepreneur eclipses the labor of working-class South Asians. For those first- and second-generation immigrants who gathered at this event, ethnicity and class were mobile constructs, constituted through the dissemination of speculative venture capital in Silicon Valley.

Yet such euphoric narratives of class and community are consistently constrained by the difference of race. Many of the young women who participate in the Miss India USA contest are aware that it is the only pageant that celebrates the distinctive talents, achievements, and skills of this immigrant group. For these contestants, the pageant offers the chance to receive public adulation on the basis of their "beauty" rather than be targets of public discrimination on account of their racial or class difference. These young women invest time and capital (in the form of the multiple rehearsals they attend and the ornate clothing and jewelry they purchase for the event) and work to embody narratives of upward mobility even if they are not themselves middle class. However, because Miss India USA celebrates those immigrants who achieve the "American dream"—a dream that is nowhere more evident than in the overnight success of Internet-based enterprises in Silicon Valley—the long years of training that it takes to become queen is marginalized in the rhetoric of the pageant. Equally important, the fact that the contestants feel as if their beauty can only be properly quantified in this contest—as opposed to mainstream events such as Miss America or Miss Teen USA—demonstrates how Miss India USA is centrally about the problem of race.[10]

Neoliberal Citizens, Secular Subjects

The exceptional conditions of capital and class movement for South Asians in Silicon Valley are directly linked to changing economic and social conditions for middle-class Indians during the same period. From 1991 onward, the socialist five-year plans that had determined Indian economic development for nearly fifty years after independence were steadily dismantled in favor of the privatization of major industries. Throughout the late 1990s the Indian government removed license restrictions on state-owned industries (in the manufacturing, telecommunications, banking, airline, and education sectors) in order to solicit foreign investment and develop private enterprises led by Indian as well as foreign corporations. The so-called liberalization of the Indian economy was accompanied by two other factors: the increasing political power of Hindu nationalist parties throughout the 1990s (including but not limited to the Bharatiya Janata Party, or BJP), and the consolidation of a middle-class identity through the social changes precipitated by liberalization and the advancement of the Hindu right.[11] The expansion of the middle class across all sectors of Indian society has amplified and distorted relations of power between urban and rural populations, religious and caste identifications, and regional and linguistic groups. Economic reform has also impacted gender relations, as media images of the "liberalized" female subject proliferate on billboards and television screens across the country, and as women's political representation is secured at a parliamentary level.[12] The "new India" of the early twenty-first century is marked by these multivalent shifts in the public and private spheres, as well as by the increasing impoverishment of the urban and rural poor.

Economic liberalization in India has also dynamically changed the relationship between the Indian state and its diasporic subjects. Since 2003, the Indian government has held annual conferences to solicit foreign investment from Non-Resident Indians (or NRIs) who reside in Europe, North America, Africa, the Caribbean, and Asia.[13] The Indian state has tapped several immigrant entrepreneurs to lead reforms in the health care, technology, and real estate sectors. The outsourcing industry that links Silicon Valley to India is one of many such areas of profitability. Corporate outsourcing takes different forms, ranging from multinational software companies led by Indians in India, call centers staffed by Indian workers in cities like Bangalore or Mumbai, or the hiring of specialized workers from India for short-term projects in the United States. As Aihwa Ong has argued in *Neoliberalism as Exception*, the outsourcing industry is based on the premise that Asian workers provide specialized knowledge for lesser pay. It enables call center workers to be paid more than workers with similar skills in India, but less than their peers in the United States. Ong notes that outsourcing relies upon "a circulating low-wage workforce entirely at the mercy of the fluctuating needs of the labor market" (164).

The 1999 Miss India USA pageant preceded some of these more-dramatic changes in labor and commodity migration that bind together South Asia and the United States. However, the global effects of a decentralized Indian economy were already visible at this ethnic beauty pageant in California. An Indian satellite media corporation was one of the major financial sponsors of Miss India USA. In turn, the pageant was a fund-raiser for a charity organization devoted to private education in India. During the course of the evening, media representatives from TV Asia, a satellite and cable television company founded by the Bollywood megastar Amitabh Bachchan, came onstage to promote their television programming for NRIs.[14] These employees of TV Asia delivered rousing speeches about the importance of creating "positive" images of Indians abroad. However, such media representations were to be generated not through television programming from within minority immigrant communities but rather from corporate offices in India, through television serials that employed Indian actors.

Likewise, representatives from the charity group Asha for Education came onstage to promote awareness of their cause. Asha is one of many nongovernmental organizations (NGOs) that currently dominate movements for educational reform in India, primarily by establishing private schools for rural and urban working-class children. Asha's model of private enterprise for educational reform is highly successful, and the organization now has chapters across the United States and in Europe, Australia, and Southeast Asia. As an NGO, Asha is independent of Indian state supervision, and the organization is largely dependent on financial and material support from Indian immigrant communities.[15] At the pageant, all proceeds after expenses were earmarked toward Asha's educational initiatives. Between musical and dance performances, representatives from Asha lectured the audience on the organization's current projects and future goals. However, the charitable orientation of the evening was secondary to the pageant proceedings. At one level, the fund-raising capacity of the event enabled audience members to imagine themselves as neoliberal subjects of the Indian state, for their tickets symbolized their investment in Indian educational and social reform. With ticket prices ranging from $75 to $250 (and tables for eight to ten attendees available for $650 to $1,500), Asha stood to collect a sizable donation. At another level, because the pageant was devoted to celebrating the accomplishments of immigrants in America, developmental initiatives in India merited little attention and even less acclaim. Ultimately Asha's fund-raising efforts at Miss India USA were of no avail. Given that the evening's proceedings ran two hours overtime, and that the ballroom rental and catering costs at the Fairmont Hotel exceeded sponsored budgets, the pageant in fact lost money—in excess of $23,000. Asha ultimately did not receive a penny.[16]

The pageant's failure as a charity event draws our attention to the ways in which Miss India USA is organized by competing rhetorics of nationalism. Because small-business owners and entrepreneurs sponsor the event, the pageant reflects the domestic (U.S.-based) capital investments of an emerging immigrant group. This community of South Asians extols its educational and economic achievements and represents itself as model U.S. citizens. However, this same group of immigrants is also incorporated into the neoliberal project of the modern Indian state, principally as a source of foreign investment. Asha's effort to raise funds for educational development in India was premised on the assumption that the audience was composed of NRIs, who are defined as diasporic subjects of the Indian state. Yet these diasporic subjects were also ethnic minorities who embodied and reproduced aspirational narratives of class, culture, and capital mobility in the United States. For Indian government officials who were guests at the pageant, Miss India USA was therefore an extraordinarily dislocating event. When Consul General R. M. Abhyankar was invited to give a speech onstage, he wryly noted, "Frankly, I'm wondering what I'm doing here." As such, the financial orientation as well as the fiscal rhetoric of Miss India USA is situated at the intersection of postcolonial projects of Indian nationhood and the multicultural demands of the U.S. state.

The complex negotiation of multiple national localities is evident not only in the organizational framework of the pageant but also in the contestants' performances. Specifically, the talent show and question-and-answer segments of the pageant showcase the ways in which the contestants embody and articulate diverse relationships of national belonging. In her study of the Miss America pageant, Sarah Banet-Weiser argues that the talent show and question-and-answer segments—which, as the most generic components of the pageant, are frequently overlooked—in fact highlight the agentive capacity of the contestants. As "the sole space and time within the pageant where the contestant makes an autonomous (in a manner of speaking) decision about her performance," the talent show and question-and-answer segments are central to understanding the diasporic localities of Miss India USA.[17] Whereas the talent show demonstrates how Hindi film songs and dances dominate the performative rhetoric of Indian national identity, the question-and-answer session highlights how contestants embody multicultural notions of citizenship as Americans.

For the pageant organizers, the talent show was a conduit for demonstrating how first-generation immigrants successfully cultivate cultural allegiance to India among second-generation youth. In his opening remarks, Rahul Roy, president of the Federation of Indian Americans, noted, "younger people are our future." Likewise Harish Panchal, a member of the executive organizing committee, downplayed the focus on physical attributes at the pageant by emphasizing its cultural value. He proclaimed that the "beauty pageant is not only for promoting beauty, but also promoting the talents, the personality, that our young girls have. It is also to promote, recognize, to build the self-esteem, to build the self-confidence for young women." Despite Panchal's emphasis on character building, the scoring method at the pageant is heavily weighted toward the physical attributes rather than the talents and personality of the contestants. According to the chief pageant organizer,

Amar Walia, the evening gown segment counts for 40 percent, the traditional wear segment for another 40 percent, and the talent show for a mere 20 percent, with the question-and-answer segment officially unscored. Although the talent show counts minimally toward the official score, these series of brief performances illuminate how "Indian culture" is produced through the sexualized bodies of young women, specifically through their embodiment of popular idioms of South Asian femininity.

Of the fifteen contestants at Miss India USA 1999, three were Kuchipudi dancers, trained in the South Indian dance tradition; eight danced to Hindi film songs; one danced to a Hindu devotional hymn; another played a Hindi film song on her flute; one contestant enacted a dramatic monologue from a Hindi movie; and yet another contestant was a brown belt in karate, who chopped planks of wood. Other than the classical dances and the martial arts performance, therefore, ten contestants performed dance, music, or monologues that explicitly referenced popular Hindi cinema. In *Beyond Bollywood*, Jigna Desai argues that these films are a primary site for "familiarity and intimacy" in diaspora (109). Notions of romance, family, and homeland that structure commercial Hindi movies are "central to thinking through pleasure and power and how they affect [diasporic] subjectivity" (112). Clearly, the power and pleasure that Bollywood films afford are critical not only to evaluating the contestants' performances, but also to understanding the audience's appreciation of their talent. Throughout the talent show, renditions of Bollywood film songs and dances were greeted with wild cheers, as young men climbed onto the tables, yelling their devotion to the contestants. Beaming parents and siblings ran frantically around the runway taking photographs, often standing in front of the official videographer for the event. As an ideology of national belonging, the performative capacities of Bollywood film engender nostalgic desire and pleasure in diaspora. Yet the performance of song and dance by diasporic subjects is also implicated in contemporary debates around religious, ethnic, and linguistic identity in India. Although Bollywood films circulate widely among diasporic communities overseas, the most popular of these films are integral to disseminating official discourses of Indian secularism—a discourse that proves to be particularly problematic in a decade dominated by the rise of the Hindu right.

At the pageant that I attended, Chitra Khanvilkar, Miss India Northern California, chose to enact a dramatic monologue against communal violence.

She performed in front of a large screen that projected images of rioting Hindus and Muslims from the blockbuster film *Bombay*. Khanvilkar appeared onstage dressed in a simple salwaar kameez with a dupatta over her head, strands of hair lying loose in anguish, a prominent bindi on her forehead. She shouted in Hindi,

> What's going on here? What's all this confusion [*tamasha*] about? Who has created this uproar? Is there anyone who can answer my question? There are so many people here but yet all are quiet. Your unmanliness [*namardangi*], your cowardice will be silent witness to the destruction of your country. [. . .] You are used to living in darkness, in slavery. First you lived as slaves of kings, then of the British, and now of some treacherous politicians.
> [Wild applause from the audience.]
> You are cutting each other's throats. Even the creator must be ashamed watching from above. The creator has created the most beautiful beings—humans, humans! But looking down upon us, we have become worms [. . .] Why isn't anyone saying anything? What do you think? Who has created this wall that's between you?
> I am a Hindu. I am a Muslim. What's the difference between us? This one prays to Ram, and that one to Allah. [Brief recitation of invocatory verses in Arabic and Sanskrit.] In which book is it written that you should make your fellow humans bleed? In which book does it say this? In the Gita or the Koran? In these books it is written that you should be a good human, but we have become demons!
> But there is still time to think. To understand. To act on these scriptures. Or else our country, which is a symbol of peace in this world, will become a sea of blood. Save this country of mine. Save this country of mine and put out these flames of animosity. Long Live India! [*Jai Hind!*][18]

Directing her tirade toward Hindu-Muslim riots in India, Khanvilkar chastised the onlookers for their apathy toward the everyday nature of communal violence. She characterized her listeners as belonging to one of two major religious traditions; they are deemed incompetent because of their inability to follow their respective scriptures. If one were to correctly practice religion, Khanvilkar implied, Indian society would naturally cohere through the operation of discrete religious units, which would in turn produce a transcendent and rational vision of the postcolonial Indian state. Central to this vision is the humanist citizen-subject, what Khanvilkar called the "good human." Conversely, those who incorrectly practice their faith shirk their responsibility as national citizens: they are described as "unmanly," or emasculated, cowards. As Khanvilkar, noticeably marked onstage as Hindu, recentered God as the ultimate mediator of civil conflict, she emphasized the rupture between the ideology of secularism that informs the postcolonial Indian state (which maintains "equal respect for all faiths") and the very public mobilization of religious identities in contemporary Indian politics.

Khanvilkar's plea for religious harmony replicated notions of religious pluralism that are established in the Indian constitution. The 1947 constitution, which defines the Republic of India as a secular and socialist state, maintains a principle of "Sarva Dharma Sambhava," often translated as "equal respect for all faiths." The term refers to the often-cited fact that the Indian subcontinent is the birthplace for four major religions (Hinduism, Buddhism, Jainism, and Sikhism), while Christianity, Judaism, Islam, and Zoroastrianism have flourished in India since the first millennium. As a principle of pluralist diversity, "Sarva Dharma Sambhava" implies that individual and private practices of diverse religious faiths should cohere harmoniously in the public sphere. The important distinction here is between religious tolerance and religious harmony. From a secular-nationalist standpoint, the notion of religious "tolerance" emphasizes the fact that there is one majority religion (Hinduism, which is the practice of over 80 percent of the Indian population) and relegates other religious groups to minority status (even though Indian Muslims, at 12 percent of the population, are numerically among the largest Muslim populations in the world). In contrast, religious "harmony" engenders an idealized notion of the national public sphere. To emphasize religious harmony eclipses the fact that many practitioners of minority religions have assimilated their practices and customs to locally dominant religious traditions. By upholding principles of religious harmony, the Indian state obscures relations of power between majority and minority religious groups. Further, the constitutional recognition of equality across religions does not translate into legal equality for all religious groups.[19] The problem with pluralist slogans like "Sarva Dharma Sambhava" is that such nationalist ideologies do not recognize the difference between majority and minority religions in India, or the unequal relations of power that shape everyday life between Hindus and Muslims, between Muslims and Sikhs, and between Hindus and Christians in South Asia.[20]

Khanvilkar's plea for religious harmony reinstated the hegemony of Hindu nationalism in contemporary India and its diasporas. She performed her speech against a backdrop of images taken from the film *Bombay*, directed by the Tamil filmmaker Mani Ratnam. Released three years after the destruction by Hindu nationalists of a mosque known as the Babri Masjid in the north Indian city of Ayodhya, the film chronicles the Hindu-Muslim riots that subsequently occurred in Bombay (now Mumbai). *Bombay* situates the riots as the backdrop to a fictional love story about Shekhar and Sheila Bano, a Hindu man and Muslim woman from the southern Indian state of Tamil Nadu. Unable to gain acceptance from their families, Shekhar and Shaila Bano migrate to Bombay to consummate their relationship through marriage. The couple have twin sons, whose names (Kamal Bashir and Kabeer Narayan) reflect the religious syncretism of their family heritage. Shekhar, a news reporter, begins to investigate the destruction of the Babri Masjid; he and Shaila Bano are separated from their children in the communal riots in Bombay that follow. The film, a commercial success, has been critiqued for its romanticization of communal violence through a sentimental focus on Shekhar, Shaila Bano, and their children, whose reunification at the end of the film secures the trope of the Indian national family.

At Miss India USA, Khanvilkar's performance against the backdrop of images from *Bombay* garnered tremendous applause. However, her dialogue, uncredited during her performance, was in fact adapted from another Hindi film, *Krantiveer* ("The Heroic Revolutionary"). While *Bombay* produces its version of communal harmony through the love story between Shekhar and Shaila Bano, *Krantiveer* is a popular action film of an entirely different genre. Released in 1994, *Krantiveer* is the story of Pratap, the grandson of a Gandhian nationalist who grows up to become a rent collector for a slumlord in Bombay. Embodying the prototype of the vigilante-hero, Pratap rebels against the nexus of real estate property developers and corrupt politicians who engineer communal riots in his basti, or slum, emerging victorious against politicians and the upper class.[21] Described as a film that explores "the relationship between capital and the riots in Bombay in 1992," *Krantiveer* makes explicit the links between globalizing capital and local manipulations of democratic government by corrupt politicians in modern India.[22] Pratap's speech, adapted by Khanvilkar, occurs at the climax of the film as he is sentenced to death for killing the property developer, politicians, and local slumlord in a bloody shoot-out. In the film, Pratap stands in front of the gallows, a white noose swaying dramatically behind him as he addresses the large crowd that has come to witness his public execution. Throughout Pratap's delivery, his body erupts in anger: his voice is agitated and harsh, and his arms extend uncontrollably. As Pratap concludes his speech, he grabs the hood from the executioner and prepares to hang himself. At that point he is miraculously granted a reprieve, and the crowd whoops and swarms toward the gallows in adulation of Pratap, signaling the close of the film.

In their synopsis of *Krantiveer*, Ashish Rajadhyaksha and Paul Willemen describe Pratap's speech as "a spine-chilling harangue ostensibly in favour of communal harmony, but in fact directly invoking the language associated with the Shiv Sena leader Bal Thackeray [. . .] its basic message [is] that Pratap's lumpen-brutalism, directly connected with Shiv Sena gangsterism, is the legitimate inheritor of the nationalist freedom struggle" (520). Rajadhyaksha and Willemen emphasize that *Krantiveer* repeatedly endorses an ideology of vigilante violence in the figure of Pratap, whose brutal protection of personal and familial interests mirrors the tactics of the Shiv Sena, the Maharashtrian regional Hindu nationalist party.[23] This representation of the Indian citizen-subject in *Krantiveer* alerts us to the ways in which the film diverges sharply from the melodramatic family romance that is *Bombay*. While *Bombay* seeks to reinstate the secular national family, *Krantiveer* endorses the right-wing ideology of Pratap, whose proclivity for bloodletting is the means through which the national family is secured.

Chitra Khanvilkar's performance onstage drew upon the idiom of both these films. Yet her adaptation of the speech from *Krantiveer* was markedly different from Pratap's delivery. Not only did she amend part of the dialogue (beginning with her question "In which book is it written [. . .]?" until the end of her monologue); she also omitted the diversity of religious groups that Pratap refers to (while he says "I am a Hindu, I am a Muslim, I am a Sikh," Khanvilkar only mentioned Hindus and Muslims). Equally important, Khanvilkar's gendered embodiment of the speech was utterly different from Pratap's performance. If Pratap is the angry young man, his wiry body and close-shaven head the focus of the camera, Khanvilkar's appearance (in white salwaar kameez) was mournful, her body fuller. Although Khanvilkar shouted her speech and pumped her arms vigorously, she could not approximate the didactic, accusatory tone of Pratap's speech. As she rendered Pratap's diatribe against politicians, industrialists, and the Indian state, Khanvilkar performed as the anonymous everywoman, while Pratap remains the iconoclastic revolutionary hero.

At the Miss India USA pageant, what did the refraction between *Bombay* and *Krantiveer* in Khanvilkar's dramatic monologue signify? The ideological confluence between these two cinematic narratives—the romantic narrative of *Bombay*, the vigilante heroism of *Krantiveer*—creates confusion over the location of the "secular" in postcolonial Indian nationalist discourse. While Khanvilkar's adaptation of the speech from *Krantiveer* ostensibly espoused a viewpoint against communal violence, her attempt to mimic Pratap in fact reinforced his masculinist and vigilante subject-position. In so doing, Khanvilkar asserted her own (and Pratap's) visibly Hindu subjectivity as the normative "secular" stance of the modern Indian state. At the same time, Khanvilkar performed against film clips from *Bombay* that depicted alternating images of Muslim and Hindu leaders as if both religious communities were equally responsible for the communal riots in Bombay in 1992 (here it is important to remember that the riots followed the destruction of the Babri Masjid by right-wing Hindu activists). If we are to follow this visual logic of *Bombay*, the postcolonial Indian state emerges as the site of rational modernity, manifest in the reunited body of the national family. The divergent representations of secularism in *Krantiveer* and *Bombay*, therefore, resolve the problem of nationalism differently: in *Krantiveer*, through the endorsement of vigilante violence; in *Bombay*, through the restored unity of the hero's interreligious family. Located between the idioms of these two films, Khanvilkar's attempt to recuperate divergent representations of "secular" nationalism into her own transcendant subject-position as an Indian (note her final cry, "Long Live India!") was untenable.

Khanvilkar's tenuous embodiment of secular nationalism was, in turn, mirrored by audience members, who applauded wildly during and after her performance. The applause highlighted the audience's belief in the responsibility of all Indians to prevent communal riots. This is the visual logic of *Bombay*, which assigns equal culpability to Hindus and Muslims for the 1992 riots and attempts to restore interreligious harmony through reuniting Shekhar and Shaila Bano with their children. However, the audience's participation in Khanvilkar's performance also demonstrated their will to believe in the ideology of *Krantiveer*, a vigilantism that reasserts the primacy of a Hindu-majority nation and the centrality of the working class as the "authentic" national subject. In this depiction of India, there is no place for religious minorities or for diasporic subjects. The audience thus participated in what the media studies scholar Ravi Vasudevan calls the "miscognition" of the narrative logic of *Bombay*, which represents both Hindus and Muslims as equally culpable for the riots. As Vasudevan proceeds to write, "Can it be because the moment of the figuration of equal culpability is also that of the coherence, reparation and renewed legitimation of Indian society in the film?" (51). In *Krantiveer*, that "renewed legitimation" comes in the form of endorsing Pratap's vigilantism, whereas in *Bombay* the legitimation comes in the triumphant form of the benevolent patriarchal state. As the hero of *Bombay* tearfully declares at the climax of the film, "Hum sirf Indian hain" (We are only Indian). Vasudevan suggests that the logic of *Bombay* works toward a "desired identity" that is "always above other identities, and this transcendental situation has a name: 'Indian'" (63). Khanvilkar's embodiment of this transcendental situation, both in her endorsement of God as a mediator of civil conflict, as well as in her final shout of "Long live India!" also attempted to produce a coherent identity as "Indian." Clearly, it was an identity deeply desired by the diasporic audience who participated, through exclamation and loud applause, in her performance.

In my reading of Khanvilkar's performance, the deeper miscognition that occurs is the ruptured ideology of secularism itself, specifically the misrecognition of the place of religious minorities in the postcolonial Indian state.[24] While contestants at the 1999 Miss India USA pageant represented a variety of religious affiliations (including Sikhs, Christians, and Jains, but not Muslims), the participation of the majority of these contestants in the song, dance, and monologues of Hindi film suggests the dominance of a particular ideology of nationalism. As I have suggested, this is a nationalist ideology that engenders confusion about the "secular," or the place of religious faith and practice in the performance of postcolonial nationhood. The two films that Khanvilkar draws upon for her performance prioritize the secular citizen-subject. However, in *Krantiveer* that citizen-subject is Pratap, whose vigilantism echoes the gangsterism of a regional Hindu nationalist party; in *Bombay* the film closes with Shekhar's universal assertion that "I am Indian," but operates through visual imagery that defines Muslims as instigators of communal violence.[25]

Khanvilkar's speech highlights the failure and fragility of secularism as a national project in postcolonial India and at the same time reproduces the dominance of Hindu nationalism in diasporic popular culture. The use of Bollywood film in her performance is "crucial in [. . .] creating a culture of imaginary solidarity across the heterogeneous linguistic and national groups that make up the South Asian (Indian) diaspora."[26] Yet if this is the case, then it is fundamentally important to understand what constitutes a "culture of imaginary solidarity." My reading of Khanvilkar's adaptation of a monologue from *Krantiveer*, set against images from *Bombay*, argues that we must be deeply attentive to the visual, rhetorical, and performative modalities through which the Hindu nationalist subject becomes the subject of secularism in postcolonial India and, via the circulation and consumption of Bollywood film, in South Asian diasporas.

Disidentifying with Multiculturalism

Whereas Khanvilkar's talent show emphasized the "secular" and "Indian" identifications of the pageant contestants and audience members, the question-and-answer segment brought into relief the contestants' locality within the U.S. state. Though the question-and-answer segment is officially unscored, the answers that the finalists provide generate an archetypal "ideal female subject [. . . one who is] intelligent, goal-oriented, independent, feisty, and committed to individualism."[27] This representation of the feminine subject is crucially reliant on liberal ideologies of selfhood, particularly liberal-feminist notions of the agentive subject. The production of an agentive self at a pageant that values the production of a coherent national community, however, is a vexed endeavor, particularly given the paternalistic format of the question-and-answer session.

At the 1999 Miss India USA contest, Priya Vij, a former beauty queen (Miss India USA 1989), and her husband, Sandeep Vij, hosted the question-and-answer segment. Sandeep was introduced by the organizers as "one of the most successful engineers in Silicon Valley," and Priya was described by her husband as "a practicing dentist, a mother of two children, and the wife of a very happy husband." In a brief speech, Priya chronicled her life history in the decade since she was crowned Miss India USA, central to which was her encounter (at the Stanford University library) with her future husband. By attending an elite institution, marrying within the Indian American community, beginning a family, and pursuing a professional career in dentistry,

Priya Vij epitomized what Rahul Roy described as "younger people [who] are our future." Her presence onstage proved that the measure of a beauty queen's success lies not only in her talent or professional credentials, but also in her value as an exchangeable commodity for marriage and her reproductive capacity to bear a further generation of children. The appearance of Priya and Sandeep Vij onstage underscored the heteronormativity of the pageant, specifically its focus on the family as a primary unit for the reproduction of culture and community. Priya Vij concluded her speech by glowingly describing her reign as Miss India USA as an opportunity to "give something lasting to our motherland"—although where exactly her "motherland" was remained unclear.

Sandeep Vij took over the microphone to host the question-and-answer session as his wife remained on the sidelines. Posing somewhat generic questions to each of the five finalists, he elicited responses from the contestants that largely extolled the virtues of being both Indian and American. However, to Miss India Southern California, Sharan Gill, Vij asked, "If you could change the outcome of any event in history, what would it be and how would you change it?" Given that this was nominally a Miss India pageant, the anticipated answer, perhaps, would concern the 1947 independence of India, or its flip side, the partition of the subcontinent. Yet Gill's response, mediated after some silence, was, "The Vietnam War [. . .] because I really believe that had we shown a little more strength back then, we would be a much stronger country right now."

How can we comprehend the sudden imposition of the Vietnam War at a Miss India USA pageant? In the midst of performing "India" onstage, Gill refers to a historical event that has radically shaped the national consciousness of contemporary America. The Vietnam War is variously narrated as the defeat of American triumphalism or the advancement of communism in East Asia. The war is an embodied memory that was deeply affective for a generation of American youth in the 1960s and 1970s but now largely circulates as a historical event, a subject taught in high school textbooks. However, within Asian American studies the Vietnam War is a flashpoint for the expansion of U.S. imperialism in Southeast Asia. Its aftereffects are multiple: millions of Vietnamese and Cambodians dead, children abandoned or forcibly given up for adoption under Nixon's infamous Operation Babylift, and the immigration of thousands of Vietnamese, Cambodian, and Hmong refugees who resettled across the United States. In her introduction to *Immigrant Acts*, Lisa

Lowe remarks that the Vietnam War is one of several entry points for the racialization of the Asian immigrant subject.[28] How then does Sharan Gill's invocation of the Vietnam War relate to her racialization as an Asian American? Alternatively, how does it signify her incorporation into the (white) American national body, one that was visibly damaged in the domestic and global arenas by losses sustained during the war?

Gill's response is more than just an anxious search for an answer. Her ambivalent use of the plural personal pronoun "we" gestures to many national bodies—Americans, Indians, Vietnamese—that signals her multiple localities. Indeed, Gill's performance can be read as a kind of "positioned performance," a performance that "is constituted and contextualized by power and history [. . .] grounded not only from the vantage of theory, but more importantly, from the actors' point of view and cultural knowledge."[29] Who is the "we" that should have "shown a little more strength," and what kind of strength was Gill referring to? During the Vietnam War, conservative U.S. political discourse called for a display of greater military strength, apparent in Nixon's decision to bomb Cambodia. But among antiwar protestors in the United States, Europe, and across Asia, "strength" was signaled through acts of resistance to the state.[30] Gill's embodied historical memory of the Vietnam War highlights the collective trauma of this national event. It also disrupts the pageant's objective to produce an identifiably "Indian" ethnic and national community overseas. By signaling her ambivalent locality—within the American national body *and* against its imperialist state formation; identifying as an Asian American *and* as part of a majoritarian U.S. public—Sharan Gill embodies a South Asian subjectivity. Although her answer during this segment was solicited in response to an idea of India, Gill's comment was situated within the imperial racial formation of America.

In my view, Gill's response was a mode of disidentification with the pageant and its rhetoric of belonging. In *Disidentifications*, the performance studies scholar José Muñoz defines disidentification as a "hermeneutic, a process of production, and a mode of performance" (25). Muñoz theorizes disidentification in relation to the performance of queers of color, as an analytic that "is meant to be descriptive of the survival strategies the minority subject practices in order to negotiate a phobic majoritarian public sphere that continuously elides or punishes the existence of subjects who do not conform to the phantasm of normative citizenship" (4). At the pageant, the strategic performance of minority subjects like Gill does not fully conform to the "phantasm of normative citizenship" that is disseminated within the U.S. public sphere, nor to the neoliberal models of nationhood advanced by the Indian state. Gill's participation in Miss India USA signals her contractual obligation to identify with multiple dominant constructs of citizenship, evident through her successful completion of several segments (the Indian dress, Western evening gown, and as I discuss below, her dance during the talent show). Yet by using the question-and-answer session to create what Muñoz calls "critical uneasiness" (115) within the ideological structure of the pageant, Gill, through her response, disidentifies with the rhetoric of ethnic belonging promulgated by pageant organizers, and ruptures coherent formations of multicultural citizenship. Her citing of the Vietnam War enables her to negotiate a public sphere that is "phobic" to heterogeneous notions of diasporic locality.

As a means of identifying with and against the state, disidentification also operates to secure the difference of diaspora. For example, in her work on the Queen of the Chinese Colony pageant held in Panama, the anthropologist Lok Siu examines how ethnically Chinese women negotiate their representation of their countries of origin (ranging from Guatemala to Honduras to Costa Rica) with their embodiment of Chinese femininity. Similar to the ubiquitous display of Bollywood dance at the Miss India USA pageant, these performances of "Chinese-ness" are modeled on the songs and fashion of contemporary Hong Kong pop stars. However, alongside these popular performances of Chinese femininity, the contestants are also expected to perform indigenous or Spanish colonial dances that represent their countries of origin. Siu argues that the contestants, lavishly bedecked in national dress, embody forms of racialized difference that cannot be recuperated into dominant discourses of nationhood within their countries of origin. As ethnically Chinese and as mixed-race subjects, they disidentify with frameworks of nationhood in Central America, which often do not account for descendants of Chinese immigrants. However, the contestants' spoken introductions in Spanish, rather than in Cantonese or Mandarin, demonstrate how they also identify with their countries of birth rather than with an abstract, imagined "China" that was promoted at the pageant.

Disidentification thus works powerfully with and alongside processes of identification. At Miss India USA, Sharan Gill's racialized and gendered performance as an appropriately "Indian" and feminine subject is secured through her seamless performance to Bollywood music, itself a transnational commoditization of Indian culture. At the same time Gill's citation of another national history, the history of the Vietnam War, locates her within the racialized parameters of U.S. citizenship. Gill occupies multiple localities: as a minority Asian American subject whose place in the United States is irrevocably shaped by memories of loss in Vietnam; as an American citizen who identifies with imperialist impulses of the U.S. state. But Gill is also South Asian, an immigrant whose ties to the subcontinent and to the United States are triangulated through the failed expansion of the U.S. empire in South and Southeast Asia. The fact that she cannot visibly resolve these contradictory localities emphasizes how South Asian subjectivities cannot be recuperated within assimilationist notions of U.S. citizenship.

Sharan Gill went on to win the 1999 Miss India USA pageant, and her final walk down the runway was greeted with loud cheers. When I asked two audience members why Gill had won, one replied, "Because her name was Sharon [sic]." And another said, "Because she was sexy. She looks like a runway model." My concern here is not to deliberate on the specific reasons for Gill's selection as the winner of the Miss India USA pageant, nor to treat the audience members' comments flippantly. Rather, I am interested in the implications of Gill's response for the embodiment and performance of locality in diaspora. If the winner of Miss India USA is doubly located in the "secular" project of postcolonial India and in the racial formation of America, simultaneously identifying and disidentifying with the rhetoric of national patriotism on both shores, what do Gill's "sexiness" and "modern" name imply? Although the performances that compose Miss India USA demonstrate how South Asian subjectivities are consistently gendered and sexualized, as the titleholder of the pageant Gill also exemplified how to embody two spatially and temporally disparate narratives of national belonging.

Being Miss India: Globalizing Sexuality and Modernity

The success of the Miss India USA pageant, an iconic community event, hinges on the tremendous popularity of Miss India contests in India. Beauty pageants have proliferated in India during the past decade, from neighborhood community events to multimillion-dollar international pageants. The first national Miss India pageant was held in 1958, just over a decade after independence. The contestants were selected as models for the national textile industry, showcasing handloomed saris and promoting India's indigenous textile fabrics. However, in the sixty years since, contestants have gone on to become professional models for multinational corporate advertising campaigns, Bollywood film stars, and media personalities. Their ubiquity in popular culture is yet another effect of Indian neoliberalism, for the success of contestants' careers—and indeed the success of the Miss India pageant itself—is reliant on the sustained growth of private enterprise. From its state-owned origins, the Miss India pageant is now sponsored by a number of media groups and multinational corporations, including the Times of India media group and Unilever.

The privatization of the beauty industry in contemporary India has coincided with the phenomenal success of Indian beauty queens at international competitions since the mid-1990s. Beginning with Sushmita Sen and Aishwariya Rai, who were crowned Miss Universe and Miss World in 1994, and including Lara Dutta, Priyanka Chopra, and Diya Mirza, who swept the international pageant world in 2000 by winning the Miss Universe, Miss World, and Miss Asia-Pacific contests, respectively, former Miss India pageant winners have become household names in India. In turn, the Indian contestant has become a recognized figure in the international pageant world. For many Indians the success of Miss India contestants abroad demonstrates the emergence of a new, "global" India. Rupal Oza has contended that beauty pageants are as much an index of globalization in India as the Indian government's declaration of nuclear capability.[31] As a commoditized representation of Indian nationhood, the glamorous figure of Miss India reflects both the sovereignty of Indian statehood and India's increasing participation in a global market.[32]

The official website for the Miss India pageant proclaims, "In the past years since 1965 when it first began, the Femina Miss India pageant has changed considerably. The focus has shifted from finding the prettiest face in the country to getting a set of girls having the level of finesse and class, required to contend internationally."[33] Since 1992, entry rules for the Miss India pageant have required candidates to be between eighteen and twenty-three years of age, at least five feet six inches tall, and unmarried, childless Indian nationals (including Indian passport holders living overseas). In recent years, the website for the pageant claims to have received thousands of applications. Out of these, three hundred are selected for previewing, and finally twenty finalists are chosen on a nationwide basis.[34] For these twenty finalists, the Times of India group sponsors an intensive six-week-long mandatory training course.[35] The candidates are coached in catwalk, diction, etiquette, and diet: as one anthropologist notes, "Young women enter the pageant fully expecting to change not only their bodies but also to emerge several months later as fundamentally altered human beings."[36] At the Miss India pageant, the professionalization of the contestants in terms of appearance, clothing, and diction eclipses markers of regional difference. The young women are announced onstage only by their first names, eliminating the possibility of guessing a contestant's regional, caste, or religious background through their surnames.

In her remarks on the Miss India pageant, the feminist historian Kumkum Sangari contends that the popularization of the beauty pageant at local, district, and state levels was synchronous with the opening of Indian markets to imported consumer products. She analyzes Indian beauty pageants as transnational productions, which recycle and subvert old nationalist ideologies for a new regrouping of patriarchies in a new global order. In this context Miss India contestants must demonstrate "double competency" by consuming both domestic and international products (evident in the multinational product endorsements received by winning contestants). In so doing, the beauty queen becomes a nationally as well as an internationally valued commodity. Because the pageant is a primary site for advertising consumer goods, the increasingly elaborate staging of the Miss India contest is instrumental to the expansion of a consumer-oriented Indian middle class. At the same time, the disciplined appetite of the Miss India contestants (both literally in terms of their underweight physique, and rhetorically through their controlled sexuality) is central to the reproduction of patriarchal and nationalist ideals of Indian womanhood. As such, the gendered figure of the Miss India pageant embodies what Sangari calls both "a classic India and a global modern."

In contrast to the steady decline in U.S. viewership for the Miss America and Miss Universe pageants, Miss India pageant winners receive prominent national media coverage in India. Along with the first two runner-ups to the pageant, Miss India competes in a variety of international pageants (such as Miss Universe, Miss World, Miss Earth) that have recently been staged in developing countries and territories including Vietnam, Cyprus, and Puerto Rico. While the standards of beauty propagated at the Miss India pageant continue to adhere to what might be called a metropolitan norm (the ideal candidate is tall and thin, has fair skin and high cheekbones), the globalization of the beauty pageant has resulted in a distinct remove from the metropolitan center. As the beauty pageant becomes an event that is locally comprehensible in India, and as the winner of the Miss India contest is transported globally, international beauty pageants are brought closer to home. Thus in 1996 the Miss World pageant was hosted, amid vigorous protests from leftist feminist and Hindu nationalist groups, in Bangalore.[37] The Miss India pageant is situated at the intersection of market reforms initiated by the Indian state that are conducive to a globalized idea of India, and the third world–ization of the pageant industry itself.

The production of the "global modern" at the Miss India pageant is also deeply vested in discourses of sexuality that shape the Indian middle class. As Vimla Patil, a former editor of *Femina*, the women's magazine that co-sponsors the pageant, comments:

> You have to agree that the reason why the Miss India contest is so prominent today [is that] not once was there any scandal about this contest. No girl has ever said she was used badly, or was exploited or was made to go to bed with a judge. To my knowledge, no girl has ever been asked to do what a decent girl ought not to do [. . .] It [the pageant] had total respectability, acceptability, and convinced parents [. . .] People have even accused me of promoting the middle-class, but what's wrong with that? It is the middle class that's making this country. It is the middle-class woman who makes her own money and changes the destiny of her children.[38]

The simultaneous censorship of young women's sexuality, alongside the promotion of the middle class as evidence of the "success" of the Femina Miss India pageant, illustrates the contradiction—indeed, the conflation—between ideologies of sexuality, class, and modernity in postcolonial India. Central to this notion of modernity is the figure of the middle-class woman, who is represented in mainstream visual culture as both a "consuming subject" and in terms of her "sexualisation as an actively desiring subject."[39]

The Miss India USA pageant is also situated within this conjuncture of sexuality, modernity, and globalization. While the winners of Miss India USA and Miss India do not overlap in terms of their participation in international competitions, Dharmatma Saran, founder of Miss India USA, is affiliated with the national pageant industry in India. Saran's official relationship with Miss India and Miss India USA establishes a certain consistency, if not coherence, between the representational form as well as the rhetorical organization of the two pageants. Both competitions are structured by overlapping ideologies of gender and sexuality, which in this case circulate between national and diasporic sites of consumption. Given the eminently exportable figure of the Indian beauty queen, the winner of Miss India USA re-inflects what it means to be a "global modern." Like the Indian beauty queen who demonstrates "double competency," the winner of Miss India USA also has a doubled resonance. She is at once implicated in a traditional-yet-modern idea of India *and* shaped by contemporary discourses of race and class in the United States. Her location in both sites relies upon circumscribed notions of femininity and sexuality.

In an online interview discussing the Miss India USA pageant, Saran states, "We will never permit vulgarity and bikini wearing in our competitions [. . .] we don't believe in the axiom [that the] shorter the dress, [the] greater will be the chances of winning the prize. We are very conservative in that. We only showcase the best of Indian culture and not the skin. We strongly oppose exhibiting women in a cheap manner on the dais."[40] Saran's refusal to exhibit female sexuality onstage reinforces the value of Miss India USA as a middle-class event. "Indian culture" is reflected in the contestants' performances, rather than the exhibition of their skin; the community rallies against the "cheap" display of women and paternalistically protects her modesty through the "conservative" nature of the pageant. Yet while the organizers attempt to preserve notions of feminine modesty, at the pageant that I attended the performances by female contestants and models onstage were explicitly sexual. During the course of the evening, fashion models representing local Indian clothing companies sashayed down the runway in low-waisted skirts and backless blouses. Their sinuous moves were choreographed to the latest Hindi film songs, eliciting roars of approval from the young men in the ballroom. Similarly, some of the most popular talent show performances were by those contestants who danced to contemporary Hindi film songs. Their performance mimicked popular cinema heroines, and their clothing accentuated the movements of their breasts, hips, waists, and thighs. However, the contestants' particular versions of performing femininity onstage were more or less coded in a form of sexual expression sanctioned by Bollywood film, itself generally approved as a form of middle-class family entertainment. Moreover, given that the entire pageant took place as a community gathering and charity fund-raiser, the hoots and hollers that contestants and models elicited from the audience were condoned as an indication of family entertainment. Saran's denial of sexuality as a trope within the beauty pageant is thus contradicted by the pageant itself, for the pageant-as-entertainment succeeds only through the performance of middle-class sexuality.

The ways in which contestants' bodies are disciplined by patriarchal norms of behavior are evident not only in their renditions of Hindi film songs but also by the eager consumption of these performances by various members of the audience. However, equally important to our understanding of the pageant are the ways in which these same norms of "respectable" behavior elicit so-called "modest" performances of sexuality. The anthropologist Malathi de Alwis writes of her experience serving as a judge for a beauty contest in Sri Lanka, where the winner was evaluated not only by the appropriateness of her attire, but also by her walk or gait. As de Alwis notes, the traditional attire of the young women—which itself stands for and constitutes a dominant notion of Sinhala-ness—operates only in relation to an "aesthetic of movement" that is embodied by the contestant. The winner, she writes, "was the woman who most successfully produced her sexuality in the movement of her body, 'not openly and blatantly, but shyly, as if embarrassed but also excited by its very production.'" Like the proliferation of Bollywood song and dance performances, de Alwis informs us, this "fraught aesthetic of 'respectability,' sensual yet submissive, is particularly well represented and valorized in the Sinhala cinema" (186–87).

At the 1999 Miss India USA pageant, the talent show performance by the winning candidate, Sharan Gill, reflected both the importance of so-called "traditional" attire and the life given to this attire through a particular aesthetic of movement. Gill's performance during the talent show was a slow and sensual folk dance to a popular Hindi film song. She appeared onstage clothed in a low-waisted long skirt and a short embroidered blouse, her head and eyes partially covered by a veil, and her midriff fully bared. Gill's consistent awareness of her bodily impact on the audience, her measured stance on the catwalk, her bashful but seductive eye movement, garnered whoops and loud cheers from the audience. Along with her subsequent response during the question-and-answer session, Gill's embodiment of a "traditional-but-modern" figure of Indian womanhood during the talent show ultimately won her the crown.

The dissonance between the rhetoric of family entertainment that structures the format of Miss India USA and the sexualized performances that characterize its content illustrates the contradiction between notions of sexuality and modernity that circulate at the pageant. Despite the organizers' repeated insistence that the beauty pageant was not about the sexualization of the female body, the contest itself was won by a young woman who had performed a highly recognizable form of popular Indian female sexuality, coded in the language of Bollywood film. Against the ongoing production of India as a global modern on the world stage, the Miss India USA beauty pageant attempts to secure a middle ground between the production of "tradition" and "modernity," particularly as this is enunciated through the sexualized bodies of young women. Although the Miss India USA pageant aspires toward the construction of a cogent ethnic and national community, this idealized vision of community is ruptured by the performances of the young women onstage. Indeed, the pageant can only be recuperated as a community event through its marketing as a form of mass entertainment.

The Futures of Miss India USA

As the judges tallied the scores late into the night at the Miss India USA pageant, winners from previous contests came onstage to entertain the audience. The emcee for the final segment of the show was Teju Patel, Mr. India Los Angeles 1998.[41] Close to midnight, Patel addressed a weary audience: "We are here to pervert—excuse me, to *preserve*—our culture." With a slip of the tongue, Patel inadvertently emphasized how Miss India USA is a site for cultural preservation *and* perversion. I take up this slippery meaning of pageantry to understand how Miss India USA impacts our understanding of South Asian localities in the United States.

As the first and only national pageant organized by the IFC in San Jose, the 1999 Miss India USA pageant was critical to consolidating an emerging middle-class narrative of South Asian immigration to the West Coast. As I have discussed, the nexus of class and capital mobility in Silicon Valley at the turn of the twenty-first century generated a narrative of South Asian immigration that is distinct from the post-1965 migration of scientists and engineers. The pageant organizers emphasized the achievements and wealth of entrepreneurs in the high-tech industry, even though pageant sponsors were mainly local small businesses that were not related to the "dot-com" boom. Nevertheless, the organizers projected a story of upward mobility, one that eclipsed the longer history of working-class South Asian immigration to the region. Throughout the twentieth century, South Asians in northern California have inhabited complex racial identities: as "Hindus" and "Mexican Punjabis," as H-1B workers as well as the more recent phenomenon of high-tech "body shopping." These heterogeneous legal and popular representations of South Asians were reconsolidated into a singular history of middle-class migration: a narrative of "success" that was widely disseminated at the pageant as the only available experience of immigration.

Such stories of class mobility travel from the United States to India, for both countries are linked through the circulation of neoliberal ideologies of capital and citizenship at the turn of this century. Whereas in Silicon Valley the exceptional conditions of class mobility generated new racial economies for Asian Americans and South Asians in particular, in India a rapid series of neoliberal economic reforms produced an expansive and powerful middle class. Likewise, the powerful effects of pluralist ideologies of U.S. multiculturalism, which purportedly reflect the ethnic diversity of the national body, are bound at the pageant to notions of secular nationhood in contemporary India. The problem with this rhetorical linkage, however tenuous it may be, is that both projects of nationhood fail to secure universal notions of citizenship. In the United States, multiculturalism operates actively to produce ethnic and racial difference, rather than simply reflecting diversity. Similarly in India, popular notions of "secularism" do not simply illustrate the ethnic, religious, and linguistic diversity of national body; instead such ideologies of nationhood can be mobilized to consolidate right-wing Hindu political and religious practice. Yet in both India and the United States, middle-class urban publics identify themselves through a shared vocabulary of citizenship: as diverse, secular, and modern subjects. This is the rhetoric of citizenship that is discordantly embodied by the pageant contestants, organizers, and audience members.

For the young contestants, the challenge is to identify the convergence between two distinct rhetorics of national belonging. On the one hand, pageant participants identify as NRIs who are integral to the project of Indian modernity. For contestants like Chitra Khanvilkar, as for many others, the performative idiom of Bollywood film becomes central to establishing a nostalgic relationship between the Indian state and its diasporas. Khanvilkar's monologue and the audience's appreciation of her performance collude in their aspiration toward a transcendent "Indian" identity, sanctioned by the postcolonial state. However, this idea of India is crucially reliant upon Khanvilkar's embodiment of a Hindu nationalist subjectivity that consistently frames the Muslim as other. The transnational circulation of Bollywood film as a popular medium of imagining community enables the complicit participation of middle-class immigrant subjects in reproducing ideologies of Hindu nationalism. These performances of popular culture critically suture the ethnic politics of diasporic communities with religious and caste politics in modern India.

As Sharan Gill reminds us, however, notions of national belonging are constantly negotiated in diaspora. While Gill's sensual dance during the talent show underscored her complicity with popular representations of Indian femininity, her unexpected response during the question-and-answer session ruptured hegemonic notions of Indian "culture" and "tradition." Gill's apparent alignment with a majoritarian national public, and its memory of the Vietnam War, engendered her vexed locality as South Asian. Her disidentification with the rhetoric of ethnic pageantry despite winning the title crown illustrates the paradox of multiculturalism. For minority subjects, the allure of liberal multiculturalism is its promise of full citizenship. Yet embodying such universalist notions of citizenship requires minority subjects to identify with a homeland outside the United States in order to make visible their ethnic difference. In turn, their embodiment of spatial, racial, and temporal difference undermines their naturalized claim to citizenship. In contrast to such discourses of multicultural citizenship, Gill identifies with a nationalist history of America, specifically the history of U.S. military intervention in Vietnam. Our inability to fix Gill's stance for or against the war requires us to move beyond representing her as either a resistant Asian American subject or as an assimilated American citizen. Her South Asian locality illustrates how, for many subcontinental immigrants, belonging to America is delineated through a prior history of U.S. imperialism in Asia. Along with her winning dance performance, Gill highlights the convergence between ideologies of multicultural citizenship and postcolonial nationhood at the pageant. Performance is thus a central modality through which we can see how ethnic identity, as Stuart Hall writes, is always "in process," and equally important, how the histories that come to support what he calls "new ethnicities" are in a constant process of becoming.⁴²

Although the Miss India USA pageant purports to be a community event, it routinely meets with several forms of dissent within local South Asian communities. Given that participation in the pageant is limited to persons of "Indian origin," those who self-identify as Pakistani, Bangladeshi, or Sri Lankan are excluded. However, multiracial contestants routinely participate in the event, as do South Asians whose parents come from other diasporic locations (the Caribbean, East Africa, and Asia). What it means to be "Indian" at the pageant, therefore, relies upon somewhat ambiguous notions of national origin. Moreover, even within local Indian communities in the San Francisco Bay area, the pageant is hardly representative of the diversity of linguistic and ethnic groups. One South Indian Tamil-speaking woman whom I spoke to after the pageant remarked, "You know, these things are for North Indian girls—Gujaratis, Punjabis. Our South Indian girls don't go for them." Notwithstanding the fact that there were South Indian contestants onstage (and that South Indians have won the pageant in recent years), the organizational rhetoric of the Miss India USA pageant reinforces an idea of India that is "North Indian," Hindu, and Hindi-speaking. Likewise, though Muslim, Christian, and Sikh women consistently participate in the pageant, no Muslim contestant has won the title since the pageant began in 1981. However, the pageant sporadically crowns Christian and Sikhs as beauty queens: Sharan Gill, a Sikh, is one such example.

In the decade since I attended Miss India USA in San Jose, the contest has continued to thrive on the East Coast. It has also been the site of other unexpected performative acts. In 2004 Kashish Chopra, Miss India New England and runner-up to the 2003 Miss India USA pageant, publicly came out as lesbian. Chopra told fellow contestants of her sexuality during rehearsals for the pageant and was subsequently profiled in several online gay and lesbian publications. As she noted in an early interview, her participation in Miss India USA makes her "a little more visible in the [Indian] community. Perhaps it makes my role as an Indian lesbian somehow more important." However, in the same article Dharmatma Saran downplays the importance of Chopra's coming out, remarking that "we have one [lesbian] every year. It's their choice. Nobody has complained to us."⁴³ Following her participation in the pageant Chopra worked as a public speaker, lecturing to South Asian and queer student groups across the country. In her public presentations Chopra consistently reiterated a middle-class narrative of immigration and identified strongly with her Punjabi background. In another interview she remarked, "Little do my parents know that I want to marry someone who is Indian, someone who is a professional, someone with the same family values. I want everything that they would have wanted for me but in a woman."[44] By staging her sexuality through the medium of pageantry, Chopra embodies a patriotic rhetoric of nationhood and upward class mobility that is articulated through the public performance of lesbianism.

At an international level, Miss India USA continues to be affiliated with beauty pageants organized by South Asian diasporic communities in Europe and elsewhere in North America. The winner of Miss India USA proceeds to the Miss India Worldwide contest, which is also organized by the India Festival Committee and presided over by Dharmatma Saran. The Miss India Worldwide contest replicates the format of Miss India USA but with one major exception. Instead of state-level contestants representing various regions in the United States, at Miss India Worldwide the contestants are third- and fourth-generation South Asians from the Netherlands, Singapore, New Zealand, Suriname, Guyana, and so on. The pageant is also held in a range of international locations, including India. However, since 1990 the most frequent winners of Miss India Worldwide have been either Miss India USA or Miss India from India.[45] Thus while Miss India Worldwide explicitly affirms the diasporic localities of South Asians, it also underscores the hegemony of so-called "authentic" notions of Indian nationhood and upwardly mobile notions of multicultural citizenship.

As a multivalent site of performance, the Miss India USA pageant is meaningful in distinct ways for organizers, audience members, and contestants. For the organizers, the pageant reproduces narratives of upward class mobility that underscore the contractual economic relationship between (model) minority subjects and the U.S. state, as well as between NRIs and the postcolonial Indian state. For audience members, including myself, the pageant is a spectacle of national belonging constituted through the glamour of song, dance, and performance. The fact that some audience members are fully engaged with the exuberant display of nationhood onstage, whereas others remain aloof, underscores the creative dissonances that mark the production of South Asian locality. For the contestants, the pageant is a rare opportunity to shine onstage, as close to a mainstream beauty contest as many will come. However, the pageant ultimately produces only one crown, held on to for only one year. For most contestants the pageant is a brief moment of public adulation, after which they retire into obscurity. Miss India USA represents the doubled specter of nationalism: she is a figure integral to a "secular" narrative of the Indian state, and an ethnic subject disciplined into the multicultural body of the United States.

In Chapter 4 I move from community pageants organized by first-generation Indian immigrants to art festivals organized by second-generation South Asians. These festivals are also celebrations of South Asian diasporic culture and community. Yet for the organizers of the art festivals, such events are central to redefining South Asians as a progressive, rather than conservative and mainstream, immigrant group. In contrast to the Miss India USA pageant, the art festivals deliberately solicit and display a diversely constituted South Asian identity. Those who attend and participate in these festivals also tend to identify as South Asian, rather than as Indian or American. Moving ahead one decade from the late 1990s to the early twenty-first century, I examine how second-generation South Asians collectively produce anti-assimilationist narratives of locality through art and performance. To what extent these strategies of cultural resistance comply with or resist pluralist ideologies of American multiculturalism is the subject of the following chapter.

FOUR

The Art of Multiculturalism
Diasporadics, Desh Pardesh, and Artwallah

At Diasporadics, a South Asian art festival held in New York City in 2000, the Seattle-based artist Ameen Gill (now Ameen Dhillon), a fourth-generation Sikh Canadian, displayed selections from her lithographic installation *The Mango Tree*. Gill's lithographs detail the long and turbulent history of her family's immigration to North America. Six panels of turban cloth are printed with portrait photographs of the artist's great-grandfather, grandfather, and father, who traveled from undivided Punjab to Mexico, Cuba, Canada, and the United States in the early twentieth century. These panels are interspersed with photolithographic prints of family members who were left behind: wives and daughters who never came to the Americas, and the sons who followed in their father's footsteps. *The Mango Tree* showcases a globalizing market for labor, binding together colonial land reforms in the Punjab with the agricultural industries of central California and the lumberyards of British Columbia. Gill draws lines of similarity and difference between Canada and India, both subjects of the British empire; between Mexico and the United States, whose borders are fluid and porous; and between Cuba and Mexico, shared destinations of political and economic revolution. As a multigenerational narrative, Gill's lithographs also enlarge the historical scale and geographical scope of South Asians in the Americas. Displayed on eight-foot-tall panels against the back wall of the exhibition hall, *The Mango Tree* encouraged collective viewing and, in turn, facilitated a shared experience of identification for the viewers.

At Diasporadics, *The Mango Tree* generated a sense of locality that "expresses itself in certain kinds of agency, sociality, and reproducibility."[1] For Gill, creating *The Mango Tree* was an agentive act, one that enabled her to come to terms with a complex patrilineal genealogy of immigration. The lithographs did not simply recuperate a lost archive of family photographs; Gill also reframed these prints by contextualizing them within transcripts of oral interviews that she had conducted with her relatives. For the young South Asians who gathered around the installation at Diasporadics, *The Mango Tree* was critical to producing a shared experience of sociality, as viewers identified—in whole or in part—with the long century of immigration captured by the portrait photographs. In turn, the collective social experience of viewing Gill's work was reproduced across time and space, as *The Mango Tree* traveled to multiple art festivals over a two-year period. After Diasporadics, *The Mango Tree* was selected for display at another South Asian art festival called Artwallah, held in Los Angeles. There too, viewers intensely identified with the visual and oral narratives of *The Mango Tree*, despite their own disparate national, linguistic, and religious backgrounds. At both Diasporadics and Artwallah, the experience of viewing *The Mango Tree* generated a notion of locality that was expressed not in relation to the history and cultural politics of the subcontinent, but in relation to a shared experience of belonging to the United States.

In this chapter I explore the relationship between the aesthetics and politics of South Asian locality at art festivals organized by second-generation immigrants. As a format for community gatherings, the South Asian art festivals that I discuss differ significantly from cultural programming offered by first-generation immigrant communities. Such cultural programs, sponsored by nonprofit religious, regional, and national associations, commemorate religious holidays and independence days and function as fund-raisers for charity organizations on the subcontinent. Often these cultural programs highlight performances by visiting classical and popular artists and serve to maintain the linguistic, ethnic, and religious boundaries that divide nations on the subcontinent.[2]

By contrast, the three art festivals that I examine were annual cultural events organized by second-generation South Asians for South Asian immigrants, rather than for a mainstream public. These festivals include Desh Pardesh, held in Toronto between 1989 and 1999; Diasporadics, which was organized in New York between 2000 and 2002; and Artwallah, which was held in Los Angeles between 2000 and 2010. All three festivals facilitated the display of art by emerging South Asian artists (including visual and performance art, spoken word, dance, and theater), the consumption of art by young South Asian viewers, and the circulation of artworks across festival sites. At the same time, the art festivals also operated as dense social networks between South Asian activists in Canada and the United States, as well as between progressive South Asian groups on the East and West coasts. Like the beauty pageants I discuss in Chapter 3, the art festivals are sites of display for notions of nationhood, ethnicity, gender, and sexuality. Yet unlike the organizational politics of Miss India USA, the art festivals function as venues for progressive activism, which the organizers define as antiracist, antisexist, and queer politics.

These art festivals reached their peak in terms of funding and audience participation between 1999 and 2005 and preceded the current proliferation of private venues for the display and consumption of South Asian art.[3] Each festival was initially funded through public grants at the state and federal levels, although over the course of ten years the organizing committees came to rely increasingly on private corporate and donor funding. Indeed, the decline in public funding for the arts was directly responsible for the closure of each festival. Desh Pardesh closed its doors in 2000, Diasporadics in 2002, and Artwallah in 2010.[4] However, all three festivals are historically significant because they provided a format for the exhibition and display of art that continues to inform smaller venues of South Asian diasporic artistic production today. The festivals are also distinguished by the ways in which organizers and audience members garnered public funding and private investment, solicited artwork by emerging and established artists, and showcased visual and performance art by diasporic artists from North America, Europe, Africa, and the Caribbean. Some of the visual artists who were first exhibited at Desh Pardesh and Artwallah have now become major figures in the art world, exhibiting their work in museums and galleries across the United States and Europe, as well as in India, Pakistan, and Bangladesh. Bringing together activists, educators, and artists, the art festivals enable us to examine discourses of immigration and identity outside the academy.

The ways in which locality is embodied by festival organizers and participants as an affective experience of belonging highlights how the art festivals operate as ethnographic, historical, and performative texts. As ethnographic texts, the festivals map a dynamic social field of primarily second-generation immigrants who self-identify as "progressive" and as "South Asian." For these immigrants, the festivals were a unique opportunity to create political networks across Canada and the United States that enabled the sharing of racial, sexual, and gendered experiences of what it means to be South Asian. As an ethnographer, I attended and participated in Desh Pardesh 1999 in Toronto, Diasporadics 2000 in New York City, and Artwallah 2001, 2002, and 2005 in Los Angeles. At each festival I interviewed organizers, artists, and other attendees, following up with participants after a gap of two to three years. By contributing my field notes and initial observations on the festivals to South Asian community newsmagazines, I also engaged in conversation with organizers who disagreed with my critique of the art festivals.[5] Nonetheless, my continued engagement (as an audience member, and later as a friend of the artists) demonstrates how the art festivals engender a compelling narrative of racial and political community.

Second, as an archive of South Asian cultural politics at the turn of the twenty-first century, the festivals can also be read as historical texts. The historical narratives engendered at the festivals were multiple and contradictory, drawing on disparate sources and points of origin. Many visual and performance artists drew upon personal memories of the subcontinent, as well as autobiographical experiences of immigration to the United States. However, because these festivals were, first and foremost, a celebration of immigrant experience, those artists whose works primarily addressed caste, religious, or class politics on the subcontinent were marginalized from the festivals' effort to create South Asian identities in diaspora. That is, the festivals were central to establishing a temporal difference between a history of South Asia and a history of South Asians in North America. These different registers of "South Asia"—as a place of cultural origin, as a racialized term of belonging, and as a geopolitical construct—became points of entry as I created an archive of festival materials including flyers, pamphlets, websites, and press kits. As I shared these artifacts with friends and colleagues in subsequent years, these fraying documents constituted a nostalgic memory of what it meant to be young, progressive, and South Asian. Yet a critical ethnographic reading of the art festivals, in relation to these archival objects, demonstrates how both organizers and participants embodied notions of progressive political community that were routinely disassociated from anticommunal and working-class politics in South Asia.

Finally, I read the art festivals as performative texts. Through close readings of installations, films, and visual art that circulated across East and West coasts and between the United States and Canada, I explore how the art festivals came to stand for "the" South Asian experience. The social field of artistic production and consumption at the festivals generated homogeneous notions of belonging, despite the heterogeneous religious, national, and class backgrounds of artists, organizers, and audience members. For those artists who display their work at such festivals, as well as for the viewers who eagerly consume these artworks, being South Asian is simultaneously a private experience and a public feeling, an affect of belonging that is generated in the company of other subcontinental immigrants. Such individual narratives of ethnic belonging are central to identifying collectively as South Asian. Exploring the performative effect of producing and consuming art at each festival enables us to understand how these progressive social venues create ideologies of ethnic community that converge with neoliberal frameworks of race and ethnic politics.

As a strategy of neoliberal politics, multiculturalism produces highly differentiated ethnic, sexual, and gendered communities and locates "culture" within the domain of individual experience. Such neoliberal forms of multiculturalism enable the art festivals to signify as iconic celebrations of South Asian community, for the festivals are largely funded through state grants for cultural diversity, corporate grants for community development, and private donations from local businesses. At the same time, the art festival is also an occasion for organizers, viewers, and artists to identify as "progressive," as immigrants whose politics oppose the practice of capital accumulation. Put another way, those who participate in and identify as South Asian through these festivals resist identifying with the state, even as the neoliberal state engenders the conditions for the formation of ethnic and racial community. As progressive South Asians identify with other subcontinental immigrants at the art festivals, they also disidentify with the exclusionary logic of multiculturalism that brought them together in the first place. Hence the art festival, as a site for the production of South Asian locality, is constituted through the display, exhibition, and consumption of multicultural belonging.

Writing on cultural festivals that feature immigrant artists and performers, Lisa Lowe remarks that such events operate as "both a mode of pluralist containment and a vehicle for intervention in that containment."[6] Desh Pardesh, Diasporadics, and Artwallah differed from state-sponsored cultural events that merely feature immigrant artists, for the ethos of these festivals was that they were social and political events for and by South Asian communities. The festivals were organized to deliberately question modes of pluralist containment by the state, and artists as well as attendees viewed their work as an "intervention in that containment." However, the intense commitment of artists, attendees, and organizers to a politics of resistance also exposes the contradiction between a logic of neoliberal multiculturalism that funds the art festivals at both the state and local levels, and acts of disidentification that create ethnic identity and community on site. These acts of disidentification are diffuse, visible in select works of art and in individual responses to the artwork. For artists and organizers who understand their work as a form of resistance, how do such acts of disidentification create "progressive" and "South Asian" communities? In turn, how might such notions of racialized community consolidate dominant ideologies of multiculturalism?

By identifying as part of a community, South Asian immigrants establish a stake in the public domain. Indeed, such affective experiences of belonging to one another are central to the ways in which second-generation immigrants express solidarity across national, religious, linguistic, and class difference. However, as the queer theorist Miranda Joseph notes, such formations of community are often implicated within, rather than positioned against, the circulation and consumption of capital. For minorities, queer and otherwise, "community" becomes a source of salvation, a site of exemption from the state. Yet rather than characterize such communities as in themselves "false or inauthentic," Joseph suggests that it is crucial to "take these invocations and practices of community at their word and to assess the complex complicity with and resistance to capitalism offered by community" (ix). Her reading of community as constituted through capital movement enables us to understand how forms of ethnic solidarity are constituted not simply through affective relations of identity but also through practices of production and consumption. At the art festivals, one such practice is the production and consumption of multiculturalism.

My concern is with the fundamental contradiction between the historical context, the performative format, and the political content of the art festivals: that is, between the rhetoric of "South Asia," the performance of being "South Asian," and the politics of community that emerges at each festival. For those South Asians who identify as progressive subjects through their participation in the art festivals, how are notions of diasporic solidarity reconciled with neoliberal formations of citizenship? In what ways does the construct of "South Asian" straddle the divide between the public identity of a minority group and a private experience of racialized difference? In their essay "The Remaking of a Model Minority," Jasbir Puar and Amit Rai critique the use of solidarity as an organizational concept for South Asian diasporas, particularly when South Asians are characterized by heterogeneity and difference. They write,

> What then is a singularity in solidarity? If we can think of solidarity as the communication of irreducible singularities that are no longer specific (i.e., identitarian) or transcended (by the economy), what fuses one community's struggles to another's is the intensity of articulated oppressions, the vibrations of contradictory joys, and the multiple experiences of becoming-other produced through its processes. We are not then speaking of a solidarity across difference, if by difference is meant something like "community identities" [. . .] We are speaking of a monstrous experience of solidarity that would be singular and intense and for that very reason multiple (or always miscegenated) and irreducible. (88)

Puar and Rai's argument against an identitarian construct of "solidarity across difference" and in favor of a "monstrous experience of solidarity" challenges neoliberal constructs of community. It also demonstrates how the category of "South Asian" operates as an intense form of belonging for progressive immigrants, who aim to celebrate the multiplicity (or miscegenation) of experiences within a community that is otherwise divided by language, religion, and class. Such a heterogeneous notion of solidarity, engendered through "multiple experiences of becoming-other," is what makes the idea of being South Asian desirable for me, as a critic and participant at the art festivals. But it is also what disrupts the relationship between the aesthetics and the politics of locality that are produced at each festival site. Even as the art that is displayed and circulated at the festivals generates monstrous and multiple narratives of immigration, the ways in which these artworks are rhetorically framed by organizers and consumed by viewers reproduce a singular construct of community: one that is located within the racial formation of the United States.

Being Young and Progressive: Producing South Asian Community

Desh Pardesh, Diasporadics, and Artwallah were characterized by their shared commitment to art and activism as a modality of creating South Asian community. Each festival was shaped by its geographical location, by different public discourses of multiculturalism in the United States and in Canada, and by the different histories that characterize South Asian migration to both countries as well as to the East and West coasts of the United States. However, all three festivals developed an aesthetic mandate that emphasized the commonality of South Asian immigrant experience, taking into account the heterogeneity of national, religious, and linguistic groups that composed their audience. For this reason, programming at all three festivals was largely oriented toward the experiences of youth growing up *in* North America, rather than focusing on reasons for immigration *to* North America. Such festivals are central to defining a sense of belonging in the public sphere, away from the private realm of family and home. Indeed, for many participants who volunteered and attended the festivals over multiple years, the community of South Asians that assembled at each festival site *was* family, for the festivals generated an alternative mode of kinship based on progressive politics. In contrast to mainstream immigrant cultural events that emphasize women's roles as carriers of "culture" and "tradition," the organizing committees for the art festivals embraced an antisexist and queer politics that challenged normative constructs of the national family. Toward this end, the festivals encouraged interactive programming and also solicited feedback from participants in order to use the arts as a form of political action rather than passive consumption. Workshops, panels, and post-performance discussions were an integral part of the festivals, as were the after-parties and other social events that ran parallel to festival programming.

An open letter to the audience at Desh Pardesh stated, "Rather than just showcasing 'art' for the audience's consumption, we are framing the artistic performance or presentation within a context that invites audiences to consider the historical, political and intellectual situation within which art occurs." Here, the encounter between artist and audience is characterized by a shared experience of immigration as well as a critical engagement with local political contexts. Similarly, the website for Diasporadics advertised the festival as straddling the "nexus between arts and activism." At Desh Pardesh and Diasporadics, the organizing committee and many of the audience members were deeply committed to public politics. Many were founding members of South Asian queer, feminist, and youth groups in the United States and Canada and had worked in immigrant rights organizations and antiracist coalitions. Several members of Desh Pardesh and Diasporadics were themselves first-generation immigrants from Pakistan, Sri Lanka, India, and Bangladesh who were also committed to secular movements for political change on the subcontinent. Likewise, program brochures from 2001 to 2005 characterized Artwallah as a "progressive" venue for South Asian art. In the case of Artwallah, many of its founding members had been involved in Indian American as well as South Asian organizations at university campuses in the Los Angeles area.

The curatorial process of the three festivals was also central to showcasing their progressive politics. Organizing committees frequently collaborated with local South Asian visual arts organizations during the selection processes (for example, Desh Pardesh collaborated with SAVAC, the South Asian Visual Arts Collective in Toronto). Artwork was selected through open calls for submissions, though many artists also created works specifically in response to the curatorial objectives of the festivals. Several artists emphasized personal stories of migration: their work depicted what it meant to leave South Asia and grow up as an immigrant in North America, Europe, or Africa. For the organizing committees as well as for many of the viewers, the self-reflexive and self-referential nature of artwork was itself a form of progressive consciousness. The artists challenged mainstream representations of South Asians as a model minority, through spoken word performances and films that called attention to working-class, feminist, and queer experiences of migration. At the same time this diverse set of personal narratives generated a singular construct of ethnic belonging, one that surpassed differences among immigrants of various class and national backgrounds.

Desh Pardesh, translated as "Home Away from Home," was the first South Asian art festival in North America. Held annually in Toronto between 1989 and 1999, Desh Pardesh grew out of "Salaam Toronto!" a one-day arts event in 1988 sponsored by Khush, the Toronto-based South Asian gay men's organization. Originally aimed at increasing gay and lesbian visibility within South Asian immigrant and mainstream Canadian communities, over the course of a decade Desh Pardesh became a multiday event, featuring gallery exhibits, workshops, and live performance. The 1999 program booklet described the festival as a forum for "artists, panelists, and cultural producers who raise complex issues around identities, gender, sexualities, technologies, fundamentalism and nationalism and transfer such passionate inquiries into the public domain."[7] The festival had three principal objectives. First, it highlighted artists from across the South Asian diaspora, including immigrants from the Caribbean, Australia, and Europe. Second, it encouraged artists and audience members to educate themselves about various nationalist movements on the subcontinent (leftist, right-wing, working-class) in order to draw links between political movements on the subcontinent and the politicization of South Asian diasporic subjects. Third, by hosting a series of feminist, queer, and labor-oriented programming in government buildings across the city, Desh Pardesh critically engaged with public discourses of Canadian multiculturalism.

In 1999 nearly five hundred people attended Desh Pardesh over four days. Daytime events included a mixed-media visual arts exhibit showcasing artists from the United States, Pakistan, and Sri Lanka; film screenings; a children's dance and yoga class; and a roundtable discussion on fundamentalism in South Asia and the diaspora. In addition, evening cultural programs included puppet shows, poetry readings, hip-hop, and spoken word performances by South Asian artists from North America, Europe, and Australia. The festival received funding from the Canadian Race Relations Foundation; the Ministry of Citizenship, Culture and Recreation; and the Toronto Arts Council. All these groups provided state grants earmarked for minority racial and sexual cultural programming.[8] Funds from these sources were augmented in small part by contributions from private donors.

Desh Pardesh's origin in Salaam Toronto! was apparent not only in its programming content, which explicitly thematized the relationship between queer sexualities and South Asian identities, but also through the queer spaces of socialization sponsored by the festival. In addition to festival programs held at the 519 Community Centre, which catered to the gay, lesbian, bisexual, and transgender community in Toronto, Desh Pardesh also featured two queer parties: "Boys Night Out in Babylon" and "Rowdy Girls and Vixens." At Rowdy Girls and Vixens, female and transgendered participants, organizers, and audience members at Desh Pardesh met to socialize and discuss professional issues. As the Desh Pardesh program booklet suggested, it was also a chance to "bat your eyelashes, talk shop, flirt and groove." Likewise, Boys Night Out in Babylon provided "sofas to lounge on and debate Desh programming, corners to snuggle in with your newest honey."[9] In contrast to the heteronormative social behavior that dominates young South Asian leisure spaces, at Desh Pardesh the festival programming enabled queer practices of socialization.[10] To this day, Desh Pardesh is frequently recalled as a utopic celebration of queer community. Queer South Asian groups such as Trikone in San Francisco continue to reference Desh Pardesh in their own cultural programming, as many organizers had been part of the festival in its early years.[11]

The queer South Asian communities that emerged at Desh Pardesh also exposed contradictory notions of national authenticity. A flyer for Desh Pardesh stated that membership to the festival board was limited to "people of South Asian origin." Here, "South Asian origin" is not a visibly racialized category (that is, it is distinct from the stipulation of "Indian origin" at the Miss India USA pageant). Desh Pardesh board members included descendants of indentured laborers from Guyana and Trinidad; immigrants from East and South Africa; multiracial South Asians; and first- and second-generation Canadian immigrants. As a historical claim to national origin on the subcontinent, being of "South Asian origin" is also about occupying a racialized experience of citizenship in Canada. The vexed relationship between embodying a minoritized racial subjectivity (as Canadians) and disparate histories of immigration (from the subcontinent via Africa and the Caribbean) belies the singularity of "South Asian origin" as a racial and national construct.

In *Racial Castration*, David Eng considers the fraught relationship that queer Asian Americans have with notions of "home," wherein home is variously configured as the heterosexual family and the U.S. state. Eng asks, "How might queerness and diaspora provide a critical methodology for a more adequate understanding of Asian American racial and sexual formation as shaped in the space between the domestic and the diasporic? What enduring role do nations and nationalism play in the delineation of such a critical project?" (206). In relation to Desh Pardesh, Eng's questions highlight the tension between the progressive rhetoric of the festival as a site for the production of youthful queer communities, and the ways in which such communities are shaped by Canadian and subcontinental nationalisms. On the one hand, the queer topography of Desh Pardesh was mapped across Toronto at publicly funded institutions such as the 519 Community Centre as well as at private downtown nightclubs for events like Rowdy Girls and Vixens. As festival attendees participated in these public events, they challenged the ways in which "home" is relegated to the private sphere of the domestic, and disassociated "homeland" from heteronormative constructs of the national family. Equally important, they produced and embodied ethnic and sexual communities within the metropolitan space of the Canadian state. On the other hand, by naming these heterogeneous communities "South Asian," participants at Desh Pardesh disidentified with the apparatus of Canadian multiculturalism. Their point of origin lay elsewhere, on the subcontinent. Despite the fact that Canadian state funding partly enabled the production of this particular community, the relationship between being South Asian and identifying as Canadian was eclipsed. Desh Pardesh provided a "home away from home" for diasporic subjects who were shaped not only by their geographical distance from the subcontinent, but also by their ideological proximity to the Canadian state.

Building upon Desh Pardesh's commitment to creating South Asian community in Canada, Diasporadics addressed the diversifying class backgrounds and national origins of subcontinental immigrants in the United States. In 1999 and 2000 the festival attracted approximately 250 people over the course of two nights and featured live performances by artists (many of whom had previously performed at Desh Pardesh) as well as a visual arts exhibition. All events were held at Riverside Church Theatre in New York City, across the road from Columbia University. Diasporadics, which was organized by an open collective of activists, educators, and artists, was cosponsored by the South Asian Lesbian and Gay Association and the progressive South Asian youth camp, Youth Solidarity Summer. Operating on a smaller scale than Desh Pardesh, Diasporadics was organized primarily through volunteered time and space, as well as with administrative support from local nonprofit feminist and queer of color organizations such as the Audre Lorde Project. The purpose of the festival, announced the Diasporadics 2000 program booklet, was to bring together "artists and activists interested in using arts as a vehicle for social change." Like Desh Pardesh, the organizing committee of Diasporadics aimed to use art as a means for direct political action. Consequently, the organizational format of the festival included an interactive visual arts exhibit, evening performance art shows, and ample opportunities for audience members to socialize with artists and festival organizers. As the Sri Lankan American hip-hop artist D'Lo wrote affectionately in the 1999 festival program booklet for Diasporadics, she has "kicked it with almost everyone on the bill, that's what you get for performing at every goddamn S.AZ. [South Asian] event." Such vibrant feelings of solidarity and kinship were actively sustained throughout the festival, characterized by the dynamic relationship forged between artists and audience members at each event.

The rhetorical organization of the festival emphasized a transnational politics of activism, as several of the organizing members were academics and activists who had long been involved in secular movements for democratic change in India, Pakistan, and Bangladesh. However, the artistic content of Diasporadics strongly relied upon a U.S.-based framework of multiculturalism. The Diasporadics 2000 festival program booklet stated: "The members of DIASPORADICS are committed to a progressive politics rooted in creative expression. We seek to provide a community forum that uses the arts to critique and resist social structures which marginalize individuals based on class, race, gender, sexuality, nationality, religion, age or physical ability." Although Diasporadics represented itself as a "community forum," the program committee nevertheless endorsed forms of creative expression that codified individual experience. Thus while the festival was committed to "progressive politics," the principal mode of political action was not through forms of collective action but rather through individual artistic production.

This neoliberal rhetoric of individual achievement secured the same social structures of race, gender, and sexuality that the festival aimed to deconstruct. For example, at the visual arts exhibition in 2000, the artist Tamara Zeta Sanowar-Makhan stood in the center of the room wearing a dress made of sanitary napkins. Titled *Ultra-Maxi Priest*, the exhibit arrived in New York City after previously being censored from a municipal art exhibition in Oakville, Ontario.[12] Her dress, which she had stitched together from commercially available sanitary napkins, was prominently white. Chaste and unstained, it did not hold traces of visible blood, excrement, or bodily waste. Covering her from neck to ankles, and across the full length of her arms, the dress approximated a priest's cassock and referenced the long history of Christian missionaries in the Anglophone and Francophone Caribbean who propagated modes of social discipline that augmented the formal colonial structures of indenture and slavery on the plantations. However, the link between a British colonial history in the Caribbean, Britain's imperial relationship to Canada, and Sanowar-Makhan's own subjectivity as a minority Canadian subject remained unaddressed at Diasporadics. Many viewers volubly spoke of Sanowar-Makhan's installation as a powerful feminist "choice," characterizing her decision to wear sanitary napkins as a liberal-feminist intervention in media images of the female body. For several viewers this live installation was an advertisement for women's empowerment, removing a specifically gendered shame about menstruation. Such reactions to Sanowar-Makhan's installation demonstrate the disparity between a reading of her artwork that emphasizes the historical context of its production, and one that focuses on the social context of its consumption. At one level, her installation showcased the global circuits of labor migration shaped by the expansion of the British empire. At another, *Ultra-Maxi Priest* brought to life colonial and Christian ideologies of gender and sexuality that were disseminated among Indian indentured laborers and African slaves on plantations. At Diasporadics, these multivalent expressions of empire and immigration were made secondary to Sanowar-Makhan's ability to wear layers of sanitary napkins in public: what appealed to many viewers was not the historical narrative that undergirded the art, but the artist's individual self-expression and creativity. Although the collective objective of the visual arts exhibition at Diasporadics was to "critique and resist" social structures of race and gender, the viewers' engagement with *Ultra-Maxi Priest* focused instead on individual acts of feminist empowerment.

Shortly after Diasporadics was installed in New York, and following the demise of Desh Pardesh, Artwallah was organized in 2000 as the first South Asian art festival on the West Coast. Literally meaning "one who makes art," Artwallah became the only annual South Asian art festival in North America. Unlike Diasporadics, which was organized by a constantly changing group of artists and academics, Artwallah initially had the institutional and financial backing of the Indo-American Cultural Center (IACC). The IACC, founded simultaneously with Artwallah, promoted the representation of South Asians in the mainstream media and performing arts. Although the IACC was initially conceived as the public face of the Indian American community in Southern California, it broadened its mandate to include artists from across the South Asian diaspora. Toward this end, Artwallah showcased work by artists of various South Asian origins from Europe, Australia, the Caribbean, and Africa. Nevertheless, IACC maintained a prominent focus on Indian immigrant art and activism. Artwallah was one of many public events sponsored by the IACC, alongside

Hindi language classes, gala literary film and musical evenings, and mentorship programs for South Asian youth. The long-term goals of the IACC, as stated on its website, included "creating a multi-media museum and cultural center focused on the South Asian American experience." From 2000 to 2004, the programming content at Artwallah was curated by the South Asian Artists' Collective (SAAC), a group that defined itself in the 2001 Artwallah program booklet as a "Los Angeles–based forum of established and emerging South Asian Artists who seek to embrace and support the progressive exploration of South Asian experiences in America and the global diaspora." In 2004 the IACC merged with Artwallah festival leadership and SAAC in order to become Artwallah, the organization. With the objective of ensuring long-term "financial and programmatic sustainability," IACC lent the Artwallah festival committee a leadership strategy, volunteers, and programming base.[13] Simultaneously, the curatorial responsibilities for Artwallah were dispersed between volunteer board members overseen by a full-time paid director of the festival.

Artwallah borrowed from the multiday programming format of Desh Pardesh, focusing on workshops, performances, and panel discussions during the day and performance art shows at night. In 2001 Artwallah was held over three days and nights at Artshare, a community arts warehouse in Los Angeles's garment district; in 2002 the festival encompassed the entire compound of the Village, the Los Angeles Gay and Lesbian Center; and in 2005 the festival was held on the spacious grounds of the Barnsdall Art Park in East Los Angeles. On all three occasions the festival included a visual art exhibition that ran for the duration of the festival; panels showcasing recent film, writing, dance, and theater by British, Canadian, and U.S.-based South Asian artists; and a cultural show that was repeated each evening, featuring artists who had previously performed at Desh Pardesh or Diasporadics.

Like its predecessors, Artwallah was committed to developing a forum for South Asian diasporic art by regularly curating emerging and established artists. In this vein the program booklet for Artwallah 2005 described the festival as a "grassroots organization" (46). As such the distinction between Artwallah, Desh Pardesh, and Diasporadics was not immediately apparent in the format and content of the festivals. However, in contrast to the two earlier festivals, Artwallah's success was largely dependent on private and corporate funds. The 2005 Artwallah festival program booklet noted the following corporate sponsors: Edison International, the energy corporation;

Washington Mutual Bank; Toyota Motor Sales; and the Boeing Company. The festival also received grants from the National Endowment for the Arts and the Los Angeles Cultural Affairs Department, as well as sponsorship from MTV Desi (fully owned by Viacom), and Anheuser-Busch.[14] Equally important, Artwallah successfully cultivated donor relations with individuals in the South Asian community in Los Angeles and beyond, with private donations accounting for almost half its funding.[15]

In an interview that I conducted in 2002, a coadministrator of Artwallah noted that the programming aimed to showcase "art that is not only political, but also personal and cultural." Because Artwallah curated a range of visual and performance art that dwelt on the emotional experience of immigration, she differentiated Artwallah from Desh Pardesh and Diasporadics, both of which she described as having "a much more political agenda." Suggesting that politics operates in a realm separate from the "personal and cultural," the administrator also acknowledged the disparity between individual narratives of experience that compose the artwork on display at Artwallah and the collective forms of political action that characterizes its "grassroots" ethos. However, her comment also indicated the vexed relationship between Artwallah's self-representation as a public celebration of ethnic identity and its increasing reliance on private funding.

Because the Toronto-based Desh Pardesh operated as a point of origin for Diasporadics and Artwallah, the relationship between the circulation of capital and the production of ethnic identity was also mediated by different public discourses of multiculturalism in Canada and the United States. The postcolonial theorist Sneja Gunew argues that working across the United States and Canada requires theorizing "situated multiculturalisms," a comparative study of multiculturalism that is attentive to "constructions of the local, the national, and the global" (2). At each level, multicultural policy in the United States and Canada impacts minority subjects differently.[16] The feminist scholar Himani Banerji demonstrates how such situated readings of multiculturalism can reveal the difference between state-mandated and populist discourses of race and citizenship. Whereas a statist ideology of liberal pluralism in Canada produces differential claims to statehood (among French and English speakers, First Nations, immigrant Canadians, and so on), Canadian state funding agencies also produce pluralist representations of racial minorities in the public media.[17] In comparison, more diffuse structures of multiculturalism in the United States highlight the difference between official multicultural policy and popular representations of race and ethnicity. Banerji writes that whereas in Canada multiculturalism is a "state-initiated enterprise," in the United States "one can speak of multiculturalism from above or from below" (538). In this context the U.S.-based Diasporadics and Artwallah are evidence of multicultural practice "from below," for both festivals were grassroots efforts for South Asian community organizing. However, the aesthetic mandate that determined the content of the festivals was also determined "from above," that is, by state-sponsored discourses of multiculturalism that promote a neoliberal ethnic politics.

At Artwallah 2005 the encounter between Canadian and U.S. discourses of multiculturalism was evident at the screening of *Continuous Journey*, a documentary by the Toronto-based filmmaker Ali Kazimi. The film, produced with public funding from the Canada Council for the Arts, was screened for the first time to a Los Angeles–based audience. Kazimi's documentary examines the infamous *Komagata Maru* incident of 1914, in which a Japanese ship carrying 376 Punjabi Sikhs, Hindus, and Muslims traveled from Hong Kong to British Columbia. On arrival in Vancouver the passengers were denied the right to land on Canadian soil. In the view of the Canadian state, the passengers had violated the law of "continuous journey," which stipulated that immigrants coming to Canada must make an unbroken voyage from their country of origin. As a legal provision, "continuous journey" was one way of limiting immigration to Canada by undesirable subjects, including immigrants from Asia. The *Komagata Maru* could not make a continuous journey from Hong Kong to British Columbia because the ship needed to refuel en route in Yokohama, Japan. However, for Gurdit Singh Sandhu, the Sikh entrepreneur who chartered the ship and recruited the men who accompanied him on this journey, the voyage of the *Komagata Maru* was a political act, a means of staking his claim, as a British colonial subject, on Canada, itself an outpost of the British empire. Like Canadians, the Punjabis on board were also imperial subjects, yet they were denied the right to land because of their racial and religious difference.[18]

Kazimi's documentary film used archival newsreels, photographs, and oral testimonials to excavate a little-known historical event and examine its implications for contemporary race relations in Canada. *Continuous Journey* received polite applause from the audience at Artwallah, many of whom learned of the *Komagata Maru* incident for the first time through the film. However, for this viewing audience in Los Angeles, the history of racial legislation in Canada appeared to be entirely divorced from a popular narrative of middle-class South Asian migration to the United States. In 2005 the dominant public image of South Asians in California was the figure of the Internet entrepreneur who had made millions in the high-tech industry. Indeed, some of these entrepreneurs were major donors for Artwallah. For the tiny audience who watched this film—only fifteen viewers sat in a theater that had capacity for two hundred people—*Continuous Journey* was a historical footnote. It represented a working-class history of South Asian migration, a history that occurred in another country at another time. Despite the fact that the *Komagata Maru* incident was integrally related to South Asian migration to California during the same period, neither the audience members nor the curators commented on Kazimi's documentary footage that linked racist attacks against Sikh immigrants in Canada to anti-Asian violence on the U.S. West Coast in the early twentieth century. Viewing *Continuous Journey* at a festival that celebrated South Asian upward mobility created a dissonance between Kazimi's production of a progressive labor history of South Asian migration and the audience's consumption of the film as entertainment.

The audience members' tepid response to *Continuous Journey* was in contrast to their enthusiastic identification with *Ganges Dreaming*, a short experimental film that immediately followed Kazimi's documentary. Directed by Usha Chohan and Eric Hiss, *Ganges Dreaming* featured the innovative electronic soundtrack of the South Asian musical artist Karsh Kale. Kale's thumping bass line was set against visual images that conjured a timeless and essential India: hordes of people gathered on the banks of the Ganges River; heat and dust on the riverbanks; women swathed in colorful saris. Mobilizing tropes of imperial travel, the film offered an encounter with India itself.[19] As Chohan and Hiss described in the Artwallah program guide, their film fuses "the images, sounds and textures of India with a compelling soundtrack [to create] a transcendent experience."[20] Yet this aestheticized rendition of India as an "experience" turned its people and landscape into ethnographic objects, silently consumed by the audience. Audience members hooted and clapped when the final credit read, "Dedicated to Mother India." Hiss and Chohan's representation of India as a "motherland" reproduces popular orientalist tropes of the East as a site of spiritual transformation and transcendence.[21] It also reinstates India as a point of cultural origin for immigrant subjects and, equally important, reasserts the hegemony of India within popular cultural representations of South Asia.

The juxtaposition of *Ganges Dreaming* with *Continuous Journey* at Artwallah 2005 illustrates the complex processes of identification and disidentification that shape South Asian communities. *Continuous Journey* delineated the broader global history of South Asian labor migration, from colonial Punjab to Hong Kong, from Hong Kong to Yokohama, and finally from Yokohama to Vancouver. It also emphasized the relation between race and citizenship by providing archival evidence of discrimination against South Asian immigrants in the early twentieth century. As a critique of multiculturalism, *Continuous Journey* located South Asians within the longer history of Canadian state formation. However, in California, in the face of early twenty-first-century discourses of South Asian entrepreneurial success, which prioritize individual achievements of capital accumulation, the film fell flat. In contrast, *Ganges Dreaming* codified a neoliberal discourse of multiculturalism within which a dehistoricized visual representation of "India" stood in for the lived experience of South Asians in the United States. The audience's enthusiastic reception of this film demonstrated the viewers' identification with notions of ethnic community that are forged through "importation, not immigration."[22]

The production of ethnic community at Artwallah, Desh Pardesh, and Diasporadics demonstrates how locality is variously conceived by young South Asian immigrants. At Desh Pardesh, immigrants of Caribbean, East African, and North American origin embodied a queer South Asian community that was mapped across the urban public space of Toronto. At Diasporadics, the organizational rhetoric of collective activism was transformed into an identity politics of ethnic and gender difference, as the curatorial program emphasized individual narratives of empowerment. At Artwallah, stories of South Asian entrepreneurial success eclipsed longer histories of labor migration to North America. Across these three festivals, the form and content of progressive politics were shaped by dominant discourses of multiculturalism from above and from below.

Archives of History, Politics of Memory

Returning to the visual art exhibition at Diasporadics, I examine how the production of ethnic community at the art festivals was challenged by a "monstrous" set of personal and national histories that emerged from the artwork on display. Ameen Gill's *The Mango Tree* was the focal point of attention at Diasporadics, as her installation of turban cloths trailed onto the floor. The series of lithographs began with a print of Gill's great-grandfather, Ganga Singh, who migrated from rural Punjab to the U.S. West Coast in 1906. He worked for twenty-five years as a groundskeeper for a California senator and never returned to see his family in India. The next lithograph was a portrait of his son, Gill's grandfather, a gambler and businessman who owned a transport company that ferried busloads of passengers to small towns across the Punjab. The handwritten backdrop to this photograph chronicled Gill's grandfather's migration from India to the United States via Cuba and Mexico in the 1920s. After joining his father in California, Gill's grandfather moved to the west coast of Canada, working in the lumberyards of Vancouver and joining an established Sikh community there. The final lithographic print in the series was a portrait of Gill's father, who migrated from Punjab to Vancouver in 1933 to work in the lumber industry but remained in Canada to establish his family.[23]

Gill's installation brings together disparate narratives of departure and arrival that were embodied by her forefathers, but she also seeks to make

The Mango Tree (lithographic installation). On display at Diasporadics 1999. Photograph by author.

visible the women and children who remained in Punjab. She uses a labor-intensive process of photo-plate lithography to digitally transfer images from old family portraits onto turban cloth. Her manual intervention in this family tree is also evident through her transcription of oral histories of migration, which are faintly visible on the backdrop of each panel and which frame the archival photographs. Gill's transcription—a series of fragmented sentences assembled through interviews with family members in India—repeats itself every two and a half panels. However, because the panels are curated differently at each exhibition site, and are arranged in terms of the visual synchrony between photographs rather than in terms of the narrative coherence between panels, Gill's work confounds viewers who expect to read a chronological narrative history across the portrait photographs.[24] Viewed against the coarse cloth of the panels, Gill's handwriting has a ghostlike quality, faint but persistent, an endlessly repeating narrative of migration from colonial India to North America.

The Mango Tree was initially conceived as a five-foot-tall accordion-folded book project, which was displayed at Artwallah 2002. As a book installation, *The Mango Tree* charted a reverse narrative of migration, chronicling Gill's first trip from Canada to India in 1996 to visit her relatives. In an interview that I conducted with Gill some months after Artwallah, she noted that the first installation of *The Mango Tree* enabled her to ask questions of "who I was, where I was from, and where I was going."[25] On each page Gill reprinted multiple images of herself riding a bicycle, as well as portrait photographs of her father, thereby layering onto the same page stories of her journey to Punjab and her father's migration overseas more than sixty years earlier. The installation unfolded to create a map of northern India that prominently linked the northwestern state of Punjab to the national capital of New Delhi. Like in the lithographs she subsequently composed, Gill's handwriting (in this case excerpts from her travel journal) pervaded the book installation, forming a relief to the repeated images of herself and her father. This early version of *The Mango Tree* engendered an intact image of post-partition India, within which Punjab—known for its agricultural revolution and the modernist architecture of its state capital, Chandigarh—assumed pride of place.[26] However, in contrast to this representation of the Punjab as a modern, indeed a "progressive," state is another set of popular representations: of Punjabis, particularly Sikhs, as terrorist and antinational subjects. The consolidation of power by Sikh nationalist groups in Punjab during the late twentieth century, as well as the emergence of a secessionist movement for an independent Sikh state of Khalistan, has led to the brutal repression of Sikhs by the Indian government, most egregiously during the army's attack on the Sikh Golden Temple in Amritsar in 1984 and in the aftermath of Prime Minister Indira Gandhi's assassination that same year. The persecution of Sikhs as a minority religious group in India is absent from *The Mango Tree*, even though anti-Sikh violence is a major cause of emigration.[27]

In the later version of *The Mango Tree*, Gill's use of lithographic printing rather than book installation portrays a different genealogy of selfhood. Rewinding back to the history of her paternal ancestors' migration out of India, the lithographs excavate the turbulent history of colonial Punjab in the early twentieth century. At that time, the province of Punjab spanned what is now Pakistan and India. From the late nineteenth century onward, British administrative control of the province, one of the most fertile regions on the subcontinent, resulted in the redistribution of land and water rights as well as new taxation laws. For independent farmers who for generations had lived off their land, these new legislative acts generated social and political upheaval.[28] For Gill's paternal ancestors, the detrimental impact of these laws on the local economy prompted their migration overseas. The photographs in the prints portray Gill's grandfather and great-grandfather as young men, representing their migration as a story of youthful ambition and hard work. Yet the oral interviews that Gill transcribes by hand against the backdrop of each print testify to the growing number of children in the family and the scarcity of money. The contradiction between image and written text in the lithographic version of *The Mango Tree* generates an alternate history of South Asian locality, one that binds together economic conditions in colonial India with the growing demand for agricultural labor in central California and lumberyard workers in British Columbia.

This later version of *The Mango Tree* narrates a story of movement out of South Asia rather than chronicling Gill's return to the subcontinent. As such, the lithographs also showcase the domestic implications of South Asian migration, specifically the conditions of racial and sexual panic that sharply delimited Asian immigration to the United States and Canada in the early twentieth century. Because Gill's great-grandfather and grandfather were barred from bringing their wives to California, the families that they left behind appear in only a single group photograph on one panel. What enlarges the absence of women in this series is Gill's own disappearance from the lithographic project. Unlike the earlier version of *The Mango Tree*, in which Gill's image was imprinted on every page of the book installation, in the lithographic version Gill is literally and figuratively absent. Her pictorial erasure from *The Mango Tree*, however, is supplanted by ghostly traces of her handwriting across the photographs, which operate as a way of inserting herself in this patrilineal and masculine story of migration. The haunting quality of the transcribed narratives underscores the sharply gendered experiences of migration for men and women in Gill's family. It also makes visible how Gill's own subjectivity dissolves and re-emerges through a series of border crossings: her ancestors' travels from colonial India to the

The Mango Tree (detail).
Image courtesy Ameen Dhillon.

Americas; from Mexico to California; from the United States to Canada; and in her own adult life, from Vancouver to Seattle.

At Diasporadics and Artwallah, the installation of *The Mango Tree* framed the rhetorical and historical context of the festival itself. Gill's lithographs remind us that the history of South Asian immigration to North America did not begin with the emigration of a professional class after the Hart-Celler Act of 1965. Instead, she telescopes back from that dominant narrative of middle-class migration to map uncommon historical linkages between pre-partition Punjab, the Caribbean, and North America over the course of a century. The dynamic aesthetic of *The Mango Tree* emphasizes Gill's autobiographical experience but also incorporates the viewer into this narrative of transnational migration. As the largely young South Asian audience stood at various heights and distances from the lithographs, the expansive visual effect of *The Mango Tree*—its eight-foot-tall panels, the large portrait photos, the repetitive narrative—generated a collective viewing experience. The scale of the installation and its representation of diaspora were larger than life, enabling viewers to inhabit a disparate set of narratives spanning several times and places. In so doing, *The Mango Tree* produced a notion of locality for young South Asian immigrants whose experiences of growing up in North America are enormously varied. *The Mango Tree* produces a phenomenology of belonging that is defined not spatially, in terms of the viewer's identification as an Indian, Punjabi Sikh, or American, but relationally and contextually, by identifying with Gill, her archival family portraits, and the incomplete narratives that spill across the panels.

Because *The Mango Tree* was printed on turban cloth, the lithographs are also an insistent reminder of the ethnic and religious differences that marked the racial segregation of Sikh immigrants in North America throughout the twentieth and into the twenty-first century. Although Sikhs in Canada and the United States in the 1920s were subject to different immigration laws, their racialization in both countries was strikingly similar. Sikh workers were mistakenly identified as "Hindoos," and their growing presence on railroads in Oregon and Washington as well as in lumberyards in British Columbia prompted anti-immigrant race riots.[29] On view at Artwallah, the long rolls of turban cloth acquired a denser historical meaning, for the lithographs also reflected the racial and religious persecution of Sikh immigrants after September 11, 2001. Across the panels what comes to life is the figure of the "turbaned Sikh terrorist," which links together the misrecognition of

Sikhs as Hindus in the early twentieth century and as a terrorists a hundred years later.[30] In *The Mango Tree*, the portraits of turbaned Sikh men acquire a spectral presence through the coarse texture of archival photographs that are reproduced onto turban cloth, and through the enlarged scale of the prints. These expansive images haunted viewers who walked through the small visual arts exhibition space at Artwallah. The ghostly photographs stood in for the bodies of Sikh men who were killed, detained, or "disappeared" after the September 11 attacks, many of whom were deported with Muslim South Asians and Arab Americans to their countries of so-called "origin."[31]

Bringing together this critique of U.S. empire with images of Sikh racialization in *The Mango Tree* highlights how Gill's lithographic prints generate multiple, monstrous narratives of migration that bind South Asia with the United States. These are the miscegenated narratives of what Puar and Rai called "becoming-other." In *The Mango Tree*, Sikh men become other to viewers through the racial and sexual panic that surrounded Asian immigrant labor camps on the United States and Canadian west coasts in the early twentieth century, as well as through media representations of Sikhs as terrorists in the aftermath of 9/11. But the figure of the turbaned Sikh also becomes other to South Asian youth—like those who gathered at Diasporadics and Artwallah—who view this set of family portraits as emblematic of their own migration history *and* as irreducibly other to their normative localities as middle-class immigrants and U.S. citizens. Thus as *The Mango Tree* circulated at art festivals on the U.S. East and West coasts, it generated relations of identification and disidentification with audience members. The fact that representations of Sikh men could simultaneously be assimilated into and become other to normative renditions of what it means to be South Asian highlights how even "progressive" sites of cultural production, such as the art festivals, cannot operate as emancipatory spaces of community. In times like these, it may be more productive to conceptualize South Asian communities not as collectivities based on racial solidarity, but rather in terms of what Puar calls a "queer assemblage" that "moves away from excavation work, deprivileges a binary opposition between queer and not-queer subjects, and [. . .] underscores contingency and complicity within dominant formations."[32]

Some distance away from *The Mango Tree* at the Diasporadics visual arts exhibition, the painter Dhruvi Acharya exhibited a handful of mixed-media paintings. Acharya's work can be viewed as a counterpoint to Gill's lithographs, emphasizing how "queer assemblages" of South Asians at the art festivals can also be complicit with dominant formations of gender, caste, and religion in South Asia as well as with notions of upward class mobility in the United States. At the time a recent art school graduate, Acharya more recently has had her work prominently featured in solo and group gallery shows. Over the past decade her paintings have steadily appreciated in value on the international art market, and she is viewed as one of India's most promising young painters.[33] Acharya was born in Bombay (Mumbai) but immigrated to the United States as a student, living in New York for several years before moving back to India. She writes in her online artist's statement, "My works focus on the psychological and emotional aspects of an urban woman's life [. . .] Just like me, my work is not overtly or obviously political [. . .] When the works are viewed, I hope the specifics of the stories and the meaning of each image become unimportant, and all that is felt and remembered is the universality of the human experience."[34]

My reading of Acharya's works focuses precisely on the "specifics of the stories and the meaning of each image," for her paintings illustrate the dissonant political and aesthetic representations of South Asian locality at the art festivals. At Diasporadics, Acharya showed three paintings, including her work *Captive*. Using acrylic paint on canvas and pasted paper images from Indian comic books, *Captive* depicts a solitary female figure reclining on a pink couch, eating potato chips. Against the luminescent blue ink of the canvas, the woman's body fully occupies the frame of the painting, her thighs and chest illuminated by the faint light of what might be a television. Pasted onto her breasts, arms, and belly are images and word bubbles from the Indian comic book series *Amar Chitra Katha*. A peacock swoops toward the bag of chips, its beak poised to peck not at the food, but at the pieces of paper pasted onto the woman's body. The unnamed woman's eyes are cast upward, as if dreaming. Her mouth sealed, what speaks across and through her body are the vivid images from *Amar Chitra Katha* comics.

Amar Chitra Katha is a popular series of comic books on Indian folklore, religious mythology, and history that was founded in 1967 with the slogan "The Route to Your Roots." An imprint of the publishing company India Book House, *Amar Chitra Katha* prides itself on educating Indian children in "their rich cultural heritage."[35] In the early 1970s *Amar Chitra Katha* began publishing graphic adaptations of popular Hindu epics such as the *Ramayana* and *Mahabharata*, along with folk tales such as the *Panchatantra*. Ini-

The Art of Multiculturalism 189

Captive (2000). Synthetic polymer paint and collage on canvas. 30 × 30 inches. Image courtesy Dhruvi Acharya.

tially published in English, the comic books were rapidly translated into a variety of other Indian languages to promote national integration in post-independence India. The publishers of *Amar Chitra Katha* pride themselves on their historical accuracy and commitment to representing a diverse Indian public. The readers of the comics are primarily middle-class, urban, and upper-caste Indians, though in the past decade the series has become increasingly popular among Indians overseas.[36] For many viewers of Indian origin at Diasporadics, therefore, seeing *Amar Chitra Katha* comics in Acharya's works generated a profoundly nostalgic identification with her paintings.[37]

The narrative content of *Amar Chitra Katha* is shaped by secular principles of national diversity and religious harmony (or "Sarva Dharma Sambhava," which I discussed in Chapter 3). The comic book series focus on a range of religious and historical figures, ranging from New Testament narratives of Jesus Christ, to Dalit (or "untouchable") political leaders such as B. R. Ambedkar, to the Mughal emperor Akbar. However, while *Amar Chitra Katha* upholds a nationalist creed of "unity in diversity," the comic books are in fact central to the reproduction of a normatively Hindu, upper-caste, and middle-class Indian public. By far the greatest number of comic book issues feature Hindu gods and religious mythologies such as the *Mahabharata* and *Ramayana*, and it is from this archive of popular representation that Acharya constructs the narrative of *Captive*.

In *Captive* the images and word bubbles pasted across the canvas are from one of the earliest issues of *Amar Chitra Katha*, titled "Savitri," published in 1970. One of the many stories that make up the *Mahabharata*, Savitri is the name of a beautiful princess who falls in love with Satyavan, a pauper she meets in the forest. The reader finds out that Satyavan is in fact a prince, whose father's kingdom was unjustly usurped after a family quarrel. Satyavan does not know that he is fated to die within a year, for at his birth his parents chose to have one noble son who must die young rather than several unworthy living sons. Despite her knowledge of his impending death, Savitri insists on marrying Satyavan. On the day that Satyavan is fated to die, Yama, the god of death, appears in the forest. Satyavan is instantly struck dead, but Savitri refuses to let Yama go. She trails him for several hours, and Yama is impressed by Savitri's persistence and beauty. Yama grants Savitri several wishes, among them the return of the lost kingdom to her husband's father. Her last wish, says Savitri, is to have many sons. Yama grants her this wish, and then Savitri asks: but how can she have sons when her husband is dead? Yama realizes that he has been tricked, but he is so impressed by Savitri's love and devotion to her husband that he grants Satyavan's life back.[38]

The tale of Savitri is replete with motifs familiar to readers of Hindu mythology: filial piety and feminine duty shape this social world in which sons are preferred over daughters, daughters obey their father's wishes, wives are driven by undying devotion to their husbands, and romantic love reproduces the sanctity of class and caste. In *Captive* the images and dialogue from this issue of *Amar Chitra Katha* are pasted in neat, round bubbles across the ample frame of the female figure. On the belly detail shown, a word bubble declares, "It is said, a father who does not give his daughter in marriage is a sinner." While Savitri initially protests—"Father, my friends say a girl must marry and go away! I will not go anywhere"—elsewhere on the painting she finally responds, "All right father, I shall do as you say." Surrounding these word bubbles are images of Satyavan's muscular torso, and of the beautiful Savitri. In the comic book version of this tale, Savitri's

Captive (detail).
Image courtesy Dhruvi Acharya.

devotion to her father and husband is rewarded toward the end of the story, when Satyavan is granted his life back and inherits his kingdom from his father and Savitri assumes her rightful place as his queen. However, in *Captive*, Acharya pastes assorted images and dialogue from the comic book across the body of the female figure, producing a disjointed and unresolved visual and literary narrative.

As Acharya's selection of images emphasizes, the myth of Savitri works only through the containment of her sexuality. Although Savitri is represented as an independent and autonomous woman in the comic book (she falls in love with Satyavan despite his poverty, much to her father's dismay), she must marry if she is to uphold her family honor. Once married, her value lies in her reproductive capacity to extend her husband's lineage by bearing sons. Savitri's decision to marry Satyavan, and her ability to persuade Yama to give Satyavan's life back, are cast in *Amar Chitra Katha* as acts of feminine agency. Yet Savitri's pursuit of Yama is also necessitated by her own knowledge that she ceases to exist outside a locus of patriarchal control. The story of Savitri underscores not only the contractual nature of her sexual and economic relationship to her husband and father, but also the mythic quality of her independence.

Laid onto the body of the female figure in *Captive*, the animated faces of Savitri, her father, and Satyavan undulate across folds of flesh, interspersed with images of equal dimension that Acharya has penciled onto the canvas: trees, leaves, lips, the pages of an open book. Stretched onto the white T-shirt that covers the female subject of the painting, the comic book characters are engaged in conversation with each other, with graphic expressions of grief, laughter, and lust on their faces. Meanwhile, the subject of the painting is alienated from that conversation: her face is turned upward, away from her body, and the white thought bubble emerging from her own head is filled with an abstract cloudy image. Against the idealized beauty of Savitri—her pert breasts, slim waist, and wide hips—the bodily comportment of the female subject is distorted and excessive.

In *Captive* the myth of Savitri informs the gendered and sexualized subject of the painting. Savitri's quest for independence, for example, is mirrored in the continuous consumption of WOW potato chips by the female figure. The prominent red package of WOW, a trademarked brand of chips made with olestra—the nonfat oil introduced (and quickly discontinued) as a miraculous invention in American junk food—promises the illusion of consumption without calories. Similarly, the story of Savitri illustrates the contradictions of gendered agency. Although she constantly attempts to assert her independence in relation to her father and husband, Savitri is ultimately recuperated into the patriarchal domestic economy of the heterosexual household. Like the open bag of potato chips that offers empty satisfaction to the female subject of the painting, Savitri's eventual restoration as queen—an event that takes place outside the frame of this painting—offers her little gratification. Despite the size and strength of her body, the female subject of *Captive* cannot take precedence over the story of Savitri; instead, she is held captive by that myth.

At Diasporadics 2000, *Captive* was a remarkable instance of the ways in which Acharya, like other artists and attendees at the festival, engaged with commodified notions of South Asian history. As an aesthetic text, *Captive* is created through layers of incommensurable narratives. The first is of the unnamed female figure that occupies the bulk of the canvas. Her diasporic subjectivity is suggested through her isolation within the painting and by her continuous consumption of the olestra-fried chips, which here represent the emptiness of the American dream of upward class mobility. The second narrative is forged through the excerpts from *Amar Chitra Katha*, which stand in for a commodified history of India that is readily consumed by middle-class youth in India and in the diaspora. The comic book panels are central to the formation of a "secular" viewing public, for the panels draw upon Hindu mythology in order to engender a common "cultural" (or religious) heritage shared by members of a diverse national body. In this context, the story of Savitri represents the centrality of women to reproducing notions of culture, heritage, and tradition. Savitri's embodiment of chastity and filial piety engenders a national morality tale: "chaste and devoted wives will ultimately bring triumph to their loved ones and themselves."[39] Using layers of opaque and translucent paint, and an alternating matte and gloss finish, Acharya creates a uniform surface on canvas that absorbs the difference in physical texture between the comic book cutouts and the larger female subject of *Captive*. Although the various mediums used in the painting provide contrasting visual depth, the uniform surface of *Captive* flattens the difference between a historical past in India (embodied in Savitri's sexual contract) and the female figure's present location in the United States (the elusive gratification provided by the WOW potato chips). At the same time, by remapping the *Amar Chitra Katha* comics onto the female subject of

Captive, Acharya revises the nostalgic and nationalist qualities of that comic book series. When placed across the body of the unnamed woman, the dialogue and image bubbles do not offer an explanation for the clouded mind of the female figure, or for the peacock that swoops menacingly toward her breasts. Instead, Acharya's use of comic books in *Captive* makes visible the incommensurate relationship between the gendered experiences of the two female subjects of the painting: between the national, mythological subject of Savitri and the equally mythic, diasporic female subject of the painting. *Captive* highlights the difference and distance that structure the relationship between the national and the diasporic, between histories of the past and memories of the present, and between real and imagined notions of "South Asia" that circulate at the art festivals.

The Mango Tree and *Captive* exemplify the phenomenological production of locality. Gill's lithographic panels draw upon her family history of migration from colonial Punjab to North America, generating nonlinear narratives of South Asian migration that are quite literally larger than life. Although Gill attempts to locate her own transnational subjectivity in relation to successive paternal migrations out of the subcontinent, she herself dissolves from view. Unlike her omnipresent image in the earlier book installation of *The Mango Tree*, Gill's absence from the lithographs can be traced only through her reproduction of oral histories across the archival images. Further, Gill's gendered and racialized experience as a Sikh woman living in America in the aftermath of September 11, 2001, is impossible to figure through this series of lithographic prints. In *Captive* the alienated female subject of the painting draws obliquely on Acharya's immigrant experience in the United States and her subsequent return to India. Yet India, as represented through the *Amar Chitra Katha* comics, is no longer the site of "home." The story of Savitri, as it is refashioned across the body of the diasporic female subject, draws the viewer's attention to Acharya's critique of Hindu nationalist mythology and the reproduction (via the transnational circulation and consumption of these comics) of an equally mythical notion of the secular Indian public.

Ameen Gill and Dhruvi Acharya's works illuminate the contradiction between aesthetic and political representations of South Asians in America. Aesthetically, both artists draw upon what Acharya describes in her artist's statement as the "universality of the human experience." From this perspective the display and consumption of their work at the festivals engender a collective experience of locality, one that is shared by South Asians across religious, regional, and national differences. However, the composition of both artworks challenges universal notions of experience and generates a multivalent critique of South Asian history, including dominant histories of British imperialism and popular representations of Indian womanhood. Gill and Acharya also make use of the tactile quality of a range of materials—archival photographs, comic books, and turban cloth—to provide texture, density, and specificity to migrant narratives. The stories of immigration embedded in these two works are specifically about working- or middle-class immigrants, Sikhs or Hindus, men or women. Together, the lithographs and the painting encompass a diverse set of migrations spanning more than a century, delineating the ties that bind colonial Punjab to imperial Canada, and postcolonial India to the United States. How then do *Captive* and *The Mango Tree* create a universal portrait of South Asian migration?

The selection of these artworks by the festival organizing committee was emblematic of hegemonic notions about the place of art in diasporic popular culture. Although the organizers of Diasporadics and Artwallah promoted a progressive rhetoric of community that emphasized difference (of class, national origin, religion, gender, and sexuality), these same festivals also deployed art to forge "universal" experiences of ethnicity and race. In this context, the fact that the painting and lithographs drew from autobiographical experience is central to the formation of an identitarian politics, or what Puar and Rai critique as "solidarity across difference." The audience members' engagement with these artworks in turn validates the function of art as a representation of ethnic community. In contrast to the audience's disidentification with the race-based immigration history that was showcased in *Continuous Journey*, many viewers intensely identified with *The Mango Tree*. Their voluble admiration for Gill's art was based on her creative rendering of her family's migration to North America, in particular her use of archival family portraits. At the same time, in order for this heterogeneous group of immigrants to incorporate Gill's work into their own identities as South Asians, they necessarily elided the specifically racialized experience of Sikh migrants to the United States across the twentieth century. In so doing, audience members were complicit in reproducing a neoliberal discourse of multiculturalism, an ideology of belonging that reconsolidates dominant notions of class, gender, religion, and nationhood within South Asian communities. At the same time, not all audience members could identify fully with the artworks on display. For those who were unfamiliar with *Amar Chitra Katha* comics or histories of early twentieth-century Punjabi migration, the exhibition and consumption of these artworks generated a profound sense of dislocation. And for those who identified as Bangladeshi, Pakistani, or Sri Lankan, the marginalization of their specific immigration and religious histories within the visual art exhibition was another experience of becoming-other, of experiencing both distance and difference within universal notions of South Asian community.

Viewing South Asia, Being South Asian

Following the visual art exhibition at Diasporadics, the evening performance featured Shonali Bose's film *Lifting the Veil*. A documentary on workers' rights in India, *Lifting the Veil* examines the effects of economic liberalization policies instituted by the Indian government in the 1990s. While depicting the rapid globalization of the Indian middle class, the film focuses on the impoverishment of the urban working class, specifically women. Bose's documentary uses interviews with corporate executives, mill workers, and laborers to comment on the social conditions of poverty in India. As a commentary on the effects of globalized capital, *Lifting the Veil* drew expressions of shock and outrage from viewers in the audience, numbering almost two hundred young South Asians. At the end of the film screening, Bose came onstage to denounce the social and political reforms that have accompanied economic liberalization in contemporary India. In a rousing voice, shaking her fist, Bose pointed to the World Bank and International Monetary Fund as institutions responsible for the continued exploitation of the Indian working class. The audience listened carefully and cheered loudly after Bose's talk. Yet there were also visible stirrings of discomfort among those present. Clearly many viewers, including myself, felt chastised and dutifully noted Bose's call to join Indian workers in a global anticapitalist movement; but several of us also felt strangely distant from the urgent geographical and political context of the film. In Bose's film and speech, India was brought closer to the United States through the economy of globalization. At the same time, her call for activism in a place far removed from New York chafed against the diasporic community of South Asians that was produced through the cultural programming of the art festival.

That night, the Riverside Church Theatre was packed to capacity with young South Asians traveling from the East and West coasts, from Vancouver and Toronto, and across New York City. Enthusiastically cheering on the artists onstage, the audience hooted and whistled their approval of the diverse cultural program: a performance of classical Indian dance set to hip-hop music, a singer-songwriter playing electric guitar and tabla, short-story readings, and comedy sketches. As part of this exuberant series of performances, *Lifting the Veil* struck a particularly unsettling note. The film's focus on India and Bose's exhortations for solidarity with Indian workers clearly discomfited many. Immediately after the screening, a friend sitting nearby wryly commented that Bose was the "authentic token" at Diasporadics. Preceded by readings and performances that celebrated the varied experiences of South Asians in the United States, Bose's film and speech were anomalous in drawing the audience's attention to political movements in South Asia.

In light of the larger rhetorical organization of Diasporadics as an art festival for and by South Asians, *Lifting the Veil* and Shonali Bose's presence onstage were strangely out of place. In Bose's documentary, the decline of workers' rights and rise of global capitalism take place elsewhere, in India. Although the audience members at Diasporadics recognized Bose's demand for solidarity with Indian workers, their collective identification as "South Asians" and as "progressive" activists occurred within the United States. While Diasporadics' organizational motto of art and activism encouraged collaborations between immigrant artists, activists, and audience members, *Lifting the Veil* demanded a form of personal and political investment in contemporary India that Diasporadics could not provide. For an audience distanced not only spatially but also temporally from the events filmed in Bose's documentary, *Lifting the Veil* produced a sense of guilt at a festival that was overwhelmingly about feeling good (feeling good about being South Asian, about being queer and South Asian, and so on).[40]

My understanding of this phenomenology of guilt arises from the different registers used to define "South Asia" at the art festivals. Rather than focusing on histories of migration to North America, or on experiences of racialized subjectivity in the United States, *Lifting the Veil* engages with the political and economic conditions of the working class in contemporary India. The real-time documentary subjects of *Lifting the Veil* are far removed from the cultural experiences that define the racialized, sexualized, and gendered identities of South Asians in the United States. At the art festival,

Bose's film produced an idea of "India" and "Indians" that was spatially and temporally distinct from the images, sights, and sounds that create the phenomenology of becoming South Asian. *Lifting the Veil* indicts the residents of the global North in the exploitation of labor in the global South, a transnational relationship that necessarily produces a political correlation between workers in late twentieth-century India and middle-class South Asians in diaspora. However, the art festivals were founded upon a rhetoric of South Asian community that operates only at a temporal and spatial remove from the subcontinent. Consequently Bose's insistence on India as a place of lived time was refuted by the very parameters of "progressive" politics at South Asian arts festivals. The festivals thus engendered "a South Asian space-time that has no time for South Asia."[41]

The audience's simultaneous investment in and distance from Bose's film demonstrated how the affective charge of being South Asian is bound by local (American) politics of community organizing. In an essay on lesbian organizing in India, "To Render Real the Imagined," Naisargi Dave explores the political impact of identifying as "lesbian," interpreted as both an imagined community of belonging and as a political category that comes to be defined by norms of proper behavior. She demonstrates how, when one of the first Indian lesbian groups was formed, scores of women who were married and single, from varying class and caste positions, from small towns and cities, wrote to each other self-identifying as lesbian. As a category of belonging, therefore, the term "lesbian" was not exclusive to urban, upper-class English speakers in India. However, as lesbian social groups became face-to-face networks, what it meant to be lesbian splintered along the lines of "the politically competent and the politically incompetent, or the proper and the less-than-proper, lesbian subject" (607). Tracking the emergence of a lesbian community in India, as Dave writes, is also a story of loss, for the emergence of community requires "a circumscription of the affective space of politics such that sex, pleasure, and desire were gradually deemed less than fit for this emergent, newly politically aspiring, lesbian community" (608).

My reading of how progressive and queer assemblages of South Asians come to be constituted at the art festivals expands upon Dave's exploration of political community. The emergence of a South Asian community at the art festivals is also circumscribed by the "affective space of politics," which deems certain kinds of political engagement (for example, Bose's virulent opposition to capitalism) "less than fit" for an aspirational ethnic community.

This affective distinction between a "political self and an apolitical other" is precisely the distinction that is reproduced at the art festivals.[42] Those who organize and participate in the festivals embody a South Asian self—a self that is politically progressive, heterogeneous, and second generation—in opposition to an apolitical other, figured as the mainstream, cultural nationalist, first-generation immigrant community. But the problem is that the production of a South Asian self at the art festivals is located within the affective space of multicultural politics in the United States. The work of sustaining South Asian community requires embodying a new understanding of space and time that is distinct from the production of class and caste-based citizenship on the subcontinent. Thus in contrast to fictional narratives of South Asian subjectivity that rely on an imagined bond with national subjects in South Asia (for example, in Jhumpa Lahiri's short stories, which I discussed in Chapter 1), at the art festivals the ethnographic production of South Asian locality relies on distance and difference from South Asia.

Not all the artistic events at Diasporadics were removed from direct political engagement with the subcontinent. On a previous night, the educator Shakil Choudhury presented the Brown Book Project, a collaborative venture between Pakistani teenagers in Lahore and young Pakistani Canadians in Toronto. As an "anti-racist educational resource" to be distributed within the Toronto public school system, the Brown Book brought together personal narratives of youth to highlight the relationship between religion and ethnic identity. A self-identified "Pakistani-Bengali Muslim," Choudhury was particularly invested in using young people's writing to generate community discussion on the rise of Islamist movements and the threat of Hindu fundamentalism on the subcontinent. Informed by bell hooks' work on representations of black men in the media, the Brown Book Project also aimed to broaden representational strategies for young South Asians, specifically Muslims. Here, autobiographical narratives of young men and women in Lahore and Toronto were deployed to correct media representations of Muslim communities in Canada. Choudhury's presentation and call for donations received strong support from Diasporadics audience members, many of whom were also educators. Though the Brown Book was transnational in content, in its form and style it was informed by U.S. race and ethnic studies. It was also emblematic of Canada's state-oriented ideology of liberal pluralism, for Choudhury's project received funding from the Canadian Race Relations Foundation as well as the Toronto District School Board.

Lifting the Veil and the Brown Book Project shared the same stage at Diasporadics. However, the audience responses generated by these two texts demonstrated the disparity between South Asia and North America, and more important, the difference between South Asia and being South Asian. Bose's documentary and her "authentic" presence onstage signified a political engagement with leftist critiques of globalization and Indian Communist Party politics. By contrast, the Brown Book Project presented a domestic framework of racial and ethnic identity, even as it emphasized the transnational formation of young Muslim subjectivities. For this audience in New York City, the Brown Book mirrored their racialized locations as South Asians. Although Diasporadics prided itself on its transnational politics, the dominant experience of the festival was to celebrate belonging to an ethnic community in North America—one that was removed from the landscape of Bose's film. The rhetorical divergence between films like *Lifting the Veil* and the majority of the artwork on display at Diasporadics—between what I have described as a feeling of guilt interrupting a sensation of feeling good—demonstrates how being South Asian is about a racialized and politicized notion of belonging to the United States.

As a site for progressive politics, the festivals were a cultural touchstone for a number of South Asian groups, including feminist, queer, antiracist, and labor organizations. Many of the festival organizers, volunteers, and attendees were active members of such groups and defined themselves and their political communities primarily in opposition to the U.S. state. By suggesting that participants and organizers at the art festivals were complicit in producing and embodying an affirmative multicultural politics, I do not wish to diminish their contributions or deny the transnational activist networks to which they belonged. My interest is in the complex cross-connections between the encouragement and sanction of certain kinds of affects (feeling good about being South Asian) and the repression and denial of others (feeling guilt). The affective nature of belonging is engendered through denying the spatial and temporal relationship that binds together economic and social conditions in South Asia with the political formation of South Asian communities in the United States. Such an emphasis on positive affect also means that those who identify as progressive and as South Asian tend to evade the political impact of other kinds of transnational organizations—for example, the emerging power of Muslim and working-class groups. It is within the delimited field of neoliberal race and ethnic politics in the United States that South Asian communities "solidify, accrue social value, and inch toward recognition."[43] It is also within this social field that the idea of South Asia becomes transformed into the cultural politics of being South Asian.

Consuming Art, Commodifying Identity

On a warm July evening in 2005, the opening reception for Artwallah took place at the Barnsdall Art Park, with a clear view of the famous "Hollywood" sign on the surrounding hills. On view were several artworks and videos by South Asian artists from across the United States and the U.K. With its outdoor seating for musical performances and indoor theater seating for five hundred people, the Barnsdall Art Park was an expansive site for Artwallah, the last remaining South Asian art festival in North America. Since the festival's founding in 2000, Artwallah had doubled the number of musical and dance performances, film screenings, and stand-up comedy. In addition to designated performance spaces, the Barnsdall Art Park was lined with stalls selling food, music, DVDs, clothing, and jewelry. Some stalls showcased immigrant-owned small businesses, such as Indian restaurants and catering companies. Others advertised glossy magazines for professional second-generation South Asians, and were operated by equally glamorous young men and women. White Americans staffed stalls that sold yoga, incense, and meditation accessories. Walking through the outdoor art exhibition or attending one of the open-air workshops required having to navigate these small businesses; actively engaging with the artwork at Artwallah necessitated the simultaneous consumption of a variety of ethnic goods. While the commercial activities of the festival drew a more heterogeneous audience, including Latinos and other Asian Americans, the visibility of these stalls demonstrated the extent to which Artwallah created a commodified experience of South Asian-ness for middle-class consumption.

Like Desh Pardesh and Diasporadics, Artwallah was explicitly committed to producing an annual "progressive South Asian arts festival."[44] Yet Artwallah was also crucially distinct from its predecessors in terms of its funding structure and political organization. In 2005 the festival committee stated its commitment to "cultivate and empower artistic voices of the South Asian diaspora."[45] Toward that end, the committee began to solicit private and corporate donations in addition to applying for state grants. In subsequent years the impact of private funding became increasingly visible as Artwallah marketed itself as an aesthetic brand rather than as a political experience: the festival's distinctive logo was endlessly reproduced on its website, official correspondence, and press and publicity materials. As a nonprofit enterprise with commercial content, Artwallah had proved to be a profitable means of marketing "South Asian" as a brand of ethnic identity.

The transformation of Artwallah from an affective experience of belonging into a commercialized celebration of being South Asian relied upon the spatial organization of the festival as well as its funding structure. As a tourist experience, Artwallah demonstrated how the culture of particular exhibitions—in this case, an exhibition of contemporary South Asian diasporic art—becomes a culture of experience, in this case the experience of being South Asian.[46] This experience was curated through a diverse array of visual and performance art, as well as a series of public forums, such as workshops on financial planning and networking events featuring South Asian actors and filmmakers. However, while Artwallah capitalized on its proximity to the Hollywood culture industry by creating a platform for emerging South Asian artists, it also consolidated the heterogeneity of artwork displayed at the festival—and the heterogeneous audience that attended festival events—into a singular narrative of upward mobility.

Such narratives of upward mobility were showcased not only through the visible celebration of "South Asian" identities via the consumption of visual art (such as the video *Ganges Dreaming* discussed above) but also through the increasingly less visible sources of labor and funding that went into creating this annual art festival. In my interviews with artists and audience members in Los Angeles at Artwallah 2005, many artists questioned the fiscal and organizational structure of the event. Did the festival make a profit or operate at a loss? Was it organized strictly on a volunteer basis, or were certain components of the organization (for example, technical support) paid for their work? While Artwallah's professionalism was evident in the high production value of its media materials (festival program booklets, websites, and press kits) it described itself as a "grassroots" organization. That enabled the organization to continue to solicit private and public donations. However, over the years the festival became increasingly professionalized in its display of art and solicitation of artists. As some artists remarked, shouldn't Artwallah have compensated artists with honoraria or travel reimbursements?[47] That these questions could not be publicly discussed or answered at Artwallah highlighted the unequal distribution of power between festival organizers, artists, and attendees. It also illustrated the contradictory relationship between the festival's commitment to progressive politics and grassroots activism and its hierarchical administrative and financial structure.

Shailja Patel, a performance artist from San Francisco, thematized the central tension between art as an expression of ethnic community and art as an ethnic commodity in her performance at Artwallah. In 2005 Patel performed excerpts from her work *Migritude*. *Migritude* (the title plays on the words migration, negritude, and attitude) delineates the long journey that Patel's family made from colonial India to East Africa, and Patel's own migration as a student from Kenya to England and subsequently to the United States.[48] Like Ameen Gill's lithographs, Patel's poems expand upon South Asian labor migration within the domain of the British empire, linking colonial India to Kenya, and postcolonial Kenya to England. Patel's work traces the intertwined history of race and class that structures South Asian localities in each of these sites. In the prose poem "Shilling Love," Patel speaks of her parents' determination to provide their children with a "world-class education." Patel's parents insist that the entire family participate toward this goal, as they take on extra hours at the workplace and their children study harder to pass their exams. The family's collective effort reflects their determination for upward mobility and capital accumulation. However, within the racial turmoil of post-independence Kenya, the pursuit of class mobility alienates Kenyans of Asian origin from black Africans, for Indian merchants are seen as allies of the British. Though Patel's parents were born and raised in East Africa, in their view their children have no place in the new Kenya. As the Kenyan economy collapses and the value of the Kenyan shilling rapidly plummets against the British pound, Patel's parents work ever harder to send their children to England:

> My parents never say / they love us / they save and count / count and save the shilling falls against the pound / college fees for overseas students / rise like flood ties / love is a luxury / priced in hard currency / ringed by tariffs

[. . .]
75 Kenyan shillings to the pound / they hug us / tearless stoic at airports / as we board planes for icy alien England / cram instructions into our pockets like talismans / [. . .] *remember remember remember the cost of your life*[49]

Countering love with money, Patel's parents work to finance their daughters' educations overseas. Their excessive labor at once reflects and compensates for the family's vexed racial and class location in Kenya. During the military coup of 1982 that threatened to take over the independent Kenyan government, the tide of anti-Asian nationalism in Nairobi taught Patel "that all my patriotic fervor / will not / turn my skin / black."[50] Patel's patriotic identification as a Kenyan citizen cannot eclipse her middle-class status in Kenyan society. Nor can she claim racial identification with a postcolonial African public, which views Patel and her family as nonblacks. Once abroad, she disidentifies with "icy / alien England," a country to which she has formal legal ties as a Commonwealth subject. This series of identifications and disidentifications maps Patel's journey to the United States, where she begins to identify as a woman of color. Many years later it is a different kind of national patriotism that delays Patel's family reunification, as her parents are detained, along with their Kenyan passports, by a U.S. immigration inspector. *Migritude* expresses the literal and psychic cost of migration across three continents, as Patel's poetry denies the romance of transnational localities. Instead, she emphasizes how the immigrant's life is valued in a global marketplace, where the exchange of bodies from third to first world is measured in the relative worth of Kenyan shillings to British pounds.

Patel is one among the many established artists who continued to showcase their work at Artwallah in the spirit of forging South Asian solidarity. Patel describes her performance as an expression of "her personal transitions as a migrant: from survival to self-expression, invisibility to activism, model minority to radical artist."[51] In many ways, *Migritude* encapsulates the dynamic and self-reflexive process of producing South Asian locality at the art festivals. Patel draws upon an autobiographical history of immigration to tell a story about race, class, and national belonging. In turn, her performance is staged as a progressive narrative of South Asian politics. At Artwallah, *Migritude* garnered scattered applause as several audience members walked in and out of the theater during the performance. It was also staged without the benefit of introduction by festival organizers and without an organized forum for questions and answers with the artist. There were, of course, those in the audience who were keenly compelled by Patel's performance, and some viewers stayed in the theater to speak with her afterward. Yet for many others, *Migritude* was just another show, a spectacle of history for those entertained by the performance of politics. *Migritude* was one of many examples of theater that was displayed for public consumption at Artwallah, and yet it was apparent that many viewers did not consider Patel's performance a profitable use of their time. Instead, the cost of watching *Migritude* was twofold. First, Patel's historicization of diasporic subjectivity within a global economy of migrant labor sharply contrasted with the upwardly mobile, professional aspirations of the young South Asians in the audience (the target group for the glossy magazines sold outside the theater). Second, Patel's politicization as a racialized subject of the state occurred elsewhere—not in the United States but in Kenya. The historical narrative of empire that emerged through Patel's performance of *Migritude* was far removed from the racial and class locations of middle-class South Asians in America.

Artwallah shut down in 2010 amid the economic downturn, which had adversely affected one of its major donors.[52] However, focusing on the exhibition culture of Artwallah demonstrates how notions of being South Asian have shifted from the formative experience of queer community at Desh Pardesh and the activist ethos of Diasporadics. As an aesthetic experience, Artwallah relied heavily on the commodification of ethnic identity. During the concluding performance at Artwallah 2005, the founder of the festival, Sarita Vasa, came onstage to solicit donations. "The real reason to give to Artwallah," declared Vasa, "is because there are amazing artists behind it." As performers joined the staff of Artwallah to take a final bow, the theater was consumed in a frenzy of music, sound, and light. Yet by that time half the audience had left the hall. The private donations that supported the festivals' growth were not used to fund the artists whose work was central to Artwallah. Nor was Artwallah entirely successful in creating a collective experience of ethnic community that reflected the heterogeneous backgrounds of festival organizers, artists, and audience members. What Artwallah did succeed in creating, however, was a distinctive brand of South Asian experience, one that transformed the festival into a venue for middle-class entertainment.

As ethnographic and historical texts, the art festivals showcase the correlation between the production of locality and the consumption of ethnicity. Festivals like Desh Pardesh and Diasporadics were initially established to provide alternatives to cultural nationalist constructs of identity. The organizing committees of these festivals, as well as artists and audience members, collaborated to produce queer and racialized narratives of diasporic identity. By curating visual and performance art, music and theater, literary readings and dance, art festivals are central to the emergence of a South Asian public culture in North America. At the same time, Desh Pardesh and Diasporadics illustrate the ways in which the art festivals make a critical intervention in neoliberal constructs of multiculturalism. At Diasporadics, the display of Ameen Gill's *The Mango Tree* and Dhruvi Acharya's *Captive* demonstrated how multivalent histories of nation and empire can be subsumed into universal narratives of diasporic experience. As the screening of Shonali Bose's film emphasized, such imaginative constructs of South Asian community occupy an entirely different space-time from political formations of citizenship on the subcontinent.

As a performative text, the art festivals also generate commodified notions of ethnic identity. Artwallah's success demonstrated how the art festivals are implicated within global circuits of capital movement—even though Shailja Patel's performance and the film screening of *Continuous Journey* explicitly critiques the transnational circulation of capital. While Artwallah was initially formed as a grassroots festival for South Asians, its growth was sustained by the concentration of capital in the hands of a few private donors. This model of financial investment also prefigured the demise of the art festival as a progressive forum for community building and as a collective experience of viewing art. In the wake of the art festivals, privately owned galleries devoted to contemporary South Asian art have proliferated across metropolitan cities in the United States and Canada. Such galleries make no distinction between artists from the subcontinent and those in diaspora.[53] The value of the artworks on display is measured not in shillings but in dollars, for only those artists whose work is profitable on the global market are displayed for public consumption.

In Chapter 5 I expand upon the commodification and consumption of South Asian identities by examining a major entertainment production: the Broadway musical. By exploring the circulation of neoliberal ideologies of nationhood in song, music, and dance, I delineate the ways in which young immigrants become South Asian through their participation in a Bollywood-themed musical. Unlike the "progressive" political ethos of the art festivals, the Broadway musical is an entirely mainstream commercial endeavor. Yet for those actors and dancers who performed in the show, the musical was an unprecedented opportunity to embody racialized, gendered, and sexualized identities as South Asians. For these performers the musical narrative highlights the intimate relationship between imaginative representations of South Asia and the everyday lives of immigrants in America. However, because the musical was staged in New York in the years immediately following the terrorist attacks of September 11, 2001, the spectacular performance of South Asia onstage cannot be divorced from the ongoing racial and religious discrimination against U.S. minority subjects offstage. The ruptured relation between performance and politics underscores the fragile production of diasporic locality. It also illustrates how for many immigrants, identifying with "South Asia" and being "South Asian" remain incommensurable objects of desire.

FIVE

"Somewhere You've Never Been Before"

The American Romance of Bombay Dreams

Bombay Dreams, a musical produced by Andrew Lloyd Webber, opened at the Broadway Theatre in New York City in April 2004. A love story between Akaash, a young man from the slums of Bombay (Mumbai), and Priya, the woman of his dreams, the musical is at once a romance, a melodrama, and homage to Bollywood films. Following a two-year run in London, *Bombay Dreams* was widely anticipated to be a success on Broadway. The musical's premiere was preceded by extensive media publicity, including billboards on Times Square and a special issue of *Time Out New York*. One of several musicals that have arrived in New York via London's West End, *Bombay Dreams* was not atypical in terms of its transcontinental travels. However, it was the first Broadway musical inspired by Bollywood films and music, and the first to feature South Asians in all its lead roles. As such, the making of *Bombay Dreams* generated an unprecedented collaboration between writers in the U.K., composers and musicians in India, and cast and crew in the United States. Despite the large budget and anticipated audience for the show, *Bombay Dreams* ran on Broadway for just eight months, closing on January 1, 2005. By most measures, *Bombay Dreams* was a flop, a financial and artistic disaster, especially when compared with Webber's other long-running musicals such as *Evita*, *Phantom of the Opera*, and *Cats*.

Rather than dismiss *Bombay Dreams* for its apparent failure on the Broadway stage, however, I focus on the extraordinary life that this musical had in New York, a life that was created and sustained by South Asians. Unlike theater critics who panned *Bombay Dreams* as an inauthentic rendition of Indians in India, I explore the musical as a social text about South Asians in diaspora. The musical was the most significant mainstream South Asian cultural production to be staged in New York in the early years of this century and generated a great deal of enthusiasm in local South Asian arts communities. For subcontinental immigrants who performed in the musical, *Bombay Dreams* emblematized the success of an immigrant group that had finally achieved widespread recognition. For many other immigrants who participated in the musical as audience members, *Bombay Dreams* represented the emergence of the Indian nation-state as a cultural and economic powerhouse at the turn of the twenty-first century. For non–South Asian audience members, viewing the musical was an exotic journey to "Somewhere You've Never Been Before," as the advertisements put it. And for those immigrants who did not view the musical but nonetheless incorporated its images, songs, and advertisements into their everyday life, *Bombay Dreams* was in fact a familiar story, a story about South Asian racialization in the United States.

Like the cultural texts that I have previously discussed, the musical is structured by a dissonance between identifying with an imaginative construct of South Asia and identifying as South Asian. However, theorizing locality at *Bombay Dreams* also highlights the problem of place. Given the transatlantic circulation of the musical between London and New York, what are the consequences of representing a locale—in this case, Bombay—in a musical story oriented toward an audience elsewhere? What are the narrative and performative strategies that bind together two distinct places, and what is gained and lost through these representations? How do South Asian immigrants who act in and watch the show identify with these representations of place, even if Bombay is not their place of origin?

Originally staged in London's West End, *Bombay Dreams* draws upon the music, narrative, and choreography of Bollywood film, itself a dominant mode of representation for notions of postcolonial Indian modernity. Translating this performative vocabulary onto the New York stage required the labor of South Asian immigrant actors and dancers. While the musical relied upon actors who appeared to be racially "authentic," the producers also quickly domesticated *Bombay Dreams* into yet another ethnic American musical. *Bombay Dreams* highlights the difference between producing a diasporic cultural text—one that was written, composed, and staffed by South Asians—and consuming a multicultural performance of ethnicity. The fact that the musical propagated a troubling vision of Indian secular nationalism also compels those South Asians who participated in the show as actors, viewers, or critics to examine closely our desire to identify with the object of representation.

For South Asian actors and dancers, largely second-generation immigrants, *Bombay Dreams* offered a chance to break through to the national stage. The musical enabled South Asians to inhabit an "ethnic" role for which their own ethnicity was an asset, not a liability. Toward this end, actors and dancers of various subcontinental origins took seriously their responsibility to embody notions of Indian "culture" and "tradition." Onstage, South Asian cast members took care to accurately reproduce dance movements from Bollywood films and deliver their lines in accented English. Offstage, they derived a powerful sense of satisfaction from expanding the role of South Asians in U.S. public culture. Many actors spoke of their work for *Bombay Dreams* as the role of a lifetime. Others spoke of the intense personal relationships that they forged with other cast members. Dancers described the approval they received from South Asians in the audience who recognized their ability to perform classical Indian and Bollywood dance. Likewise, actors spoke of how achieving their long-cherished dreams of performing on Broadway enabled their immigrant parents to finally approve of their career choice. For these young South Asians, the nature of their work in *Bombay Dreams* extended far beyond their racial identification with their roles.

Yet while *Bombay Dreams* showcased South Asians in all its lead roles, the musical was about Indians in India, not about South Asians in America. As such, among first-generation immigrants who viewed the show, the musical generated mixed reactions. Some audience members were disappointed that the musical did not feature well-known Hindi film actors and actresses. Others admired the musical precisely because it employed young South Asians in starring roles and thus projected high-achieving immigrants into the spotlight. Almost all the South Asians who went to view the show during its run on Broadway were middle-to-upper-class immigrants. Not only were the tickets prohibitively expensive (ranging from eighty dollars to more than twice that amount); the musical was never advertised in the working-class Indian, Pakistani, and Bangladeshi neighborhoods in and around New York City.

For those viewers who were disappointed by the lack of "real" Bollywood stars in *Bombay Dreams*, the musical nevertheless came to represent the arrival of a modern India on the world stage. Specifically, the musical propagated an idea of Bombay (as Mumbai was called in the musical) as a city that was secular, diverse, and urbane: in short, like New York. By equating Bombay with cities such as New York and London, *Bombay Dreams* represented the cultural and social effects of Indian neoliberalism. Indeed, that story of transformation was mirrored in the musical narrative itself, which showcases the heroic rise of Akaash from the slums to the glamorous circuits of the Hindi film industry. In the musical, Akaash's individual achievement triumphs over interreligious and class violence in contemporary Bombay. Likewise, in the rhetoric of the neoliberal Indian state the private citizen triumphs over "premodern" differences of class and caste. That *Bombay Dreams* featured a score by the renowned Indian composer A. R. Rahman (who subsequently received an Oscar for his work on the film *Slumdog Millionaire*) also underscores how the musical represents the globalizing aspirations of modern India.

For South Asian actors as well as audience members, *Bombay Dreams* emerges as a multivalent site for the production of locality. However, because the musical is characterized by a central contradiction between its performative style and narrative content, I highlight how locality is difficult to place. The musical is styled through the performative idiom of contemporary Bollywood film, particularly its rhetoric of globalization. The storyline of the musical reflects the ascendence of a global Indian middle class characterized by its upward mobility and capital accumulation.[1] At the same time, the musical transforms this story about contemporary India into a "universal" narrative of individual achievement and assimilation. Such a narrative is at once specific to the neoliberal aspirations of the Indian state and central to a neoliberal narrative of the U.S. state. In both India and the United States, neoliberal discourses of national diversity emphasize the difference between ethnic, religious, racial, and caste groups, and simultaneously require their cohesion as citizen-subjects in the public sphere. Strategies of managing difference, whether ethnic, racial, or religious, are of course distinct to each country. In India the national body coheres through a public rhetoric of "unity in diversity," a slogan popularized after independence by the first prime minister, Jawaharlal Nehru. By comparison, in the United States, difference is managed through the rhetoric of multiculturalism, which has shifted over the past three decades from the "melting pot" to ideologies of a "post-racial" or "color-blind" America. Despite their rhetorical distinction, notions of pluralist diversity in India and in the United States share a common investment in disciplining the unruly subject of the nation. In *Bombay Dreams* the unruly subject is not Akaash, the hero who disrupts social order as he pulls himself out of poverty; rather it is the Muslim, the Sikh, and the queer subjects in the musical who are eliminated from the text. From the viewpoint of the Indian as well as the U.S. state, these are precisely the terrorizing figures of the national public, the religious and sexual minorities who disrupt the sanctity of citizenship.[2]

Linking the performative style of the musical with its narrative content thus entails exploring how *Bombay Dreams* draws upon multiple notions of nationhood. *Bombay Dreams* was glossed in the national media as a musical that brings "Indian" style together with "American" content. Yet attending to the multivalent narrative of the musical requires moving beyond a vocabulary of cultural mixing or fusion. I delineate the overlapping histories of imperialism and citizenship that bind together the United States, the U.K., and South Asia in order to showcase how representations of "India" are made equivalent to representations of "America" in the musical. *Bombay Dreams* is a West End production that arrived on Broadway via choreographic and musical composition in India; it aimed to reproduce an "authentic" portrayal of India via the performative rhetoric of Bollywood films; it draws upon the labor of first- and second-generation U.S. immigrants who are required to act as "Indians"; and these same immigrants identify as "South Asian" through their performance.

As a transnational musical production, *Bombay Dreams* was also a product of translation. Because the producers aimed for *Bombay Dreams* to have "crossover" or mainstream success, they rewrote the script as it traveled from London to New York. In the U.K., the writer Meera Syal drew upon the long history of British imperialism on the subcontinent, which popularized an orientalist vision of "India" in the British imagination. Further, a substantial Asian immigrant population in London itself guaranteed the financial success of the musical.[3] In the United States the prospect of a largely non–South Asian audience, composed primarily of tourists, posed a different challenge. For this broader viewership, the musical was pitched as a journey to an unknown destination (India), though this imagined India was domesticated through the narrative idiom of a universal (or American) story. In this respect, for the producers of *Bombay Dreams* the musical was not so different from award-winning "ethnic" Broadway musicals such as *Miss Saigon*, *Flower Drum Song*, or *Fiddler on the Roof*.

What makes *Bombay Dreams* distinct from other so-called ethnic musicals is its location within the racial and political landscape of New York City in 2004. That summer, New York was host to the Republican National Convention (RNC). *Bombay Dreams*, along with long-running musicals such as *Phantom of the Opera* and *Aida*, was one of the featured entertainment programs for RNC attendees. While RNC participants were encouraged to attend musicals as a means of contributing their tourist dollars toward New York's ailing economy, musicals like *Bombay Dreams* were promoted as "family friendly" entertainment. In the context of the convention, "family friendly" translated into "nonpolitical" and stood in for heterosexual and white notions of the national family. However, *Bombay Dreams* turned out to be an explicitly political event, for the Broadway Theatre was the site of pitched battles between RNC attendees and protestors, the two groups embodying contesting notions of nationhood. For the RNC attendees, the September 11, 2001, terrorist attacks shadowed the entire convention, which was cloaked in an anti-immigrant rhetoric of keeping America safe and secure. For the hundreds of protestors who thronged the theater, the irony of keeping America "safe" at a musical that was produced through the labor of immigrants was unmistakable. Situating *Bombay Dreams* within this charged political landscape elucidates the ways in which a musical that was nominally about India became a spectacular performance about contemporary America.

Drawing upon my own participation in the musical as an audience member and interviews with cast members, I situate *Bombay Dreams* as an ethnographic and performative text integral to the production of South Asian locality. Reading the narrative of the musical in relation to contemporary Bollywood films demonstrates how the musical generates a fictional construct of India onstage that is "secular" and "modern." Like popular films in India, the performative idiom of the musical relies upon the visible erasure of the Muslim. Muslim characters onstage initially contribute to the spectacle of Bombay's ethnic and religious diversity, but their presence (along with Sikhs) is gradually eroded from the musical narrative. Likewise, the presence of sexual minorities, such as the transgendered hijra who is Akaash's best friend, is also ejected from the plot in order to secure the heteronormative romance of the musical. These elisions trouble the staging of the musical as a politically accountable representation of contemporary India, and yet, as I demonstrate through ethnographic interviews, even those actors who played the roles of these minority characters reveled in their performances. As an audience member, I went to see *Bombay Dreams* four times over the course of its run in New York in 2004. The first time was during previews of the musical; the second, immediately after the opening night; finally, in late December after the principal cast had substantially altered, I saw *Bombay Dreams* twice.[4] For several years after the closure of the musical I interviewed cast members from the original Broadway production, now based in New York, Chicago, Toronto, and California. Their personal and professional reflections generate a vivid account of how this Broadway production was central to their own identification as South Asians. Even though cast members came from diverse national backgrounds (Australians, Canadians, Americans), religious groups (Hindu, Muslim, and Christian), and subcontinental origins (Pakistani and Indian), they felt bound to each other through their common investment in the musical. Given the racial politics of casting in musical theater and the commercial constraints of Broadway productions, these cast members viewed *Bombay Dreams* as a rare opportunity to perform *as* South Asians. Through interviews with these cast members, I examine not only how these actors are integral to the production of the musical but also how their labor is central to understanding the act of consumption.[5]

My engagement with *Bombay Dreams*, its cast, and other audience members is as much an attempt to understand the pleasure that saturates my own experience of the musical as it is an analysis of the rhetoric of national subjectivity that informs it. On the first two occasions that I saw the musical, the mood inside the theater was radiant. The audience erupted into a spontaneous standing ovation following each performance, moved if not by the quality of the musical then at least by the earnest enthusiasm of the actors. At each viewing I anticipated with great delight the musical's hit numbers, "Shakalaka Baby" and "Chaiyya Chaiyya," as well as the kiss shared between Akaash and Priya onstage.[6] At the matinee and evening performances I attended, the musical attracted crowds of ticket-holders. The audience included families with children and grandparents; South Asians, Latinos, African Americans, and Asian Americans; and a large contingent of white senior citizens. My enthusiasm for *Bombay Dreams* derived not only from the energetic dance numbers but also from the extraordinary sensation of watching a Broadway stage full of young South Asian actors as well as other actors of color. Although on numerous previous occasions I had attended films, literary readings, and plays in New York City featuring South Asians, *Bombay Dreams* was the first mainstream event that brought South Asians in such vast numbers to the American entertainment industry. My compulsion to return several times to see a production that was predicted to fail during its opening week was an attempt to develop a sustained engagement with a memorable, if short-lived, form of diasporic popular culture. It was also a means of exploring the contradictory affect that I experienced, as a viewer who identified with the performers onstage and who disidentified with the ideological representations of Indian and U.S. nationhood generated through their performances. My inability to reconcile this public representation of South Asia with my private identification as a South Asian highlights the predicament of identifying with mainstream South Asian diasporic popular culture, specifically in terms of its racial, sexual, class, and caste politics.

Bombay, London, New York: Making an American Story

Bombay Dreams is a love story that centers on the class difference between its protagonists. Akaash, a boy raised in the slums of Bombay, and Priya, the daughter of a wealthy film director, meet when Akaash's slum, Paradise, is threatened with demolition. A private real estate company plans to acquire Paradise in order to construct a multiplex cinema at the same location. The residents of Paradise have two choices: purchase the land themselves, or be evicted from their home. Priya visits Paradise to make a documentary about what she calls the "real" Bombay. Her fiancé, Vikram, a lawyer, offers to defend the slum's residents against the demolition project. When Priya and Vikram meet Akaash, he has no desire to be a documentary subject; instead he wants to be a movie star. His primary advocate is a childhood friend, the hijra Sweetie, whose love for Akaash is sidelined when Akaash falls in love with Priya. Through a string of coincidences engineered by Sweetie, Akaash becomes the new hero of Bollywood cinema in a film directed by Priya's father. Meanwhile, we find out that Vikram is not an altruistic lawyer but the owner of the real estate company that plans to demolish Paradise. In rapid succession the musical charts Akaash's rise to fame, his affair with the screen goddess Rani, his romantic relationship with Priya, and his reconciliation with his family in the slums. By the end of the musical, Paradise is saved, Sweetie is killed, Vikram's duplicity is revealed, and Priya and Akaash get married.

Bombay Dreams is one in a series of musical productions that have featured Asian Americans in lead roles, beginning with the 1958 Broadway production of *Flower Drum Song*. Based on the novel by C. Y. Lee, *Flower Drum Song* was originally directed on Broadway by Gene Kelly and later released as a Hollywood film in 1961 (it was restaged for Broadway in 2005 by David Henry Hwang). In *The Melancholy of Race*, Anne Anlin Cheng writes eloquently about *Flower Drum Song*, a musical that, as she notes, elicits both "the pleasure of identification" and "its immediate renunciation." For those who recall the flashy dance routines of Linda Low or the demure manner of the Chinese immigrant Mei Li, the musical operates as a "public memory" of Asian American subjectivity, one that produces an "involuntary delight that finds itself slightly unseemly" (31). For the Asian American viewer who simultaneously identifies and disidentifies with the gendered and racial subject of *Flower Drum Song*, the musical generates an uncanny memory of belonging. Likewise in *Bombay Dreams*, a musical replete with ironic references to Bollywood film, the viewer identifies (perhaps bashfully) with the racialized and sexualized subjects onstage, even while disidentifying with the popular narrative conventions of Bollywood cinema. Both *Flower Drum Song* and *Bombay Dreams* are also preoccupied with the romance of belonging, articulated through the genre of the love story. In *Flower Drum Song* the narrative follows the love triangle established between Wang-Ta, a wealthy second-generation Chinese American, and his prospective brides: Linda Low (the vamp) and Mei Li (the virgin). There is also a third woman, Helen Chao, a seamstress who unsuccessfully solicits Wang-Ta's attention. Though Linda Low entrances Wang-Ta, particularly through her performance of explicit sexuality, Wang-Ta ultimately chooses Mei Li as his partner. She embodies both the "traditional" and "modern" China, and their union represents the upward mobility and legality of the Asian American immigrant subject. Similiarly in *Bombay Dreams*, the plot revolves around Akaash's attraction to the vamp Rani and the virgin Priya. But the third wheel in this love triangle is the transgendered figure of Sweetie, the hijra who is neither man nor woman, neither Hindu nor Muslim. Sweetie consistently interrupts Akaash's affair with Rani and his romance with Priya, even though Sweetie's love for

Akaash remains unrequited. In the final scenes of the musical Sweetie is murdered, thereby allowing Akaash to secure his love for Priya. By the conclusion of *Bombay Dreams*, Priya and Akaash's marriage consolidates the modern Indian family, triumphing over differences of class, caste, and sexuality.

The narrative parallels between *Flower Drum Song* and *Bombay Dreams*, however, did not translate into commercial success for the latter. *Flower Drum Song* preceded the 1965 Hart-Celler Act and showcased the first generation of naturalized Asian Americans (specifically Chinese Americans) after World War II. By contrast, *Bombay Dreams* culminates four decades of South Asian migration to the United States and was staged in New York just a few years after 9/11. The discourses of race and nationhood that shaped the reception of both musicals, therefore, dramatically diverge. Whereas *Flower Drum Song* is one more example of the all-inclusive nature of Broadway as a "melting pot" where ethnic subjects transform into American citizens, *Bombay Dreams* literally exceeds the temporal and spatial boundaries of the United States.[7] The geographic location of the story line in Bombay, as well as the fact that the musical traveled from London to New York, engenders a different history of postcoloniality, one that is not immediately recuperable within a U.S.-based framework of race and ethnicity. The postcolonial history of *Bombay Dreams* is performed through the idiom of Bollywood cinema, and as such the Broadway musical is altered in relation to a popular vocabulary of dance, movement, and music on the subcontinent. Moreover, unlike musicals such as *Miss Saigon* that re-create scenes of U.S. military intervention in Asia, there is no public history of U.S. imperialism in South Asia that binds viewers to the plot conventions of *Bombay Dreams*.

On the opening night in April 2004, an eclectic parade of celebrities streamed into New York's Broadway Theatre, including Salman Rushdie, Donald Trump, and Miss America Erika Harold. In spite of these celebrity endorsements, the mainstream press panned *Bombay Dreams*. The *New York Times* called the show "an expensive model of blandness" that is "never, ever compelling," while the *Washington Post* described the musical as something that "exists to be endured, like a bad date."[8] The only enthusiastic and unabashedly supportive reviews of the musical came from the immigrant press, as well as from Indian newsmagazines. In a typical cover story, the North American edition of *India Today* displayed a beaming Ayesha Dharkar as Rani, arms outstretched, drenched in the blue glow of stage lights, with the headline "Staging a Coup [. . .] A. R. Rahman's *Bombay Dreams* Storms

Broadway."⁹ Notably, *India Today* erased Andrew Lloyd Webber's signature from the musical, presenting it as an entirely "Indian" production.

In fact, the musical was a transnational creation, conceived during a meeting in London between Andrew Lloyd Webber and the filmmaker Shekhar Kapur. In his introduction to the program guide for *Bombay Dreams*, Webber remarks that a recent fascination with Bollywood music provided inspiration. He writes that he was cooking lunch at home when

> a song [on the television] lured me away from the stoves: Three lines of gorgeous girls were dancing for a few seated blokes with turbans whilst one girl moved demurely and sang in an abnormally high chest voice. Very good this song was too. Unfortunately I forgot to write down the name of the movie. To this day I haven't traced it.

Webber mentioned his newfound discovery of Hindi films to Kapur, who in turn sent Webber some compilations of Bollywood musical hits. Webber took these videocassettes with him on holiday "and chucked them on in the background whilst the kids were playing in the garden." The songs he heard convinced him that Bollywood film music signified "the revitalization of popular melody from somewhere far removed from Western Europe and America."[10]

The setting of Webber's initial encounter with Bollywood—at home in London, attending to the kitchen stove—domesticates South Asian popular culture within the spatial geography of Britain. The tapes are "chucked" on in the background while Webber's attention remains on his children. At the same time, however, Webber contends that the music revitalizes popular melody from "somewhere far removed," that is, external to the homeland that he inhabits. The fact that Hindi film music is both intrinsic to and marginalized from British popular culture was further highlighted when Webber brought A. R. Rahman, the composer of these hit songs, to London. Rahman, who has sold more than one hundred million albums worldwide, was an unknown entity to Webber but not to the South Asian immigrants who eagerly awaited the composer. During one of the music rehearsals, Webber found that "most of the Asian head waiters of Soho [were] awaiting him outside the stage door."[11] Like the forgettable "blokes with turbans" that Webber saw on television, his casual description of "Asian head waiters" dismisses the ethnic and class diversity of Asian immigrants in Britain, now the largest nonwhite minority group in the country.[12] He also reproduces the spatial and temporal difference between South Asia and South Asians, even as the two sites are linked through the circulation of music and film. For Webber, whose exposure to popular Bollywood music was limited to a single television show, the world of immigrant fans awaiting A. R. Rahman provocatively expanded his conceptions of what it meant to be British. Webber's collaboration with Rahman tapped into the expansive musical imagination of an increasingly multicultural Britain.[13]

While *Bombay Dreams* was conceived as an homage to Bollywood film, it was also forged in response to the increasing racial diversity of the audience for musical theater. Multiculturalism, in this context, operated both as a commercial means for marketing the musical and as a neoliberal form of race management that was integral to casting the show. In the West End as well as on Broadway, actors of subcontinental origin had all the principal speaking roles, and the ensemble cast was also composed primarily of South Asians as well as other actors of color. In New York, Manu Narayan played the lead role of Akaash, Anisha Nagarajan played Priya, Ayesha Dharkar played Rani, and Sriram Ganesan was Sweetie. With the exception of Narayan, who had performed in other Broadway productions, and Dharkar, whose roles in independent films had received international acclaim, amateur actors held the remaining lead roles. In interviews that I conducted, principal and ensemble cast members endorsed the producers' efforts to promote racial diversity, which in their view enabled relatively unknown actors to break through to the Broadway stage. Anjali Bhimani, who played Rani during the last two months of the production, declared that "every single speaking character in that show was of South Asian descent—and that was quite a coup." Sheetal Gandhi, a dancer in the ensemble cast, likewise spoke of *Bombay Dreams* as an unparalleled opportunity. Reflecting on the audition process, she commented, "[I thought] here's a musical where I look exactly like what they want. I just want to be in a room with other Indian artists. On a whim, a week before auditions, I bought a ticket and flew into New York." For Gandhi, *Bombay Dreams* was not only the first time that she was able to work with other South Asian artists; it was also the first time that she was able to perform as a South Asian onstage.

In Gandhi and Bhimani's words, their individual achievements override the commercialized representation of racial diversity onstage. However, the producers' insistence on hiring South Asians for the principal roles also reflects the growing debate over multiracial casting in mainstream theater, particularly following the casting debacle of *Miss Saigon*, the show that immediately preceded *Bombay Dreams* at the Broadway Theatre. In that musical the highly sexualized and racialized encounter between Kim (a Vietnamese prostitute) and Chris (an American GI) was embodied onstage by a Filipina actress, Lea Salonga, and a white American actor, Willy Falk. Salonga was a well-known singer in the Philippines, but her role in *Miss Saigon* marked her debut on the Broadway stage. However, for the lead role of the Engineer—one of two biracial roles in the musical—producer Cameron Macintosh retained the white British actor Jonathan Pryce, who had played the Engineer in London's West End. As Karen Shimakawa has detailed in her book, *National Abjection*, Macintosh's insistence on retaining Pryce was vigorously protested by Asian American performing artists and activists. As a result, Pryce was banned from the production by Actors' Equity. However, shortly thereafter he was reinstated in the role of the Engineer, for Macintosh threatened to cancel the musical production on Broadway. Shimakawa contends that Pryce's performance, playing a Eurasian man "in yellowface, with taped eyelids, blackened teeth, greased hair, and bronzed skin," constituted one of the most visually satisfying sequences of the musical for many audience members (48).

The problem with the New York production of *Bombay Dreams* was not white actors playing brownface, as multiracial casting had been resolved through hiring South Asian immigrants. Instead, the problem of race arose when the producers attempted to circumvent falling revenues by bringing in a name-brand star, the African American singer Tamyra Gray. Gray, who had achieved minor celebrity status as a contestant on the television show *American Idol*, was recruited to play the lead role of Priya for the final eight weeks of the show. According to ensemble cast members, the decision to cast Gray in the musical was clearly a means of attracting a larger audience as well as generate ticket sales during the peak winter holiday season. Gray's professional demeanor and talent was acknowledged by all the cast members, but her presence as an African American in an "Indian" musical that was otherwise populated by South Asians elicited contradictory remarks. In my interview with Suresh John, a second-generation South Asian Canadian actor in the ensemble cast, he dismissed the significance of race for the role of Priya. John claimed, "A lot of people didn't kind of notice [Gray]—as far as the 'Indian-ness' of it goes. There's nothing that Priya does that's particularly

'Indian.' "[14] In contrast, Anjali Bhimani, though noting Gray's dedication to the role, conceded that Gray "changed the flavor of the play." In either case, Gray's participation in *Bombay Dreams* was short-lived. Although her role was widely advertised and succeeded in drawing a number of fans to Broadway, her performance could not single-handedly turn around the financial prospects of the show. The main problem, according to Bhimani and John, was not that Gray was African American. It was the fact that the musical featured a largely unknown cast and a story line set in India, and thus could not attract the mainstream audience necessary to keep the show running. As Bhimani said, "It wasn't like we needed to bring in more South Asians to the audience—we needed to bring in more Americans." Although Gray brought a level of celebrity to the musical, her casting amplified the narrative dissonance between a national show like *American Idol* and a transnational musical production such as *Bombay Dreams*. The former is a televised competition to find the next American pop star, and its popularity has generated numerous international franchises. The latter was a multimedia production created in consultation with writers in the U.K., musicians in India, and actors in the United States. The particular challenge of *Bombay Dreams* was not to expand the show overseas but rather to domesticate it. Because the producers were finally unable to reconcile the relationship between the domestic audience and the transnational narrative of the musical—or what Webber might describe as the difference between "home" and "somewhere far removed"—*Bombay Dreams* closed after ten months.

Some South Asian audience members suggested that the musical failed because it did not feature established Bollywood stars. In an Op-Ed article for the *New York Times*, Prashant Agrawal argued that the musical should have starred mainstream Hindi film actors such as Amitabh Bachchan and Aishwariya Rai.[15] Without star power, the producers of *Bombay Dreams* missed their chance to capitalize on the global popularity of Bollywood and thereby attract a large Indian American audience, whom Agrawal erroneously described as "America's richest ethnic group." By hiring unknown South Asian immigrants, Agrawal noted, *Bombay Dreams* failed to reproduce an authentic version of Indian culture. Agrawal's comments elucidate the ways in which Bollywood films stand in for representations of "national culture" in diaspora, similar to the role of Bollywood songs and dance at the Miss India USA pageant. His demand to see Hindi film stars on Broadway also illustrates the dissonant uses of Bollywood in Indian popular culture and in diasporic cultural productions. Even though *Bombay Dreams* drew upon the song, music, and dance forms of commercial Hindi films, the musical itself was oriented toward a non–South Asian audience. Thus while *Bombay Dreams* was advertised as a journey to a time and space outside the United States, it is Agrawal's desire to see a so-called "authentic" representation of India that is out of place.

The casting of the musical only partially resolved the question of how to domesticate a transnational production for an American audience. The challenge still remained in translating the script from the original British production to focus on the rags-to-riches story of the musical's hero, Akaash. According to Elizabeth Williams, a coproducer of the musical, for *Bombay Dreams* "to succeed on Broadway, it has to be like any other mainstream musical that had roots in another country." Listing the success of *Evita*, *Zorba the Greek*, and *Fiddler on the Roof*, Williams noted that the show should "move the audience here or anywhere in the world."[16] Likewise Steven Pimlott, who directed both the New York and London productions, characterized the musical as a "universal" form of entertainment and described *Bombay Dreams* as "a great all-singing, dancing show. It could make you remember the MGM musicals."[17] Rewriting the musical as it traveled from London to New York was central to this project of translation, for *Bombay Dreams* could not rely on audience members familiar with Bollywood cinema. Instead, Pimlott and Williams sought to represent *Bombay Dreams* as an "ethnic" narrative that ultimately transcends precisely its ethnic difference in order to become an American story.

The difficulty of translating a story about Indians in India into a "universal" narrative about immigration was prefigured during the musical's run in the West End. The novelist and comedian Meera Syal wrote the original script for a British audience, who she assumed would be familiar with India, given the long history of British imperialism on the subcontinent. As she remarked, "with colonization there's been a love-hate relationship between us for over 300 years."[18] Yet Syal's assumption of a naturalized historical relationship between South Asia and Britain requires further interrogation, for the fact of colonialism does not translate into a familiarity with Indian history or culture. At the time Syal wrote *Bombay Dreams*, the British media continued to draw upon colonial representations of India as "The Jewel in the Crown," as depicted by the popular 1980s television series of the same name. To a large extent Syal's ongoing work for television and film, in collaboration with the publications of numerous other British Asian writers, has reoriented British imperial nostalgia for the subcontinent in order to focus on postcolonial Asian migration to Britain.[19] Yet even in this regard the story line of *Bombay Dreams* does not account for the heterogeneity of Asians in Britain. Although subcontinental immigrants constitute over half of Britain's nonwhite population (and in London composed nearly half the audience for the musical), within this group 22 percent identify as Indians, 16 percent as Pakistani, and 6 percent as Bangladeshi.[20] The majority of British Asians identify as Muslims (a minority are Hindus and Sikhs).[21] India is not the dominant point of cultural origin even for those Asians of Indian origin, many of whom are the descendants of immigrants from Kenya and Uganda. Despite the diverse national, religious, and class composition of Asian immigrants in Britain, the musical was rather incongruously staged as part of a larger orientalist representation of India. For example, in London the premiere of *Bombay Dreams* was accompanied by a mass shopping campaign launched by the department store Selfridges, which announced that May 2002 was "India month." Indian fashion and interior designers, Bollywood makeup artists, and celebrities were recruited to transform Selfridges into an exotic destination for shopping that recalled the imperial fantasies of the British Raj.[22] At the same time, the mainstreaming of Bollywood popular culture underscored the emergence of a global Indian middle class. Selfridges' "India month" was one in a series of media events that recuperated *Bombay Dreams* into a peculiarly British imagination of colonial and postcolonial India.

In the United States the premiere of *Bombay Dreams* was not tied into a larger campaign for Indian goods or commodities. However, the musical was dramatically redesigned for the Broadway stage in terms of narrative, music, choreography, and set design. As opposed to Asian immigrants who composed nearly 50 percent of the West End audience for *Bombay Dreams*, in New York only an estimated 15 to 20 percent of the audience was South Asian.[23] Given the small numbers of South Asians who would view the musical as "native informants," the Waxman Williams production group hired Thomas Meehan (who wrote the scripts for *Annie*, *Hairspray*, and *The Producers*) to rewrite the musical for Broadway.[24] Unlike Syal, who had grown up with an intimate familiarity with popular Hindi film and its idiom of romance and tragedy, Meehan had never seen a Bollywood film before working on *Bombay Dreams*. "In London," Meehan noted, "it was more of a parody of a Bollywood movie. But mainstream America does not know so much about Bollywood [. . . we had] to turn it into a traditional, old fashioned romantic story."[25]

Negotiating the competing narrative conventions of what Pimlott described as "MGM musicals" and contemporary Bollywood film, the scriptwriters adjudicated between multiple musical idioms. Syal and Meehan eliminated the satirical elements of the West End production in order to produce a classic romantic narrative of poor-boy-meets-rich-girl. Likewise, the musical score featured additional compositions by A. R. Rahman that introduced American audiences to a combination of Punjabi bhangra and hip-hop music. Given the unfamiliarity of most cast members with the movement language of dance sequences in Bollywood films, the Indian choreographer Farah Khan collaborated with the West End choreographer Anthony van Laast to translate Bollywood dance moves from screen to stage. Finally, the stage set was elaborately redesigned: the pivotal "wet sari" sequence of the musical now featured thirty-two nozzles of water, creating what the set designer Mark Thompson described as a stage effect similar to the grand hotel fountains of Las Vegas. The total production cost for the U.S. version of *Bombay Dreams* came to fourteen million dollars, double that of the London production.[26]

The cost of translating *Bombay Dreams* to an American audience, however, was much more than the financial investment poured into this Broadway show. By transforming the musical plotline, Meehan overrode the historical relationship between the United States and South Asia. At no point did the musical's producers acknowledge the increasing exchange of labor, capital, and commodities that bind the subcontinent with the United States, particularly in terms of the globalization of South Asian popular culture. Instead of drawing South Asia closer to America (like the visual works created by South Asian artists that I discussed in Chapter 4), the revised production of *Bombay Dreams* imagined South Asia as a place entirely outside the boundaries of the United States. The writers of *Bombay Dreams* sought to create an idea of India that was foreign to the U.S. public, even as the musical relied on performances by South Asian immigrants and an audience base that was nearly 20 percent South Asian. At the same time, this idea of India was domesticated into an "American" story through a so-called universal narrative of romantic love. By adjudicating between different rhetorics of national belonging, the writers and producers prioritized the narrative of American multiculturalism and marginalized the politics of caste and class in contemporary India.

The Queer Romance of Modernity: Caste, Class, and Sexuality in Bombay Dreams

Reorienting *Bombay Dreams* in order to read it as a story of postcolonial and multicultural nationhood requires approaching the musical at a slant, for it requires examining not only how the musical represents racial minorities in the United States, but also how such representations are bound by the narrative conventions of popular culture produced outside the United States. *Bombay Dreams* engenders a particular representation of South Asia in America, one generated through the transnational circulation of Bollywood films. In turn, the performative conventions of Bollywood shape how immigrant actors and dancers identify as South Asian on Broadway. Their labor makes visible the ways in which notions of modernity and globalization on the subcontinent are refracted through practices of U.S. multiculturalism. As South Asian immigrants creatively embody this performative rhetoric of Indian nationhood, they bind and warp ideologies of national belonging on the subcontinent as well as in America. Reading the dialectical relationship between Bollywood (as a global representation of Indian modernity) and Broadway (as the "melting pot" of America) distorts the temporal and spatial framework within which we locate South Asian diasporas.[27]

Drawing upon an ethnographic reading of the Broadway production, I explore three distinct aspects of the musical narrative. First, differences of religion, caste, and class are elided in order to represent Bombay as a site of Indian secular modernity. Second, the ongoing project of economic liberalization in India is central to establishing equivalence between Bombay and New York, both metropolitan sites of capital. Finally, the romantic narrative between Priya and Akaash secures the musical's representation of a heteronormative national body. In the latter context, I explore the pivotal location occupied by minority religious and queer subjects in *Bombay Dreams*. The primacy of the heterosexual compact between Akaash and Priya is enabled through the queer—but ultimately not modern—figure of the hijra Sweetie.

In a preproduction video of the musical, the director Steven Pimlott insists that *Bombay Dreams* "is its own thing—it's not a Bollywood movie."[28]

A closer reading of *Bombay Dreams*, however, reveals that it duplicates the complex sequence of subplots and extended song sequences that are integral to Bollywood films. At the Broadway Theatre, the curtain rose to taped recitations from Hindu Sanskrit scriptures followed by the Muslim call to prayer. As the scrim dissolved, the backdrop of the stage came prominently into view, featuring the silhouette of a mosque and a temple rimmed by an expansive vista of skyscrapers and shacks. A large beehivelike set descended onto the stage. This was the slum of Paradise, home to Akaash and his family. Two drummers aloft on either side of the set introduced the title song, "Salaa'm Bombay." In an upbeat tempo, Bombay came to life as a paradise of slums, where people living in poverty dreamed of fame and stardom to the beat of Bollywood film music. Act 1 begins with Akaash introducing himself to the audience: he is not only the hero of the musical but also Sweetie's childhood friend and a beloved prankster in his slum community. The first act progresses rapidly as Akaash meets the filmmaker Priya and her fiancé, the lawyer/real estate developer Vikram; joins Sweetie in gate-crashing the Miss India beauty pageant; and falls into the arms of the Bollywood siren Rani, who implores Priya's father to cast Akaash in his next movie. The movie is a resounding success, and Akaash becomes a film star overnight, but success comes at the cost of relinquishing his ties to Paradise. In act 2, Akaash must prove his loyalty to Paradise and its residents. When Sweetie realizes that Vikram is responsible for the impending destruction of Paradise, she confronts him and is killed. Akaash finally comes to the rescue by offering to buy Paradise on behalf of its inhabitants, thereby deposing Vikram and securing Priya's love. The musical ends with a spectacular wedding finale and a long kiss between Priya and Akaash.

One of the world's most populated cities and the commercial heart of post-independence India, Bombay is the subject of several literary and historical accounts on Indian modernity.[29] Renamed Mumbai in 1995 by regional political parties, Bombay continues to be represented in the Indian media as a cosmopolitan city, teeming with ethnic, religious, and linguistic diversity. In the souvenir program for the musical, Meera Syal describes Bombay in relation to other metropolitan locales. She writes that Bombay is "the richest, most vibrant city in India boasting more expensive real estate and more millionaires than Manhattan, and a new MTV generation whose style and pizazz would make your average London socialite look like a plodding country bumpkin. [The city has] 16 million people of every single faith and income level." Syal proceeds to contend that like Manhattan, Bombay "is a city of enterprise [. . .] these people may be poor but no-one starves as there is enough work for everyone." Here, Bombay mirrors the economic and social diversity of New York City, with a vibrant black-market economy that provides employment, including for slum residents who are described by Syal as "fiercely organized and independent." In Syal's view the rapid growth of the Indian middle class exceeds the wealth of New Yorkers and Londoners, thereby establishing Bombay as an emerging "global city" in the twenty-first century.[30]

Syal's comparison of Bombay with London and New York pointedly fails to mention another fundamental similarity between the three cities: namely, the rise in violent attacks against racial and religious minority groups. Like New York and London, which saw an increase in race-based hate crimes against Arab Americans and South Asians after the terrorist attacks of September 2001 and July 2005, Bombay is also characterized by religious and ethnic violence. During the 1990s the hegemony of the regional political party Shiv Sena led to targeted violence toward Muslims and other minority groups. For example, during riots between Hindus and Muslims following the destruction of the Babri Masjid, the Shiv Sena actively supported the destruction of Muslim-owned businesses and residential communities in Bombay (a history of communal violence that is reflected in the film *Bombay*, which I discussed in Chapter 3). More recently, in 2008, Bombay was the target of terrorist attacks, allegedly by Pakistani militants fighting for a free Kashmir. Although these attacks did not result in mass rioting across the city, Muslim residents and businesses in Bombay were targeted by state and federal agencies and became subjects of surveillance and interrogation by the Indian state.

Such intensive government efforts to profile religious minorities, along with tacit state support for anti-Muslim riots, reflect the ascendance of Hindu nationalist ideologies in contemporary India. As the political theorist Thomas Blom Hansen has argued, Hindutva (a Hindu-centric ideology of belonging) has emerged as a dominant identity of selfhood in Bombay across the past three decades. The rise of Hindutva stands in opposition to the historically diverse urban identities of Bombay's inhabitants, which include large populations of Sikhs, Muslims, Christians, and Zoroastrians. Such Hindu-centric ideologies emerge out of the deep tension between regional and national identity, between "vernacular" languages such as Marathi and national languages such as Hindi and English, as well as between local manifestations of economic underdevelopment and the ongoing growth of the Indian middle class. The emergence of a regionalist (Maharashtrian) and Hindu communal identity is also directly linked to the Shiv Sena's tactics of political intimidation and economic control.[31] The Shiv Sena makes no appearance in *Bombay Dreams*, but the musical's representation of ethnic and religious diversity in Bombay draws upon the recent history of communal violence in the city. The ways in which the romantic narrative of the musical hinges upon the threat of violence contained within notions of a diverse national public illuminates the tangled relationship between representations of "secular" Indian citizenship and discourses of religious and ethnic difference.

In *Bombay Dreams*, Akaash's childhood home of Paradise is deliberately represented as a slum in Bombay, rather than a generic slum in any other Indian city. What makes Paradise so distinctive is its use of visual markers to signify Bombay's ethnic and religious diversity. Among the residents of Paradise is a Sikh man wearing his turban and a Muslim distinguished by his white filigreed cap. But these are the only two people onstage who are visually distinct from the rest of the slum's thirty-odd inhabitants, whose names, dress, and bindis on the women's foreheads mark them as Hindu. The cultural critic Tejaswini Niranjana draws our attention to the visual rhetoric of clothing in popular Indian cinema, particularly as it is used to mark ethnic minorities. Discussing *Roja*, a Tamil film by the director Mani Ratnam, Niranjana notes that the hero, Rishi, "usually appears only in jeans and a shirt or sweater." On the other hand, the Kashmiri militants who kidnap Rishi "always appear in clothes which mark them as ethnically Muslim; it is an ethnicity which reveals them as anti-modern (therefore anti-national or anti-Indian), intolerant and fundamentalist, while Hindu ethnicity as displayed by [. . .] Rishi is merely part of the complexity of being Indian" (152). Like Rishi in *Roja*, Akaash always appears onstage in jeans and a shirt, embodying the modern Indian man. His female counterpart, Priya, is likewise made modern and feminine through her clothing. Priya frequently wears salwaar kameez, but equally often appears onstage in a pair of trousers and a blouse. In contrast, the remaining inhabitants of Paradise wear "Indian" clothes (saris and kurta pyjamas), and within this group the Muslim and Sikh characters are consistently demarcated as religiously "other" by their clothing. In contrast to Priya and Akaash, the Muslim and Sikh inhabitants of Paradise are not only not modern; they are unnamed, nonverbal subjects who are extraneous to the plot development of the musical.

I focus on the representation of non-Hindu others onstage in *Bombay Dreams* because they rupture the visual logic of a musical that is otherwise dominated by Hindu iconography. For example, in act 2 Akaash rescues Priya from her impending marriage to Vikram during Ganesh Chaturthi, a major regional Hindu festival celebrating the elephant-headed god, Ganesh. Four large illuminated floats of Ganesh dominate the stage, and the city's rich and poor rejoice together in celebration. Conspicuously absent in this scene are the filigreed cap of the Muslim man and the turban of the Sikh man (though the actors who play these roles are in fact onstage). Likewise, Akaash's marriage to Priya takes place on a stage set drenched in orange and pink silk, presided over by two priests who bless the couple as the curtain falls. The wedding scene that closes the musical—by now so familiar to Western audiences—is constituted through Hindu rituals that are "so normalized that we do not pay them any special attention, or even mark them as 'religious.'"32

The ubiquity of Hindu ritual and practice obscures the narrative tension between the musical's representation of ethnic and religious diversity and its affirmation of universal citizenship. In order for Bombay to be made equivalent to New York or London, the city must be made visually recognizable onstage through its representation of a diverse (or multicultural) national public. The visible differentiation of religious and ethnic others also engenders a modern idea of India. Yet the larger problem that remains unaddressed in the musical is its desire to establish equivalence, if not equity, between majority and minority subjects onstage. As I described earlier, *Bombay Dreams* opens with recitations of Hindu scriptures and the Muslim call to prayer; the backdrop to Paradise contains the outlines of a Hindu temple and a Muslim mosque. But this false equivalence between Hindus and Muslims is undermined by the disproportionately large number of Hindu subjects in the principal cast of the musical, and the fact that the Muslim and Sikh characters literally disappear from the final scenes. The result of this assimilative process is the erasure of a history of communal violence between Hindus and Muslims in the slum and the subsequent recuperation of Paradise as an icon of Indian "secularism."

The debate around representations of religious diversity in *Bombay Dreams* is compounded by the musical's representation of class and caste difference.

Throughout the musical the protagonists' class positions are consistently conflated with their caste status. For example, the poverty-stricken Akaash and his grandmother Shanti refer to themselves as "untouchables," so low in the caste hierarchy that they literally cannot be touched. In the context of modern Indian politics, Shanti and Akaash would be categorized as Dalits, rather than "untouchables," but identifying with this political category appears to be beyond the historical scope of the musical.[33] Conversely, the lawyer/industrialist Vikram is taunted as "the brahmin in the suit," as his wealth is perceived to be synonymous with upper-caste status. Because Shanti and Akaash's representation as "untouchables" is conflated with their working-class lives, Akaash and Priya's courtship is portrayed as a romance across caste lines, rather than as a negotiation of class difference. Supplementing the absence of class dynamics is the fact that Shanti, Akaash, and Sweetie are never portrayed engaging in any kind of work. In fact, "labor" in the musical is only approximated through song and dance.[34] The heterogeneous class, caste, and religious composition of Paradise thus functions in the musical as a mere backdrop to the primacy of heterosexual romance.

However, the violent intersection of class, caste, and religious identities is not fully contained by a "secular" representation of India's national diversity onstage. Instead, the musical narrative illustrates how ongoing neoliberal economic reforms in India impact the tense relationship between upper and lower castes, as well as between working- and middle-class subjects. The conflict around class and caste is centrally staged as a question of property—more specifically, a question of who has the right to inhabit public property. At the outset of act 1, we learn that Akaash is an orphan from Mahim, whose parents died during a slum clearance program. Mahim, a district in western Bombay, was one of the nodal points of the 1992–93 Hindu-Muslim riots. The slums of Mahim were also targeted in a government demolition project in 1999, part of a public works program to construct highways for urban commuters. The death of Akaash's parents in a (real) slum clearance project demonstrates how working-class citizens are literally erased from public land through state-sponsored projects for modernization. During Akaash's life, control over public property shifts from the state to the hands of private real estate developers. Priya and Akaash meet when Paradise is about to be demolished, for Vikram's real estate company plans to bulldoze the slum in order to build a multiplex theater complex replete with multinational fast-food chains. As one of the construction managers describes it, the new luxury complex will feature "twenty-five screens [. . .] and a Pizza Hut." Faced with the destruction of their home and livelihood, the slum's residents pool their money to buy back their home but fall short by several thousand rupees. Akaash (now a Bollywood superstar) comes to the rescue of Paradise and announces that he will buy back the slum with his own money.

The absence of the Indian state in these debates over public land is a telling instance of the privatization of property and the globalization of capital in contemporary India. Vikram and Akaash are in different ways model subjects of the neoliberal Indian state. Vikram's plan to develop Paradise into a luxury leisure complex reflects the increasing power of the Indian middle class, whose self-identity is forged through acts of consumption. Moreover, the preponderance of fast-food chains like Pizza Hut reflects the Indian government's solicitation of foreign investment from multinational corporations. Vikram is thus at the vanguard of the modern and global India, an India whose successes are reflected in the rapid redevelopment of metropolitan cities. By contrast, Akaash is an "untouchable," a man from the slums. He has risen to power through the private circuits of the Bollywood film industry, which has enabled him to amass enough wealth to buy back the slum. Akaash's commitment to Paradise reflects a sense of national patriotism, substantiated through his capital investment in the nation and solidified through his identification with the masses. In the musical the battle between Akaash and Vikram is eventually resolved when Vikram's duplicity is revealed and Akaash heroically comes to the rescue. Yet even this narrative resolution highlights how both male leads represent neoliberal conceptions of citizenship that rely on individual achievement and capital accumulation.

The narrative of Indian modernity in *Bombay Dreams* is also shaped by a gendered and sexualized discourse of Indian femininity. While Akaash and Vikram fight over Paradise, the larger battle is in fact over Priya, Vikram's fiancée and Akaash's paramour. As a traditional-yet-modern Indian woman, Priya is the grounds for debate over the market value of Paradise, as her value as bride and wife is equated with the cost of saving the slum. Significantly the other women in the musical, including Rani (with whom Akaash has an affair) and the hijra Sweetie (his childhood friend) are noticeably absent from these negotiations. Rani deploys her own sexuality as a means of climbing the rungs of the film industry; in her case the sexual economy of her body translates into capital for upward mobility. By contrast, Sweetie is stigmatized for being transgendered. Though hijras also use their bodies as a means of accumulating capital—many hijras labor as sex workers in towns and cities across the subcontinent—Sweetie's queer sexuality does not gain her class mobility within the heteronormative economy of *Bombay Dreams*.

Sweetie's performance highlights the ways in which liminal sexual and religious subjectivities are contained by the musical. As Akaash's confidante, Sweetie is the moral force of *Bombay Dreams*. Her presence is a consistent comic relief onstage, as her lines sparkle with sarcasm and sexual innuendo. During the performances I attended, Sweetie's performance was consistently met with surprise, laughter, and empathy from the audience. Sriram Ganesan, who played the role of Sweetie on Broadway, was acclaimed for his sensitive portrayal of her character. Many reviews of the musical proclaimed that Sweetie, rather than Akaash or Priya, was the star of the show.[35] It was clear that audience members, whether South Asian or non–South Asian, maintained an empathetic relation with Sweetie, visible in the standing ovation that Ganesan received at the conclusion of each performance. Yet Sweetie is also, rather predictably, the tragic queer whose death secures the heterosexual compact of the musical. While the speech, dress, and comportment of hijras have operated as a source of comic relief in Hindi films over the past several decades, on Broadway Sweetie's performance carries a different impact. Onstage, her affect reads as drag or camp, even though hijras do not identify as male or female. Equally important, Sweetie is represented onstage as Hindu, though hijras are integral to the popular practice of Islam as well as Hinduism, and frequently participate and worship in both religious traditions.[36] Despite the fact that hijras occupy a distinct social and economic function in modern India, popular representations of hijras continue to employ orientalist tropes of sexual difference.[37] Indeed, as the anthropologist Lawrence Cohen writes, "*Hijras*—like *sati*, sacred cows, fakirs on beds of nails, and 'the caste system'—[have] become essentialized icons of India" (279).

By prioritizing Sweetie's role in *Bombay Dreams*, my objective is not to reify her sexual difference. Instead, it is to understand what it means to have a queer character at the locus of the romantic narrative in the musical. Like the unnamed Sikh and Muslim men who are visually marked as religiously and ethnically "other," Sweetie is marked as sexually other by her costume, makeup, and choreography. During the preproduction tour that the crew made to India, the choreographer Anthony van Laast commented on the distinctive physicality of hijras: their heavy walk and gait, the sexualized hip thrusts used to court customers for sex work, and the ritually loud hand clapping. Translated onto Broadway, Sweetie and the four other hijras onstage who accompany her in nonspeaking roles perform these gestures in the form of high camp. Sweetie's performance of femininity is consistently characterized as sexual parody, specifically in relation to the demure and self-contained femininity that is exhibited by Priya. In the two ballads that bookend the musical ("Love's Never Easy" and "Hero"), Priya and Sweetie sing of their love for Akaash from opposite ends of the stage, occupying different spaces and differently feminine bodies. As Sweetie begins to sing, "Love's never easy / Take it from a girl who knows [. . .] / All we women want in life is to find a man that's kind and true / We see life through men's eyes / So we know what pleases you," Priya's voice and gestures take over the song as Sweetie recedes from the center of musical attention. Elsewhere in the musical, Sweetie's sexuality is consistently triangulated through Priya and, to a more limited extent, Rani. While Priya and Rani compete for Akaash by occupying polarized sexualities—the virgin and the vamp—Sweetie's own sexual desire for Akaash cannot be adequately categorized and is never fully realized.

Though Sweetie is rendered "female" and "Hindu" in the musical, her presence undermines stable categories of gender, sexuality, and religious subjectivity. As neither man nor woman, incorporated into both Hindu and Muslim religious practices, Sweetie embodies what the film critic Ravi Vasudevan calls a "multi-communal agency" (59). Because Sweetie has verbal exchanges with all the characters, irrespective of class, caste, religious, or ethnic difference, her performance is central to embodying the cosmopolitan character of Bombay. She is also the public face of the city, for her desire to protect Paradise against urban redevelopment ultimately leads to her death. At the same time, her desire for Akaash must be contained within the narrative parameters of the musical. In the final scenes Sweetie confronts Vikram about his intent to destroy Paradise. In response Vikram taunts Sweetie by insinuating that she is physically repellent to Akaash. Sweetie refuses to believe Vikram and is shot and killed by him; she is rewarded when Akaash finally arrives to cradle her dying body. Ultimately, Sweetie's death reconciles Akaash with his grandmother and more broadly with the inhabitants of Paradise. The death of Sweetie also serves a utilitarian purpose, for by dying she secures the romantic love between Akaash and Priya.

The difficulty of locating Sweetie's brief life within the heterosexual and nationalist parameters of the musical signals what Gayatri Gopinath calls the "impossible desires" of queer femininity. In her discussion of Shyam Selvadurai's novel *Funny Boy*, Gopinath examines the cross-gender identification of the young male protagonist Arjie, who is immersed in playing games of "bride-bride." For Arjie, "dressing up as the bride—complete with shimmering white sari, flowers and jewelry—is a way of accessing a particular mode of hyperbolic femininity embodied [. . .] by the popular Sri Lankan female film stars of the day."[38] Gopinath reads Arjie's queer desire to be the bride (rather than the groom) as a means of interrogating "different South Asian nationalist narratives that imagine and consolidate the nation in terms of organic heterosexuality."[39] Like Arjie, Sweetie's performance on Broadway is also enunciated through her embodiment of hyperbolic femininity, one that is deployed toward her dreams of becoming Akaash's bride. However, in my reading of *Bombay Dreams*, Sweetie's queer femininity does not necessarily destabilize the patriarchal relations of the national family; rather it is deployed as a means of reconsolidating the "organic heterosexuality" at the heart of the musical. Sweetie's multi-communal identity brings to life the complex relationship between Hindus and Muslims, upper and lower castes in contemporary Bombay, and thus critiques the musical's depiction of Akaash and Priya's love as a victory across caste boundaries. Yet Sweetie embodies not the beautiful bride but the stigmatized hijra, a character whose femininity is the object of ridicule, not worship. The hypervisibility of Sweetie onstage—her prominent gait, clothing, and loud voice—is what makes her the target of sexual violence. That her murder is readily assimilated into the story line (and in fact hastens its conclusion) illustrates how the figure of the hijra remains extraneous to a musical narrative of modern India. Though the audience mourns Sweetie's death—at each performance I attended, the gunshot that kills her was met with stunned silence—as viewers, we are also complicit in acknowledging the centrality of heterosexual romance to the representation of Indian modernity in *Bombay Dreams*.

The debate over who should own Paradise, therefore, is not simply a question of the slum dweller versus "the brahmin in the suit." It is also a question of the complex transactional relationship between gender, sexuality, and capital mobility. In the musical, these relationships are glossed as competing stories of love between Akaash, Priya, Sweetie, and Rani. By prioritizing these individual love stories, the musical evades the larger problem at the heart of the narrative: namely, the absence of the Indian state in disputes over claims to property. Though Paradise remains intact, the state's role in abetting the privatization of the slums remains unaddressed. The absence of the state is central to the musical's representation of neoliberal India, a place where private citizens debate the use of public property. Indeed, throughout the musical, claims to citizenship are determined by access to property. Such privatized notions of citizenship emphasize the neoliberal relationship between the postcolonial Indian state and its diverse subjects.

As the director Steven Pimlott comments, "Bombay is the hero of the story, really, rather than any one character."[40] As the hero of the musical, Bombay is made to stand in for an idea of India that is at once traditional and modern, local and global. Likewise Meera Syal writes in the program guide that "like Manhattan, this is a city of enterprise and in-your-face wheeler-dealing [. . .] It's the Bombay way, and the motor that keeps the city speeding along, humming its brash optimistic tune." Yet the optimism reflected by Syal and embodied by the characters gives me pause, for it overrides the problematic representation and erasure of religious, sexual, class, and caste difference in the musical. The fact that Akaash and Priya's marriage remains central to the musical narrative demonstrates how this performance of romantic love stands in for "the highest form of secularism" in postcolonial India.[41]

Multicultural Dreams off Broadway

The imaginative national landscape of *Bombay Dreams* was not limited to the spectacular representation of India onstage at the Broadway Theatre. Throughout its run in New York City, the musical also generated an equally cosmopolitan representation of America, celebrated for its racial and ethnic diversity. Moving from a close reading of the musical that emphasizes how *Bombay Dreams* produced a neoliberal narrative of India, to an ethnographic reading of its consumption by South Asians and non–South Asians, requires us to take account of how the musical engendered a sense of place in the United States. For weeks in advance of its premiere, advertisements for the musical proliferated in subway stations, on buses, and on billboards across Manhattan. For the journalist Aseem Chhabra, the posters featuring "steamy and hot-looking young *desi* actors" locked in a passionate embrace were a turning point:

> Living in New York I have rarely felt different from other New Yorkers. But looking at these posters I felt proud to be a *desi* in the city [. . .] with the arrival of *Bombay Dreams*, it seemed as if Bollywood and popular Indian culture was finally here.
> "That is my culture," I felt like proclaiming to the morning commuters at Times Square, as they passed by those two posters. "I grew up watching Bollywood movies. [. . .] And now you have a show that celebrates the movies of my childhood and teenage years."

An immigrant himself, for Chhabra *Bombay Dreams* signified the arrival of South Asians in American popular culture. Amid New York City's historically diverse immigrant population, Chhabra claims that he rarely feels any different from other New Yorkers. Yet seeing these "hot" images of South Asians on the billboards of Times Square enables him to inhabit a specifically racialized and sexualized sense of belonging.[42] By declaring that Bollywood is "my culture," Chhabra claims commercial Hindi cinema as a primary source of his Indian national identity. At the same time, by identifying as a "*desi* in the city," Chhabra inhabits a localized form of ethnicity that is specific to being in diaspora. Though the posters advertised *Bombay Dreams* as a journey to "Somewhere You've Never Been Before," for viewers like Chhabra the musical produced a collective experience of belonging, one rooted in the geography of New York City.

Coinciding with previews of the musical, the March 25, 2004, edition of *Time Out New York* presented a special collection of articles on "South Asian New York," guest edited by the novelist and musician Tanuja Desai Hidier. The cover of the special issue featured the actresses Anisha Nagarajan and Ayesha Dharkar (who played Priya and Rani, respectively), dressed in the attire of the 1970s' Bollywood vamp. This special issue of *Time Out* was a guide to all things South Asian in New York City: restaurants and clubs, theater and music, film and dance, literature and art. In her introduction, "Salaam! New York," Hidier celebrated the increasing numbers of first- and second-generation South Asians across the United States. She wrote that the children of immigrants are no longer "American Born Confused Desis" but rather "American-born Creative Desis. That neither-here-nor-there space between cultures is at last a You are Here" (14). *Bombay Dreams* was one example of "You are Here," but *Time Out* situated the musical within a larger cultural landscape of New York thoroughly inhabited by South Asians. From galleries and museums that showcased art from the subcontinent, to the long-established Pakistani, Bangladeshi, and Indian restaurants and grocery stores in Manhattan and Queens, South Asia was everywhere in New York City. The articles emphasized the incipient emergence of a South Asian diasporic literary landscape, shaped by familiar resonances of the subcontinent as well as by new communities produced through migration. Describing a group of immigrant writers from India, Pakistan, and Kashmir who met weekly in Brooklyn, the journalist Suketu Mehta noted the "real sense of camaraderie and the idea that in this country so far away [from] home, that this is also a home."[43]

As a travel guide to New York City, *Time Out* was also another medium of "Somewhere You've Never Been Before." Yet the special issue also domesticated all things South Asian squarely within the confines of New York City. New York was defined by the ethnic, racial, and religious diversity of its inhabitants, by its artistic and commercial productivity, and above all by its modernity. Within the urban landscape, the regional and national diversity of South Asia had become part of the multicultural terrain of New York City. In turn, New York mirrored the city of *Bombay Dreams*. Locating *Bombay Dreams* within this creative imagination of a South Asian New York highlighted how the musical was incorporated by diasporic subjects into their version of the American dream, as an example of American multiculturalism that enabled writers like Chhabra and Mehta to claim New York as "home."

In the summer of 2004, however, a different kind of New York came into public view as the Republican National Convention took place in midtown Manhattan. Following the terrorist attacks of 9/11, the U.S. invasion of Iraq, and ongoing war in Afghanistan, the convention reaffirmed a dominant public rhetoric of national safety and security, even as the U.S. state expanded into new imperialist ventures overseas. As then-governor of California Arnold Schwarzenegger declared at the convention, "America is back. Back from the attack on our homeland, back from the attack on our economy, back from the attack on our way of life [. . .] To those critics who are so pessimistic about our economy, I say, 'Don't be economic girly men! The

U.S. economy is the envy of the world.'"[44] Poised to nominate the incumbent George W. Bush as candidate for the upcoming presidential elections, the RNC generated a rhetorical fiction of the American national body, one that was primarily white, aggressively heterosexual, and economically and militarily self-reliant. Despite the posturing of candidates and speakers, the entire convention site was heavily fortified by police security provided by the federal and city governments.

Outside the convention center, the RNC provided a full slate of entertainment programming for its delegates. *Bombay Dreams* was one of eight selected musicals for conventioneers, along with popular shows such as *Beauty and the Beast*, *Aida*, and *Phantom of the Opera*.[45] Specially priced group tickets for matinee shows to these musicals were offered to conventioneers, who were encouraged to take part in reviving the tourist economy of New York City. Like the nationalist rhetoric of the convention itself, which grew out of the terrorist attacks of 9/11, the decline in New York's tourism and business industry was also attributed to the destruction of the World Trade Center. Attending the musicals enabled conventioneers to feel as though their consumption of these popular cultural texts was a patriotic act that stimulated the local economy and produced a sense of national pride.

However, the conventioneers were completely unprepared for the unprecedented scale of mass protests against the RNC. Protest groups of every size coordinated to offer six days of counterprogramming to the RNC, including mass demonstrations, marches, and face-to-face confrontations with delegates across Manhattan. One such protest was staged in front of the Broadway Theatre during a specially scheduled matinee show of *Bombay Dreams*. In "Bollywood Spectacles," Gopinath writes about watching television coverage of RNC delegates emerging from the theater:

> The show was apparently a hot ticket among the RNC delegates, and its tag line—"Somewhere You've Never Been Before"—provided a colorful backdrop as the camera captured delegates admonishing protesters for preventing the police from doing their job of "keeping America safe." It seemed particularly ironic to me that the delegates occupied themselves [. . .] with xenophobic calls for a never-ending "war on terror" while they diverted themselves [. . .] with a brief foray into Bollywood glamour." (157)

"Somewhere You've Never Been Before" 239

While Gopinath offers this anecdote as a prelude to examine the popularity of Bollywood films during a period of increasing U.S. aggression overseas, I expand upon this domestic scene to consider its implications for the location of the musical in New York City. By focusing on the interaction between the delegates who attended the show, the protestors who massed outside the theater, and the actors onstage, I unravel the politics of race and nationhood that structured the consumption of *Bombay Dreams*.

Though television coverage of the protests was minimal, several online blogs detail police violence against protestors during the 2004 RNC, including the demonstration that took place outside *Bombay Dreams*. On that day, protest groups called for demonstrators to converge in front of each musical venue where RNC delegates gathered and to confront delegates as they emerged during the intermissions and after the matinee performances. Throughout the afternoon at the Broadway Theatre, a standoff took place between protestors, delegates, and the police. With at least two arrests that night in front of the Broadway Theatre (and more than two hundred throughout Manhattan and Brooklyn during the course of the convention), *Bombay Dreams* became one in a series of entertainment venues that were sites for the production of domestic law and order.[46] The verbal protests and poster campaigns against the conventioneers engaged with a wide range of national and international issues: the wars in Iraq and Afghanistan, terrorism and torture, human rights, global warming, abortion rights, and gay and lesbian civil rights. None of these issues were explicitly addressed by any of the musicals the conventioneers attended, and there was nothing specific to *Bombay Dreams* that required the presence of riot police at the Broadway Theatre. How then did this musical about postcolonial Indian modernity become a site for violent confrontation over U.S. national politics?

In conversation with actors who performed in *Bombay Dreams* during the RNC, I came to realize why the musical was selected as appropriate programming for a convention whose theme was "Fulfilling America's Promise by Building a Safer World and a More Hopeful America." Like *Phantom of the Opera*, *Bombay Dreams* was an Andrew Lloyd Webber musical, a "family friendly" form of entertainment. Focusing on the story of Akaash's rise from rags to riches meant that *Bombay Dreams* could be viewed as a quintessentially American story of upward mobility. Further, the pageantry of love and marriage offered by the musical transported conventioneers to another "culture," one that rather remarkably resonated with their own investment in the sanctity of heterosexual marriage. For RNC delegates, the musical was an aesthetic experience, divorced of political context. By framing the musical as mainstream entertainment, the RNC programmers eclipsed the relationship between the representation of South Asia onstage and the everyday lives of South Asian immigrants in New York offstage.

The troubled relationship between the aesthetics and politics of the musical became apparent in my conversation with Suresh John, the Canadian ensemble cast member of *Bombay Dreams*. Speaking of the RNC-sponsored matinee performance, John related an incident involving Manu Narayan, who played Akaash:

> Manu was like, "Republicans, are you with me?"—in the hip-hop bhangra scene in the beauty pageant—and he got a letter the next day. He got a fine and a letter [. . .] well maybe not a fine but a letter. But they [the audience] loved it, they ate it up, and it was a ninety-nine percent Republican house. And when Manu said that, they all went crazy, but the next day he got a letter from someone higher up, probably the producers. The reason they said [that Narayan could not reference Republicans] was that they were probably thinking that we [the cast] would do something anti-Republican or something.

Narayan was reproached for his shout-out to the audience during this special performance of *Bombay Dreams* not because he had improvised on the musical lyrics, but because his comments were directed toward an audience of RNC attendees. His improvisation in this scene of the musical was in fact consistent with other performances, when he shouted out to Punjabis, New Yorkers, and so on in the audience. Though the audience at the special matinee performance apparently "loved" being called out, the letter that Narayan received from the producers chastised him for referencing Republicans and, more broadly, for incorporating references to American politics in the show. Yet Narayan's shout-out occurred in a performance that was specifically organized as entertainment programming for the RNC, itself a political event. The producer's fear that cast members would retaliate against their audience both recognizes the politicization of this special performance of *Bombay Dreams* and simultaneously denies the place of U.S. and Indian politics in the aesthetic production of the musical.

The producers' attempt to control a potentially unruly cast of South Asians resonates with the ongoing domestic surveillance of South Asian and Arab American immigrants after September 11, 2001. Just one year prior to the premiere of *Bombay Dreams*, the U.S. Immigration and Naturalization Service demanded the "Special Registration" of male noncitizen immigrants from the Middle East and South Asia, including Pakistan and Bangladesh, who had entered the United States as tourists, students, and workers. Special Registration procedures included compiling fingerprints, photographs, and residential addresses of immigrants, as well as personal details on their marital status, religious affiliation, and family members. Part of a larger government intervention that prioritized the racial profiling of Arab Americans and South Asians, Special Registration procedures curtailed the domestic residence, international travel, and legal status of noncitizens.[47] A 2004 Asian American Legal Defense and Education Fund report on the impact of Special Registration, based on a survey of New York City, noted that 95 percent of registered immigrants were Muslim and 59 percent were working class. More than half the immigrants who registered by the government deadline were put into deportation proceedings (2). The impact of Special Registration procedures can be measured through the distorted geography of South Asian immigrant communities in New York City. Several Pakistani-owned businesses in Brooklyn were shut down, and Pakistani families in Coney Island moved away from New York as immigrants were subject to deportation procedures. Likewise, a number of Bangladeshis who operated small businesses in Manhattan and Queens closed down their businesses and moved out of the country.

These Muslim South Asian immigrants were the direct target of the RNC, and yet the conventioneers who attended the special performance of *Bombay Dreams* could not relate their consumption of the Broadway musical to the production of state surveillance procedures. Instead, as John noted, the conventioneers delighted in being part of a show that, in their view, took place elsewhere, outside the United States. At the same time, while middle-class South Asian immigrants such as the prominent writers and artists featured in *Time Out New York* claimed that New York was "home," the magazine did not profile those working-class immigrants who were ejected from the United States because of their legal status, religious backgrounds, and national origin. As one New York–based immigrant put it, "Special Registration makes me feel like this country is not mine."[48]

Keeping the dream of America safe and alive at *Bombay Dreams* thus required consistently producing a spatial and temporal distance between the musical's representation of a secular India onstage and the rhetoric of American multiculturalism that structured the consumption of the musical offstage. These two discourses of neoliberal citizenship are linked through their strategic deployment of ethnic, sexual, and religious difference to connote national diversity and through the erasure of difference to promote national unity. In the musical's fictional India as well as during the RNC in New York, the difference of being queer and Muslim was simultaneously made visible and obscured. As a performative text, *Bombay Dreams* illustrates the contradictions that characterize the production of locality for South Asian immigrants. The musical was integral to an upwardly mobile narrative of South Asians in New York, as illustrated by the special issue of *Time Out* magazine. At the same time, the disappearance of working-class Muslim South Asians due to Special Registration procedures distorts this middle-class and multicultural topography of New York City. It is precisely the erasure of Muslim, Sikh, and queer figures from the musical that enabled many viewers, including RNC conventioneers as well as middle-class Indian immigrants in the audience, to enjoy the show. Exploring why the musical continued to be compelling for South Asian cast and audience members despite its apparently conservative domestic and global politics demands that we pay close attention to the relationship between racial identity and representation.

Embodying South Asia, Performing America

The Broadway version of *Bombay Dreams* drew together a cast of young South Asians from across North America as well as Europe and Australia. These first- and second-generation immigrants identified as Indian, Pakistani, and Sri Lankan, and as Muslims, Hindus, and Christians. In my interviews with cast members, several participants characterized the musical as a unique opportunity to perform *as* South Asians onstage. For these actors, dancers, and singers, the musical generated new notions of racial identity. At the same time, the actors I spoke with made clear that their own racial identification with the role was not the sole reason they were selected for the musical. They described their talent as unbound by race, and refuted notions of being identified onstage primarily by race. Their complex relationship with race as a category of performance as well as their recognition of themselves as racialized subjects corresponds with Celine Parreñas Shimizu's reading of race and sexuality in the Broadway musical *Miss Saigon*. Discussing her interviews with Asian American cast members in the show, Shimizu writes,

> To understand acting as simply re-presentation of corresponding phenotypes and national identities is to say that actors and actresses play roles as non-creating beings. [. . .] Acting requires filling the role with parts of themselves: their specific bodies and histories [. . .] In the process, they [the actors] articulate a different relationship to sexuality than the one offered by the producers and the one expected by the audiences. They also present an understanding of their work as a political critique. (59)

For the cast members I spoke with, their labor for the musical (including their preparation for auditions) was central to their understanding of themselves as creative and agentive subjects. They did not see themselves as simply corresponding with the phenotypes of their characters onstage. At the same time, their investment in representing their characters "authentically" emerged from their own experiences as minority subjects, specifically as South Asian immigrants who grew up with few images of South Asian identity and sexuality in mainstream public culture. As a result the actors and dancers, especially those in lead roles, took seriously their responsibility to "articulate a different relationship" to race, one that was performed (if not narrated) as a form of political critique. Because *Bombay Dreams* was the first musical prominently featuring South Asians on Broadway, it was vested with the personal histories, professional ambitions, and life stories of its cast members.

Sheetal Gandhi, the dancer from northern California, described *Bombay Dreams* as a means of coming to terms with her racial and national identity. Trained in Western modern dance as well as classical Indian dance, Gandhi was one of only two South Asians present at the Actors' Equity Association audition for the musical. During an interview that I conducted with her, Gandhi spoke exuberantly about her experience:

> Just the audition [for *Bombay Dreams*] itself, I'll never forget. They break you up and you do a dance combination, and the rest of the group is watching when you audition. And I remember when I went and the rest of

the group is watching, I could hear people say things like, "Oh, so *that's* what it's supposed to look like," and "Go girl, that's fierce!" [So] it's not just about the movement at this point, it's about the roots and the culture and the style, and this is what I grew up with. [. . .]

[I thought] if this show is going up there, then they need me. [. . .] it was really important for me to be out there, to deliver the spirit, because without that it's just another musical.[49]

Gandhi perceived the unique choreography of the musical, which drew upon both jazz ballet and classical Indian dance, as a means of claiming her South Asian subjectivity. Central to this notion of becoming South Asian is Gandhi's embodiment of authenticity, "the roots and the culture and the style," as well as her ability to demonstrate what a dance combination is "supposed to look like." When Gandhi danced in front of her peers, they cheered her on but also stood corrected by her embodiment of "culture" and "race." Her role as a principal dancer was integral to delivering the spirit of the show and to conveying the authenticity of the dance movement. Without her unique contribution *Bombay Dreams* would be "just another musical." As a dancer Gandhi took pride in her ability to generate new vocabularies of movement rather than simply embodying fixed constructs of identity. In this context, to be able to dance as a South Asian on Broadway enabled her to inhabit new bodily meanings. Because Gandhi was able to reconcile the specific movement vocabulary of Bollywood dance with the format of the Broadway musical, she identified *Bombay Dreams* as pivotal to her racial subjectivity as South Asian.

Though *Bombay Dreams* was powerfully enabling for Gandhi, she also discussed the work of her peers in terms that exposed the contradiction between racial identity and racial authenticity. In the same interview Gandhi commented, "For a lot of the actors who were of mixed ethnicity, half Indian or a quarter Indian, there was a chance for them to get in touch with themselves, a part that they could more easily shrug off than those of us who were first- and second-generation." In her view, an authentic embodiment of race was critical to preserving the ethos of the musical and dance narrative. Given the extensive revision of the choreography, lyrics, and plot development from the original London production to the Broadway stage, Gandhi emphasized her unique responsibility as a South Asian to "maintain any of the gestures that we could [. . .] to bring the authentic flavor on stage." She further claimed that her efforts to preserve the "authentic flavor" of the choreography was appreciated by "people of South Asian descent in the audience" who recognized her performance of classical dance forms. Gandhi's comments illustrate how actors and dancers of diverse backgrounds identified as South Asian through their work for the show. She also underscores how, in her view, first- and second-generation immigrants have a unique responsibility to maintain racial authenticity in order to reproduce an accurate representation of South Asia onstage, one inflected with an understanding of "roots" and "culture."

Despite Gandhi's awareness of the phenotypical differences among South Asians who worked on the show, the experience of working with other subcontinental immigrants was central to her feelings of belonging. Gandhi mentioned that in the aftermath of the Broadway production, "A lot of us stayed in touch, and there's a network there that I now realize is so important to be connected to. Before *Bombay Dreams*, I was just solo: I'm an artist, and I'm South Asian. Not 'I'm a South Asian artist' [. . .] now knowing that there's a community, it's neat." Though the musical was staged for only ten months, Gandhi cites the lasting impact of her work for the musical in terms of the racialized communities that she forged with other actors, dancers, and singers. Moving from a "solo" to collective identification of being South Asian, Gandhi demonstrates an emerging political awareness, one that moves from an identitarian construct of ethnicity to a politicized condition of racial subjectivity. Her description of herself as a "South Asian artist" demonstrates how she embodied a professional identity as a racial minority in the world of musical theater. Equally important, it delineates a collective social experience centered on the fact of racial difference.

However, working in *Bombay Dreams* was not simply an affirmative experience for immigrant actors and dancers. For some cast members the professional obligation to embody racial difference onstage led them to deny the difference that race makes offstage. Their narratives showcase how the experience of becoming South Asian entails a relationship of profound disidentification with the multicultural politics of the musical. For example, the actress Anjali Bhimani, who played Rani in the final months of the Broadway production, argued that her racial identity was secondary to her performance in *Bombay Dreams*. In my interview with her, Bhimani noted that her previous roles in musical theater had not been "ethnic specific," and remarked,

The other thing is that people often want to hear that—do you feel like paving the way for future South Asian actors, or a responsibility to be representative of the South Asian community. And in a sense that does a disservice to the South Asian community. How about we say that I'm just an actor who does this. How about we forget about the fact that—yeah, it's great I'm an Indian, but I'm certainly not the only [. . .] and I don't feel like—hey look at me, I'm Indian. I'm another actor trying to make a living. That's how I've made a living, by being an actor, not by being Indian.[50]

In contrast to Gandhi, Bhimani rejects identifying as a South Asian actor and disidentifies with the notion of a larger South Asian community. Instead she views her work outside of categories of racial representation and prefers that critics and audience members "forget" the fact that she is Indian. Although Bhimani's work onstage is precisely about "hey look at me," she aims to displace the look of the audience from the fact of her racialized body. In her view her professional qualifications lie in her capacity to transcend rather than embody race. As Bhimani contends, she is not paid for being an Indian but rather for being an actor, one who is able to move away from the constraint of race.

Bhimani and Gandhi's commentaries reveal the tense negotiation between embodying race and performing multiculturalism onstage. As Cheng writes in the context of *Flower Drum Song*, "For the denigrated racialized subject, self-representation must finally be much more complicated than either denying or assenting to stereotypes. In other words [. . .] the question of the stereotype does not expose the difference between East and West; rather, it *announces* the active engagement between the ideological constructions of the two, which in turn articulates a profound anxiety about one's own racial difference and national position" (35). In distinct ways Bhimani and Gandhi demonstrate their "active engagement" with ideological constructs of South Asia and America, assenting to certain racialized representations as well as denying the difference of race. For Gandhi the opportunity to dance in a production that called attention to her "roots" enabled her to inhabit, in her words, an "authentic" subjectivity as a South Asian artist. Although Bhimani, like Gandhi, endorsed multicultural casting in *Bombay Dreams*, she argues that race was irrelevant to her professional work as an actor. By insisting on demarcating her own racial subjectivity from her onstage performance, she encourages us to consider the musical entirely in terms of the professional qualifications of the cast. Both Bhimani and Gandhi appear to have resolved their engagement with the racial politics of the musical: Gandhi by embracing her identification as a South Asian, Bhimani by denying the particularity of race. Yet both women also articulate what Cheng calls a "profound anxiety" about their locality within the parameters of the Broadway musical. Bhimani described *Bombay Dreams* as "essentially a Bollywood movie on stage, which means, it's not going to have a whole lot of substance. It's about spectacle, it's about fun." Characterizing the musical as a form of mass entertainment, Bhimani rejects the significance of race within the narrative and describes her own labor as creating "fun" for the audience, just like any other Broadway show. For Gandhi, however, her work in *Bombay Dreams* prompted her to ask a political question: "What does it mean to be a South Asian artist in the West, and what is our responsibility?" Negotiating between the universal form of the musical and their racial difference as minority subjects, Gandhi and Bhimani demonstrate the complexity of inhabiting the Broadway stage as South Asians. The difficulty of reconciling these divergent notions of race (as phenotype or as phenomenology) within the musical is reflected in the ways in which *Bombay Dreams* is commonly understood as either an aesthetic or political text.

Bombay Dreams was also deeply informed by the affective experience of audience members, myself included, who were overwhelmed by the spectacle of racial recognition onstage. Through the performances of actors and dancers such as Gandhi, Bhimani, and John, South Asian immigrants in the audience found ways of producing a sense of locality in relation to the musical. In my interview with Manu Narayan, who played the leading role of Akaash throughout the Broadway production, he elucidated the transformative effects of *Bombay Dreams* on audience members, particularly on second-generation South Asians:

> For the first time [South Asian] audiences, which are a minority audience, who were coming from all over the world to see the show, to see South Asians all playing the lead. And these weren't South Asians like Shah Rukh Khan or Rani Mukherjee, and weren't necessarily the most attractive people in the world. And if I'm a five-year-old child or ten-year-old child and recognize that the majority American audience is looking at the same thing onstage and recognizing me, through their laughs, through their applause. And that is the *most* important thing about the show.[51]

In contrast to Prashant Agrawal, whose Op-Ed article bemoaned the absence of "real" Bollywood stars, Narayan argues that it is precisely the lack of Indian actors such as Shah Rukh Khan and Rani Mukherjee that creates a close encounter between the audience and performers, both diasporic subjects. Through their desire for and incorporation into the universal format of the Broadway show, *Bombay Dreams* establishes an intimate relationship of belonging. It is an intimacy evoked through the fictional second-generation immigrant child in the audience, who recognizes not only that all the lead roles are played by South Asians (thereby racially identifying with the actors) but also the fact that a majority white audience is looking at the same racialized object onstage and "recognizing me." Like the affective charge of identifying as South Asian at art festivals like Diasporadics and Artwallah, here too locality is produced through applause and laughter. Witness to this effusive outpouring of positive affect, the young child—the "denigrated racial subject"—is transformed into a recognizable self.

However, Narayan's imagination of the visible racial self relies upon the heteronormative romance enshrined in the musical. He proceeds to note that "children in this country don't [get to] see [. . .] people just like them [in order to say] hey, I can identify with that person, and that person is getting applauded by one thousand eight hundred people every night [. . .] for singing, for dancing, for kissing, for falling in love. To say, "hey, it's ok to be me."

For children unable to see "people just like them"—for those who are racialized subjects in American popular culture—*Bombay Dreams* offers the consolation of identity. But this form of racial identification disidentifies with the queer romance of the musical, for the kiss that culminates the show is between Akaash and Priya, not between Sweetie and Akaash. What produces a sense of national belonging *as Americans* is not simply the fact that South Asians are singing and dancing onstage. More precisely, it is by witnessing the performative idiom of heterosexual romance that the fictional child begins to embody his/her locality in the United States. It is by establishing a triangulated relationship between the heterosexual hero onstage, the racialized child offstage, and the "one thousand eight hundred" Americans who applaud the performance in the theater that *Bombay Dreams* secures the normative locality of South Asians in the United States.

The Consolation of Identity

On each occasion that I went to see *Bombay Dreams*, my own pleasure in viewing the musical derived from the extraordinary sensation of seeing young South Asians perform in leading roles on the Broadway stage. Certainly, *Bombay Dreams* was not the first instance of multiracial casting: recent musicals such as *The Lion King* and *Rent* have also relied on actors of color in principal roles. Yet what was unique about *Bombay Dreams*, and what I uneasily desired, was its consistent representation of a "secular" and "modern" idea of South Asia onstage, a representation that secured my own subjectivity as a South Asian offstage. That this representation of secular modernity was constituted through the steady erasure of queer, Muslim, and Sikh subjects from the musical, and that my subjectivity as a South Asian relied upon the recognition and disavowal of this erasure, strains the boundaries between nationalist and diasporic modes of identification. The incommensurable relationship between performing South Asia and being South Asian became evident in the ethnographic interviews that I conducted, as actors and dancers expressed their vexed location between popular representations of "India" and the embodied experience of being a racial minority in the United States. However, the fact that mainstream popular cultural texts like the Broadway musical remain objects of desire, for critics and audience members offstage as well as for the actors and dancers onstage, reveals how middle-class South Asians are deeply invested in multicultural narratives of belonging.

The musical is a place from which we can begin to "imagine otherwise." I borrow the term from Kandice Chuh, whose incisive readings of Asian American cultural politics demand a renewed attention to the powerful relationship between nation, identity, and race. Chuh deconstructs a narrative of Asian American subjectivity that claims to originate in the civil rights movement for Asian American studies in the academy, a movement that relies on the visibility and autonomy of the Asian American subject. While she acknowledges the "vitality of this narrative," she also points to the ways in which this originary moment has "tended to overshadow other possible narratives of the field's emergence" (5). She concludes by calling on us to "disown" America, a critical move that in her words requires "the imperative to disarticulate 'nation' from 'home,'" in order to "further the work of creating home as a space relieved of states of domination" (124). Between these two points—a cultural nationalist history of Asian American emergence, and a disavowal of nationalism that reconceptualizes the location of immigrant subjects—Chuh delineates the alterity of Asian America as a form of critical engagement with fictional narratives of Asian American subjectivity and historical narratives of U.S. empire.

The popular cultural texts in this book also map the alterity of Asian America by bringing the field into intimate historical and political contact with the Indian subcontinent. But instead of disowning nationalism, I have explored the ways in which South Asian cultural productions are bound by multiple ideologies of nationhood. These include ideologies of Hindutva; neoliberal constructs of citizenship; progressive antiracist coalition politics; and liberal multicultural notions of ethnicity. Framing immigrant cultural productions in relation to such discourses of belonging is not simply a means of reinscribing diasporic subjects within the domain of the nation-state. Instead, it is a method of articulating how deeply and creatively South Asians engage with the politics of representation and the politics of identity, on the subcontinent as well as in the United States. Tying together these disparate modes of identification highlights the unexpected encounter between rhetorics of diversity and difference in both national sites. In this context, recognizing how middle-class South Asian immigrants are complicit with producing and consuming dominant modes of representation—as upwardly mobile, autonomous, and visible subjects—is one way of deconstructing what Chuh describes as "states of domination" that characterize each of our "homes."

In an interview one year after the closure of *Bombay Dreams*, Suresh John remarked that the Broadway musical was never intended for a South Asian audience in the first place:

> The people who would've enjoyed the show the most couldn't afford a ticket—cab drivers, waiters, workers, people who work in Edison and Jackson Heights and Queens—those people didn't even know about the show. And they couldn't afford it, a hundred dollar ticket. And I'd be in a cab and I'd show them stuff from the musical and they'd be like [. . .] they didn't even know it was going on [. . .] And I had a friend [who said] that in Jackson Heights and Edison, New Jersey, there was no advertising whatsoever, and that's where Indian people live, and there's not even one poster. There are so many people living there and they're not even advertising [the musical].

John's anecdotal evidence about the lack of advertising in northern New Jersey and Queens—areas where there are dense concentrations of Pakistanis and Bangladeshis as well as Indians—contrasts sharply with Aseem Chhabra's description of the posters prominently displayed in Times Square. Whereas Chhabra embraced the advertisements for *Bombay Dreams* as representations of "my culture," John's comment amplifies how the musical was out of reach for working-class South Asians. But his remarks also illustrate a larger dissonance, a dissonance within the national imaginary of America itself. For the South Asian actors and viewers who identified with *Bombay Dreams*, the musical offered the consolation of identity: a means of claiming this popular representation of South Asia as if it were true to one's experience of being a racial minority in the United States. That such forms of identification are only ever partial and momentary is a perpetual reminder of the fact that diasporic subjects never fully belong within this national construct. The "cab drivers, waiters, workers" whose underpaid and unrecognized labor is central to the U.S. economy are among those immigrants more obviously denied access to such representations of multiculturalism. But middle-class South Asians who work hard to be part of this show, either as actors or as viewers, also occupy a contingent place within the national romance of America. The fact that *Bombay Dreams* was repetitively performed but never secured a lasting place on Broadway demonstrates how this diasporic cultural text could not be recuperated into narratives of U.S. citizenship.

Stories of becoming South Asian enjoin us to imagine other ways of thinking, inhabiting, and practicing transnational futures. The narratives of locality that I have examined draw upon a heterogeneous group of immigrants divided by their religious, national, gender, sexual, and class identities. Together, the cultural texts produced by these immigrants constitute an unwieldy and affective experience of belonging. For many South Asians, such a desire to belong engenders a profound feeling of identification. It also produces a capacity to disidentify with normative representations of citizenship. The fact that subcontinental immigrants have created literature, film, art, and performance that are integral to popular representations of America demonstrates how South Asians have dynamically reshaped the multicultural landscape of the United States. At the same time, the fact that many of these texts draw upon dominant ideologies of nationhood on the subcontinent illustrates how diasporic populations are central to reproducing notions of postcolonial citizenship. The everyday lives of South Asians are marked by this consistent negotiation of local narratives and global histories: what I have described as a movement of perversion and preservation that binds together South Asia with America. As first- and second-generation immigrants produce cultural texts that imagine an "elsewhere," I delineate the ways in which their consumption of these texts unexpectedly creates a critical feeling of belonging here.

Epilogue

Throughout this book I have positioned myself in relation to an archive of South Asian cultural production as reader, viewer, participant, and critic. The disparate locations that I have occupied within this field of public culture have been shaped by various methods of critical analysis, not all of which adhere to disciplinary conventions. By using ethnography in order to read literature and documentary films, performance studies in relation to visual art, and social theory as a means of understanding performance cultures, I examine the affective conditions through which immigrants identify and disidentify with popular culture. Turning these cultural texts toward the question of locality highlights how a politics of representation fails to account for the difference of being South Asian. To read literature, film, and performance in terms of what it represents—assimilation or resistance, belonging or marginalization—negates the complex processes of identification that immigrant subjects forge with popular texts. Because such representational frameworks of analysis are tethered to the domestic parameters of race and ethnic politics in the United States, they also evade the ways in which diasporic popular culture is produced in relation to contemporaneous social and political movements in South Asia. These include anticolonial and independence movements in Bangladesh, Pakistan, and India; the rise of right-wing Hindu nationalism; secular democratic and leftist movements; as well as neoliberal forms of globalization. By reorienting popular cultural texts in relation to these varied discourses of nationalism on the subcontinent, I have highlighted the ties of capital and cultural movement that bind South Asia to the production of race and ethnicity in America.

Theorizing locality is thus both a framework within which to grapple with the vexed narratives of racial and class mobility that characterize the stories of middle-class South Asians, and a means of reconceptualizing the historical scale and political scope of Asian American studies. As I see it, the challenge of working with South Asian diasporic popular culture is twofold. First, reframing Asian American cultural production in relation to contemporaneous events in South Asia produces a different temporality of diaspora, one that is disjointed from teleological narratives of migration from the subcontinent. Exploring these narratives of becoming South Asian requires taking into account the embodied experience of other imperialisms, specifically those produced outside the domain of the U.S. empire. These include not only the legacy of British colonialism, but—as in *The Namesake*— the experience of identifying with a literary history of Russian imperialism and participating in the Non-Aligned Movement. Woven through each of these distinct histories is a growing cognizance of the United States as a global power, an event that is signified in Lahiri's "The Third and Final Continent" through the 1969 lunar landing. Our ability to recognize the postcoloniality of South Asian immigrants requires being able to read popular cultural texts in relation to these multiple temporalities, not all of which are synchronous with the time of U.S. citizenship.

Second, locality makes it incumbent on us to examine the heterogeneous modes of production and consumption through which immigrants engage with popular cultural texts, including those that we may consider, at first glance, to be regressive or retrograde. As I have discussed, beauty pageants and Broadway musicals are frequently depicted as derivative forms of mass culture, and yet they become important venues for immigrants to stage their racial, gender, and sexual identities. Conversely, documentary films and art festivals that are staged as "progressive" representations of immigrant identity reveal the dissonances of class and citizenship that structure South Asian communities. The disparity between the narrative content and rhetorical form of these cultural texts reflects the contradictory locations that South Asians have occupied in the United States across the turn of this century. In this book I focus specifically on the decade between 1999 and 2009, which was witness to a surge of South Asian writers, filmmakers, and actors in the mainstream media, as well as the widespread appeal of Bollywood songs and dance. Equally important, this period is marked by the legislative effects of September 11, 2001, which targeted South Asians who were identified (and misrecognized) as Muslim, undocumented, non–English-speaking, and working class. Yet as I have argued, the events of 9/11 are not exceptional in terms of their impact on South Asian communities. Instead, each text that I have examined reflects a longer history of race-based legislation, ranging from the 1914 *Komagata Maru* incident to the 1923 Supreme Court case of Bhagat Singh Thind, as well as the 1965 Immigration and Naturalization Act and the 2003 Patriot Act. By historicizing social practices around the consumption of popular culture in relation to these legislative acts, I showcase how the experience of locality is not singularly about the present (or post-9/11) moment, but an uneven process of identifying with and embodying narratives of racialization in the United States.

As I posit a broader geographical and historical perspective on contemporary experiences of race and identity, I also recognize how such a methodological approach makes it incumbent to clarify my own stakes in this project. My objective has been to show how transnational experiences of belonging are "relational and contextual," a phenomenological experience that is forged in relation to dominant discourses of nationhood.[1] By exploring the alignment between middle-class experiences of immigration, multicultural narratives of American citizenship, and notions of nationhood on the subcontinent, I have become increasingly drawn to the ways in which immigrants engage with the neoliberal state. For those of us whose critical consciousness of race and class politics has been shaped by working with South Asian immigrant communities, such complicities are often abjured or deferred by our commitment to an antiracist and antinationalist politics. Indeed, it is precisely through identifying as South Asian that we believe we can advance a progressive politics, one that creates coalitions across differences of national origin, religion, gender, and sexuality. Yet this, too, requires a complicit engagement with nationalist narratives, because such collective experiences of belonging are frequently generated through a multicultural rhetoric of identity politics.

Such contradictory expressions of selfhood and community characterize my own experience of locality. In many ways this book emerges from the peculiarities of being born in Bombay (Mumbai), raised in Tokyo, and educated at universities in the United States and in India. From this perspective, locality offers a framework of understanding how immigrants identify with the popular culture that they create, and a means of coming to terms with relations of disidentification that bind us, as scholars of race and ethnicity, to the subjects that we study. If locality is a phenomenology of belonging, then one of its more important conclusions is to reframe the affective conditions that generate our own desires to belong. My experiences as an Indian national in Japan, a foreign student in the United States, and a diasporic subject in India reflect the ways in which these disparate identifications collude with dominant structures of gender and class, citizenship and nationhood in multiple sites. It is this series of intimate engagements with the state that has shaped my attachment to the field of South Asian diasporic public culture at the heart of this book.

As with many South Asians I interviewed over the course of my research, my immigration to the United States was not a straightforward process. Growing up in what Saskia Sassen calls "the global city," I was raised within one of the smallest Indian communities in East Asia. Over the course of my childhood, the number of Indian citizens in Tokyo grew from five hundred people in the 1970s to three thousand in the 1990s, and to nearly twenty thousand residents today. In a city of twelve million people, these Indians abroad composed an intimate community of family and friends. My parents' acquaintances included small-business owners, diplomats, teachers, journalists, and missionaries. The intricate web of personal and professional relationships that defined our community in Japan was linked in turn to a larger web of familial and business associates on the subcontinent as well as across Southeast Asia, the Middle East, and in increasingly larger numbers, the United States.

As a child I felt peripheral to these dense networks of diaspora. I was only aware of how far we were from India, and how much my parents invested in the place they had left behind. Our private experience of temporal and spatial distance from the subcontinent translated into the public labor of embodying national identity. In 1976 my father established an organization called the Indian Community Activities Tokyo (ICAT), which brought together Indians from different regional, religious, and linguistic backgrounds.[2] While ICAT's objectives were primarily social, it also provided an important political function. Often newly arrived immigrants would call my house from Narita airport, inquiring about visas, job opportunities, and places to stay. For this group of newfound kin, my parents wrote and mailed newsletters that contained important information on local governmental regulations and community events. They also took it upon themselves to inform the Japanese media about Indian "culture" and "customs." At its inception, the community was so small that my parents did not restrict their socializing to those who shared their religious beliefs or language. Instead, they forged close friendships with Zoroastrians, Muslims, and Christians, attended festivities for a variety of religious groups, and resisted attempts to build houses of worship that catered only to certain segments of the immigrant population. Like the Nehruvian slogan of "unity in diversity," ICAT was also invested in secular and nonsectarian models of community. Because ICAT operated entirely out of my house, I came to identify this diverse network of diasporic subjects as my home.

As Indian nationals abroad, our shared sense of community was consolidated not through a common narrative of history and culture, but rather through middle-class notions of citizenship. Throughout my childhood I was charged with performing classical and popular dances at ICAT's annual Diwali celebrations, clothed in saris, lehengas, or salwaar kameez. Since there were no local resources for Indian dance classes, these performances were choreographed entirely by watching videotapes of contemporary films and listening to audiocassettes of popular songs. As a teenager, I increasingly experienced these Diwali dance performances as a source of anxiety and shame, yet my parents never wavered in insisting on these rituals of performance. Such public performances became the means through which a group of Indians could identify themselves *as* Indians, even in a faraway land.

Following my parents' lead, I always described myself as "Indian, from Bombay," despite the fact that India was a tourist destination and that I knew Tokyo, not Bombay, like the back of my hand. At the international school I attended, each student was charged with representing her "culture," despite the fact that most of us were more familiar with Japanese popular culture than any other national media. On the annual United Nations day at school I dutifully wore a sari; later these clothes became popular with my friends, who were enamored of bindis and bangles. I knew very few other immigrants from the subcontinent who shared my experience. Sri Lankans were even fewer in number than Indians, and included small-business owners as well as refugees from the civil war who had applied for asylum. Occasionally I met Pakistanis and Bangladeshis whose parents were diplomats, briefly living in Tokyo before moving elsewhere. Although these classmates were from neighboring countries on the subcontinent, I felt no kinship with them. When my friends teased us for speaking strange languages, or when teachers confused our names, I was unable to understand why so many people thought we were alike.

The Japanese government also fostered differences of class and national origin among immigrants from the subcontinent. Indians and Pakistanis were subject to strict visa regulation and were required to enter Japan with guaranteed employment as professionals, or had designated short-term positions as service industry or domestic workers. A Japanese passport was nearly impossible to acquire. Until recently the government demanded that naturalized citizens change their surnames into names legible in Chinese characters. As dependents of a middle-class professional, neither my brother nor I was aware of the impact of these bureaucratic processes. Yet we were in constant contact with the surveillance of the Japanese state, which required us to carry alien registration cards, register with immigration authorities whenever we traveled overseas, and inform our local police station of changes in residential address.

By the early twenty-first century, the landscape of immigration had altered dramatically in response to Japan's growing labor requirements. The new immigrants include thousands of Indian citizens who are engineers and scientists. Many Sri Lankans, Afghanis, and Bangladeshis have opened small businesses. Multinational corporations have also hired professional workers of South Asian origin, largely second-generation immigrants from Australia, Europe, and North America. Meanwhile, undocumented workers from every country on the subcontinent work in the manufacturing and recycling industries. The Indian Embassy, which for fifty years was a dilapidated building occupying prime real estate, was recently transformed into a glass and steel tower rivaling any corporate headquarters. Like *Slumdog Millionaire*, the film chosen to inaugurate the new embassy premises in 2009, the history of subcontinental migration was represented as a tale of rags to riches.

The peculiar decision to screen a British movie at the opening of the new Indian embassy highlights the Indian state's investment in narratives of upward mobility. The young protagonist of the film moves from the margins to the mainstream, catapulting to fame through his wits, luck, and love. *Slumdog Millionaire* has been rightly critiqued for emphasizing the autonomy of its protagonists while downplaying the structural effects of neoliberalism and caste/class violence in India.[3] At the same time, the romantic narrative of the film, particularly its focus on mobility across class, cannot be underestimated. The promise of upward mobility propelled my parents from rural to urban India, from Bombay to Tokyo, and motivated my own travel for education overseas. Equally important, this shared aspiration for mobility linked my experience to the lives of middle-class immigrants I subsequently met in the United States. The experience of upward mobility is not universal to subcontinental immigrants in Japan, nor is it representative of South Asians in America. Yet the transnational circulation of a film like *Slumdog Millionaire* (from the U.K. to the United States, from the United States to India, and from India to Japan) demonstrates the intricate ties that bind diasporic subjects to class and caste politics on the subcontinent. The film's popularity is also evidence of the enduring hegemony of the middle class, which continues to shape representations of South Asians in diaspora.

Such transnational reproductions of class privilege structured my initial experience in the United States. In the early 1990s, pluralist frameworks of multiculturalism shaped my education as a college student, determining course content, residential life, and campus social events. My university was host to a number of ethnic student groups, including a South Asian Students Association (to my confusion, distinct from the Asian Students Association). In this environment I met for the first time other young men and women who had spent their entire lives outside their parents' homelands. However, unlike my experience of identifying as a "foreigner" in Tokyo, many South Asian students I met had grown up in predominantly white American suburbs and identified as racial "minorities." Though subcontinental immigrants on campus were differentiated by national origin, gender, sexuality, and religious faith, as peers we also worked to understand the similarities that characterized our shared experience. At the university I attended, one major commonality was our tacit identification as middle class. In my conversations with peers, I came to realize that "middle class" had a loose definition, used equally by students who took on multiple jobs and loans to support their education, as by those bolstered by trust funds. Accompanying this class identification was our self-representation as "South Asian." A term borrowed from the campus group to which my friends and I belonged, the meaning of "South Asian" proved to be as elastic as the term "middle class." Though most of us agreed where South Asia was located on a world map, our practices of becoming South Asian were entirely positioned within the United States. Becoming South Asian was engendered through participating in bhangra dance competitions, campus fashion shows, and being at parties with people who looked like us. It rarely referred to a region of the world that few of us knew in historical detail, or to countries with which we had limited contact. Although identifying as South Asian almost always invoked the sensation of an "elsewhere," it was an identification that, strangely enough, belonged here.

As part of the social experience that accompanied campus multiculturalism, I was consistently reminded that subcontinental immigrants shared the same process of racialization, even if we did not share the same national, religious, or class affiliation. Hate crimes committed by the so-called "Dotbusters" in New York and New Jersey had left a violent imprint on South Asian communities on the East Coast. The white youth who perpetrated these crimes targeted Indians who wore the "dot," or bindi, which symbolizes matrimony for Hindu women. The victims of their crimes, however, included men and women, Sikhs and Muslims, Indo-Caribbeans, Bangladeshis, and Pakistanis across class backgrounds. In 1993 I actively followed a trial involving a survivor of a Dotbuster hate crime, Kaushal Saran, who had been brutally beaten by three men. Federal prosecutors accused the men of violating Saran's civil rights. The all-white jury acquitted the defendants, despite the fact that one of the assailants had confessed to his crime. The outcome of the trial sparked public protests across the East Coast, drawing attention not only to Saran's case but also to violence against racial minorities more generally. On a cold February night, I joined hundreds of college students from Asian American, African American, and other campus groups to protest the outcome of Saran's assailants' trial.[4] Participating in this rally a few months after leaving Japan was a means of claiming my place in the United States, an attempt to situate myself in relation to the frameworks of race and ethnicity that defined what it meant to be South Asian.

In retrospect, my participation was also a performance of belonging. Like my youthful dance recitals, this protest was also fraught with anxiety. Joining a progressive coalition of college students, I was convinced that we were fighting against racial and religious discrimination, as we protested against being marginalized as "dots" on America's racial landscape. But what I came to realize several years later was that South Asian college students had mobilized for Kaushal Saran precisely because he was, like many of us, middle class. Saran's qualifications as a physician had contributed to national media coverage of his case; his attackers gained public sympathy because they were perceived as native to New Jersey, being both white and working class.

That the Dotbusters brutally attacked Saran not just on account of his racial difference but also because of his class, and that South Asian college students came together because their own class standing had been threatened, became evident while reading critical accounts of the Dotbusters many years later.[5] Though I remembered the rally as my first attempt to publicly claim my rights as a minority subject in the United States, the protests were also the modality through which rights-based claims of belonging were made analogous with class-based claims to citizenship.

There were other ways in which my identity as a South Asian threatened to unravel. After college I began a graduate program in India, at a moment when the socialist state economy was steadily being dismantled. In the mid-1990s my experiences in Delhi were marked by the aftermath of the destruction of the Babri Masjid, a time when religious and communal politics came to the forefront of the Indian public sphere. Compounding this sense of rupture were the economic "liberalization" policies instituted by the state, which, though still in their infancy, had already begun to reconfigure notions of class and urban geography. Embodying a progressive national subjectivity in this context required disidentifying with the dominance of the Hindu right and identifying with the failure of the middle class to advance social and economic reform. Such secular identities also required taking into account the different histories of postcolonial citizenship that shaped political and economic relations on the subcontinent. What it meant to be a "local" in this context alerted me to the dissonances between my childhood as an "Indian" in Japan and as a "South Asian" in the United States, especially when in India I was identified not only by my class position but also by caste, religion, and region of origin.

Since returning to the United States fifteen years ago—first as a student, and now as a permanent resident—I have been motivated by the contradictions and solidarities that characterize diasporic communities. How immigrants realign transnational structures of class and citizenship to create new forms of identity, and in what ways such identifications reproduce hegemonic structures of power, is central to my analysis of South Asian diasporic public cultures. I continue to be compelled by the creative works that are produced, circulated, and consumed among South Asian immigrants, many of which propagate a shared narrative of multicultural identity. Yet these same narratives consistently elide the heterogeneity of religious practice, class, national origin, gender, and sexuality that characterizes subcontinental immigration. Equally important, such popular cultural texts are often disengaged from contemporaneous events in South Asia, even as structures of postcolonial nationhood impact the form, content, and genre of these texts. Locality emerges at precisely these disjunctures of time and space, shaping the affective relations between author and reader, filmmaker and viewer, performer and audience. As a capacious modality of understanding how immigrants are sutured to one another in a particular place and time, it enables us to understand the fragile formation of community. Together with the literary, cinematic, and ethnographic texts that I have gathered in each chapter, my writing of this book is part of the creative and critical process of becoming South Asian.

Reference Matter

Notes

INTRODUCTION

1. On how Asian American beauty pageants promote idealized representations of immigrant communities see King-O'Riain, *Pure Beauty*.

2. Theories of cultural citizenship have had a widespread impact on ethnographic studies of race and ethnicity: see Ong, "Cultural Citizenship as Subject-Making"; Siu, *Memories of a Future Home*; and Maira, *Missing*.

3. On how middle-class South Asians are represented as the "solution" to U.S. race relations, particularly in relation to African Americans, see Prashad, *Karma of Brown Folk*.

4. See Kymlicka, *Multicultural Citizenship* for arguments in favor of pluralist paradigms of multicultural diversity. Feminists of color have rigorously critiqued essentialist notions of identity which undergird liberal multiculturalism: see Mohanty and Alexander, *Feminist Genealogies*, and Spivak, *Critique of Postcolonial Reason*. In *End of Racism*, Dinesh D'Souza anticipates the so-called "postracial" moment in U.S. politics.

5. In *Neoliberalism as Exception*, Aihwa Ong writes that neoliberal economic policy "conceptually unsettles the notion of citizenship as a legal status rooted in a nation-state, and in stark opposition to a condition of statelessness" (6).

6. On the evolving political relationship between the Indian state and its diasporas see Mani and Varadarajan, "Largest Gathering."

7. On Tamil diasporic mobilization to effect regime change in Sri Lanka see Ismail, *Abiding by Sri Lanka*, as well as Jegannathan, "eelam.com." On Sikh immigrant advocacy for an independent state of Khalistan see Axel, *Nation's*

Tortured Body. On Indian American support for right-wing Hindu nationalism in India see Rai, "India On-line."

8. On the relation between Asian American and African American civil rights movements see Prashad, *Everybody Was Kung-Fu Fighting*. Avtar Brah, in *Cartographies of Diaspora*, writes about participating in the ethnic studies movement at UC Berkeley during the 1970s. Brah's account is one of the few published references to South Asians who participated in movements for Asian American self-determination.

9. For example Shankar and Srikanth, *A Part, Yet Apart*; Purkayastha, *Negotiating Ethnicity*; and Joshi, *New Roots*.

10. David Palumbo-Liu explicates this transnational turn toward the study of the U.S.-in-Asia by focusing on the Asia-Pacific as a zone of border crossings. Similarly, in *Imagine Otherwise*, Kandice Chuh reframes Asian America as a site for political critique of the U.S. empire in Southeast and East Asia, including Hawai'i, Korea, and the Philippines.

11. On gendered and sexualized representations of East and Southeast Asian Americans see Shimizu, *Hypersexuality of Race* and Eng, *Racial Castration*. On literary representations of Asian American masculinity see Kim, *Writing Manhood*.

12. The debate between Asian American studies as a primarily U.S.-centered discourse of racial politics, and scholars who advocate for a diasporic and transnational perspective, has defined the field for nearly two decades. See Wong, "Denationalization Reconsidered," for an argument in favor of prioritizing the domestic sphere of racial production; and Eng, "Out Here and Over There," on the analytical possibilities gained by a queer diasporic perspective. Susan Koshy's essay, "Category Crisis" is among the early scholarly works that situate South Asian Americans within a domestic racial framework and considers their transnational political affiliations.

13. The phenomenology of resistance is integral to early volumes on South Asian Americans, including Women of South Asian Descent Collective, *Our Feet Walk the Sky*; Das Dasgupta, *Patchwork Shawl*; Srikanth and Shankar, *A Part, Yet Apart*; and Srikanth and Maira, *Contours of the Heart*. Each of these volumes also aims to incorporate a diversity of South Asian immigrant experience, across national origin, class, gender, and sexuality.

14. Early quantitative sociological surveys of Indian Americans that fostered representations of South Asians as an assimilated immigrant group include Saran, *Asian Indian Experience*, and Saran and Earnes, *New Ethnics*.

15. On South Asians as resistant ethnic subjects see Prashad, *Karma of Brown Folk*; Das Gupta, *Unruly Immigrants*; Maira, *Desis in the House*; Shankar, *Desi Land*; and Sharma, *Hip Hop Desis*.

16. In *Race and Resistance*, Nguyen also makes the case for "good" and "bad" subjects of Asian American studies. Our arguments overlap insofar as we both contend that our fields are shaped by a bifurcated response to Asian American identity formation: namely, resistance or accommodation. See Nguyen, 143–72.

17. See Maira, *Missing*, on the implications of "dissenting citizenship." I discuss how dissent and complicity structure South Asian identities in Chapter 2.

18. See Muñoz, *Disidentifications*, on the performative possibilities offered by disidentification. I explore the centrality of disidentification for the production of South Asian locality in Chapter 3.

19. Self-identified progressive South Asian groups include South Asian Lesbian and Gay Association (SALGA), Desis Rising Up and Moving (DRUM), South Asian Women's Creative Collective (SAWCC), Narika, and Trikone.

20. See Islam, "In the Belly of the Multicultural Beast," for her critique of the term "South Asian" and its association with multicultural identity politics.

21. On how "South Asia" emerged as a construct of area studies in the aftermath of World War II see Cohn, *Colonialism*, 13–14. In his archival investigation of regional area studies programs, Cohn establishes historical links between what he calls the "investigative modalities" of the British colonial administration in India and the creation of the Human Relations Area File (HRAF) in the United States. The HRAF was tasked with creating a "taxonomy of cultures," South Asia being one among many world regions under investigation.

22. See Leonard, *Making Ethnic Choices*, on early twentieth-century Punjabi migration to California and the "Mexican Hindu" families created through marriage.

23. See Koshy, "Category Crisis," and Mazumdar, "Politics of Religion and National Origin" on the implications of *United States v. Bhagat Singh Thind* for South Asian racialization.

24. On the *Komagata Maru* incident see Jensen, *Passage from India*.

25. Das Gupta, *Unruly Immigrants*, 29.

26. See Palumbo-Liu, *Asian/American*, parts 2 and 3, for the historical conditions of the model minority thesis. On changing visual representations of Asian Americans from "yellow peril" to "model minority" see Lee, *Orientals*.

27. The 2000 U.S. Census report lists 2,195,569 people who identify as part of one or more South Asian immigrant group. South Asian countries specified in the census include India, Pakistan, Bangladesh, Sri Lanka, Nepal, Bhutan, and the Maldives. Respondents include both "foreign-born" South Asians as well as people of South Asian origin born in the United States. Pakistanis, Bangladeshis, and Sri Lankans are chronically undercounted in the census, in part because the census form makes no provision for their nationalities, which must be written

down under the category "Other." See Burnes and Bennet, "Asian Population 2000."

28. On the relationship between neoliberal economic policies in India and the emigration of workers overseas, particularly to the Persian Gulf region, see Lukose, *Liberalization's Children*.

29. For a discussion of the overlapping racial and religious histories that produce the figure of "the Muslim" in the United States see Rana, *Terrifying Muslims*. Rana argues that in the aftermath of 9/11, "'the Muslim' emerged as a category of race that was policed through narratives of migration, diaspora, criminality, and terror" (66). On the consequences of reading working-class South Asians as "Muslims" and "terrorists" see Kumar, *Foreigner Carrying*.

30. South Asian actors who currently have recurring roles on cable and network television programs include Aasif Mandvi, Kal Penn, Aziz Ansari, Padma Lakshmi, and Archie Punjabi.

31. On the prominence of Indian middle-class subjects in the national media see Mankekar, *Screening Culture, Viewing Politics*; Vasudevan, "*Bombay* and Its Public"; and Niranjana, "Nationalism Refigured."

CHAPTER 1

1. On the exclusion of South Asians from normative parameters of Asian American studies see Shankar and Srikanth, *A Part, Yet Apart*.

2. In *The Invention of Tradition*, Eric Hobsbawm writes, "'Invented tradition' is taken to mean a set of practices, normally governed by overtly or tacitly accepted rules and of a ritual or symbolic nature, which seek to inculcate certain values and norms of behavior by repetition, which automatically implies continuity with the past. In fact, where possible, they normally attempt to establish continuity with a suitable historical past" (1).

3. See Lowe, *Immigrant Acts*, 1–36.

4. For an extensive discussion of the Hart-Celler Act and its implications for South Asian labor migration see Prashad, *Karma of Brown Folk*, 74–80.

5. On the Indian state, its elite educational institutions, and their relation to postcolonial projects of modernity see Srivastava, *Constructing Post-Colonial India*.

6. Asian American studies scholars and queer scholars of color have deconstructed this linear teleology of queer politics: see in particular Manalansan, "In the Shadow of Stonewall."

7. Lahiri, "Intimate Alienation," 199.

8. See U.S. Supreme Court, *Takao Ozawa v. United States*, 260 U.S. 178 (1922). http://caselaw.lp.findlaw.com/scripts/getcase.pl?court=US&vol=260&invol=178 (accessed May 7, 2010).

9. On the relationship between the *Ozawa* and *Thind* cases see Shankar and Srikanth, *A Part, Yet Apart* (especially chapters 3 and 4); on *Thind*, see Das Gupta, *Unruly Immigrants* (chapter 1). Both Ozawa and Thind had argued that they should be considered "white," Ozawa on the basis of his skin color and Thind on the basis of racial origin theories that considered Indians to be of the "Aryan race."

10. Chuh, *Imagine Otherwise*, 122.

11. Given the recruitment of Afro-Caribbean and South Asian workers to British factories after World War II, Powell predicted a future in which "the black man will have the whip hand over the white man." His pronouncement provoked widespread racial harassment of Asian and Caribbean immigrants. See "Enoch Powell's 'Rivers of Blood' Speech."

12. Chuh, "Imaginary Borders," 281.

13. Anita Mannur notes in *Culinary Fictions* that food preparation is central to the "very processes of abjection" that Lahiri's protagonists experience in the United States (161).

14. The anthropologist Lisa Malkki highlights the political implications of color-coded spatial boundaries on world maps for refugees, exiles, and other migrants.

15. Lahiri uses the English spelling "Dacca," which was prevalent in the 1960s and 1970s. I use "Dhaka," the contemporary spelling of the city, reflecting its pronunciation by Bengalis.

16. On Indo-Pakistan relations during the 1971 war see Sumit Ganguly, *Conflict Unending*, 51–78.

17. For a secular-leftist perspective on the movement for liberating Bangladesh see Mukul, *Pictorial History*.

18. In 1971 George Harrison and Joan Baez organized "The Concert for Bangladesh," which raised nearly $240,000 for Bangladeshi refugees. Similarly, the Beat poets Allen Ginsberg and Peter Orlovsky organized a poetry recital that same year to draw attention to the Bangladeshi liberation movement, following Ginsberg's tour of refugee camps in India. See Brown, *A Blue Hand*, 213–16.

19. For Nixon's interventionist policy in South Asia as a strategy of the cold war see Rahim and Rahim, *Bangladesh Liberation War*.

20. Nayanika Mookherjee extensively documents human rights abuses perpetuated on Bangladeshis by the Indian and Pakistani military, and examines the repercussions of the war on contemporary Bangladeshi public culture in "*Muktir Gaan*, the Raped Woman and Migrant Identities of the Bangladesh War," 92.

21. India officially declared war on Pakistan on December 3, 1971, although the Indian government began funding Bengali liberationist guerrilla groups many months earlier.

22. In 1905, the British viceroy Lord Curzon partitioned Bengal province into East and West Bengal, ostensibly for better administrative control of the region. Following violent protests by Bengali nationalists, his decision was reversed in 1911. See Bose and Jalal, *Modern South Asia*. The 1905 partition is allegorically represented in Rabindranath Tagore's 1916 novel, *The Home and the World*.

23. Caesar, "Beyond Cultural Identity," 85.

24. Kaul, "Separation Anxiety," 280.

25. My interpretation of "imagined community" is indebted to Benedict Anderson's work by the same name.

26. Lilia remarks, "Several people told me that they had never seen an Indian witch before. Others performed the transaction without comment" (*Interpreter of Maladies*, 39). Although Lilia herself does not identify as Indian (much less as an "Indian witch"), my argument is that Lilia's identification as South Asian has less to do with her own recognition as a racialized subject than with her participation in another time.

27. Until 1972 Shillong was the capital of Assam, a state created in the aftermath of the 1947 partition of India. For Bangladeshi refugees, both Hindus and Muslims, Shillong was one of many destination points along the border of West Bengal (India) and Sylhet (East Pakistan). The absorption of Bengali-speaking refugees in this region of India, however, provoked violent disputes over land and language between Bengali speakers and indigenous (adivasi) populations in the area. These regional and linguistic battles for sovereignty precipitated the division of Assam and the reappropriation of Shillong as the state capital of Meghalaya in 1972.

28. Like the young Gogol Ganguli, Jhumpa Lahiri also goes by her "pet" name in public, disregarding her two "good" names, Nilanjana and Sudeshana. See Glassie, "Crossing Over."

29. See Terrazas, "Indian Immigrants."

30. For example, Kakutani and Metcalf's reviews in the *New York Times* (Kakutani, "From Calcutta to Suburbia," and Metcalf, "Out of the Overcoat"). The *San Francisco Chronicle* noted, "Names have always been contested territory in immigrant families [. . .] any Fernando who went by "Freddy," any Lefkowitzes or Shmulovitzes who became Lakes and Smalls, can take a seat at the Ganguli table and feel right at home." See Kipen, "Indian Immigrant's Son."

31. For a critique of the intensive focus on "intergenerational conflict" in South Asian immigrant families see Maira, *Desis in the House*, 18.

32. Prashad, *Darker Nations*, 34.

33. In his blog posting on *The Namesake*, Amardeep Singh also discusses Akaky's "parthogenetic birth" and suggests Gogol Ganguli's name as a form of

catachresis. However, Singh's focus is on finding a name for a diverse community of second-generation subcontinental immigrants, not all of whom may identify as "South Asian."

34. Caesar, "Gogol's Namesake," 104.

35. Ibid., 105.

36. For a cultural history of the Indian railways see Laura Bears, *Lines of the Nation*. Similarly, Manu Goswami, in *Producing India*, discusses the railways as an infrastructural edifice that shaped the political imagination of colonial India. It is important to note that the British railways were also central to demarcating the postcolonial boundaries between India and Pakistan during partition in 1947.

37. Nehru's speech was delivered on the eve of Indian independence, during the partition riots. His remarks have often been cited as a manifesto for India's national unity.

38. Grewal, *Transnational America*, 46.

39. See Karlinsky, "Gogol, Nikolai," for this account of Gogol's death.

40. *Concise Oxford Dictionary*, 10th ed., s.v. "Namesake." See also Oxford English Dictionary, online ed., s.v. "Namesake."

41. On Elihu Yale's imperial ventures in India see Gandhi, "Yale, India, and the Failure of the 'Global University.'"

42. Spivak, *Critique of Postcolonial Reason*, 188.

43. Mankekar, "Reflections on Diasporic Identities," 368.

44. Prashad, *Karma of Brown Folk*, 85–108.

45. Lowe, "Intimacies of Four Continents," 192.

46. Ibid., 207.

47. Representing migration as a movement between two worlds (from "old" to "new," if not from third world to first world) is a dominant literary trope that Lahiri herself draws upon. For an autobiographical account of her own family's migration see Lahiri, "My Two Lives."

CHAPTER 2

1. Asian American documentaries have consistently highlighted the violent racial and political formation of Asian America (such as the 1982 murder of Vincent Chin in Detroit and the 1992 Los Angeles riots), in addition to provoking public debate on the representation of women and queer subjects. I am particularly interested in those documentaries that acquire canonical value, even as these films question the "truth" of documentary. These include *Slaying the Dragon*, *Sa-I-Gu*, and *Who Killed Vincent Chin?*

2. See Shimizu, *Hypersexuality of Race*, for a critique of these dominant representations of Asian American femininity and sexuality.

3. Some of the earliest documentaries made by U.S.-based filmmakers include those by Bald (*Taxi-valah/Auto-biography*), Khurana and Murgai (*Julpari*), Sikand (*The Bhangra Wrap*), and Nidhi Singh (*Khush Refugees*).

4. Online viewer responses to both *Calcutta Calling* and *B.E.S.* are available on websites such as *Sepia Mutiny*, a U.S.-based South Asian group blog, as well as on the PBS websites for television programs such as *Frontline*.

5. On the AIA and its petition for a new census category of "Asian Indian" see Das Gupta, *Unruly Immigrants*, 27–55.

6. Ibid., 61.

7. On the economic transition from colonial to independent India and state rationale for public holdings see Kumar, *Cambridge Economic History of India*.

8. *Knowing Her Place* is distributed by the feminist media arts organization Women Make Movies.

9. Within South Asian American studies, the narrative of a "balance between two cultures" is widely disseminated in feminist anthologies such as Women of South Asian Descent Collective, *Our Feet Walk the Sky*; Srikanth and Maira, *Contours of the Heart*; and Das Dasgupta, *Patchwork Shawl*. Reclaiming "choice" is central to these liberal-feminist accounts of embodying ethnicity, all of which foreground women's agentive capacities.

10. Lata Mani's critique expands upon Partha Chatterjee's discussion of "the women's question" in nineteenth-century India. Chatterjee argues that the problem of how to maintain Indian "tradition" in the face of the colonial state was resolved within the patriarchal discourse of Indian nationalism by aligning women with the spiritual and private domain of the home rather than in the material and public domain of the state. Women's bodies became the site for the reproduction of an essentially "Indian" nation, as women's dress, education, religiosity, and comportment were disciplined into this idealized notion of national culture. See Chatterjee, *Nation and Its Fragments*, 116–34.

11. The terms "spiritual" and "material" worlds draw from Chatterjee, *Nation and Its Fragments*.

12. Rajan situates her scholarship on sati in relation to two seminal texts in the field: Lata Mani's *Contentious Traditions* and Spivak's "Can the Subaltern Speak?" Whereas Mani's monograph focuses on colonial discourses that evaded the subject of sati, Spivak contends that the sati cannot speak, and that in fact the subject is annihilated.

13. In her discussion of the 1995 British feature *Bhaji on the Beach*, Desai discusses the feelings of homesickness experienced by the South Asian immigrant women in the film. Desai suggests that homesickness is "the gendered embodi-

ment and subjective experience of nostalgia" (*Beyond Bollywood*, 136). As a somatic experience, sickness is expressed in various ways by the female protagonists of *Bhaji*, including through physical signs of domestic abuse. Yet in contrast to the absence of physical evidence of abuse in *Knowing Her Place*, Desai notes that abuse must be made legible through visible marks on the body in order for the viewer to recognize the immigrant subject as "homesick," that is, as dislocated from home.

14. In *Politics of Piety*, Mahmood elaborates on her argument against the "prescriptive" conditions of liberal-feminist theory, specifically in terms of its incapacity to engage with gendered practices of religious piety in non-Western contexts.

15. Lata Mani, "Gender, Class, and Cultural Conflict," 35.

16. Rajan, *Real and Imagined Women*, 50.

17. The Ties Program website advertises itself as "helping children know the people with whom they share their heritage are warm, wonderful, genuine people." See "The Ties Program."

18. See Piper, "What Age Is the Right Age?"

19. See Dolgin and Franco, *Daughter from Danang*, and Liem, *First Person Plural*. Both films are widely circulated as educational resources on Asian adoption by the Public Broadcasting System (PBS) and the Center for Asian American Media (CAAM).

20. See Dorow, *Transnational Adoption*.

21. Between 1989 and 2004 the United States issued 78,188 immigrant visas to Asian adoptees; Indian adoptees were 7.2 percent of this total. See "Adopted Asian Americans," *Asian Nation*, June 28, 2006 (available at www.asiannation.org/adopted.shtml).

22. See "IMH History."

23. For current regulations regarding Indian adoption, see "Guidelines Governing the Adoption of Children, 2011." Adoption of infants and children is regulated by the Central Adoption Resource Authority (CARA), a division of the government of India.

24. Barbara Yngvesson, in "Going 'Home,'" compellingly discusses the experiences of such "roots trips" for adoptive parents as a journey that "marks the child as not-me, as fundamentally other-than-me" (24).

25. Eng, "Transnational Adoption," 9.

26. On the psychic relations of identity that structure forms of kinship between birth parent, adoptive mother, and adoptive daughter in *First Person Plural* see Eng, *Feeling of Kinship*, 93–137.

27. See Sachi Cunningham, "Behind the Lens: Interview with Sasha Khokha."

28. All comments posted on "Rough Cut—India: Calcutta Calling." Comments on the website are continuously updated, though authors of anonymous postings cannot be verified.

29. Ibid. The website functions as an archive of posts left by viewers who saw the online and televised versions of *Calcutta Calling.*

30. See Mauss, *Gift*. The classic gift economy demands reciprocal giving, which poses a quandary in the film. For their family members, the adoptees are spiritual gifts from God, and therefore the gift cannot be reciprocated. Yet the adoptive families also make charitable contributions to Indian orphanages as a means of reciprocating the "gift" they have received.

31. On *Sepia Mutiny* as a "political" rather than cultural or social community blog for second-generation immigrants see Ahmed, "So Long."

32. Abhi, "All-American Girls in Calcutta," *Sepia Mutiny*, January 23, 2006 (available at www.sepiamutiny.com/sepia/archives/002883.html, accessed February 17, 2006). All comments cited follow the initial blog posting. Given the online nature of this forum, Abhi's name and the names of the commentators cannot be verified.

33. Eng, "Transnational Adoption," 13.

34. For another instance of marking gendered, ethnic, and sexual solidarity through piercing one's nose see Ganatra, *Junky Punky Girlz*, and B. Mani, "Queer Films, Straight Desis."

35. See "Census Profile: New York City's Bangladeshi American Population."

36. See Lee and Peng, "Census-Based Profile."

37. I take the evocative phrase "imaginary homeland" from Salman Rushdie's essay by the same name.

38. On the concept of downward mobility see Ameeriar, *Downwardly Global.*

39. See Maira's discussion of multiculturalism and public school programming in *Missing*, 174.

40. See Khan, *Callaloo Nation*, 5. Although Khan's ethnography focuses on South Asian diasporic communities in Trinidad, my reading of *B.E.S.* expands upon her argument for the mutually constitutive nature of religious and racial identities.

41. Quoted in Shukla, *India Abroad*, 239.

CHAPTER 3

An earlier version of this chapter was published as "Beauty Queens: Gender, Ethnicity, and Transnational Modernities at the Miss India USA Pageant," in *Positions: East Asia Cultures Critique* 14.3 (2006): 717–47. Copyright Duke University Press. Reprinted by permission of the publisher.

1. On Indian H-1B visa holders in the San Francisco Bay area see Mankekar, "India Shopping."

2. By "Bollywood" I refer to commercial Hindi-language cinema that circulates widely across India and its diasporas in North America, Europe, the Caribbean, Southeast Asia, and Africa. On the global reach of Bollywood film see Punathambekar and Kaveri, *Global Bollywood*.

3. Cohen, Wilk, and Stoeltje, "Introduction," 2. The authors emphasize the similarities in terms of form, content, and organization that structure beauty pageants in the United States and around the world.

4. Ibid., 8.

5. In 1999 the invited judges included Elaine Alquist, Assembly member of the twenty-second district of California; the film directors Jag Mundra and Krishna Shah; the actresses Sita Thompson and Rajashree; and Sonia Nikore, a casting director for NBC.

6. At the 1999 Miss India USA pageant, contestants represented the following states: California, Delaware, Florida, Georgia, Massachusetts, New Hampshire, New Jersey, New York, Texas, and Virginia. States where regional Miss India competitions are held but which were not represented at the pageant include Illinois, Indiana, Kentucky, Maryland, Michigan, Mississippi, Ohio, Oklahoma, Oregon, South Carolina, and Wisconsin. See Friedman and Grimberg, *Miss India Georgia*, for an excellent documentary on state-level beauty pageants sponsored by Indian American communities.

7. See Swamy, "Making Beauty."

8. See Rudrappa, *Ethnic Routes*, chaps. 4–5, on the transformation of Indian immigrants into ethnic subjects within the U.S. state, specifically through the uses of clothing and performance.

9. See Subramaniam, "Indians in North Carolina," on Indian high-tech industry workers.

10. As a pageantry of American multiculturalism, the title of Miss America has been held by African American, Asian American, and Arab American contestants since the late 1980s. However, though South Asians participate as state representatives, no South Asian has been crowned Miss America since the pageant's inception.

11. Oza, *Neoliberal India*, 2.

12. Although India has had a female prime minister, women (specifically Muslims and Anglo-Indians, as well as marginalized caste and indigenous groups) have been underrepresented in the government. The passage of the Constitution Bill (108th Amendment) in March 2010 now reserves one-third of Lok Sabha and state assembly seats for women, and one-third of existing seats

for so-called Scheduled Caste / Scheduled Tribe groups are also reserved for women.

13. See Mani and Varadarajan, "Largest Gathering," on the historical context of the annual Pravasi Bharatiya Divas conference and its implications for the contemporary economic and political relationship between the Indian state and its diasporas.

14. See Mankekar, *Screening Culture*, on the impact of satellite television programming on Indian public culture in the late twentieth century.

15. As detailed on its website, Asha for Education maintains links to educational and social initiatives in India.

16. See "Glamour-Beauty Queens."

17. Banet-Weiser, *Most Beautiful Girl*, 106. See also Watson and Martin, "There She Is," on the evolution of the Miss America beauty pageant format.

18. My gratitude to Javid Syed for his translation of this speech.

19. On the Uniform Civil Code and its implications for Indian religious minorities see Rajan, *Scandal of the State*, 147–73.

20. On Sarva Dharma Sambhava and its impact on notions of Indian secularism see Jaffrelot, *Hindu Nationalism*, 315–40.

21. In *Krantiveer*, Pratap (played by Nana Patekar) is raised in a basti that is the site of Hindu-Muslim riots. As depicted in the film, the riots are engineered by contracts drawn between the property developer Yograj, the slumlord Lakshmi, the ganglord Cheetah, and a pair of corrupt politicians who use the basti as an electoral vote-bank. Patekar's delivery of this speech, in the context of his vigilante acts of violence, has been described as "searing jingoism." See Verma, "Rediff Review."

22. Mishra, *Bollywood Cinema*, 230–31.

23. Thackeray is the founder of the Shiv Sena, the regional Hindu nationalist party affiliated with the nationwide Bharatiya Janata Party. On the rise of the Shiv Sena see Hansen, *The Saffron Wave*.

24. In *Liberalization's Children*, Ritty Lukose emphasizes the "descriptive and normative" quality of popular critiques of Indian secularism. Specifically, she draws attention to how such critiques argue for the "containment of caste politics in the name of a unified Hindu identity" (170). Reading Khanvilkar's performance as simply "Hindu" thus elides the fact that her embodiment of Hinduness is upper caste and regionally specific to northern India.

25. In "*Bombay* and Its Publics," Vasudevan emphasizes "the degree to which Muslim aggression is visibly more pronounced, especially in the film's tendency to fetishize their image in the white filigreed cap. I believe that this indicates the premise of a mainstream, and therefore necessarily *Hindu* secularist narrative

dealing with cultural difference as its central theme [. . .] the narrative cannot neutralize constructions of the Muslim as other" (49). I discuss further popular representations of the Muslim-as-other in Chapter 5.

26. Mishra, *Bollywood Cinema*, 237.

27. Banet-Weiser, *Most Beautiful Girl*, 88. Banet-Weiser's description refers to the question-and-answer segment of the Miss America pageant, which provides a model format for many of the young women participating in Miss India USA.

28. Lowe's *Immigrant Acts* opens with an epigraph that highlights the contentious debate over Maya Lin's design for the Vietnam War Memorial in Washington, D.C. Lin's memorial was chosen through an open national selection process, but Vietnam War veterans' groups protested against the seemingly abstract quality of her design as well as her Asian heritage (Lin is Chinese American). Though Lin's memorial was eventually built, the veterans' groups successfully campaigned for an additional memorial, a classical bronze sculpture that depicted a group of male soldiers as well as an American flag.

29. Manalansan, "*Biyuti*," 158.

30. For visual documentation of global protests against the Vietnam War, see Ali and Watkins, *1968*.

31. See Oza, *The Making of Neoliberal India*, chaps. 4–5.

32. The mission of Indian export promotion is integral to the Miss India pageant. In 2003 the first two rules for pageant contestants were "(1) I am a proud Indian. I shall devote fifteen days a year to promote domestic tourism, Indian heritage, and Indian jewelry and handicrafts. (2) I am expected to be successful in all that I undertake. I will help the Government of India promote the textiles and handicrafts of India." See Dewey, *Making Miss India*, 23.

33. See "Catch-up with the ex-Miss India's." This website is no longer accessible. The name "Femina" comes from the Indian women's magazine of the same name, which is published by the Times of India media group. See "Femina Miss India." The Miss India contest is now cosponsored by Pond's, a division of Unilever.

34. "Most-Often Asked Questions about the Femina Miss India Contest." The final twenty contestants for the title of Miss India do not represent states or regions within India, in line with the pageant's secular mission.

35. See "Pond's Femina Miss India 2006—Training Schedule."

36. Dewey, *Making Miss India*, 2. Dewey was a backstage participant in the 2003 Miss India pageant, whose travel with, and access to, contestants was sponsored by the Times of India media group.

37. In "Showcasing India," Oza discusses political movements for and against the 1996 Miss World pageant in Bangalore, highlighting how Marxist feminist protests (against the pageant industry's imperialism) converged with right-wing

Hindu nationalist protests (against the sexualized representation of women). The 1996 Miss World pageant was sponsored by ABCL corporation, which was later an investor in TV Asia, the media company that sponsored the Miss India USA pageant.

38. Quoted in Khambatta, *Pride of India*, 211.

39. John, "Globalisation," 382. John's critique of visual depictions of the Indian middle class emphasizes the ways in which women's bodies are represented through acts of voracious consumption.

40. See Swamy, "Making Beauty."

41. A sporadic occurrence in the mid-1990s, Mr. India Los Angeles is now defunct. Although local South Asian business communities in Southern California sponsored this pageant, it did not have a national component.

42. See Hall, "New Ethnicities," as well as Hall, "Cultural Identity and Diaspora," 222.

43. Quoted in Spence, "Miss India Is Out."

44. Quoted in Nishioka, "Miss India Comes Out."

45. Only four winners in the past twenty years (from Hong Kong, South Africa, the United Arab Emirates, and Suriname) have been exceptions to this rule.

CHAPTER 4

1. Appadurai, *Modernity at Large*, 178.

2. One such example of first-generation immigrant cultural programming is the 1991 Festival of India in Edison, New Jersey. See Shukla's analysis of this festival and its implications for Indian American identity in *India Abroad*, 25–77.

3. The South Asian art festivals I discuss gave rise to events such as the Minneapolis-based progressive Sri Lankan conference Diaspora Flow, and Desi-Q, a conference for queer South Asians in San Francisco. The visual arts component of Diasporadics, Artwallah, and Desh Pardesh preceded the current proliferation of private galleries for the display of contemporary South Asian art.

4. In 2010 the founders of Artwallah terminated their work because of lack of funding. However, in June 2010, the former staff of Artwallah mounted a daylong event, "Afterlife." Afterlife's prospect as an annual South Asian art festival is contingent on funding.

5. See B. Mani, "Destination Culture."

6. Lowe, *Immigrant Acts*, 85. Unlike my focus on art festivals that are created for and by ethnic communities, Lowe's critique of cultural festivals focuses on state-sponsored displays of multiculturalism, such as the 1990 Los Angeles Festival of the Arts.

7. SAVAC continues to thrive as a center for the production and display of South Asian diasporic art in Toronto: see www.savac.net/.

8. See *Desh Pardesh*, 1999.

9. Ibid., 11.

10. In *Desis in the House*, Maira details heteronormative patterns of social behavior that dominate the interaction between young South Asian men and women at dance clubs.

11. Gopinath notes that Desh Pardesh is frequently recuperated into an imaginative geography of queer South Asian diasporas ("Funny Boys and Girls," 122). An example of queer cultural programming that drew directly from the influence of Desh Pardesh was Queer Filmistan, a South Asian film festival held in San Francisco in 2001. On the rhetoric of "progressive" and "queer" programming at Queer Filmistan see B. Mani, "Queer Films, Straight Desis."

12. *Ultra-Maxi Priest* was pulled from a South Asian group art exhibition at the Oakville Municipal Building in Ontario for not conforming to "public standards." In protest Sanowar Makhan performed a live installation outside the municipal building. See Kelly, "Banned Art Work."

13. See www.iacc.org. The IACC is now defunct.

14. See funding sources listed in *Artwallah 2005*, 40–46.

15. Names of donors and sponsorship amounts obtained from DevDugal.com. The website currently hosts a blog unrelated to Artwallah.

16. Gunew's thesis diverges from political theorists such as Kymlicka, who argues that both the United States and Canada are "multinational and polyethnic states," composed largely of "voluntary" migrants. Such liberal ideologies of multiculturalism (expressed through popular metaphors such as "mosaic" or "melting pot") flatten distinct histories of colonization, imperialism, and race relations in North America. See Kymlicka, *Multicultural Citizenship*, chap. 2.

17. The Canadian National Film Board funded several feature films by South Asian directors that were screened at Desh Pardesh, 1999.

18. See Johnson, *Voyage of the Komagata Maru*. See also Jensen, *Passage from India*, on anti-Asian race riots and court cases in Canada, as well as anticolonial movements in India that emerged in the aftermath of the *Komagata Maru* incident.

19. On the aesthetic value and power of travel narratives see Pratt, *Imperial Eyes*, 201–27.

20. *Artwallah 2005*, 9.

21. On orientalist representations of Indians in America see Prashad, *Karma of Brown Folk*, 21–68.

22. Lowe, *Immigrant Acts*, 87.

23. Ameen Gill, telephone interview, February 14, 2001.

24. Ameen Gill, e-mail to author, June 19, 2001.

25. Early images of *The Mango Tree* are available at "Contemporary Art and Identity."

26. See Kamdar, "Bread Basket Case," on the agricultural revolution in Punjab, and R. Brown, *Art for a Modern India*, on the modernist aesthetics of Chandigarh.

27. On Sikh diasporic movements for Khalistan see Axel, *Nation's Tortured Body*.

28. On British colonial redistribution of land and water rights in Punjab see Mukherjee, *Colonizing Agriculture*. On land rights under British rule see Washbrook, "Law, State and Agrarian Society."

29. See Leonard on early Punjabi migration to the West Coast.

30. See Puar, "Queer Times, Queer Assemblages" on the representational economy of the "turbaned Sikh" and the rhetorical deployment of Sikh and Muslim male bodies by the U.S. state after September 11, 2001.

31. On hate crimes against Sikh and Muslim South Asians after September 11 see Leong and Nakanishi, *After Words*.

32. Puar, "Queer Times," 122.

33. See "Youth Power." Acharya's work has been featured in a number of solo and group shows including at the Kravets/Wehby Gallery, New York; the Queens Museum of Art, New York; Gallery Chemould, Mumbai; and Nature Morte, Delhi.

34. See Dhruvi Acharya, "Statement," April 15, 2010 (available at http://dhruvi.com/statement.htm).

35. On *Amar Chitra Katha*'s history of publication as well as its narrative representation of India see MacLaine, *India's Immortal Comic Books*.

36. See also "Big Idea." Recent issues of *Amar Chitra Katha* have focused on a number of prominent nonresident Indians (NRIs) in the United States and the U.K.

37. Kirin Narayan examines the intergenerational uses of *Amar Chitra Katha* within South Asian families as a means of crafting a South Asian (Hindu) identity. See also MacLaine, *India's Immortal Comic Books*, 198–214.

38. Acharya, e-mail to author, March 12, 2001. MacLaine (*India's Immortal Comic Books*, 53–86) has described the sexualized representation of Indian women as mythological and historical heroines, particularly in terms of their revealing costumes.

39. The moral of the Savitri fable is displayed on the website for *Amar Chitra Katha*, under the title page "Savitri."

40. The affective experience of feeling "good" may be considered in relation to Sara Ahmed's critique of the politics of good feeling. In her essay "Happy Objects," Ahmed examines those feminist subjects who are identified by the heterosexual family as the cause of unhappiness, whom she calls "affect aliens." Shonali Bose is one such "affect alien," whose film provokes discord

(or bad feelings) within the ethnic community (or family) that is produced at Diasporadics. As Ahmed writes, "What concerns me is [. . .] the very distinction between good and bad feelings that presumes that bad feelings are backward and conservative and good feelings are forward and progressive. Bad feelings are seen as orientated toward the past, as a kind of stubborness that 'stops' the subject from embracing the future. Good feelings are associated here with moving up and getting out" (50). Similarly, Bose's film is seen as stopping the sensation of "feeling good" at Diasporadics, a feeling that is aligned with the forward-oriented movement of progressive South Asian activism.

41. Dave, "South Asia in the Diasporic Imagination."
42. Dave, "To Render Real," 612.
43. Ibid., 616.
44. *Artwallah 2005*, 45.
45. Ibid., 46.
46. On exhibition cultures and the "agency of display" see Kirshenblatt-Gimblett, *Destination Culture*.
47. The artists participating in this conversation requested anonymity in order to avoid offending Artwallah festival organizers.
48. South Asians of East African origin are often described as "twice migrants." See Bachu, "New Cultural Forms."
49. Patel, *Migritude*, 27–29.
50. Ibid., 28.
51. Patel, *Shilling Love*, 23.
52. Sarita Vasa, "Artwallah's Closure and Legacy," e-mail to author, February 17, 2010.
53. I have discussed the exhibition cultures that shape the consumption of contemporary South Asian art in Mani, "Viewing South Asia."

CHAPTER 5

1. On the fantasies of class, gender, and globalization that shape contemporary Bollywood films see Mankekar, "Brides Who Travel," and Uberoi, "Diaspora Comes Home."
2. On the racialized and sexualized figure of Sikh and Muslim immigrants in U.S. public culture see Puar, *Terrorist Assemblages*.
3. The word "Asian" is popularly used in Britain to refer specifically to immigrants of Indian, Pakistani, and Bangladeshi origin.
4. The original cast of the Broadway production of *Bombay Dreams* featured Manu Narayan (Akaash), Anisha Nagarajan (Priya), Sriram Ganesan (Sweetie),

Ayesha Dharkar (Rani), and Madhur Jaffrey (Shanti). Six months later the principal cast was altered to include Yolande Bhave as Shanti, Tamyra Gray as Priya, and Anjali Bhimani as Rani.

5. In his remarks on queer Filipino beauty pageants, Martin Manalansan notes that the performances on stage are "part of the consumption or audience-related, scriptwriting, and autoethnographic processes." See Manalansan, "*Biyuti*," 155.

6. Both songs were originally composed by A. R. Rahman and featured in blockbuster Indian films. "Shakalaka Baby" was translated from the Tamil film *Mudalvan*; likewise "Chaiyya Chaiyya" was taken from the Hindi film *Dil Se*.

7. On Broadway as a "melting pot" of American theater see Sollors, *Beyond Ethnicity*, 66–100.

8. See Brantley, "Coloring by the Numbers," and Marks, "Bombay Dreams."

9. See *India Today International* for the cover image featuring Ayesha Dharkar as Rani.

10. Webber's encounter with popular Bollywood film music is described in *Bombay Dreams Souvenir Program*. This souvenir guide to the U.S. version of the musical was available for purchase at the Broadway Theatre.

11. Ibid.

12. Office for National Statistics, "British Asian Demographics."

13. On the relationship between music and multiculturalism among young British Asians see Bakrania, *Re-fusing Identities*.

14. Suresh John, telephone interview, December 1, 2005.

15. See Prashant Agrawal, "Dream On," *New York Times*, May 29, 2004 (available at www.nytimes.com/2004/04/29/opinion/dream-on.html, accessed April 29, 2005).

16. See "It's Also an American Story," *India Abroad*, April 2, 2004, M11.

17. Quoted in Pais, "Bombay Dreams Brings Bollywood to Broadway," A7.

18. Quoted in Piepenberg, "Hooray for Bollywood," 16.

19. For example, Syal's novels *Life Isn't All Ha Ha Hee Hee* and *Anita and Me*, as well as her screenwriting and acting for the television series *Goodness Gracious Me!* and *The Kumars at No. 42*, have been central to developing mainstream media representations of Asian immigrants as British subjects.

20. Office of National Statistics, "People and Migration."

21. Office of National Statistics, "Religion."

22. See Bhasi, "Living: Indian Summer," on the transformation of the Selfridges department store for "India month."

23. Quoted in Pincus-Roth, "Extreme Makeover."

24. I borrow the phrase "native informants" from Gayatri Chakravorty Spivak. See her use of the term as a biographical, pedagogical, and philosophical device in *The Post-Colonial Critic*.

25. Quoted in Padmanabhan, "Touching the Stars," 38.

26. See Pincus-Roth, "The Extreme Makeover of 'Bombay Dreams.'"

27. On Bollywood films and music as a vehicle of Indian globalization see Punathambekar and Kavoori, *Global Bollywood*, and Gopal and Moorti, *Global Bollywood: Travels of Hindi Song and Dance*.

28. See *Salaam Bombay Dreams*. The DVD features extensive interviews with the British cast and crew of the musical, as well as documentary footage of the crew's visit to India and their collaboration with A. R. Rahman.

29. For example, Rushdie's classic *Midnight's Children*; Mistry, *Fine Balance*; Chandra, *Love and Longing*; and Mehta, *Maximum City*.

30. The term is taken from Sassen, *Global City*.

31. On the emergence of regionalist Marathi identities, the rise of the Shiv Sena, and the prominence of Hindutva identity in Indian national politics, see Hansen, *Wages of Violence* as well as *The Saffron Wave*.

32. Niranjana, "Nationalism Refigured," 153. The spectacular Hindu Indian wedding scene is central to a number of recent South Asian diasporic films, such as *Monsoon Wedding* and *Bend It Like Beckham*.

33. Recent scholarship on Dalit movements has redefined the politics of caste and class in India. See in particular Rao, *Caste Question*, and Ilaiah, *Why I Am Not a Hindu*.

34. Niranjana, "Nationalism Refigured," 147. In her reading of *Roja*, Niranjana points out how contemporary Bollywood film obscures depictions of labor and of the working class, especially in comparison to social realist films of the 1950s–70s.

35. See Murray, "Talkin' Broadway's." But Lisa Tsering ("'Bombay Dreams' on Broadway") describes Ganesan as "squeaky-clean, campy, and Queer-Eyed," in contrast to Raj Ghatak's "poignant and tragic" performance in the West End production.

36. See Reddy, *With Respect to Sex*, on the multireligious social practices of hijras in the southern Indian city of Hyderabad.

37. Such orientalist representations of the sexuality of hijras are evident in Alexander Shiva's recent documentary film, *Bombay Eunuch*.

38. Gopinath, *Impossible Desires*, 171.

39. Gopinath, "Nostalgia, Desire, Diasporas," 474.

40. See *Salaam Bombay Dreams*.

41. Niranjana, "Nationalism Refigured," 158. Likewise in *Roja*, the ultimate reunion of the (Hindu) married protagonists following a terrorist attack assures

the viewers of the "secular" character of the film and strengthens the dominance of Hindu nationalism within popular depictions of modern India.

42. The posters featured models Gerard Lobo and Pooja Kumar instead of actual cast members. Two posters advertised the musical in Times Square: the first depicts Lobo and Kumar gazing into each other's eyes; the second shows Kumar in a wet blouse leaning against Lobo's bare chest.

43. Quoted in Chhabra, "Let's Play Fair," 23.

44. Quoted in Purdum, "Upbeat Republicans."

45. See Peterson, "How New York Is Defying Convention."

46. Information about the RNC protests is from New York Indymedia, available at "Andrew Paprocki's Home Page."

47. The anthropologist Junaid Rana situates Special Registration (also known as the National Security Entry-Exit Registration System) within a longer history of the detention and deportation of immigrants in the United States. Rana argues that the USA Patriot Act of 2001 (of which Special Registration is a part) draws from the McCarran-Walter Act of 1952, and was also preceded by the Illegal Immigration Reform and Immigrant Responsibility Act of 1996. Both these acts were central to the construction of the undocumented immigrant as "enemy alien." See Rana, *Terrifying Muslims*, 158–59.

48. Asian American Legal Defense and Education Fund, 16. The AALDEF report notes that by the conclusion of Special Registration procedures in April 2003, over eighty-two thousand immigrant men had been fingerprinted and questioned under oath.

49. Sheetal Gandhi, telephone interview, November 30, 2005.

50. Anjali Bhimani, telephone interview, November 21, 2005.

51. Manu Narayan, personal interview, February 8, 2006.

EPILOGUE

1. Appadurai, *Modernity at Large*, 178.

2. See the website for Indian Community Activities Tokyo at www.manicat.org/main.html for ICAT's current activities. My father retired from his position as the executive convenor of the organization in 2010.

3. In the United States, press reviews critiqued the aestheticization of poverty in the film and its glossy take on neoliberal reforms in India. See Lim, "What, Exactly, Is Slumdog Millionaire?" and Stevens, "Slumdog Millionaire."

4. The 1993 protest at the University of Pennsylvania against the verdict issued in the federal civil rights trial is documented in Suzanne Gordon, "300 Protest Racism Against South Asians," *Philadelphia Inquirer*, February 15, 1993, B4, as well as Tanamachi, "300 Brave the Cold."

5. Vijay Prashad discusses the Dotbusters and their assault on Kaushal Saran in *The Karma of Brown Folk*, 85–107. Prashad's argument is that these hate crimes are formative for a politicized racial consciousness among first- and second-generation immigrants, although he also points out that Saran's case was exceptional in that most victims of race-based hate crimes are working class rather than professionally skilled immigrants.

Works Cited

Ahmad, Muneer. "Homeland Insecurities: Racial Violence the Day After September 11." *Social Text* 20.3 (2002): 101–15.

Ahmed, Sara. "Happy Objects." In *The Affect Theory Reader*. Eds. Melissa Gregg and Gregory J. Seigworth, pp. 29–51. Durham, NC: Duke University Press, 2010.

Ahmed, Tanzila. "So Long. Farewell. Go Vote." *Sepia Mutiny*. May 2, 2006. Available at www.sepiamutiny.com/sepia/archives/cat_blog.html (accessed May 10, 2006).

Alam, Fariba, and Swati Khurana, dirs. *B.E.S. (Bangla East Side)*. New York: Third World Newsreel, 2004.

Ali, Syed. "Understanding Acculturation Among Second-Generation South Asian Muslims in the United States." *Contributions to Indian Sociology* 42.3 (2008): 383–411.

Ali, Tariq, and Susan Watkins. *1968: Marching in the Streets*. New York: Free Press, 1998.

"All About the Miss India U.S.A. Pageant." Available at www.worldwidepageants.com/aboutU.S.A.htm (accessed May 16, 2002).

Alwis, Malathi de. "'Respectability,' 'Modernity' and the Policing of 'Culture' in Colonial Ceylon." In *Gender, Sexuality and Colonial Modernities*. Ed. Antoinette Burton, pp. 177–92. New York: Routledge, 1999.

Ameeriar, Lalaie. Downwardly Global: Multicultural Bodies and Gendered Labor Migrations from Karachi to Toronto. Unpublished diss., Stanford University, 2008.

Anagnost, Ann. "Scenes of Misrecognition: Maternal Citizenship in an Age of Transnational Adoption." *positions* 8.2 (2000): 389–421.

Anderson, Benedict. *Imagined Communities: Reflections on the Origin and Spread of Nationalism*. London: Verso, 1991.
"Andrew Paprocki's Home Page." 8-27-04 Critical Mass. August 29, 2004. Available at http://amp.ishiboo.com/rnc/ (accessed September 2, 2011).
Appadurai, Arjun. *Modernity at Large: The Cultural Dimensions of Globalization*. Delhi: Oxford University Press, 1997.
Artwallah 2001. [Los Angeles:] n.p.
Artwallah 2005. [Los Angeles:] n.p.
Asha for Education. Available at www.ashanet.org (accessed September 2, 2011).
Asian American Legal Defense and Education Fund. *Special Registration: Discrimination and Xenophobia as Government Policy*. New York: AALDEF, 2004.
Axel, Brian Keith. *The Nation's Tortured Body: Violence, Representation, and the Formation of a Sikh "Diaspora."* Durham, NC: Duke University Press, 2001.
Bahri, Deepika, and Mary Vasudeva, eds. *Between the Lines: South Asians and Postcoloniality*. Philadelphia: Temple University Press, 1996.
Bakrania, Falu. *Re-Fusing Identities: South Asian Youth and Politics of Popular Music in Britain*. Durham, NC: Duke University Press, forthcoming.
Bald, Vivek, dir. *Taxi-valah/Auto-biography*. New York: Third World Newsreel, 1994.
Banet-Weiser, Sarah. *The Most Beautiful Girl in the World: Beauty Pageants and National Identity*. Berkeley and Los Angeles: University of California Press, 1999.
Bears, Laura. *Lines of the Nation: Indian Railway Workers, Bureaucracy, and the Intimate Historical Self*. New York: Columbia University Press, 2007.
Bhabha, Homi, ed. *Nation and Narration*. London: Routledge, 1990.
Bhachu, Parminder. "New Cultural Forms and Transnational South Asian Women: Culture, Class, and Consumption Among British Asian Women in the Diaspora." In *Nation and Migration: The Politics of Space in the South Asian Diaspora*. Ed. Peter van der Veer, pp. 222–44. Philadelphia: University of Pennsylvania Press, 1995.
Bhan, Niti. "Community Profile: Indian Americans." Asians in America Project. Available at www.asiansinamerica.org/museum/comm_ind.html (accessed April 20, 2006).
Bhasi, Ishara. "Living: Indian Summer; Set for Bollywood." India Today on the Net. April 22, 2002. Available at www.india-today.com/itoday/20020422/uk-cinema.shtml (accessed July 20, 2011).
"The Big Idea." *Amar Chitra Katha*. Available at www.amarchitrakatha.com/about_us/iindex.asp (accessed December 24, 2005).
Bombay Dreams. By Meera Syal and Thomas Meehan. Dir. Steven Pimlott. Broadway Theatre, New York, April 2004–January 2005.

Bombay Dreams Souvenir Program [New York:] n.p., n.d.
Bose, Shonali, dir. *Lifting the Veil*. Jonai Productions, 1997.
Bose, Sugata, and Ayesha Jalal. *Modern South Asia: History, Culture, and Political Economy*. New York: Routledge, 1998.
Brah, Avtar. *Cartographies of Diaspora: Contesting Identities*. London: Routledge, 1997.
Brantley, Ben. "Coloring by the Numbers." Review of *Bombay Dreams* by Meera Syal and Thomas Meehan. Broadway Theatre, New York. *New York Times*, April 30, 2004, E1.
Brown, Deborah. *A Blue Hand: The Beats in India*. New York: Penguin, 2008.
Brown, Rebecca. *Art for a Modern India, 1947–1990*. Durham, NC: Duke University Press, 2009.
Burnes, Jessica S., and Claudette E. Bennet. "The Asian Population 2000: Census 2000 Brief." U.S. Department of Commerce. February 2002. Available at www.census.gov/prod/2002pubs/c2kbr01-16.pdf (accessed April 20, 2006).
Burton, Antoinette. *The Postcolonial Careers of Santha Rama Rau*. Durham, NC: Duke University Press, 2007.
Caesar, Judith. "Beyond Cultural Identity in Jhumpa Lahiri's 'When Mr. Pirzada Came to Dine.'" *North Dakota Quarterly* 70.1 (2003): 82–91.
———. "Gogol's Namesake: Identity and Relationships in Jhumpa Lahiri's *The Namesake*." *Atenea* 27.1 (2007): 103–19.
"Catch-up with the Ex-Miss India's." Femina Miss India. Available at www.feminamissindia.com/flashback.html (accessed May 16, 2002).
"Census Profile: New York City's Bangladeshi American Population." Asian American Federation of New York Census Information Center, 2005. January 26, 2005. Available at www.aafny.org/proom/pr/pr20050126.asp (accessed February 5, 2011).
Chadha, Gurinder, dir. *Bend It Like Beckham*. Fox Searchlight, 2003.
———. *Bhaji on the Beach*. Channel Four Films, 1995.
Chakrabarty, Dipesh. *Provincializing Europe: Postcolonial Thought and Historical Difference*. Princeton, NJ: Princeton University Press, 2000.
Chandra, Vikram. *Love and Longing in Bombay*. New Delhi: Penguin, 1997.
Chatterjee, Partha. *The Nation and Its Fragments: Colonial and Postcolonial Histories*. Princeton, NJ: Princeton University Press, 1993.
Cheng, Anne Anlin. *The Melancholy of Race*. New York: Oxford University Press, 2000.
Chhabbra, Aseem. "Let's Play Fair." *India Abroad*, May 14, 2004, M10.
———. "Writers' Bloc." *Time Out New York*, March 25–April 1, 2004, 23.

Choy, Christine, dir. *Who Killed Vincent Chin?* New York: Filmmakers Library, 1988.
Chuh, Kandice. "Imaginary Borders." In *Orientations: Mapping Studies in the Asian Diaspora.* Ed. Kandice Chuh and Karen Shimakawa, pp. 277–95. Durham, NC: Duke University Press, 2001.
———. *Imagine Otherwise: On Asian Americanist Critique.* Durham, NC: Duke University Press, 2003.
Chuh, Kandice, and Karen Shimawaka, eds. *Orientations: Mapping Studies in the Asian Diaspora.* Durham, NC: Duke University Press, 2001.
Cohen, Colleen Ballerina, and Richard Wilk, with Beverly Stoeltje. "Introduction." In *Beauty Queens on the Global Stage: Gender, Contests, and Power.* Ed. Colleen Ballerina Cohen, Richard Wilk, and Beverly Stoeltje, pp. 1–12. New York: Routledge, 1996.
Cohen, Lawrence. "The Pleasures of Castration: The Postoperative Status of Hijras, Jankhas, and Academics." In *Sexual Nature, Sexual Culture.* Ed. Paul R. Abramson and Steven D. Pinkerton, pp. 276–304. Chicago: University of Chicago Press, 1995.
Cohn, Bernard. *Colonialism and Its Forms of Knowledge: The British in India.* Princeton, NJ: Princeton University Press, 1996.
"Contemporary Art and Identity: South Asian Diaspora in North America." Asian Art.com. Available at www.asianart.com/exhibitions/diaspora/gill.html (accessed September 2, 2011).
Cooper, Peta, and Tasmia Khan. "Kashish Chopra—Miss (Lesbian) Congeniality." DesiClub.com. May 15, 2006. Available at www.desiclub.com/community/culture/culture_article. cfm?id=192 (accessed July 10, 2011).
Cunningam, Sachi. "Behind the Lens: Interview with Sasha Khokha." *Frontline.* Available at www.pbs.org/frontlineworld/rough/2006/01/india_calcuttaint.html (accessed September 2, 2011).
Daiya, Kavita. *Violent Belongings: Partition, Gender, and National Culture in Postcolonial India.* Philadelphia: Temple University Press, 2008.
Das DasGupta, Shamita. *A Patchwork Shawl: Chronicles of South Asian Women in America.* New Brunswick, NJ: Rutgers University Press, 1998.
Das Gupta, Monisha. *Unruly Immigrants: Rights, Activism, and Transnational South Asian Politics in the United States.* Durham, NC: Duke University Press, 2006.
Datta, Jyotirmoy. "Narayan, Lead of 'Bombay Dreams,' Speaks of 'Role of the Decade.'" *News India–Times,* March 5, 2004, 26.
Dave, Naisargi N. "South Asia in the Diasporic Imagination." South Asia: Histories of the Present. Department of History and Anthropology, University of Michigan at Ann Arbor, March 17, 2001.

———. "To Render Real the Imagined: An Ethnographic History of Lesbian Community in India." *Signs* 35.3 (2010): 595–619.
Desai, Jigna. *Beyond Bollywood: The Cultural Politics of South Asian Diasporic Film*. New York: Routledge, 2004.
Desh Pardesh 9th Annual Festival/Conference. [Toronto:] n.p., 1999.
DevDugal.com. Available at www.devdugal.com/artwallah/Donate.asp (accessed December 27, 2005).
Dewey, Susan. *Making Miss India Miss World: Constructing Gender, Power, and the Nation in Postliberalization India*. Syracuse, NY: Syracuse University Press, 2008.
Dhingra, Pawan. *Managing Multicultural Lives: Asian American Professionals and the Challenge of Multiple Identities*. Stanford, CA: Stanford University Press, 2007.
Diasporadics. [New York:] n.p., 1999.
———. [New York:] n.p., 2000.
Dolgin, Gail, and Vincente Franco, dirs. *Daughter from Danang*. San Francisco: Center for Asian American Media, 2003.
Dorow, Sara. *Transnational Adoption: A Cultural Economy of Race, Gender, and Kinship*. New York: NYU Press, 2006.
D'Souza, Dinesh. *The End of Racism: A New Vision for a Multiracial Society*. New York: Free Press, 1995.
Ebron, Paulla. *Performing Africa*. Princeton, NJ: Princeton University Press, 2002.
The 18th Annual Miss India USA Pageant. [San Jose, CA] n.p., February 6, 1999.
Eng, David. *The Feeling of Kinship: Queer Liberalism and the Racialization of Intimacy*. Durham, NC: Duke University Press, 2010.
———. "Out Here and Over There: Queerness and Diaspora in Asian American Studies." *Social Text* 15.3–4 (1997): 31–52.
———. *Racial Castration: Managing Masculinity in Asian America*. Durham, NC: Duke University Press, 2001.
———. "Transnational Adoption and Queer Diasporas." *Social Text* 21.3 (2003): 1–37.
"Enoch Powell's 'Rivers of Blood' Speech." *Telegraph* (U.K.), November 6, 2007. Available at www.telegraph.co.uk/comment/3643823/Enoch-Powells-Rivers-of-Blood-speech.html (accessed February 4, 2011).
Femina Miss India. Available at http://feminamissindia.indiatimes.com/ (accessed February 5, 2011).
Frankenberg, Ruth, and Lata Mani. "Crosscurrents, Crosstalk: Race, 'Postcoloniality' and the Politics of Location." In *Contemporary Postcolonial Theory: A Reader*. Ed. Padmini Mongia, pp. 347–64. New York: Arnold, 1997.

Friedman, Daniel, and Sharon Grimberg, dirs. *Miss India-Georgia*. Hohokus, NJ: Urban Life Productions, 1998.
Ganatra, Nisha, dir. *Junky Punky Girlz*. New York: Mata Films, 1996.
Gandhi, Ajay. "Yale, India, and the Failure of the 'Global University.'" Hindu, May 4, 2005. Available at www.hindu.com/2005/05/04/stories/2005050400441000.htm (accessed May 11, 2010).
Ganguly, Keya. *States of Exception: Everyday Life and Postcolonial Identity*. Minneapolis: University of Minnesota Press, 2002.
Ganguly, Sumit. *Conflict Unending: India-Pakistan Tensions Since 1947*. New York: Columbia University Press, 2002.
Gee, Deborah, dir. *Slaying the Dragon*. San Francisco: Asian Women United, 1988.
Ghosh, Amitav. "The March of the Novel Through History: The Testimony of My Grandfather's Bookcase." In *The Imam and the Indian: Collected Prose*, pp. 287–304. New Delhi: Ravi Dayal, 2002.
———. *The Shadow Lines*. Educ. ed. Delhi: Oxford University Press, 1995.
"Glamour-Beauty Queens." India in New York. February 19, 1999. Available at www.indiainnewyork.com/iny021999/glamour/missindiaU.S.A.html (accessed October 1, 1999).
Glassie, John. "Crossing Over: Questions for Jhumpa Lahiri." *New York Times Magazine*, September 7, 2003, 19.
Gogol, Nicolai. "The Overcoat." Trans. David Magarshack. London: Merlin Press, 1964 [1956].
Goodness Gracious Me. British Broadcasting Corp., 2002.
Gopal, Sangita, and Sujata Moorti, eds. *Global Bollywood: Travels of Hindi Song and Dance*. Minneapolis: University of Minnesota Press, 2008.
Gopinath, Gayatri. "Bollywood Spectacles: Queer Diasporic Critique in the Aftermath of 9/11." *Social Text* 23.3–4 (2005): 157–69.
———. "Bombay, U.K., Yuba City: Bhangra Music and the Engendering of Diaspora." *Diaspora* 4.3 (1995): 303–21.
———. "Funny Boys and Girls: Notes from a Queer South Asian Planet." In *Asian American Sexualities: Dimensions of the Gay and Lesbian Experience*. Ed. Russell Leong, pp. 119–30. New York: Routledge, 1996.
———. *Impossible Desires: Queer Diasporas and South Asian Public Cultures*. Durham, NC: Duke University Press, 2005.
———. "Nostalgia, Desire, Diasporas: South Asian Sexualities in Motion." *positions* 5 (1997): 467–89.
Goswami, Manu. *Producing India: From Colonial Economy to National Space*. Chicago: University of Chicago Press, 2004.
Grewal, Inderpal. "Reading and Writing the South Asian Diaspora: Feminism and Nationalism in North America." In *Our Feet Walk the Sky: Women of the*

South Asian Diaspora. Ed. Women of South Asian Descent Collective, pp. 226–36. San Francisco: Aunt Lute Books, 1993.

———. *Transnational America: Feminisms, Diasporas, Neoliberalisms*. Durham, NC: Duke University Press, 2005.

Grewal, Inderpal, and Caren Kaplan, eds. *Scattered Hegemonies: Postmodernity and Transnational Feminist Practices*. Minneapolis: University of Minnesota Press, 1994.

"Guidelines Governing the Adoption of Children, 2011." Central Adoption Resource Authority, Ministry of Women and Child Development, Government of India. Available at http://adoptionindia.nic.in/guideline-family/new _guideline.html (accessed July 17, 2011).

Gunew, Sneja. *Haunted Nations: The Colonial Dimensions of Multiculturalisms*. London: Routledge, 2004.

Hall, Stuart. "Cultural Identity and Diaspora." In *Identity: Community, Culture, Difference*. Ed. Jonathan Rutherford, pp. 222–37. London: Lawrence and Wishart, 1990.

———. "New Ethnicities." In *Stuart Hall: Critical Dialogues in Cultural Studies*. Ed. David Morley and Kuan-Hsing Chen, pp. 441–49. London: Routledge, 1996.

Hansen, Thomas Blom. *The Saffron Wave: Democracy and Hindu Nationalism in Modern India*. Delhi: Oxford University Press, 1999.

———. *Wages of Violence: Naming and Identity in Postcolonial Bombay*. Princeton, NJ: Princeton University Press, 2001.

Hidier, Tanuja Desai. "Salaam, New York!" *Time Out New York*, March 25–April 1, 2004, 14.

Hobsbawm, Eric, and Terence Ranger, eds. *The Invention of Tradition*. Cambridge: Cambridge University Press, 1983.

hooks, bell. *Yearning: Race, Gender, and Cultural Politics*. Boston: South End Press, 1999.

Ilaiah, Kancha. *Why I Am Not a Hindu*. Delhi: Samya, 2005.

"IMH History." Available at http://imh-vn.org/welcome.htm (accessed June 28, 2006).

India Today International, North American ed., May 10, 2004.

Indian Community Activities Tokyo. Available at www.manicat.org/main.html (accessed July 20, 2011).

"Indo-American Community Center." December 18, 2005. Available at www.iacc -la.org/details.html.

Isaac, Allan Punzalan. *American Tropics: Articulating Filipino America*. Minneapolis: University of Minnesota Press, 2006.

Islam, Naheed. "In the Belly of the Multicultural Beast I Am Named South Asian." In *Our Feet Walk the Sky: Women of the South Asian Diaspora*. Ed.

Women of South Asian Descent Collective, pp. 242–45. San Francisco: Aunt Lute Books, 1993.

Ismail, Qadri. *Abiding by Sri Lanka: On Peace, Place, and Postcoloniality.* Minneapolis: University of Minnesota Press, 2005.

Jaffrelot, Christophe, ed. *Hindu Nationalism: A Reader.* Princeton, NJ: Princeton University Press, 2007.

Jegannathan, Pradeep. "eelam.com: Place, Nation, and Imagi-Nation in Cyberspace." *Public Culture* 10.3 (1998): 515–28.

Jensen, Joan M. *Passage from India: Asian Indian Immigrants in North America.* New Haven, CT: Yale University Press, 1988.

John, Mary E. "Globalisation, Sexuality and the Visual Field: Issues and Non-Issues for Cultural Critique." In *A Question of Silence? The Sexual Economies of Modern India.* Ed. Mary E. John and Janaki Nair, pp. 368–96. London: Zed Books, 1998.

Johnson, Hugh. *The Voyage of the Komagata Maru: The Sikh Challenge to Canada's Color Bar.* New Delhi: Oxford University Press, 1979.

Joseph, Miranda. *Against the Romance of Community.* Minneapolis: University of Minnesota Press, 2002.

Joshi, Khyati. *New Roots in America's Sacred Ground: Religion, Race, and Ethnicity in Indian America.* New Brunswick, NJ: Rutgers University Press, 2006.

Kakutani, Michiko. "From Calcutta to Suburbia: A Family's Perplexing Journey." Review of *The Namesake* by Jhumpa Lahiri. *New York Times*, September 2, 2003, E8.

Kamdar, Mira. "The Bread Basket Case." OutlookIndia.com. May 7, 2008. Available at www.outlookindia.com/article.aspx?237388 (accessed July 10, 2011).

Karlinsky, Simon. "Gogol, Nikolai (1809–1852)." Available at www.glbtq.com/literature/gogol_n.html (accessed September 25, 2005).

Kaul, Suvir. "Separation Anxiety: Growing Up Inter/National in *The Shadow Lines*." In *The Shadow Lines.* Ed. Amitav Ghosh, pp. 268–86. Delhi: Oxford University Press, 1995.

Kelly, Deirdre. "Banned Art Work Takes to the Street: Maxi-Pad Robe Deemed 'Offensive.'" *Globe and Mail* (Canada), September 30, 1999, C1.

Khambatta, Persis. *Pride of India: A Tribute to Miss India.* Mumbai: Parijat Media, 1997.

Khan, Aisha. *Callaloo Nation: Metaphors of Race and Religious Identity Among South Asians in Trinidad.* Durham, NC: Duke University Press, 2004.

Khokha, Sasha, dir. *Calcutta Calling*. San Francisco: Center for Asian American Media, 2004.
Khurana, Swati, and Leith Murgai, dirs. *Julpari*. New York: Khuragai Productions, 1996.
Kim, Daniel. *Writing Manhood in Black and Yellow: Ralph Ellison, Frank Chin, and the Literary Politics of Identity*. Stanford, CA: Stanford University Press, 2005.
Kim-Gibson, Dai Sil, dir. *Sa-I-Gu: From Korean Women's Perspectives*. San Francisco: Center for Asian American Media, 1993.
King-O'Riain, Rebecca Chiyoko. *Pure Beauty: Judging Race in Japanese American Beauty Pageants*. Minneapolis: University of Minnesota Press, 2006.
Kipen, David. "An Indian Immigrant's Son Who Is Neither Here Nor There." Review of *The Namesake* by Jhumpa Lahiri. *San Francisco Chronicle*, September 14, 2003, M1.
Kirshenblatt-Gimblett, Barbara. *Destination Culture: Tourism, Museums, and Heritage*. Berkeley and Los Angeles: University of California Press, 1998.
Koshy, Susan. "Category Crisis: South Asian Americans and Questions of Race and Ethnicity." *Diaspora* 7.3 (1998): 285–320.
Krishnan, Indu, dir. *Knowing Her Place*. New York: Women Make Movies, 1990.
Kumar, Amitava. *Bombay—London—New York*. New York: Routledge, 2002.
———. *A Foreigner Carrying in the Crook of His Arm a Tiny Bomb*. Durham, NC: Duke University Press, 2010.
Kumar, Dharma. *The Cambridge Economic History of India*. Vol. 2, *c. 1757–c. 1970*. New York: Cambridge University Press, 1983.
Kumar, Mehul, dir. *Krantiveer*. 1994.
The Kumars at No. 42. London: Hat Trick Productions and BBC Two, 2001–6.
Kymlicka, Will. *Multicultural Citizenship: A Liberal Theory of Minority Rights*. New York: Oxford University Press, 1995.
Lahiri, Jhumpa. *Interpreter of Maladies*. New York: Houghton Mifflin, 1999.
———. "Intimate Alienation: Immigrant Fiction and Translation." In *Translation, Text and Theory: The Paradigm of India*. Ed. Rukmini Bhaya Nair, pp. 113–20. New Delhi and Thousand Oaks, CA: Sage Publications, 2002.
———. "My Two Lives." *Newsweek*, March 6, 2006, 43.
———. *The Namesake*. New York: Houghton Mifflin, 2003.
Lavenda, Robert H. "It's Not a Beauty Pageant! Hybrid Ideology in Minnesota Community Queen Pageants." In *Beauty Queens on the Global Stage: Gender, Contests, and Power*. Ed. Colleen Ballerina Cohen, Richard Wilk, and Beverly Stoeltje, pp. 31–46. New York: Routledge, 1996.

———. "Minnesota Queen Pageants: Play, Fun, and Dead Seriousness in a Festive Mode." *Journal of American Folklore* 101.400 (1988): 168–75.
Lee, Anna, and Carol Peng. "Census-Based Profile Depicts Poverty, Language Barriers and Other Hurdles amid Rapid Growth for New York City's Bangladeshi American Population." Asian American Federation of New York. January 26, 2005. Available at www.aafny.org/proom/pr/pr20050126.asp (accessed May 11, 2006).
Lee, Robert G. *Orientals: Asian Americans in Popular Culture*. Philadelphia: Temple University Press, 1999.
Leonard, Karen. *Making Ethnic Choices: California's Punjabi Mexican Americans*. Philadelphia: Temple University Press, 1992.
Leong, Russell, and Don T. Nakanishi. *After Words: Who Speaks on War, Justice, and Peace?* Spec. issue of *Amerasia Journal* 27.3/28.1 (2002).
Liem, Deann Borshay, dir. *First Person Plural*. San Francisco: Center for Asian American Media, 2000.
Lim, Dennis. "What, Exactly, Is *Slumdog Millionaire*?" Slate.com. January 16, 2009. Available at www.slate.com/id/2209783 (accessed May 3, 2010).
Lowe, Lisa. *Immigrant Acts: On Asian American Cultural Politics*. Durham, NC: Duke University Press, 1996.
———. "The Intimacies of Four Continents." In *Haunted by Empire: Geographies of Intimacy in North American History*. Ed. Ann Laura Stoler, pp. 191–212. Durham, NC: Duke University Press, 2006.
Lukose, Ritty. *Liberalization's Children: Gender, Youth, and Consumer Citizenship in Globalizing India*. Durham, NC: Duke University Press, 2009.
MacLaine, Karleen. *India's Immortal Comic Books: Gods, Kings, and Other Heroes*. Bloomington: Indiana University Press, 2009.
Mahmood, Saba. "Feminist Theory, Embodiment, and the Docile Agent: Some Reflections on the Egyptian Islamic Revival." *Cultural Anthropology* 16.2 (2001): 202–36.
———. *Politics of Piety: The Islamic Revival and the Feminist Subject*. Princeton, NJ: Princeton University Press, 2005.
Maira, Sunaina Marr. *Desis in the House: Indian American Youth Culture in New York City*. Philadelphia: Temple University Press, 2002.
———. *Missing: Youth, Citizenship, and Empire After 9/11*. Durham, NC: Duke University Press, 2009.
Malkki, Lisa. "National Geographic: The Rooting of Peoples and the Territorialization of National Identity Among Scholars and Refugees." In *Culture, Power, Place: Explorations in Critical Anthropology*. Ed. Akhil Gupta and James Ferguson, pp. 52–74. Durham, NC: Duke University Press, 1997.

Manalansan, Martin F. IV. "*Biyuti* in Everyday Life: Performance, Citizenship, and Survival Among Filipinos in the United States." In *Orientations: Mapping Studies in the Asian Diaspora*. Ed. Kandice Chuh and Karen Shimakawa. Durham, NC: Duke University Press, 2001.

———. *Global Divas: Filipino Gay Men in the Diaspora*. Durham, NC: Duke University Press, 2003.

———. "In the Shadow of Stonewall: Examining Gay Transnational Politics and the Diasporic Dilemma." *GLQ: A Journal of Lesbian and Gay Studies* 2.4 (1995): 425–38.

Mani, Bakirathi. "Destination Culture." *SAMAR: South Asian Magazine for Action and Reflection* 14 (2001): 11–14.

———. "Queer Films, Straight Desis." *Subcontinental* 3.1 (2007): 1–12.

———. "Viewing South Asia, Seeing America: Gauri Gill's *The Americans*." *American Quarterly* 62.1 (2010): 135–50.

Mani, Bakirathi, and Latha Varadarajan. "'The Largest Gathering of the Global Indian Family': Neoliberalism, Nationalism, and Diaspora at Pravasi Bharatiya Divas." *Diaspora* 14.1 (2005) [2008]: 45–74.

Mani, Lata. *Contentious Traditions: The Debate on Sati in Colonial India*. Berkeley and Los Angeles: University of California Press, 1998.

———. "Gender, Class and Cultural Conflict: Indu Krishnan's *Knowing Her Place*." In *Our Feet Walk the Sky: Women of the South Asian Diaspora*. Ed. Women of South Asian Descent Collective, 32–36. San Francisco: Aunt Lute Books, 1993.

Mankekar, Purnima. "Brides Who Travel: Gender, Transnationalism, and Nationalism in Hindi Film." *positions* 7.3 (1999): 731–62.

———. "'India Shopping': Indian Grocery Stores and Transnational Configurations of Belonging." In *The Cultural Politics of Food and Eating: A Reader*. Ed. James L. Watson and Melissa L. Caldwell, pp. 197–214. Malden, MA: Blackwell, 2004.

———. "Reflections on Diasporic Identities: A Prolegomenon to an Analysis of Political Bifocality." *Diaspora* 3 (1994): 349–71.

———. *Screening Culture, Viewing Politics: An Ethnography of Television, Womanhood, and Nation in Postcolonial India*. Durham, NC: Duke University Press, 1999.

Mannur, Anita. *Culinary Fictions: Food in South Asian Diasporic Culture*. Philadelphia: Temple University Press, 2010.

Marks, Peter. "'Bombay Dreams': Belly-Up in Bollywood." Review of *Bombay Dreams* by Meera Syal and Thomas Meehan. Broadway Theatre, New York. *Washington Post*, April 30, 2004, C1.

Mathew, Biju, and Vijay Prashad. "Introduction." In *Satyagraha in America: The Political Culture of South Asian Americans*. Ed. Biju Mathew and Vijay Prashad. Spec. issue of *Amerasia Journal* 25 (1999/2000): x–xv.

Mauss, Marcel. *The Gift: Forms and Functions of Exchange in Archaic Societies*. Trans. Ian Cunnison. New York: Norton, 1967.

Mazumdar, Sucheta. "The Politics of Religion and National Origin: Rediscovering Hindu Indian Identity in the United States." In *Antinomies of Modernity: Essays on Race, Orient, Nation*. Ed. Vasanth Kaiwar and Sucheta Mazumdar, pp. 223–60. Durham, NC: Duke University Press, 2003.

Mehta, Suketu. *Maximum City: Bombay Lost and Found*. New York: Knopf, 2004.

Metcalf, Stephen. "Out of the Overcoat." Review of *The Namesake* by Jhumpa Lahiri. *New York Times Book Review*, September 28, 2003.

Mishra, Vijay. *Bollywood Cinema: Temples of Desire*. New York: Routledge, 2002.

"Miss India U.S.A.: Rules and Regulations." worldwideEpageants.com. Available at www.worldwide pageants.com/randrU.S.A.htm (accessed May 16, 2002).

Mistry, Rohinton. *A Fine Balance*. New York: Viking, 1997.

Mohanty, Chandra, and M. Jacqui Alexander, eds. *Feminist Genealogies, Colonial Legacies, Democratic Futures*. London: Routledge, 1997.

Mookherjee, Nayanika. "*Muktir Gaan*, the Raped Woman and Migrant Identities of the Bangladesh War." In *Gender, Conflict and Migration*. Ed. Navnita Chadha Behra, pp. 72–96. New Delhi and Thousand Oaks, CA: Sage Publications, 2006.

"Most-Often Asked Questions About the Femina Miss India Contest." *Femina Miss India*. May 16, 2002. Available at www.feminamissindia.com/pageant.html.

Mukherjee, Mridula. *Colonizing Agriculture: The Myth of Punjab Exceptionalism*. New Delhi and Thousand Oaks, CA: Sage Publications, 2005.

Mukul, Kazi. *Pictorial History of the Nirmul Committee's Movement*. Dhaka: Nirmul Committee, 2004.

Muñoz, José Esteban. *Disidentifications: Queers of Color and the Performance of Politics*. Minneapolis: University of Minnesota Press, 1999.

Murray, Matthew. "Talkin' Broadway's Broadway Reviews: Bombay Dreams." Review of *Bombay Dreams* by Meera Syal and Thomas Meehan. *Talkin' Broadway*. April 29, 2004. Available at www.talkinbroadway.com/world/BombayDreams.html (accessed July 20, 2011).

Nair, Mira, dir. *Mississippi Masala*. New York: Mirabai Films in association with MovieWorks and Black River Productions, 1990.

———. *Monsoon Wedding*. New York: IFC Productions and Mirabai Films, 2001.

———. *So Far from India*. New York: Filmmakers Library, 1982.

Narayan, Kirin. "Haunting Stories: Narrative Transmissions of South Asian Identities in Diaspora." In *South Asians in the Diaspora: Histories and Religious Traditions*. Ed. Knut A. Jacobsen and P. Pratap Kumar, pp. 415–31. Leiden, Netherlands: Brill, 2004.

Nguyen, Viet Thanh. *Race and Resistance: Literature and Politics in Asian America*. New York: Oxford University Press, 2002.

Niranjana, Tejaswini. "Nationalism Refigured: Contemporary South Indian Cinema and the Subject of Feminism." In *Subaltern Studies XI*. Ed. Partha Chatterjee and Pradeep Jeganathan, pp. 138–66. New York: Columbia University Press, 2000.

Nishioka, Joyce. "Miss India Comes Out." *Asian Week*, November 21, 2003. Available at http://news.asianweek.com/news/view_article.html?article_id=7ec4ddd3ebdd981ab135f1355a88c00e (accessed May 15, 2006).

Office of National Statistics. "British Asian Demographics." April 2005. Available at www.bl.uk/collections/business/asiandemographics.html (accessed November 16, 2005).

———. "People and Migration—Archived in Dec. 2005." Available at www.statistics.gov.uk/CCI/nugget.asp?ID=764&Pos=4&ColRank=1&Rank=176 (accessed April 19, 2010).

———. "Religion." Available at www.statistics.gov.uk/cci/nugget.asp?id=954 (accessed April 19, 2010).

Ong, Aihwa. "Cultural Citizenship as Subject-Making: Immigrants Negotiate Racial and Cultural Boundaries in the United States." *Cultural Anthropology* 37.5 (1996): 737–62.

———. *Flexible Citizenship: The Cultural Logics of Transnationality*. Durham, NC: Duke University Press, 1999.

———. *Neoliberalism as Exception: Mutations in Citizenship and Sovereignty*. Durham, NC: Duke University Press, 2006.

Oza, Rupal. *The Making of Neoliberal India: Nationalism, Gender, and the Paradoxes of Globalization*. New York: Routledge, 2006.

———. "Showcasing India: Gender, Geography, and Globalization." *Signs* 26.4 (2001): 1067–95.

Padmanabhan, Anil. "Touching the Stars." *India Today International*, North American ed., May 10, 2004, 38.

Pais, Arthur J. "Bombay Dreams Brings Bollywood to Broadway." *India Abroad*, March 12, 2004, A7.

Palumbo-Liu, David. *Asian/American: Historical Crossings of a Racial Frontier*. Stanford, CA: Stanford University Press, 1999.

Patel, Shailja. *Migritude*. New York: Kaya Press, 2010.

———. *Shilling Love*. [San Francisco:] Fyrefly Press, 2002.

Peterson, Thane. "How New York Is Defying Convention." *Business Week*, August 27, 2004. Available at www.businessweek.com/bwdaily/dnflash/aug2004/nf20040827_1856.htm (accessed July 20, 2011).

Piepenburg, Eric. "Hooray for Bollywood." *Time Out New York*, March 25–April 1, 2004, 16.

Pincus-Roth, Zachary. "The Extreme Makeover of 'Bombay Dreams.'" *New York Times*, April 18, 2004, E8.

———. "Extreme Makeover of 'Bombay Dreams' Which Opened on Broadway on April 29." *News India-Times*, May 7, 2004, 29.

Piper, Becca. "What Age Is the Right Age? Travelling to Your Child's Land of Birth." Available at www.adoptivefamilytravel.com/news_resources.asp#75 (accessed March 11, 2010).

"Pond's Femina Miss India." Femina Miss India. Available at http://feminamissindia.indiatimes.com (accessed June 28, 2006).

"Pond's Femina Miss India 2006—Training Schedule." Femina Miss India. Available at http://feminamissindia.indiatimes.com/articleshow/1418878.cms (accessed June 26, 2006).

Prashad, Vijay. *The Darker Nations: A People's History of the Third World*. New York: New Press, 2007.

———. *Everybody Was Kung-Fu Fighting: Afro-Asian Connections and the Myth of Cultural Purity*. Boston: Beacon Press, 2001.

———. *The Karma of Brown Folk*. Minneapolis: University of Minnesota Press, 2000.

Pratt, Mary Louise. *Imperial Eyes: Travel Writing and Transculturation*. New York: Routledge, 1992.

Puar, Jasbir. "Queer Time, Queer Assemblages." *Social Text* 23.3–4 (2005): 121–39.

———. *Terrorist Assemblages: Homonationalism in Queer Times*. Durham, NC: Duke University Press, 2007.

Puar, Jasbir, and Amit Rai. "The Remaking of a Model Minority: Perverse Projectiles Under the Specter of (Counter)Terrorism." *Social Text* 22.3 (2004): 75–104.

Punathambekar, Aswin, and Anandam Kavoori, eds. *Global Bollywood*. New York: NYU Press, 2008.

Purdum, Todd. "Upbeat Republicans Revive Bush Theme of Compassion." *New York Times*, September 1, 2004. Available at www.nytimes.com/2004/09/01/politics/campaign/01campaign.html (accessed April 21, 2010).

Purkayastha, Bandana. *Negotiating Ethnicity: Second-Generation South Asian Americans Traverse a Transnational World*. New Brunswick, NJ: Rutgers University Press, 2005.

Rahim, Enayetur, and Joyce L. Rahim. *Bangladesh Liberation War and the Nixon White House, 1971*. Dhaka: Pustaka, 1999.

Rai, Amit. "India On-line: Electronic Bulletin Boards and the Construction of a Diasporic Hindu Identity." *Diaspora* 4.1 (1995): 31–57.

Rajadhyaksha, Ashish, and Paul Willemen. *Encyclopedia of Indian Cinema*. Rev. ed. Delhi: Oxford University Press, 1999.

Rajan, Rajeswari Sunder. *Real and Imagined Women: Gender, Culture and Postcolonialism*. London: Routledge, 1993.

———. *The Scandal of the State: Women, Law, Citizenship in Postcolonial India*. Durham, NC: Duke University Press, 2003.

Rana, Junaid. *Terrifying Muslims: Race and Labor in the South Asian Diaspora*. Durham, NC: Duke University Press, 2011.

Rao, Anupama. *The Caste Question: Dalits and the Politics of Modern India*. Berkeley and Los Angeles: University of California Press, 2009.

Ratnam, Mani, dir. *Bombay*. Mumbai: ABCL and Madras Talkies, 1995.

———. *Dil Se*. Mumbai: India Talkies and Madras Talkies, 1998.

Reddy, Gayatri. *With Respect to Sex: Negotiating Hijra Identity in South India*. Chicago: University of Chicago Press, 2005.

"Rough Cut—India: Calcutta Calling." *Frontline World Rough Cut*. January 17, 2006. Available at www.pbs.org/frontlineworld/rough/2006/01/india_calcutta.html#react (accessed May 25, 2010).

Rudrappa, Sharmila. *Ethnic Routes to Becoming American: Indian Immigrants and the Cultures of Citizenship*. New Brunswick, NJ: Rutgers University Press, 2004.

Rushdie, Salman. *Imaginary Homelands: Essays and Criticism, 1981–1991*. New York: Viking, 1991.

———. *Midnight's Children*. London: Viking, 1995 [1981].

Salaam Bombay Dreams. London: Really Useful Productions, 2004.

Sangari, Kumkum. "Modern-but-Not-Western: Beauty Queens, Ethnicity, New Patriotisms." Centre for South Asian Studies. University of California at Berkeley. November 28, 2000.

Saran, Parmatma. *The Asian Indian Experience in the United States*. Cambridge, MA: Schenkman, 1985.

Saran, Parmatma, and Edwin Earnes, eds. *The New Ethnics: Asian Indians in the United States*. New York: Praeger, 1980.

Sassen, Saskia. *The Global City: New York, London, Tokyo*. Princeton, NJ: Princeton University Press, 2001.

"Savitri." *Amar Chitra Katha*. Available at www.amarchitrakatha.com/store/mainpage.asp (accessed December 24, 2005).

Shankar, Lavina Dhingra, and Rajini Srikanth, eds. *A Part, Yet Apart: South Asians in Asian America*. Philadelphia: Temple University Press, 1998.

Shankar, S., dir. *Mudhalvan*. Chennai: Sri Surya Films, 1999.

Shankar, Shalini. *Desi Land: Teen Culture, Class, and Success in Silicon Valley*. Durham, NC: Duke University Press, 2008.

Sharma, Nitasha Tamar. *Hip Hop Desis: South Asian Americans, Blackness, and a Global Race Consciousness*. Durham, NC: Duke University Press, 2010.

Sharpe, Jenny. "Is the United States Postcolonial? Transnationalism, Immigration, and Race." *Diaspora* 4:2 (1995): 181–99.

Shimakawa, Karen. *National Abjection: The Asian American Body Onstage*. Durham, NC: Duke University Press, 2002.

Shimizu, Celine Parreñas. *The Hypersexuality of Race: Performing Asian/American Women on Screen and Scene*. Durham, NC: Duke University Press, 2007.

Shiva, Alexander, Sean MacDonald, and M. Gucovsky, dirs. *Bombay Eunuch*. New York: Gidalya Pictures, 2001.

Shukla, Sandhya. *India Abroad: Diasporic Cultures of Postwar America and England*. Princeton, NJ: Princeton University Press, 2003.

Sikand, Nandini, dir. *The Bhangra Wrap*. San Francisco: Center for Asian American Media, 1994.

Singh, Amardeep. "The Nameless: Jhumpa Lahiri's *The Namesake*." July 21, 2004. Available at www.lehigh.edu/~amsp/2004/07/nameless-jhumpa-lahiris-namesake.html (accessed February 25, 2011).

Singh, Nidhi, dir. *Khush Refugees*. San Francisco: Center for Asian American Media, 1994.

Siu, Lok C. D. *Memories of a Future Home: Diasporic Citizenship of Chinese in Panama*. Stanford, CA: Stanford University Press, 2005.

———. "Queen of the Chinese Colony: Gender, Nation and Belonging in Diaspora." *Anthropological Quarterly* 78.3 (2005): 511–42.

Sollors, Werner. *Beyond Ethnicity: Consent and Descent in American Culture*. New York: Oxford University Press, 1986.

Spence, Kevin. "Miss India Is Out." *New York Blade*. September 5, 2003. Available at www.nyblade.com/2003/9-5/arts/main/ (accessed May 15, 2006).

Spivak, Gayatri Chakravorty. "Can the Subaltern Speak?" In *Marxism and the Interpretation of Culture*. Ed. Cary Nelson and Lawrence Grossberg, pp. 271–315. Urbana: University of Illinois Press, 1988.

———. *A Critique of Postcolonial Reason: Toward a History of the Vanishing Present*. Cambridge, MA: Harvard University Press, 1999.

———. *The Post-Colonial Critic: Interviews, Strategies, Dialogues.* Ed. Sarah Harasym. New York: Routledge, 1990.
Srikanth, Rajini. *The World Next Door: South Asian American Literature and the Idea of America.* Philadelphia: Temple University Press, 2004.
Srikanth, Rajini, and Sunaina Maira, eds. *Contours of the Heart: South Asians Map North America.* New York: Asian American Writers Workshop, 1996.
Srivastava, Sanjay. *Constructing Post-Colonial India: National Character and the Doon School.* London: Routledge, 1998.
Stevens, Dana. "Slumdog Millionaire." Slate.com. November 13, 2008. Available at www.slate.com/id/2204544 (accessed May 3, 2010).
Subramanian, Ajantha. "Indians in North Carolina: Race, Class and Culture in the Making of Immigrant Identity." *Comparative Studies of South Asia, Africa, and the Middle East* 20.1–2 (2000): 105–14.
Swamy, Prakash M. "Making Beauty to Help the Needy." worldwidEpageants.com. Available at www.worldwidepageants.com/helpneedy.htm (accessed May 16, 2002).
Syal, Meera. *Anita and Me.* New York: New Press, 1996.
———. *Life Isn't All Ha Ha Hee Hee.* New York: Doubleday, 1999.
Tagore, Rabindranath. *The Home and the World.* Trans. Surendranath Tagore. London: Penguin, 1985.
Tanamachi, Cara. "300 Brave the Cold to March Against Racism," *Daily Pennsylvanian*, February 15, 1993. Available at www.dailypennsylvanian.com/node/33264 (accessed July 10, 2011).
Terrazas, Aaron. "Indian Immigrants in the United States." *Migration Information Source.* July 2008. Available at www.migrationinformation.org/USfocus/display.cfm?id=687 (accessed February 27, 2010).
"The Ties Program: Adoptive Family Homeland Journeys." *Ties Program.* June 28, 2006. Available at www.adoptivefamilytravel.com/india.asp (accessed February 5, 2011).
Time Out New York, March 25–April 1, 2004.
Tsering, Lisa. "'Bombay Dreams' on Broadway: A Couple of Spices Shy of a Perfect Masala." *India-West*, May 14, 2004. Available at http://members.tripod.com/~LisaTsering/bombaydreams.html (accessed May 24, 2006).
Uberoi, Patricia. "The Diaspora Comes Home: Disciplining Desire in *DDLJ*." *Contributions to Indian Sociology* 32.2 (1998): 305–36.
"The United States v. Dr. Bhagat Singh Thind." *Bhagat Singh Thind.* Available at www.bhagatsinghthind.com/usvs.html (accessed April 22, 2006).
Vasudevan, Ravi. "*Bombay* and Its Public." *Journal of Arts and Ideas* 29 (1996): 44–65.

Verma, Sukanya. "The Rediff Review: Kitne Door, Kitne Paas," Rediff.com. March 29, 2002. Available at www.rediff.com/movies/2002/mar/29kitne.htm (accessed June 28, 2006).

Visweswaran, Kamala. *Fictions of Feminist Ethnography*. Delhi: Oxford University Press, 1996.

Warn, Sarah. "Interview with Kashish Chopra." AfterEllen.com. September 2003. Available at www.afterellen.com/People/chopra-interview.html (accessed May 15, 2006).

Washbrook, David. "Law, State and Agrarian Society in Colonial India." *Modern Asian Studies* 15.3 (1981): 649–721.

Watson, Elmood, and Darcy Martin, eds. *"There She Is, Miss America": The Politics of Sex, Beauty, and Race in America's Most Famous Pageant.* New York: Palgrave Macmillan, 2004.

Wong, Sau-ling Cynthia. "Denationalization Reconsidered: Asian American Cultural Criticism at a Theoretical Crossroads." In *Postcolonial Theory and the United States: Race, Ethnicity, Literature*. Ed. Peter Schmidt and Amritjit Singh. Jackson: University Press of Mississippi, 2000.

Wu, Judy Tzu-Chun. "'Loveliest Daughter of Our Ancient Cathay!' Representations of Ethnic and Gender Identity in the Miss Chinatown U.S.A. Beauty Pageant." *Journal of Social History* 31.1 (1997): 5–31.

Yngvesson, Barbara. "Going 'Home': Adoption, Loss of Bearings, and the Mythology of Roots." *Social Text* 21.1 (2003): 7–27.

"Youth Power." *India Today*, nat. ed., January 31, 2005, 150.

Index

Abhi (blogger), 108–109
Abhyankar, R. M., 139
Acharya, Dhruvi, 187–195
activism: art festivals and, 165, 196–201; community and, 170–181; groups, 267n19; against racially based violence, 260–261
adoptions, transnational, 97–111, 273nn21,23
"affect aliens," 280–281n40
agency, 92–94, 97, 192–193, 272n9
Agrawal, Prashant, 221–222
Ahmad, Muneer, 20
Ahmed, Sara, 280–281n40
AIA (Association of Indian Americans), 81–82
Alam, Fariba, 80, 81, 111, 112–113, 119
Ali, Syed, 120
Alquist, Elaine, 134
Alwis, Malathi de, 156
Amar Chitra Katha comics, 188–194
Anagnost, Ann, 98
Appadurai, Arjun, 4, 79
art festivals: commodification of identity and, 201–206; community and activism and, 170–181; introduction to, 163–169; overview of, 26–27; personal and national histories at, 181–196; spatial and temporal separation from South Asia and, 196–201
Artwallah art festival, 164–165, 170–171, 176–181, 201–206
Asha for Education, 137–138
Asian American studies, 9–16, 31–32, 266n12, 267n16

"Asian Indian" census category, 81–82
Association of Indian Americans (AIA), 81–82
authenticity, and identity in *Bombay Dreams*, 244–245

bad feelings, 281n40
Baez, Joan, 269n18
Banerji, Himani, 178, 179
Banet-Weiser, Sarah, 125, 139
Bangladeshi immigrants, 111–118
Bangladesh Liberation War (1971), 34, 46–56, 269nn18,20,21
beauty pageants, 124, 130, 150. *See also* Miss India USA pageant
belonging: through activism, 260–261; art festivals and, 167, 186, 195; in *B.E.S. (Bangla East Side)*, 117–118; *Bombay Dreams* and, 216–217, 225, 236, 245, 248; disidentification with, 149–150; in documentary films, 85–86, 106–107, 108, 110; experiential qualities of, 26; Hindutva, 227; in Lahiri works, 19; locality and, 4, 7–8, 23, 73, 256; Miss India USA pageant and, 1–3, 124, 161; multiculturalism and, 13–16; in *The Namesake*, 56–69; postcoloniality and, 52; queer activism and, 198; resistance and, 12
B.E.S. (Bangla East Side), 80, 81, 111–120
betrayal, 95–96, 119
Bhimani, Anjali, 219, 221, 245–247
birth mothers, of Indian adoptees, 103–104

305

Index

Bollywood: *Bombay Dreams* and, 215–226, 236; Miss India USA pageant and, 125–126, 140, 147, 159
Bombay, 143, 145–146
Bombay Dreams: American multiculturalism and, 235–242; caste, class, and sexuality in, 225–235; challenges of, as transnational production, 216–225; conclusions on, 249–252; introduction to, 208–215; overview of, 20–21, 27–28; plot of, 215–216; racial identity and, 242–248
Bose, Shonali, 196–198, 200, 280–281n40
Boys Night Out in Babylon, 172–173
Broadway musicals. See *Bombay Dreams*
Brown Book Project, 199–200
Bub, Heidi, 104
Burton, Antoinette, 11, 52

Caesar, Judith, 49, 61
Calcutta Calling, 80–81, 97–111, 119
Canada, *Komagata Maru* migration and, 18, 179–180
Captive (Acharya), 188–195
caste: in *Bombay Dreams*, 229–231; transnational adoptions and, 99, 104
"catachresis," 65–66
census categories, 81–82, 267n27
Chakrabarty, Dipesh, 55
Chatterjee, Partha, 272n10
Cheng, Anne Anlin, 216, 246
Chhabra, Aseem, 236, 251
Chinese indentured laborers, 71
Chohan, Usha, 180
"choice," 84, 88–94, 97, 118–119, 135, 272n9
Chopra, Kashish, 160–161
Choudhury, Shakil, 199
Chuh, Isaac, 32
Chuh, Kandice, 32, 40, 249–250, 266n10
citizenship: claims to, 17–20; class mobility and, 22; community and, 257; disidentification and, 149–150; in documentary films, 78, 97–111, 117; locality and, 14, 73; Miss India USA pageant and, 123, 125–126, 158, 159; modernity and, 70; multiculturalism and, 178–179; in *The Namesake*, 62–63, 67–69; neoliberal ideologies of, 6–8; postcoloniality and, 35–43, 52; religious faith and, 53; in "When Mr. Pirzada Came to Dine," 48–51, 56

Clark, Cherie, 99
class: activism and, 260–261; in *Bombay Dreams*, 229–231; identity and, 5–6; Miss India pageants and, 154; Miss India USA pageant and, 123, 125, 127–136, 155–156; postcoloniality and, 35; in *So Far from India*, 76, 82; in South Asian demographics, 20
class mobility: art festivals and, 202, 203–204; *Bombay Dreams* and, 211, 231–232; citizenship and, 6–7, 22; in documentary films, 78; identity and, 21; immigration and, 19; Miss India USA pageant and, 125, 131–133, 136, 157–158, 161; Muslims and, 114–115; in *The Namesake*, 67; *Slumdog Millionaire* and, 258–259; in *So Far from India*, 84
Coetzee, J. M., 65
Cohen, Lawrence, 232
colonialism. See imperialism
community: activism and, 170–181; art festivals and, 187, 195; capitalism and, 168; identity and, 2–3; Indian Community Activities Tokyo as, 256–257; locality and, 3–5, 14; and neoliberal ideologies of citizenship, 7–8; organizing, 198–199; political movements and, 43–45; resistance and, 12; solidarity and, 169; South Asian American studies and, 14–15
consumption: art festivals and, 168, 201–206; examining modes of, 254–255; rituals of, 34, 44
Continuous Journey, 179–180, 181
coolies, 71–72
cultural capital, 127–136, 139–140
cultural programs, 164–165
cultural texts, 5–6, 18, 254–255
culture: beauty pageants and, 124–125; identity and, 5–6; locality and, 4–5; preservation and perversion of, 1–3
Curzon, Lord, 270n22

Daiya, Kavita, 55
Daughter from Danang, 104
Dave, Naisargi, 198
demographics of South Asian communities, 19–20, 57, 77, 78, 112, 223, 267n27
Desai, Jigna, 140, 272–273n13
Desh Pardesh art festival, 164–165, 170–174, 181

Dhillon, Ameen, 163–164, 182–187, 194–195
Dhillon-Kashyap, Parminder, 118
Dhingra, Pawan, 125
Diasporadics art festival, 163–165, 167–168, 170–171, 174–176, 178–179, 181
disidentification: art festivals and, 167–168, 187; in *Calcutta Calling*, 101, 110; with multiculturalism, 14, 147–151, 159; in *The Namesake*, 68–69
dissenting citizenship, 117
D'Lo, 174–175
documentary films: conclusions on, 118–121; family, race, and citizenship in, 97–111; feminist subjects in, 81–97; introduction to, 75–81; Muslim identity in, 111–118; overview of, 25
"Dotbusters," 260–261, 285n5

economic liberalization, in India, 136–137, 196–198, 225–226, 230–231, 234, 261
education, 133–134, 137–138
Eng, David, 98, 103, 109, 173
ethnicity. *See* race and ethnicity
ethnographic texts: art festivals as, 165–166, 206; documentary films as, 78–79

fear, 53–54
feelings, good and bad, 280–281n40
feminist subjects, in documentary films, 81–97
First Person Plural, 104–105
Flower Drum Song, 216–217
Foe (Coetzee), 65–66
food preparation, 34, 269n13
Frankenberg, Ruth, 32, 51
Frontline, 106–108
Funny Boy (Selvadurai), 234

Gandhi, Sheetal, 219, 243–247
Ganesan, Sriram, 232
Ganges Dreaming, 180–181
Ganguly, Keya, 34
gender: and agency in *Captive*, 192–193; art festivals and, 175–176; *Bombay Dreams* and, 231–235; liberalization and, 136; Miss India USA pageant and, 123, 125–126; and perspectives on immigration, 87–88
gendered subjectivity, 91–93
Ghosh, Amitav, 53, 63
Gill, Ameen, 163–164, 182–187, 194–195
Gill, Sharan, 149–151, 156, 159, 160

Ginsberg, Allen, 269n18
globalization: *Bombay Dreams* and, 225, 231; Indian exploitation and, 196–198; locality and, 4; Miss India pageants and, 151–157
Gogol, Nikolai, 24, 58, 59, 60–65
good feelings, 280–281n40
Gopinath, Gayatri, 12–13, 234, 238
Gray, Tamyra, 220–221
Grewal, Inderpal, 63, 87
Gunew, Sneja, 178
Gupta, Monisha Das, 129

H-1B workers, 123
Haley, Nikki, 22
Hall, Stuart, 159–160
Hansen, Thomas Blom, 227
Harrison, George, 269n18
Hart-Celler Act (1965), 19, 36–37
hate crimes, 260–261, 285n5
heritage journeys, 97–111, 273n24
Hidier, Tanuja Desai, 236–237
hijras, 232–233, 234
Hindutva, 227
Hiss, Eric, 180
historical texts: art festivals as, 166, 206; documentary films as, 78
history, personal and national, at art festivals, 181–196
Hobsbawm, Eric, 268n2
homesickness, 272–273n13
HRAF (Human Relations Area File), 267n21
Human Relations Area File (HRAF), 267n21

IACC (Indo-American Cultural Center), 176–177
ICAT (Indian Community Activities Tokyo), 256–257
identity: art festivals and, 167–169, 181, 195; of author as South Asian, 259–261; in *B.E.S. (Bangla East Side)*, 111–118, 120; *Bombay Dreams* and, 227–228, 236–237, 242–252; in *Calcutta Calling*, 97–111; class and, 82; commodification of, 201–206; as cultural construct, 2–3; in cultural texts, 5–6; in documentary films, 78, 80–81, 118–119; in *Knowing Her Place*, 85–86, 97; locality and, 3–5, 7–8, 73; Miss India USA pageant and, 124, 127–136; multiculturalism and, 178–179; in

identity (*continued*)
  The Namesake, 57–59, 66–69; in *The Overcoat*, 60–61; political movements and, 43–45; postcoloniality and, 32–34, 35; representation and, 253; resistance and, 12; as South Asian, 16–17, 196–201. *See also* disidentification
IMH (International Mission of Hope), 98–99, 105
immigration and immigrants: *Bombay Dreams* and, 209; Canadian laws on, 18, 179–180; and citizenship in "The Third and Final Continent," 35–43; depicted in artwork, 175–176, 182, 184–187, 195, 203–205; engagement with neoliberal state, 255–256; gendered perspectives on, 87–88; "good" and "bad" subjects of, 14; H-1B workers and, 123; intergenerational conflict and, 57–58; Islam and, 111–118; in Japan, 256–258; locality and, 16–21; *The Mango Tree* and, 163–164; Miss India USA pageant and, 124, 133–134, 157–158; postcoloniality and, 34–35; Punjabi migration, 134–135; Special Registration for South Asian, 241, 284nn47,48; transnational adoptions and, 100, 102–103, 109–110; in United States, 259–261
Immigration and Nationality Act (1965), 19, 36–37
imperialism: Asian American cultural production and, 254; *Bombay Dreams* and, 222–223; depicted in artwork, 175–176; Human Relations Area File (HRAF) and, 267n21; immigration and, 17–18; locality and, 10–11, 23; postcoloniality and, 31–33, 51–52, 71–73. *See also* U.S. imperialism
indentured labor, Chinese, 71
India Festival Committee (IFC), 128–130
India Festivals, 128–130
Indian adoptees, 98–111, 273nn21,23
Indian Community Activities Tokyo (ICAT), 256–257
Indian economic development, 136–137, 196–198, 225–226, 230–231, 234, 261
Indo-American Cultural Center (IACC), 176–177
International Mission of Hope (IMH), 98–99, 105
Interpreter of Maladies (Lahiri): citizenship and, 35–43; connection to homeland and, 43–56; overview of, 24

"invented tradition," 34, 268n2
Isaac, Allan, 32
Islam, Naheed, 16

Japan, author's youth in, 256–258
Japanese American beauty pageants, 130
Jindal, Bobby, 22
John, Suresh, 220–221, 240, 250–251
Johnson, Kaylan, 97–98, 100, 101, 105, 108–111, 119
Joseph, Miranda, 168

Kale, Karsh, 180
Kaplan, Caren, 87
Kapoor, Reena, 107
Kapur, Shekhar, 218
Kaul, Suvir, 52, 54
Kazimi, Ali, 179
Kenya, 203–204
Khanvilkar, Chitra, 140–147, 159
Khokha, Sasha, 80, 81, 97–111, 119
Khurana, Sarita, 80, 81, 111, 112–113, 119
King-O'Riain, Rebecca, 124, 130
Knowing Her Place, 79–80, 81, 84–97, 118–119
Komagata Maru, 18, 179–180
Krantiveer, 143–146, 276n21
Krishnan, Indu, 79–80, 81, 84–97, 118–119

Lahiri, Jhumpa: citizenship and, 35–43; connection to homeland and, 43–56; introduction to, 30–35; and naming and belonging, 56–69; overview of, 24–25; and perspectives on diaspora, 70–74
Lavenda, Robert, 131
Leonard, Karen, 134–135
liberalization, of Indian economy, 136–137, 196–198, 225–226, 230–231, 234, 261
Lifting the Veil, 196–198, 200
Lin, Maya, 277n28
locality: and Asian American studies, 9–16; class mobility and, 7; defined, 3–5; identity and, 7–8; immigration and, 16–21; theorizing, 253–256
Lowe, Lisa, 11, 35, 71, 148–149, 167
Lukose, Ritty, 276n24

Macintosh, Cameron, 220
Mahmood, Saba, 92–93
Maira, Sunaina, 13, 57–58, 114–115, 117
Manalansan, Martin, 282n5

Mango Tree, The (Gill), 163–164, 182–187, 194–195
Mani, Lata, 32, 51, 87, 90, 95, 120
Mankekar, Purnima, 70
Mannur, Anita, 269n13
Mathew, Biju, 12
McCarran-Walter Act (1952), 284n47
Meehan, Thomas, 223–224
Mehta, Suketu, 237
Merrill, Lizzie, 97–98, 100, 105–106, 108–111, 119
Mexican Punjabis, 134–135
migration. *See* immigration and immigrants
Migritude (Patel), 203, 204–205
Miss India pageants, 125, 126, 151–157
Miss India USA pageant: conclusions on, 157–162; description of event, 127–128; disidentification with multiculturalism and, 147–151; identity and regulations for, 129–136; introduction to, 122–127; Miss India pageants and, 151–157; neoliberalism and, 136–141; origins of, 128–129; overview of, 26; preservation and perversion of culture in, 1–3; secularism and, 141–147
Miss India Worldwide contest, 161
Miss Saigon, 220, 243
modernity: *Bombay Dreams* and, 225–235; citizenship and, 70; immigration and, 37–38; Miss India pageants and, 126, 154–157; postcolonial, 61–62
Mookherjee, Nayanika, 46, 269n20
"Mrs. Sen's" (Lahiri), 30–31
multiculturalism: activism and, 170–181; art festivals and, 167–168; belonging and, 13–16; *B.E.S. (Bangla East Side)* and, 115–118; *Bombay Dreams* and, 219, 225, 235–242; citizenship and, 11–12; class and, 6; Miss India USA pageant and, 147–151, 158, 159
Muñoz, José, 149
Muslim identity, 111–118, 120

Nair, Mira, 75–77, 81–84
name changing, 66–67, 73, 270n30
Namesake, The (Lahiri), 24–25, 56–69, 72–73
Narayan, Manu, 240, 247–248
National Security Entry-Exit Registration System, 241, 284nn47,48

nationhood and nationalism: *Bombay Dreams* and, 212, 217, 239; Miss India USA pageant and, 125–126, 132, 138–140, 159, 161–162; queer activism and, 173–174; secular, 141–147; women and, 87–88
Naturalization Act (1906), 40
Nehru, Jawaharlal, 37, 62, 211
neoliberalism: art festivals and, 167–168; *Bombay Dreams* and, 211; Miss India USA pageant and, 136–147
Nguyen, Viet Thanh, 6, 267n16
Niranjana, Tejaswini, 228
Nixon, Richard, 46–47
Non-Aligned Movement, 59–60, 62, 64

Ong, Aihwa, 137, 265n5
Orlovsky, Peter, 269n18
outsourcing, 137
"Overcoat, The" (Gogol), 24, 58, 59, 60–65, 68–69
Oza, Rupal, 152
Ozawa, Takao, 40, 269n9

Palumbo-Liu, David, 266n10
Panchal, Harish, 139
Patel, Shailja, 203–205
Patel, Teju, 1, 2, 157
Patil, Vimla, 154
Patriot Act (2003), 112, 284n47
Pimlott, Steven, 222, 225, 235
Pitzenberger, Anisha, 97–98, 101–103, 105, 108–111, 119
political movements, 36, 43–56
postcoloniality: American imperialism and, 32–33, 254; Asian American studies and, 31–32; and citizenship in "The Third and Final Continent," 35–43; introduction to, 30–31; Lahiri and, 33–35; in *The Namesake*, 56–69; and perspectives on diaspora, 70–74; in "When Mr. Pirzada Came to Dine," 43–56
Powell, Enoch, 41, 269n11
Prashad, Vijay, 12, 36–37, 71, 285n5
Pryce, Jonathan, 220
Puar, Jasbir, 14–15, 169, 187
Punjab, 183–184
Punjabi migration, 134–135

Queen of the Chinese Colony pageant, 150
queer activism and subjects, 12–13, 171–173, 198, 232–234

race and ethnicity: art festivals and, 195; *Bombay Dreams* and, 210, 217, 219–221, 227–229, 239, 242–252; in *Calcutta Calling*, 97–111; "choice" and, 272n9; citizenship and, 40, 42, 51; ethnic transformation, 132–133; legislation based on, 179–180, 181, 186–187, 255; locality and, 17–20; Miss India USA pageant and, 123, 127–136; postcoloniality and, 32–33; progressive representations of, 15; representation and, 253–254; social change and, 13; terrorism and, 20–21
Rahman, A. R., 211, 218–219
Rai, Amit, 14–15, 169
railways, Indian, 62, 271n36
Rajadhyaksha, Ashish, 144
Rajan, Rajeswari Sunder, 91
Rana, Junaid, 284n47
religion: *Bombay Dreams* and, 227–229, 232; citizenship and, 45, 53; pluralism and tolerance, 141–146, 190
Republican National Convention, 213, 237–242
resistance, 12–14, 266n13
rituals of consumption, 34, 44
Roja, 228
Rowdy Girls and Vixens, 172
Roy, Rahul, 139

SAAC (South Asian Artists' Collective), 177
Salonga, Lea, 220
salvation narrative, 80, 102–103, 104, 110, 119
Sandhu, Gurdit Singh, 179
Sangari, Kumkum, 153
Sanowar-Makhan, Tamara Zeta, 175–176, 279n12
Saran, Dharmatma, 129, 154, 160
Saran, Kaushal, 260–261, 285n5
"Sarva Dharma Sambhava," 142, 190
sati, 91, 272n12
"Savitri" comic, 190–193
Schwarzenegger, Arnold, 237–238
secularism, 142–147, 276–277nn24,25
self-representation, 77–78, 246
Selfridges department store, 223
Sepia Mutiny blog, 108–109
September 11 terrorist attacks, 20–21, 111–112, 120, 186–187, 241, 255
sexuality: in *Bombay Dreams*, 231–235; in *Captive*, 192–193; Miss India USA pageant and, 125–126, 131, 154–157, 160–161

Shadow Lines, The (Ghosh), 53
Shah, Nileem, 131
Shankar, Shalini, 13, 133
Sharma, Nitasha, 13
Sharpe, Jenny, 32, 51
Shekhar, Vidya Chandra, 127–128
"Shilling Love" (Patel), 203–204
Shillong, 54, 270n27
Shimakawa, Karen, 220
Shimizu, Celine Parreñas, 243
Sikhs: racial segregation and persecution of, 186–187; repression of, 183–184
Silicon Valley, 132–136, 157–158
Singh, Ganga, 182
Siu, Lok, 150
Slumdog Millionaire, 258–259
social change, 13, 22–23, 36
So Far from India, 75–77, 81–84
solidarity, 169, 195
South Asian American studies, 9–16, 31–32
South Asian Artists' Collective (SAAC), 177
spatial boundaries and divides: art festivals and, 196–201; *Bombay Dreams* and, 209; in documentary films, 79–80; in *Knowing Her Place*, 89; in *So Far from India*, 83–84; in "When Mr. Pirzada Came to Dine," 48–50
Special Registration, 241, 284nn47,48
Spivak, Gayatri, 65–66, 67
Srikanth, Rajini, 39, 41–42
Stonewall rebellion, 38–39
subjectivity, gendered, 91–93
Sukarno, 59
Syal, Meera, 222–223, 224, 226–227, 235

Takao Ozawa v. United States (1922), 40, 269n9
temporal dissonance: in Lahiri works, 30–31; in *The Namesake*, 58, 65–67, 72–73; in "The Third and Final Continent," 39–42; in "When Mr. Pirzada Came to Dine," 45, 48–50, 55–56
terrorism. See September 11 terrorist attacks
Thind, Bhagat Singh, 17–18, 40, 269n9
"The Third and Final Continent" (Lahiri), 36–43, 71–72
Ties Program, 103–104
Time Out New York, 236–237, 241
"To Render Real the Imagined" (Dave), 198
"tradition, invented," 34, 268n2

transnational adoptions, 97–111, 273nn21,23
TV Asia, 137

Ultra-Maxi Priest (Sanowar-Makhan), 175–176, 279n12
United States: author's education in, 259–261; Bangladesh Liberation War and, 46–47; spatial difference between India and, 76–77, 79–80, 83–84
United States v. Bhagat Singh Thind (1923), 17–18, 40, 269n9
U.S. census, 81–82, 267n27
U.S. imperialism: Asian American cultural production and, 254; Bangladesh Liberation War and, 34; *Bombay Dreams* and, 217; Maira on, 114; postcoloniality and, 31–33, 52; Sikh persecution and, 186–187; in "The Third and Final Continent," 40; Vietnam War and, 148–149

Vasa, Sarita, 205
Vasudevan, Ravi, 146, 276–277n25
Vietnam War, 47, 148–149, 159
Vietnam War Memorial, 277n28
Vij, Priya, 147–148
Vij, Sandeep, 147, 148
violence: *Bombay Dreams* and, 227–228, 229; communal, 140–146; against racial minorities in U.S., 260–261, 285n5; against Sikhs in Punjab, 183–184
Visweswaran, Kamala, 95

Walia, Amar, 133–134, 135
Webber, Andrew Lloyd, 218–219
"When Mr. Pirzada Came to Dine" (Lahiri), 36, 43–56, 70–71
widow burning, 91
Willemen, Paul, 144
Williams, Elizabeth, 222
women, 81–97, 272nn9,10,13, 275–276n12. *See also* Miss India USA pageant
Wu, Judy, 124

Yahya Khan, Agha Mohammad, 46
Yale, Elihu, 67
Yngvesson, Barbara, 273n24

The authorized representative in the EU for product safety and compliance is:
Mare Nostrum Group
B.V Doelen 72
4831 GR Breda
The Netherlands

www.ingramcontent.com/pod-product-compliance
Lightning Source LLC
Chambersburg PA
CBHW030335240426

43661CB00052B/1634